# Private Markets for Public Goods

## Raising the Stakes in Economic Reform

CAROL GRAHAM

Brookings Institution Press
*Washington, D.C.*

*Copyright © 1998 by*
THE BROOKINGS INSTITUTION
1775 Massachusetts Avenue, N.W.
Washington, D.C. 20036

*Library of Congress Cataloging-in-Publication Data*

Graham, Carol, 1962–
Private markets for public goods : raising the stakes in
economic reform / Carol Graham.
p. cm.
Includes bibliographical references and index.
ISBN 0-8157-1026-7 (alk. paper)
ISBN 0-8157-1025-9 (pbk. : alk. paper)
1. Human services—Contracting out—Developing countries.
2. Municipal services—Contracting out—Developing countries.
3. Privatization—Developing countries. 4. Capitalism—Developing
countries. 5. Developing countries—Social policy.
6. Developing countries—Economic policy. I. Title.
HV525 .G72 1998                    98-19723
338.9′009172′4–ddc21                    CIP


9 8 7 6 5 4 3 2 1


The paper used in this publication meets the minimum requirements of the
American National Standard for Information Sciences—Permanence of
Paper for Printed Library Materials,
ANSI Z39.48-1984

Typeset in Palatino

Composition by AlphaWebTech
Mechanicsville, Maryland

Printed by R. R. Donnelley and Sons Co.
Harrisonburg, Virginia

# Foreword

AS COUNTRIES around the world create market economies, they are also incorporating market incentives for providers and beneficiaries of systems that deliver such public goods as health care and education. In many countries, the debate over whether a more market-oriented approach is acceptable is settled; the salient issue is how to incorporate incentives so as to improve the performance of public institutions and at the same time guarantee widespread public access and at least minimum quality standards. This study examines the way market incentives can function in the delivery of education, health care, social security, and the privatization of state-owned enterprises in poor or developing countries in Latin America, Africa, and eastern Europe.

A common element among all the reforms is their reliance on "exit" and "voice" strategies to improve institutional performance and to create new stakeholders in the reform programs. Exit strategies such as school vouchers or private social security systems provide new private alternatives to receiving public services. Voice strategies such as local management boards endow recipients of public services with new power and responsibilities to oversee the delivery of health care and education.

Case studies of programs in Bolivia, Chile, the Czech Republic, Peru, and Zambia show that such strategies can improve the performance of public institutions. They can also significantly broaden the base of stakeholders in market reform, which is critical to its political sustainability. But the efficiency gains of market strategies often entail short-term losses of services and other benefits for the poorest groups in society. In the long term, however, the damage to social equity is usually counterbalanced by the benefits of improved performance by public institutions. The trade-offs are the most serious for economies with large numbers of very poor people. Yet it is precisely in these economies that public institutions are the least effective and the returns to improving their performance are the greatest. The issues explored in this study, particularly the reform of public institutions and their role in influencing the distribution of services, have relevance for advanced industrial societies as well as developing economies.

The author wishes to thank Roberto Abusada, Alan Angell, Patricia Arregui, Nancy Birdsall, Varun Gauri, Ricardo Godoy, Merilee Grindle, Michael Jacobs, Estelle James, Steen Jorgensen, Cheikh Kane, Mitchell Orenstein, Lant Pritchett, Jeffrey Sachs, Geoffrey Shepherd, Jose Valdez, Jiri Vecernik, and Carol Wise for their helpful comments and support.

At Brookings, John Steinbruner supported this project from its inception and provided intellectual guidance throughout. Richard Haass lent important support in the concluding phase. Kris McDevitt provided invaluable research and logistical assistance. Gualberto Rodriguez and Mary Stokes also provided research assistance. Charlotte Baldwin and Monique Principi gave administrative assistance. Jim Schneider edited the manuscript, Bridget Butkevich and Maya Dragicevic verified its factual content, Carlotta Ribar proofread the pages, and Deborah Patton compiled the index.

Finally, the author thanks her husband, John Mann, and son, Alexander, for holding down the fort during a number of field trips.

The author and Brookings are grateful to the John D. and Catherine T. MacArthur Foundation, the Tinker Foundation, the Council on Foreign Relations, the Inter-American Development Bank, the Carnegie Corporation of New York, and the Poverty

Group and the Office of the Chief Economist at the World Bank for generous support for this project.

The views expressed in this book are those of the author and should not be ascribed to any of the persons or organizations acknowledged above, or to the trustees, officers, or other staff members of the Brookings Institution.

Michael H. Armacost
*President*

*May 1998*
*Washington, D.C.*

*For my father*

# Contents

# Private Markets
# for Public Goods

Chapter 1

# Private Markets for Public Goods: Politics, Equity, and Institutional Performance

W HAT ARE THE EFFECTS of vouchers and school choice on public education systems? Could private business manage the national social security system? What is an appropriate role for the private sector in delivering water, electricity, transport, and other public services? All these questions are the subject of prolonged and often divisive debate in countries ranging from the former communist and developing nations to advanced industrial nations. Proponents of increased private sector involvement in realms previously reserved for public institutions cite efficiency and the reduction of fiscal burden as the primary benefits. Opponents raise concerns about equity and access. There is little agreement about how to reform public institutions or what the role of the state versus the private sector should be.

In many advanced industrial economies, this debate is often academic. But many emerging market countries have already launched full-fledged experiments with private sector delivery of public services. Most of these experiments have generated broad support from the public as large numbers of people acquire direct stakes in new systems for delivering public goods and services. Yet the equity effects of these experiments are less clear. There are usually some people that at least initially are left behind by the reforms. Regardless of the transition costs, however, the reform of public institutions is essential to the sustainability of market reform in most countries.

The move toward market economics in the arena of public institutions and public goods has directly affected large numbers of people at least as dramatically as macroeconomic reforms. The effects on politics and on new stakeholders, equity, and the performance of public institutions in various countries are the subject of this book. Its lessons are directly relevant to countries undertaking transitions to market economies. They also provide insights for the continuing debates over the private provision of public goods in the advanced industrial societies.

## The Rationale for Private Markets for Public Goods

An unprecedented number of countries are adopting market-oriented economic policies, and most are doing so under democratic auspices. Although there is increasing consensus on the policy framework essential for market-oriented growth, there is far less consensus on what is necessary to make such growth politically sustainable and broadly shared. The benefits of initial macroeconomic reforms, such as stabilization of inflation, are immediately clear and widespread in most societies. But the benefits of most other reforms, particularly those that require changing the manner in which institutions function, are some years away. In many countries there is increasing concern that short-term costs will make it difficult to sustain public support for reforms long enough for them to yield results.

Few regions have made as much progress in implementing market-oriented reforms under democratic regimes as Latin America has. And recent evidence shows that the increases in poverty and inequality of the crisis years of the 1980s were halted and even reversed by the reforms of the late 1980s and 1990s.[1] Yet there is a widespread perception that market-oriented reforms have increased poverty and inequality and fear that these trends will lead to a voter backlash against reform.[2] Similarly, market reforms in eastern Europe are widely blamed for increasing poverty, inequality, and unemployment, even though in most cases the declines in output and fiscal deficits responsible for these trends predated market reforms and made their implementation unavoidable. Those countries that have moved the furthest toward full implementation of reforms are making strong strides toward reducing poverty and unemployment.[3] In Africa, meanwhile, there is a broad perception that market reforms have failed altogether, even though they have yet to get off the ground in most countries.[4]

Thus regardless of actual trends, in many regions there is a broadly shared *perception* that market reforms are to blame for increased poverty and inequality. This perception is the result of the intangibility of many of the benefits of reform and the very visible costs. Higher rates of economic growth and better social security systems in the future, for example, have little appeal for those whose income is limited in the present, while reductions in public employment tend to create widespread anxiety. Although the development of stock exchanges and capital markets very quickly gives wealthy groups a stake in reform, there has been far less progress in the areas that will give the rest of the public, particularly the poor, a similar stake. To make reforms *politically* sustainable, the majority of the public—which in the developing countries is also poor—must believe that they have a direct stake in market-led growth and be active participants in it.[5] Achieving inclusive and sustainable growth will entail improving the performance of the institutions that deliver education, health care, and other essential services and those that provide services essential to maintaining fair and efficient markets, such as regulation and tax collection.[6]

Institutional reform requires more implementation capacity than does macroeconomic reform, which can be initiated by a small and insulated group of policymakers and entails very different political dynamics.[7] The providers of public services tend to be politically powerful and highly organized, while the users of those services, although numerous, are usually politically weak and poorly organized.[8] Thus it is no surprise that most governments, already faced with the political challenges of macroeconomic reform, postpone or avoid more difficult reforms of public institutions and choose shorter-term solutions such as social safety nets.[9]

Explicit strategies to increase the number of stakeholders in reform—what this study terms the stakeholders approach—can be crucial in overcoming these political constraints and creating a new base of support for reform. This approach cuts across a variety of issues and types of reform. In all cases it applies to the so-called second stage of economic reforms. The first stage of reforms focuses primarily on establishing macroeconomic equilibrium and entails changing economic policies. The second stage aims to establish or reform the institutional framework necessary to sustain macroeconomic equilibrium and growth and requires reforms of institutions ranging from public finance to social security, health care, and education.

In some cases the approach entails increasing the voice or choice of users of public services as a means of improving quality and extent of coverage as well as directly involving the beneficiaries in the process. In other cases the approach entails soliciting the participation of low-income groups in the privatization process. It always entails reorienting the behavior of public sector institutions and the beneficiaries of services by introducing new market incentives into areas that were previously the domain of the state, that is, private markets for public goods. The objective is ultimately to increase the capacity of public institutions to deliver the services essential to growth and poverty reduction, thereby contributing to the political and economic sustainability of market-led growth and ultimately to stronger civic participation and possibly even to stronger democracies.

"The definition of what needs to be done to build capacity . . . include[s] actions and processes that link the public sector, the market, and civil society."[10] The stakeholders approach involves soliciting the active participation of the beneficiaries of particular reforms in their implementation. This means changing the design of the reforms so that significant parts of society benefit if they are carried out, for example, through the acquisition of shares in public companies or improvements in the education system, and so that the beneficiaries are motivated to take steps such as voting, lobbying, and protesting to prevent the reversal of reforms. In essence they become stakeholders in the reform. Programs that merely compensate people or give away benefits at well below their market costs are far less successful at generating long-term stakes in reform, as several examples in this study demonstrate.[11]

Critical to the success of such an approach is increasing public awareness and understanding of the process. In political terms this approach seeks to counterbalance the array of incentives that encourage groups within the public sector to oppose reform.[12] An underlying assumption is that involving citizens in reform will change their perception of how its benefits are produced and distributed, with consequent effects on their attitudes and behavior toward public institutions and the market process more generally.[13] Anecdotal evidence suggests that reforms have proven more politically sustainable in countries where such an approach has been incorporated, while the absence of attention to issues of public understanding, participation, and ownership has undermined political support for reforms in others.[14]

Despite the strong potential of this approach, a note of caution is in order. It cannot substitute for coherent macroeconomic policies and a reform strategy. There are wide differences in the extent of reforms undertaken among countries and in the social protection mechanisms in place to ease transition costs. There are also wide differences among countries' development strategies as they reform their macroeconomies. Some are able to rely on labor-intensive exports to both expand their economies and reduce poverty, while others remain more dependent on capital-instensive primary product exports, which rarely generate widespread labor gains. Finally, there are strong differences among countries' social welfare systems. Some are able to provide basic services effectively for all income groups, particularly the very poor. Others maintain distorted public expenditure allocations that subsidize higher-level services such as university education for the wealthy at the same time that they fail to provide the most basic services for the poor. The stakeholders approach is a tool for facilitating reforms that can correct such distortions. Yet it alone cannot compensate for extreme underdevelopment or poor policies. At times the stakeholders approach may be successful in improving reform efforts in education or privatization in a country where policies in other areas such as the health care system or the labor code remain highly skewed.

This study examines the effects of the stakeholders approach in three critical areas: the political sustainability of reform, equity, and the performance of previously public enterprises and institutions. It seeks to help fill a gap in our knowledge of the factors that make economic reforms politically sustainable across a range of countries.

## The Stakeholders Approach and Its Theoretical Underpinnings

The stakeholders approach applies to reforms that are part of the adjustment process and complement its macroeconomic and fiscal rationale. The approach tries to create winners by increasing the public's participation in and benefits from reform.[15] Although at times this entails short-term fiscal costs, in the longer term it contributes to more efficient state performance as well as indirectly to public savings and economic growth. Reform of the pension system that raises individual stakes and contributions, for example, can increase national savings capacity and help capital market development. Reform of the education system, which relies on increased local responsibility in managing schools, can result in more efficient *and* equitable distribution of public resources while encouraging private alternatives.[16] Equally important, reform of education systems is often essential to the ability of countries to sustain open economies and operate competitively in the international arena. Privatization of large parastatal enterprises reduces the fiscal burden on the state and can encourage private sector development.

This feature of the stakeholders approach contrasts with the standard view of compensation: that of relaxing fiscal constraints during adjustment in order to placate losers whose opposition poses a significant obstacle to reform. Instead, by increasing the number of individuals and local groups with a stake in change, the approach can improve the sustainability of the reform. It does so by increasing the welfare of significant numbers of stakeholders over the long term. It also contributes to sustainability by making resources and responsibilities available to new stakeholders, motivating them to take action to prevent the reversal of reforms and at the same time educating them about the broader approach underlying market reform.[17]

The approach entails government communication and marketing of reforms so that the public understands how to participate and benefit. This is distinct from the government's initial need to convince the public to acquiesce to adjustment-related losses to overcome the economic crisis and implement stabilization policies. At this stage the government is asking for participation and contribution and at the same time offering tangible benefits; the success of the reforms hinges on this participation. A government strategy of active communication is necessary to overcome the obstacles to collective action by users and reduce asymmetries in information between users and providers. Communication efforts are particularly important in the contexts of weak institutions and poor government credibility because public skepticism of government commitments and the legitimacy of new institutions will have to be overcome before soliciting broad participation in reforms based on new incentives. The effects of government communication efforts, meanwhile, may vary in different societies, particularly among those with different overall levels of educational attainment.[18]

In theory the stakeholders approach should improve equity, and this study explores the extent to which it does. Stakeholders are distributed throughout society, and benefits are not restricted to elites. None of the reforms under study is specifically directed to the poor, but almost all can involve and affect large numbers of poor. In addition, a higher proportion of the poor than the wealthy rely on public services and thus stand to benefit from reform. And increasing the participation of the poor through this approach will ultimately strengthen their political voice, which will make shifts of public expenditures in their direction more sustainable over the long term.

In contrast, the effects of the approach on the poorest of the poor are much less clear. The poorest groups tend to be distinct from the poor more generally. Their poverty tends to be structural rather than income related, and their ability to respond to new incentives and policies may be restricted by deprivation. If the poorest are malnourished, for example, they may not be able to take advantage of increased expenditures on education.[19] An approach that sought to create stakeholders among only the poorest groups would be far more difficult to implement financially and would be unlikely to improve political sustainability.[20] To some extent stakeholders reactions to new incentives and reforms are endogenous to particular societies and countries.[21] In some stakeholders reforms the poorest may be excluded because they lack time, resources, education, and information. In other cases the poorest may benefit as free riders. This is most likely to occur in social service reforms if and when the introduction of new incentives results in better systemwide performance.

Although the approach relies to a large extent on individual or local responses to new market incentives, it by no means eliminates an active role for the state in providing public goods and services. The government must not only communicate and explain the reforms, but it must maintain an integral role in regulation and public finance. Local participation and private contribution in the delivery of services can improve efficiency, but it cannot substitute for adequate public financing of essential services. And the introduction of new providers and methods of providing services is likely to require more rather than less regulation, at least in the short term.

In addition, implementing the stakeholders approach requires overcoming significant political obstacles. Yet by increasing the number of people with stakes in change, the approach may overcome some of the traditional obstacles to institutional reform. These include asymmetries in political power between providers and users, and the incentives influencing the political behavior of providers.[22] Broader public participation in and support for reform are likely to evoke a response from service providers in public institutions. For such a dynamic to develop, however, the government must have sufficient political capital at least to initiate changes—for example, devolving some resources and management autonomy to local and community levels, regardless of opposition from interest groups in central institutions.[23] In the absence of such a commitment, it is very difficult to implement significant reforms, as the failure of the education reform efforts in Peru demonstrates. Once such a commitment exists, external technical or financial support for reforms can facilitate government efforts. And once these efforts are begun, reforms can develop a momentum of their own that can counterbalance political opposition within the public sector or in other parts of the government, as the experience with health reforms in Zambia suggests (see chapter 6).

### The Theory: Exit, Voice, and Public Goods

Although there are many ways of conceptualizing the increase of individuals' stake in change, this study focuses on two: *exit* and *voice*. Both concepts involve changing the rules according to which the public acquires access to public services or public goods and providing new channels through which people can exert pressure for change. *How* the rules are changed—through exit or voice—will have different effects on who participates, on the equity of outcomes, and on the performance of public sector institutions.

Exit and voice were first elaborated as integrally related strategies by Albert Hirschman, who defined them as related responses to decay in firms, organizations, or states.[24] The concept of exit has been used by economists for decades: dissatisfied consumers exit firms, for example, by switching to products sold by other firms. The decision to exit is clean: one leaves or one does not. Exit is fairly anonymous, with the exception of well-known or centrally involved persons (for example if the chairman of the school board decides to send his or her children to a private school).

Voice, however, is ultimately a political act, and is a messier concept that may comprehend actions from faint complaint to violent and organized protest. Voice is also an art that develops over time. It requires open articulation as opposed to private exit and depends a great deal on the bargaining power of particular actors vis-à-vis the organizations they are trying to change. "Hence, in comparison to the exit option, voice is costly and conditioned on the influence and bargaining power customers and members can bring to bear within the firm from which they buy or the organization to which they belong."[25] Existing political and social structures are likely to affect particular social groups' propensity to take up opportunities to exercise voice. And the context will also affect the potential of voice to improve institutional performance.[26]

Exit and voice will differ in their relevance across various contexts in which stakeholders strategies are put into practice. When alternative private mechanisms are widely available, as with several pension and some education reforms, much of the public can choose to exit, thus creating stakes in new private systems. Yet there are also equity effects because there are transaction costs to exiting that the poorest may not be able to afford. These costs, such as extra bus fares or new uniforms required to attend private schools, may seem marginal but can be prohibitive for the poor. Exiting also requires consumers to be informed and, as many examples in this study demonstrate, the poor tend to have less access to information.

The existence of exit can discourage the development of voice, particularly if wealthier, better educated, and more articulate groups disproportionately exit. In education, many observers predict that competition from private schools will inevitably result in a deterioration of the quality of public schools as the most active and educated parents put their children in private schools. Yet recent evidence suggests that public schools perform better in areas where there are private schools than in areas where there is no competition, even when controlling for socioeconomic differences.[27] Private options in education are usually more expensive than public ones, and thus exit is more costly than voice and discourages at least some parents from exiting. But even if they do choose not to exit, the existence of the option may encourage parents who remain in the public system to use voice to exert pressure on public schools to match the performance of private ones.

Sometimes an exit option is not available because of economies of scale, legal barriers or government monopoly, or constraints of distance (as in the case of public school students in remote rural areas). Under these conditions voice is the only option, and reforms must restructure incentives to increase individuals' stake in the public system. Voice can be exercised in ways that range from increased participation in the management and delivery of services to payment of user fees.[28] Exercising voice may also entail transaction costs (opportunity costs of time, for example) and legal or institutional barriers to participation. Thus, encouraging voice options entails overcoming the standard obstacles to collective action. Not surprisingly, middle-class groups or better-off groups among the poor often dominate voice arrangements.[29] Yet despite asymmetries in political power and access to education, the poor can and do exercise their political voice if there are adequate incentives and information. The introduction of accessible channels through which they can make themselves heard (for example demand-based safety nets) can enhance their organizational potential and their political voice in general.[30]

Strategies to increase the number of stakeholders through exit and voice cannot succeed without complementary change at the center. Introducing an exit option without a concurrent central government effort to increase public awareness of the process, for example, will limit participation and is likely to have inequitable outcomes because the poor are least likely to have adequate information. And encouraging voice without expanding public institutions' capacity to respond to new demands will only result in the public's frustration. To begin exit and voice-based stakeholder reforms, governments often have to override the opposition of teachers or health care workers or obtain their acquiescence through compensation or cooptation.

An alternative approach, although we know much less about it, is to solicit the cooperation of these people through loyalty. Although this study focuses on exit and voice, loyalty is also very important in the performance of public institutions and is often undervalued. One study sheds new light on how the loyalty and performance of lower-level bureaucrats can be increased by according them more responsibility and providing nonfinancial rewards for good performance.[31] One can envision a similar dynamic occurring in areas such as education, where regional competitions and awards for public school performance might improve teacher performance and increase parental involvement, including the exercise of voice.

In addition, loyal members of communities, public school systems, and public sector firms are much more likely to attempt to exercise voice in response to organizational or systemic decline than they are to exit. Studies of pilot programs with vouchers in education in the United Kingdom, for example, have found that middle-class parents are likely to use their vouchers to choose new private schools for their children, while the working poor are less likely to exit and tend to identify strongly with their neighborhood schools. This does not mean that they are always willing to settle for schools of inferior quality; in many cases parents are loyal to their schools because they regard them as crucial to their communities.[32]

The role of loyalty raises another concept relevant to the stakeholders approach: social capital. Robert Putnam's research comparing the economic performance of different regions of Italy over a long time finds that a community's capacity to organize autonomously and remain cohesive is directly related to better-performing economies and polities. "Citizens in civic communities expect better government, and (in part through their own efforts), they get it. They demand more effective public service and they are prepared to act collectively to achieve their shared goals."[33] This contrasts with citizens in less "civic" communities, who are more likely to act as alienated and cynical supplicants of government services. In an analogous fashion, the stakeholders approach attempts to encourage a broad base of citizens (both individually and collectively) to contribute to and at the same time benefit from market-oriented reform. Different levels of social capital among communities are likely to affect the potential of stakeholders approaches, particularly those based on increased voice. At the same time, an implicit objective of the stakeholders approach is to encourage citizens to demand, individually or collectively, more accountability from public institutions, an objective analogous to that of building social capital.

The concept of social capital is important for its own sake, but it also brings up the critical role of institutions in the potential benefits of stakeholders approaches. A broad definition of institutions that encompasses those of several authors in various disciplines defines institutions as the regulations that stem from repeated human interaction and that generate credible commitments affecting specific behavior.[34] The institutional framework is structured by rules, norms, and shared strategies as well as by how those evolve from and interact with the physical environment.[35]

This definition suggests two rather distinct traits of institutions. On the one hand, to be credible and effective and serve their regulatory functions, institutions have to maintain a certain independence and neutrality. On the other, they are to some extent outside the social, economic, and cultural contexts in which they operate. Institutions reflect societal values and differ across societies. In some societies they reflect underlying agreement on more equity, while in others they reflect tolerance for higher levels of inequality, patterns that are then perpetuated by the institutional framework.[36]

The institutional framework affects the credibility of government initiatives and commitments to new stakeholders strategies. It also affects the propensity of individuals to participate in new institutional structures that result, such as new private pension systems or plans to encourage buying shares in privatized enterprises. It will also affect people's potential to act collectively and exercise voice in the administration or delivery of public services. A major challenge and indeed objective of the stakeholders approach is to reestablish the credibility of institutions in contexts in which that credibility has been eroded, as in eastern Europe, or was very weak to begin with, as in Latin America and even more so in Africa. In the past in Latin America, for example, the unpredictability of government intervention and the lack of consistent enforcement of private contracts and property rights have had devastating effects on investment and growth.[37]

Finally, an important aspect of the definition of the stakeholders approach is a fairly liberal interpretation of the term *public good*. The classic definition of a public good is a good that is "consumed by all those who are members of a given community, country, or geographical area in such a manner that consumption or use by one member does not detract from consumption or use by another."[38] In the purest sense, public goods are distinguished by indivisibility and publicness. They are indivisible in that for the entire public to enjoy public goods at all, they must—in theory—each enjoy the same amount. The quantity produced cannot be divided up and purchased by individuals according to their preferences for more or less of them as private goods can.[39]

In practice, public goods have a range of publicness that is in large part determined by how divisible they are. Some goods, such as national defense, are completely indivisible: no single consumer can purchase national defense individually. Other goods are more divisible, such as education, even though certain traits of the goods, such as regulation and monitoring of quality, remain indivisible. In addition, even though individual parents can purchase private education for their children, and more or less of it as they like, they usually live in a community that relies on the public education system, and thus they have some stake in it.[40] The benefits that public education provides the community (beyond the benefits to individual students), which range from shared values and common interpretations of history to a better-educated labor force, are the benefits that justify the state's role in education. In contrast, it is far more difficult to identify beneficial externalities generated by public ownership of cement or steel factories, for example. The more public the public good, the greater—and the less divisible—the positive externalities it provides.[41]

With the worldwide move to market-oriented economic policies, the private sector is taking on a greater role in producing and delivering education, social security, health care, and other goods that have traditionally been considered primarily public. Yet certain goods remain public in nature even if they are delivered by private providers because they have an indivisible value for the community at large. Theorists of public goods recognized long ago that although the supply, financing, distribution, and regulation of public goods had an inherent public or collectivized character, this did not apply to the production of the same goods, which might be produced more efficiently in the private sector.[42] The example of education is again relevant. Even if an entire community chooses private education, it will still have a stake in the state's regulating and at least partially financing the system so that it maintains minimum standards. "The monitoring of the public provision of services is a public good (and this is true even if the publicly provided public service is itself a private good as long as quality cannot be individually differentiated)."[43]

This study considers education, health care, and social security as public goods. In addition, some of the services provided by state-owned enterprises, such as water, utilities, and telecommunications, have a public element to them, although they vary in how essential or indivisible they are. The stakeholders approach incorporates market incentives in the form of exit and voice into the delivery of goods and services that are considered public, thereby giving individuals a stake in bettering the quality of services. In most cases this entails a major departure from a situation in which beneficiaries receive services free or with a significant subsidy but have no say in how services are delivered and no alternative options.

## Stakeholders and Political Sustainability

It is difficult to measure the effects of the stakeholders approach on the political sustainability of macroeconomic reforms in a definitive, much less quantitative, manner. For this study, political sustainability will be defined in two ways. The first is a simple definition, which is delineated by how people vote (that is, do they vote in favor of continuing reforms by selecting a proreform candidate, who may or may not be of the same party as the government that initiated the reforms) and by how politicians campaign (are most candidates running on a proreform platform and do any candidates proposing a reversal of reforms pose a realistic challenge). Recent evidence from Peru, for example, suggests that government efforts to reform the public sector and related expenditure patterns, particularly in education, can have a direct impact on voters' level of support for reform.[44]

The second definition is a much broader concept that hinges on attaining a balance between the objectives of market reform and those of achieving a socially sustainable allocation of the benefits of reform.[45] The first objective—achieving economic stability and stable growth and making basic service delivery operational—involves changing the incentive structures in both the macroeconomy and in the delivery of public social services: the creation of new stakeholders in the market process. The second objective—achieving a sustainable allocation of reform benefits—depends to a large extent on the capacity of particular societies to respond to new market incentives and therefore on the potential of stakeholders strategies to solicit the participation of a broad base of society in the market reform.

The potential of stakeholders strategies can be severely limited by deep poverty and related structural obstacles to the ability of the poor to respond to new incentives such as education, social or cultural marginalization, access to information, and inability to pay transaction costs. These constraints usually exclude them from participating in market-oriented growth more generally. Although the concepts of marginalization and social exclusion have slightly different implications in developed and developing economies, in general they describe the inability of particular individuals or groups to integrate into the market economy and gradually society at large.[46] Not surprisingly, it is particularly difficult to reach these groups through strategies that depend on individuals' capacities to take advantage of new incentives, such as opportunities for voice and choice. Although many policies directly address the causes of extreme poverty and social exclusion, they take time to yield results. In the short term they will do little to help these groups participate in new private markets for public goods.

Thus the second definition of political sustainability is inextricably linked to problems of poverty and equity and will vary according to the level of poverty in particular societies as well as differences among them in tolerance for inequality. There may at times be trade-offs between political sustainability and equity goals. In some countries, governments may succeed in building a broad base of new stakeholders in new private systems for the delivery of public goods and services and thereby create a significant base of support for reform, yet still fail to reach the poor.[47] In others, some of the poor may participate and have their positions and opportunities improved as a result, while other poor are excluded and are left with public sector services that have deteriorated and have little public support. For example, "If social insurance is an important motive for politically determined redistributive taxation, then it seems possible that thicker insurance markets could reduce social welfare. As middle class voters become more able to diversify in private markets, they may no longer see their welfare as dependent on social insurance and reduce their political support for it as a result."[48]

In instances where the excluded poor are a minority, one can envision a majority of the population supporting new private market approaches, with the votes of the very poor having little effect on electoral outcomes. In other situations in which a broader segment of the population is excluded from the benefits of reforms, the votes of those excluded would have more weight and could undermine support for market reforms more generally. In this study the contrasting experiences of Chile and Peru with education reform suggest that either outcome is quite possible.

How the poor fare in stakeholders approaches is part of the political sustainability equation, but it is by no means all of it. Stable macroeconomies are indispensable, and governments' records in achieving economic reforms are determining factors in achieving institutional reforms and therefore of the potential of stakeholders approaches.[49] Countries that proceed rapidly and extensively with macroeconomic reform in response to extreme crisis and that rebuild their economies quickly can often take advantage of the ensuing political momentum to proceed with institutional reforms.[50] Rapid and far-reaching reform also tends to undermine the position of entrenched interest groups in the public sector, allowing governments political opportunities to introduce changes in the way public institutions operate, changes often based on the introduction of new actors or stakeholders. In contrast, stalled or gradual reform allows those opposed to reform more opportunities to come together to protect their privileged access to public expenditures.[51] All of the stakeholders strategies examined in this study have been implemented during far-reaching and rapid economic reform programs, with the underlying assumption that without this context, the possibilities for creating significant numbers of new stakeholders are minimal.

The many studies on the politics of economic reform have for the most part focused on the factors explaining politicians' decisions to launch reforms rather than on the factors that influence the public's decisions to continue to vote for reforms. Still, several broad conclusions from the studies illuminate the potential effects of stakeholders approaches on the sustainability of reforms.[52]

The first is that authoritarian governments have no advantage over democracies in implementing and sustaining policy reforms. The relatively large number of authoritarian regimes in the 1960s and 1970s led to the assumption that they were better equipped to carry out market-oriented reforms than were democratic regimes. Yet since 1980 a worldwide trend toward democratic regimes has provided many examples of successful reform. By the early 1990s these examples equaled or outnumbered the successful outcomes under authoritarian regimes. Empirical studies support this conclusion, and some indicate that elections improve economic policymaking.[53]

The second conclusion is that the quality of the state bureaucracy affects the results of reform. Even when economic policymakers are insulated from a state bureaucracy, they need to rely on the political-administrative framework to implement reforms. Reform measures that are technically sound often get bogged down when they are put into practice, particularly later-stage measures such as privatization that require more institutional capacity than do first-stage reforms such as stabilization. Not coincidentally, the effects of stakeholders approaches on the performance of public institutions is a focus of this study.

The third conclusion, on which there is slightly less consensus, is that the discernible effects of interest groups on policy reform are small, or at least much smaller than had once been predicted. Evidence from a number of countries indicates that the influence of such groups on policy *choice* is minimal. Their primary influence is retrospective: they can force the abandonment of policies through votes, demonstrations, strikes, and capital flight. The chances that a reforming government, or at least reformist candidates, will be reelected seem to rest more on the overall success of the adjustment efforts than on the costs to the popular sectors.[54] Meanwhile, public expenditure patterns can influence the voting patterns of particular groups, especially if previously neglected groups receive benefits for the first time, but these effects are less significant than those of overall economic trends.[55] This suggests that the primary influence of new stakeholders will also be retrospective; that is, they will support reforms after they are carried out, rather than have a direct influence on policy choice. Yet most analysis has focused on the political behavior of interest groups acquiescing to losses incurred during macroeconomic reforms. If new stakeholders are, as expected, more active political supporters of the reforms they have benefited from, it is likely that their support will influence the direction if not the details of future policies.

A fourth conclusion is that to sustain reforms, governments usually must build political coalitions to support the measures. Spain and Mexico, for example, relied on pacts with business and labor to carry out important structural reforms as well as stabilization. The viability of such an approach, however, depends on the particular party and institutional structure as well as the credibility of future government promises.[56] The stakeholders approach is a less institutionalized but possibly longer-lasting method of creating a broad base of support for reform.

Many strategies to build support through compensation have been tried. Direct compensation to powerful and organized opponents of reform is less likely to be successful than safety net or compensatory programs, which may not be taken up by those interest groups. Given the limited public resources available for compensation during reform, it is unlikely that compensatory strategies will make "losers" who were previously privileged by statist policies as well off as they were before reform. In contrast, reaching poor and vulnerable groups with benefits for the first time has much more value added from reducing poverty and can also contribute to popular support for reform.[57]

The stakeholders approach is more likely than compensation to have longer-term effects on the sustainability of reform efforts. And creating new stakeholders among the most vocal opponents of reform may be more feasible than compensating them. This study provides examples—public enterprise workers in Bolivia, for instance—in which potential opponents of reform were transformed into supporters via stakeholders strategies. There are also examples in which opponents of reform were critical to ensuring good institutional performance but were excluded from the reform and thus had no stake in it. Teachers in Chile, for example, were able to jeopardize the sustainability of reforms several years after they were begun.

Finally, leadership matters. Studies of the politics of reform have focused on the leadership capacity of crucial policymakers as well as on the political incentives that frame the behavior of politicians. This study does not analyze leadership in detail. Yet it assumes that leadership is important to carrying out stakeholders strategies. Most successful strategies in this study had strong executive commitment. Creating new stakeholders often requires altering the positions of powerful and organized opponents of reform. Without a strong central commitment to do so, the opponents are likely to overwhelm nascent initiatives to solicit new participants.

Because studies of political economy are only beginning to shift focus from the factors that explain the launching of reforms to those that explain their consolidation, there is, as yet, no conclusive definition of political sustainability. This study of various governments' attempts to create new stakeholders in reform and the effects of those attempts on political behavior seeks to contribute to that new focus as well as to the formulation of a more complete definition of the sustainability of market reforms.

## Equity and Market Reforms

This book explores the effects of stakeholders reforms on equity. *Equity* and *equitable* are often used interchangeably. They have distinct but related definitions. *Equity* is both descriptive and functional. At one level it implies an amount of equality that is deemed optimal by particular societies. At another level, equity norms and standards allow societies to make decisions in certain realms where market criteria are insufficient, such as the distribution of the tax burden. *Equitable* is a descriptive term that implies a distribution as fair and as equal as possible. Both terms suggest a movement toward greater equality in societies with great inequality, a primary concern of this analysis.

Before evaluating the effects of the stakeholders approach on equity, it is important to ask why equity matters at all. A number of philosophers have made compelling cases for the importance of equity from the perspective of social justice. Although there are variations in their views and in their definitions, and different societies tolerate different levels of inequality, there is fairly wide agreement that very large differentials in the distribution of income inhibit social cohesion.[58]

Government policy is rarely driven by concerns about social justice. Yet equity has a distinct functional role: it guides and legitimates distributive choices, thereby making them sustainable and setting precedents for future allocative decisions. Societies and their economic institutions reflect equity norms and standards that have evolved over time. "Moreover, the social system shapes the wants and inspirations that its citizens come to have.... Thus an economic system is not only an institutional device for satisfying existing wants and needs but a way of creating and fashioning wants in the future."[59]

Although different priorities among societies result in variations in equity norms and practicies, the very existence of these standards increases economic efficiency. Peyton Young demonstrates how they help resolve day-to-day decisions about the optimal allocation of jointly produced goods. There is a wide range of such decisions for which the market alone is an insufficient guide: for example, who should receive scarce organ transplants and how should the tax burden be distributed? Equity norms and standards help resolve issues of *priority*, as in the case of organ transplants, and *proportionality*, as in the case of the tax burden.[60] The absence of established guidelines for resolving these matters, which arise every day, would result in continuous and costly distributive conflicts.

In societies undertaking far-reaching market-oriented reforms, equity norms and standards are often restructured entirely. In many developing countries, standards were deemed fair by a privileged part of the population, and the resulting institutional structures redistributed public goods among this group, while the poor majority had limited access or none. In others such as the former communist economies, norms that dictated complete equality of outcomes created disincentives and distortions on such a scale that economies became unsustainable. For both groups of countries the introduction of market reforms takes place where equity norms are in flux, and there is little agreement on how the costs and benefits of reform should be allocated.

Improving equity during market reform, which increases the chances that most people will perceive the process as fair, is not only a matter of social justice, but one essential to the sustainability of reform. It will also establish important trends in the course that future reforms take.[61] It is difficult to address concerns about equitable distribution during the implementation of certain macroeconomic reforms, such as the stabilization of inflation, where the effects (good or bad) are immediately felt by all social groups. Yet in later stages of reform, particularly those that affect the manner in which important public goods are delivered, there is much more room for incorporating equity objectives into the design. Paying attention to equity concerns when reforms are designed is likely to reduce the number of costly and potentially destabilizing distributive conflicts as reforms are carried out.

Beyond the matters of allocative efficiency, there is increasing evidence that too much inequality limits growth, which is the primary objective of market-oriented reform. Recent cross-regional comparisons by Nancy Birdsall, David Ross, and Richard Sabot show that widespread public access to assets such as land and basic education is particularly important to growth. A number of cross-country surveys show that countries that start out with less inequality, particularly with respect to these assets, grow faster.[62]

It is also important to distinguish between constructive and destructive inequality. Some inequality is necessary and constructive: it rewards productivity and innovation. Destructive inequality blocks the productive potential of the poor. When inequality is too great, the poor have neither the capacity nor the incentive to make human capital investments that, in the aggregate, increase growth. Two types of problems then perpetuate the effects of inequality on investments in human capital and, more generally, on growth: market failures and government failures.[63]

The most common example of market failure is imperfect capital markets. Access to capital depends on collateralizable wealth. Thus individuals' initial assets may be important determinants of their ability to borrow. This poses a particular problem for human capital investments because future earnings are not an effective form of collateral. The implications of this, unless compensated for, are that initial assets determine productive potential, and great initial inequality results in both great subsequent inequality and slower growth, which is perpetuated by inadequate human capital investments by the poor majority.[64]

Classical welfare theory provides a normative view of government as a benign actor whose role to is correct for market failure by funding public goods and to compensate for market or insurance failures. But the reality in most countries is that government behavior, and thus the allocation of public goods, reflects the distribution of political power and the organizational capacity of different societal groups.[65] Unequal distribution of political power can perpetuate or concentrate asset inequality. The results of formal econometrics research indicate that great inequality encourages voters to choose more redistribution or populist economic policies or both, which hinders economic growth. More recent research questions the so-called median voter approach, and suggests that the distribution of political voice as well as that of income is skewed toward the wealthy in highly unequal societies. This unequal access to political rights can increase the likelihood of continuing inequality in many countries.[66]

Market and government failure can lead to social exclusion, a concept of poverty that extends beyond income poverty and includes relative deprivation, lack of access to goods and services, and precarious social rights. Exclusion can be thought of in terms of three paradigms that have different levels of relevance depending on the country. The first, the solidarity paradigm, defines exclusion as the result of economic and political failures that leave certain parts of the population outside the concept of citizenship and social solidarity. Those who are excluded may be completely dependent on social safety nets provided by society, yet for a variety of reasons they are excluded from normal political and productive processes. This concept is perhaps most applicable to the underclass or to disadvantaged minorities in advanced industrial societies.[67]

The second paradigm is that of specialization, in which exclusion is a consequence of economic specialization and social differentiation resulting from technological change and market-led growth. This kind of exclusion reflects "voluntary choices, patterns of interests and contractual relationships between individuals, and various 'distortions' to the system—discrimination, market failures, and unenforced rights."[68] Third, in the monopoly paradigm the special-interest groups monopolize access to public goods and deny them to the poor majority. The experience of the poor in most developing countries reflects a combination of these last two paradigms.

## Implications for Market-Led Growth and Stakeholders Reforms

The discussion of equity and exclusion has obvious implications for the stakeholders approach. Despite the common perception that market reforms have negative effects on income distribution, they may often reduce distortions in factor markets such as land and credit, increase access to and the quality of such public goods as education, and reduce rent seeking in the public sector.[69] Introducing new market incentives in the provision and use of public goods may result in better service and broader access for the poor, reducing exclusion of the monopoly type. At the same time, the incentives can also make exclusion worse by creating more barriers to the participation of the already excluded poor in education and health care, increasing exclusion of the specialization type.

The varying results affect the potential and sustainability of market-oriented reforms. The same policies, when carried out under conditions of very great inequality, are likely to yield slower growth than they would in more equal societies. The evidence suggests that voters reward governments when fully implemented reforms yield growth and vote out of office those that are unable to carry them out and achieve growth.[70] In addition to the pace of growth, how *inclusive* it is matters. One interpretation of East Asia's economic success over several decades is that institutions that spread the benefits of growth policies widely "made the reversibility of policies costly, and, consequently, gave individuals and firms confidence that they would share in the growth dividend."[71] In more unequal contexts, where significant parts of the population do not benefit directly from economic growth, volatility in policies is much more common because voters are more likely to support even empty promises of change and redistribution than continuation of the status quo. Latin America's long line of populist leaders bears witness to this.[72] Policy volatility, in turn, severely limits long-term growth.[73]

Great inequality can result in a vicious political and economic spiral that hinders growth, political stability, and the reduction of poverty. Countries in the midst of delicate transitions to the market, often under the auspices of new or reestablished democratic

institutions, can face serious long-term setbacks if matters of equity are ignored and policies establish such cycles. In the former
socialist economies, where the distribution of income is usually
much flatter than that in most advanced industrial democracies,
the challenge for policymakers is to ensure that reforms introduce constructive rather than destructive inequality.[74] In areas
such as Latin America with very unequal societies, merely improving efficiency in how public services are allocated, that is, removing distortions that favor privileged groups, can improve the
poor's access to services, even if they are not free.[75] The same is
true of efficiency improvements in factor markets and in some
economic sectors such as finance, former public utilities, and social security.[76]

Yet much more remains to be done. Failure to resolve inequities during market reform will not only have implications within
societies and result in the exclusion of significant parts of the
population from participating in market growth, but will also
have implications among societies. It is difficult to imagine a very
poor country, where much of the population is excluded from
participating in market growth and has limited access to public
goods or access only to public goods of inferior quality, being
competitive in an increasingly technologically advanced global
economic system.

The equity outcomes of stakeholder reforms will vary from
country to country. First, which members of society participate
and the benefits they receive will affect equity. Second, the availability and quality of public goods will be affected by the reforms, and the access of the poor to goods such as education is
crucial in achieving growth with equity. Third, reforms may
work at cross-purposes on equity, which makes it very difficult to
predict the outcomes. The introduction of new incentives, such as
exit and voice, in the operations of public institutions may well
improve the institutions' performance and services, which overall should increase equity. And on balance the poor rely more on
public goods than do the wealthy. Thus, even if they do not participate in reforms because they are too poor, they may benefit as
free riders from improvements to public services that result from
other groups' exercising exit and voice. If, however, exit results in
the flight of most of the articulate and motivated people from the

public to the private sectors, services may deteriorate and the poor who remain dependent on them will suffer disproportionately.

If the size of the excluded groups is small and their needs can be addressed through corrective policies such as cross-subsidies, public education, and targeted programs, and if new market incentives and stakeholders strategies improve institutional performance, the overall effects on equity are likely to be beneficial. But if the number of those excluded is very large—perhaps even a majority, as it is in some countries studied here—inequality may increase in the short term, even if public institutions improve. Yet if there is potential for even greater institutional improvement and better public services and development of affordable private sector alternatives for the poor, some of the negative effects may ultimately be reversed. In addition, the introduction of new intermediary institutions in service delivery, such as nongovernment organizations and local governments, may help overcome some kinds of exclusion. The wide range of possible equity outcomes is best demonstrated in this book in the discussion of Bolivia's Popular Participation reform, which devolved responsibility for social services to the local level and introduced innovative voice mechanisms for the users of those services. The outcomes in terms of both equity and institutional performance were extremely varied across municipalities.

The diverse experiences described in the country studies will shed light on these issues. The studies provide examples of the stakeholders approach in countries with high levels of poverty and inequality and those with very low levels to discover the extent to which the approach itself affects equity, the extent to which equity outcomes are driven by other trends, and the longer-term trends that the reforms set in motion or reinforce.

## A Note about Method

The choice of countries in this study is intended to provide regional diversity and also survey various sectors—education, health care, social security, and so on. But the countries share some common elements: a continuing and relatively successful macroeconomic adjustment, adoption of the stakeholders approach in initiating one or more reforms, a certain degree of compatibility among the reforms, and the feasibility of conducting field research in a reasonable period of time. It is not a systematic comparison of examples of reform with and without a stakeholders approach, but rather an attempt to learn from and analyze instances of relatively successful programs in which such an approach has been used. The countries vary widely in per capita income and poverty: Zambia is one of the poorest countries in the world, while the Czech Republic is one of the wealthiest in eastern Europe and one of the most egalitarian countries in the world. Chile has a slightly higher per capita income than the Czech Republic, but also substantially greater poverty and inequality.[77] The case studies also reflect differences in types of public goods. Privatized state-owned enterprises are the least "public" of the goods, and education and health care are the most (figure 1-1).

In addition to a balance of income and poverty levels, the selection of countries reflects regional diversity. Three are from Latin America, the region that has gone the furthest in applying second-stage institutional reforms and using stakeholders approaches for a variety of public goods. The Czech Republic was one of the most rapid economic reformers in eastern Europe, and the first former communist economy to carry out a stakeholders strategy on a wide scale. Zambia was the first country in Africa to initiate far-reaching economic reform under democratic auspices and sweeping reforms in a social service: health care.

The study examines three kinds of stakeholders reforms. The first and least public seeks the participation of low-income groups in the privatization process; examples are taken from Chile, Peru, Bolivia, and the Czech Republic. The second is social security reform based on exit options provided through private social security plans in Chile, Peru, and Bolivia. Both the Chilean and Bolivian reforms linked social security reform to strategies to broaden participation in privatization. The third is the most "public," and in the social sectors. There are two studies of education reform: Chile's distribution of vouchers for education and Peru's increased local autonomy in managing school resources. There is also one example of health care reform based on in-

Figure 1-1. *Stakeholder Reforms: Incomes and Public Goods*

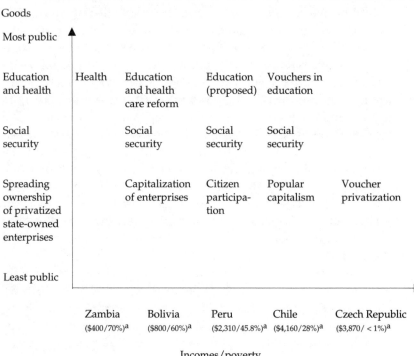

a. Per capita income in U.S. dollars and poverty ratio.

creased local responsibility for resources and management in Zambia as well as a brief description of a similar pilot program in Peru.

There are some differences in the relative success of the stakeholders approach, both within the particular sectors where the reforms were undertaken and in the effects on overall reform. Success in terms of institutional performance was evaluated by the reform's ability to increase quality and coverage of the particular service and to solicit the active participation of new stakeholders. Effects on political sustainability were primarily assessed by voting behavior and by more specific opinion surveys where they were available. To indicate improved political sus-

tainability, electoral results did not have to favor the specific parties or governments carrying out reforms, but rather the continuation of economic reform programs more generally. Equity
effects were evaluated in two ways: the effects of the reforms on
overall equity, that is, the balance of costs and benefits among all
members of society, and the effects on the poorest groups. These
latter merit particular attention because access to education,
health care, and other public goods is one of the principal means
they have to overcome extreme poverty.

Before discussing stakeholder reforms, each chapter analyzes
the political economy of macroeconomic reforms in a country,
then describes recent trends in poverty and inequality. The chapters attempt to evaluate the effects of poverty and inequality in
the country on the implementation and outcome of the reforms,
particularly on the political support or opposition they receive. In
some cases, as with education and social security reforms in
Chile and Peru, similar reforms were carried out in very different
poverty contexts and with very different outcomes as a result. A
particular focus is the effects of such poverty-related constraints
as unequal access to information, inability to pay transaction
costs, and expectations or other behavioral traits in the response
of potential beneficiaries to new market incentives.

The method for the study is inductive and based on case
studies. The aim was to evaluate the effects of the stakeholders
approach in three broad areas critical to the sustainability of market reforms. By bettering our understanding of a new approach
to the delivery of public goods and the reform of public institutions, the research aims to provide a starting point for more specific and theoretical analysis in what remains largely uncharted
territory in the realm of political economy.

## Case Study: Chile

Chile was a pioneer in initiating social reforms in the midst of
macroeconomic adjustment and in relying on private alternatives
and giving people the choice to increase their stakes in the reform

process. The Chilean reforms have captured international attention and have been widely copied. The three reforms discussed here—education, social security, and broad-based privatization—created a significant number of new stakeholders in the systems, and the reforms remained intact during the 1990 transition to democracy and after. Yet their equity effects are the subject of a great deal of controversy, particularly within Chile.

In educational reform, people were allowed to choose private instead of public schools through a system of government-subsidized vouchers that were accepted by either. A significant proportion of schoolchildren moved into the private system, which is of high, although not uniform, quality. But for various reasons, including lack of adequate information and lowered expectations, the poorest people chose the exit option much less frequently. And while public systems in urban areas for the most part benefited from the reforms, the quality of education in poor rural schools deteriorated until corrective policies were introduced in 1990. This deterioration was less the result of the voucher system per se than the decreasing real value of education vouchers in the 1980s and the lack of alternative funding options in poor rural areas. Regardless, the outcome was harmful for the poorest people. The primary focus of policymakers since the democratic transition has been to improve quality in poor rural schools while leaving the basic voucher model intact.

The privatization of Chile's pension system has received perhaps the most attention of any of the reforms under study. It was the first attempt by any country to completely privatize social security. Switching to the private system was voluntary for workers previously in the public plan, but new entrants to the labor force had to join the private system. There is a minimum pension provision for those who earn pensions under a minimum income level. Those in charge of carrying out the reforms maintain that their public relations campaign, designed to educate the public about the reform as well as to encourage participation, was critical to its success.[78] There were clear material incentives for choosing the private plans, and most workers did so. Although the reforms entailed an initial and substantial fiscal cost, the system is now credited with raising the national savings rate. And while there is no clear evidence yet for Chile, studies in other countries suggest that the distribution of wealth may be more equitable with the existence of private plans.[79] With the transition to democracy, there was no mention of reversing the reform and returning to a public system. A number of countries in and outside the region have since attempted to copy Chile's system in a modified form.

Despite the overall success of the reform and the high participation rate, the poorest workers disproportionately chose to remain in the public system. Low-income workers refrained from joining the private pension funds for many of the same reasons poor parents did not take up the education voucher option, suggesting the difficulties of creating new stakeholders among the very poor.

In the early 1980s a crisis in Chile's financial sector forced the government to reverse a round of privatizations that were begun in the late 1970s. Lack of regulation of the process, among other factors, contributed to a high level of ownership concentration, weakness in the financial sector, and expensive state bailouts of wealthy debtors. In the mid-1980s a new economic team launched a second round of privatizations with the explicit objective of broadening the base of stakeholders. By the end of 1988, nearly 170,000 people had become direct shareholders of privatized enterprises through popular capitalism and direct bidding at auction. Another 3 million, out of a labor force of 4.8 million, became indirect shareholders through the AFP system. The accumulation of shares in former state-owned enterprises was worth 2.2 percent of GDP and provided a redistribution of wealth to middle-income people at a time when the benefits of public social expenditures were being redirected to the poorest people. This second round of privatizations was important in establishing a reform that was politically as well as economically sustainable.

## Case Study: Peru

During one of the most dramatic and far-reaching stabilization and adjustment programs in the region, the government of Alberto Fujimori began a pilot reform of Peru's education system in 1983. The reform was focused on the poor and based on a stakeholders approach: increasing local control over resources and management for primary education in poor areas throughout the country. The program set up local school boards, which were to be composed of school directors and representatives of the parents' associations and the communities, and gave them greater autonomy in decisionmaking. The traditionally strong and controversial teachers' union, the Sindicato de Trabajadores en Educacion del Peru (SUTEP), was excluded from the boards in the original reform proposal, as were teachers in general, which resulted in the continued opposition of the teachers' unions to most reforms. Ultimately, the government's reluctance to devolve power fully to the local level eroded the viability of the reform. Instead the president launched a major program, directed and funded by his Ministry of the Presidency and coinciding with the April 1995 elections, to build school infrastructure throughout the country. Many schools were built in areas where there were no teachers to staff them, and broader educational reform was abandoned. The Peruvian experience in educational reform demonstrates the difficulty of achieving institutional and stakeholder reforms without executive commitment to overcoming political opposition from central public sector institutions.

The Peruvian experience with social security reform was far different. In 1992 the government introduced a private pension system ultimately intended to replace the insolvent public pension program, the IPSS (Instituto Peruano de Seguridad Social), and stimulate the local capital market. The plan was modeled on the Chilean system of encouraging workers in the state system to switch to new, contribution-based private pension funds, but had substantial problems in implementation. One reason was the incentives, which initially imposed a higher contribution rate and later retirement age for workers switching to the private program (those differences between the private and public plans have since been narrowed). In addition, because of the generally low incomes of workers and the severe budget constraints on the state, there is no state-guaranteed minimum pension as there is in Chile. This has discouraged low-income workers from switching. Other limitations are that only 40 percent of the labor force is covered by either private or public plans, and average salaries are low ($250 a month).

Nevertheless, a remarkable 1.2 million workers are now in the new private system, while 800,000 remain in the public plan. The distribution of those shifting to the private program is closely related to age and income levels, with younger, wealthier workers more willing to switch. Poorer workers cited the absence of a minimum pension or inadequate access to information as the primary reasons for not switching, which again suggests some of the difficulties of overcoming poverty-related constraints to participation in stakeholders approaches. At the same time, the speed with which the new system became operational and the major increases in workers joining after perverse incentives were eliminated suggests the broad appeal of new private alternatives, particularly in countries where the government has performed very poorly in the past. As the system develops, the number of workers with tangible stakes in it is likely to increase.

Finally, in mid-1994, the Peruvian government announced a "citizen participation" program designed to broaden national involvement in privatization. The objective was to promote popular participation by encouraging half a million citizens, many of whom had never previously held shares, to invest. The program was intended to consolidate privatization by creating a broad base of stakeholders. The major obstacles to the success of the programs were the lack of public awareness of the role of capital markets, too little disposable income among the lower and middle classes, and a widespread distrust of savings schemes following the collapse of many savings and loan institutions in 1992–94.

The program offered shares on an installment plan with a 10 percent initial cash payment and a subsidized interest rate of 1 percent a month for subsequent installments. It also provided investors with protection against falling share prices for the three-year period during which shares were being paid off. Participation was far greater than the government expected: more than 250,000 middle-income and low-income investors had participated by June 1996. Several more rounds of citizen-based privatizations were planned for mid-1988. Active public promotion of the program and favorable terms for small investors were responsible for the high participation rate. A large percentage of investors have kept their shares, which is a remarkable record in a population as poor as Peru's and suggests that while stakeholders approaches have difficulty in reaching the very poor, they have a great deal of potential and appeal for many low- and middle-income people.

## Case Study: Bolivia

In 1985 Bolivia began the first experience with successful stabilization of hyperinflation under democratic auspices. Since then two successive elections have yielded proreform governments. Yet it is also evident that the poor—the majority of Bolivians—are not fully incorporated in the market economy. As a response and a means to build political support for the beleaguered privatization process, the 1993–97 government of Gonzalo Sanchez de Lozada launched a major attempt to spread the benefits of privatization to all adult Bolivians. Under "capitalization," as the government's approach was christened, 50 percent of the shares of the major state-owned enterprises were to be sold to international investors who agreed to invest a certain amount in the enterprises rather than buying them from the government. The other 50 percent of the shares were to be deposited in a collective fund in the name of all Bolivians older than age 21. The collective fund is managed and invested by new private pension funds. The dividends are distributed as an annual payment or solidarity bond of $250 to all citizens older than 65, thus for the first time providing a form of universal social security in Bolivia.

The government departed from the usual practice of using the proceeds from privatization as fiscal revenue, instead choosing to invest the bulk of the money in the economic growth of the country. The reform increases equity because most Bolivians did not have access to the highly subsidized public pension system. And since most of the people are poor, many more poor Bolivians than rich ones will receive solidarity bonds, which represents an unprecedented transfer of resources for most poor families. Meanwhile, the privately managed individual capitalization-based pension system for workers previously affiliated with the state system is expected to boost Bolivia's underdeveloped capital markets and savings mechanisms.

The Sanchez de Lozada government also introduced a program to decentralize and democratize local government. The "Popular Participation" program changed the allocation of municipal government resources from one based on local tax revenues to a redistributive, per capita–based plan that channels unprecedented levels of resources to poor and remote communities. It also gives them primary responsibility for administering health care and education services. The resources are administered by municipal governments—many of them newly established—in conjunction with locally elected "vigilance committees." The program has had notable effects on the living standards in poor communities and on local government in Bolivia, which previously did not exist in most communities. As with all experiments in decentralization, there have been strong differences in the outcomes among communities. A remaining equity concern is the lack of managerial and administrative capacity in the poorest communities, which can result in poor management of critical health care and education services and worsen existing inequalities. Yet no other program better demonstrates the variety of outcomes that can occur from a widespread adoption of voice as a way to improve the performance and delivery of important public goods.

Regardless of the programs' flaws, they demonstrate that even in a very poor country it is possible to create a significant number of new stakeholders and improve overall equity (benefit the poor on balance, if not the poorest groups) and the political sustainability of reform at the same time.

## Case Study: Czech Republic

The Czech Republic was one of the pioneers in building a market system in eastern Europe, and its citizens have consistently supported the market approach. Part of this situation results from cultural factors and part from the conditions at the time of transition, which were far better than many in neighboring countries. However, success is also due to political leadership and to the presentation and marketing of reforms. Increasing individual stakes through a mass privatization plan was very early a major element of this process. The plan gave people vouchers in privatized enterprises that could either be kept or sold at auction. The system had a very high public participation rate. According to the officials who carried it out, a major component of success was Prime Minister Vaclav Klaus's extensive public relations and education effort, in which he traveled countrywide to explain and build support for the program. The effects of the approach on the management of the enterprises have been less successful, however, because of collusion between the banks and the investment funds that ultimately purchased a large proportion of the public's shares.

The reform was, without a doubt, critical to the political sustainability of reform in the Czech Republic. It was not a coincidence that it was implemented one month before the decisive June 1992 elections, in which Klaus received a broad public mandate that allowed him to begin the reforms necessary for the republic's turn to a market economy. The reform also redistributed resources from the state to the Czech population. However, many of the vouchers were ultimately sold off to the investment funds for profit. The selling of shares for immediate profit was directly related to lower income and education levels, which is somewhat surprising in a country with as flat an income distribution and as low a poverty ratio (less than 1 percent) as the Czech Republic. Those that sold off their shares were also more likely to vote for the left opposition than for the continuation of reform policies. While a number of reasons explain these trends and are discussed in chapter 5, the results suggest that some of the obstacles to creating stakeholders among the poorest people seem to confront all income and distributional contexts unless governments are prepared to make a strenuous effort to provide additional incentives and education to encourage participation.

## Case Study: Zambia

In 1991 Zambia initiated both an extensive adjustment program and a transition to democracy. Soon after the economic reforms began, a major health care reform was launched. The increasing involvement of communities in the management of health projects, including control over resources, distinguishes the relative success of programs in health care from lack of progress in reforming education. Raising the stakes at the local level gave the reforms a momentum that was virtually irreversible, and the process has continued despite several attempts by a new minister to reestablish central control. In education, in contrast, the central ministry was unwilling to devolve responsibility and resources.

A fundamental flaw in reforming health care, however, was the government's failure to explain the reforms to the public. Although reform was first advocated through the 1991 election campaign, the government's failure to communicate with the public adequately since then has resulted in some severe and damaging mistakes in implementation, in particular the introduction of user fees. Fees were introduced in a haphazard manner, and an exemptions policy for children and those unable to pay was poorly understood and carried out. As a result, the poor (which make up about 70 percent of the population) failed to participate. This eroded popular support for the reforms, and possibly for economic reform more generally. It may also help explain high levels of failure to vote that characterized the October 1996 elections. Ironically, the drop in usage of the public health system by the poorest people occurred at a time when major strides were made in reforming the structure of service delivery. It is to be hoped that the falloff can be reversed once flaws in the exemptions and other main policies are corrected. And the results suggest the very significant gains that can be made by increasing the participation and responsibility of local people—via voice—in the delivery of the most important public goods. Yet they also suggest there is little to gain from exit or voice options that are based on payment of fees in places where such a high percentage of the population is impoverished.

## Concluding Comments

Each of the case studies helps show how and when stakeholders strategies can improve the performance of public institutions in delivering public goods and services and also support the sustainability of reforms. They also show how these strategies affect equity, although these effects are often specific to the particular context and to the mix of exit and voice strategies adopted. The final chapter summarizes the lessons and conclusions from all the chapters and discusses their theoretical and practical implications.

All the case studies point to the contributions private market approaches can make to improve the delivery of public goods in virtually all contexts. They also emphasize the importance of the state in providing adequate regulation and financing, as well as correcting for the many impediments that the poorest people face in responding to new market incentives. Although equity trade-offs are the greatest for the poorest countries because there are many poor people who may be excluded from the reforms, the potential gains from improved institutional performance are also greater, particularly since state-centered programs have failed in many of them. Ultimately, market-led growth will be difficult if not impossible to sustain in any country that lacks public institutions capable of fulfilling their essential functions. Strengthening that capacity and contributing to the sustainability of market-based economic policies is the objective of the reform efforts that are described in the following chapters.

Chapter 2

# Markets and Public Goods in Chile: Schools, Pensions, and Popular Capitalism

C HILE WAS the first country in Latin America to carry out extensive macroeconomic reforms. It also led the region in restructuring its social services based on private sector participation and on new incentives for individual choice. The Chilean reforms have been discussed extensively elsewhere, and this chapter does not attempt a comprehensive evaluation.[1] It is intended to serve as a point of departure for the more detailed discussion of less well known examples of reform in the other countries in the study, which were based on or are variations of the Chilean approach to providing public goods and services. The chapter provides an overview of how the introduction of market incentives and individual choice created significant numbers of new stakeholders in a new model for the delivery of public goods and services in Chile. It focuses on two reforms, in education and social security. It also briefly discusses Chile's efforts to broaden the base of stakeholders in the privatization of state-owned enterprises. The chapter examines the effects of these new market incentives on the political sustainability of the reforms and their effects on equity.

The Chilean reforms were begun under the authoritarian regime of Augusto Pinochet in the early 1980s and were maintained by successive democratic governments after the 1990 transition to democracy. This is not surprising, because by 1990 a significant number of moderate-income people as well as the wealthy had stakes in the new private education and social security systems, in newly privatized state-owned enterprises (SOEs), and more generally in the market-oriented economic model. Yet despite broad coverage by the new education and social security systems, the reforms failed to incorporate the poorest of the population as full participants, leaving them with limited access to or inferior quality of crucial public services. As a result, a primary focus of policymakers in Chile in the 1990s has been to address equity issues.

The results of Chilean attempts to reform equity are of particular relevance to this study because in many other countries—several discussed in this study—similar reforms are being attempted in contexts of much higher poverty and much weaker administrative capacity than in Chile. In addition, most reforms are now being carried out under democratic auspices, which present a very different political economy dynamic than Chile did in the early 1980s. As a result, different choices or compromises are often made in designing reforms. An important first step in analyzing the reforms in other countries is to review Chile's efforts, its record in providing privatized public goods and creating new stakeholders, and the effects on equity.

## The Context for Social Policy Reform

The education and social security reforms in Chile were part of an extensive package. In 1973 General Pinochet overthrew the elected Marxist government of Salvador Allende, with the explicit objective of saving Chile from the threat of communism, social unrest, and economic chaos. By 1975 a group of economic advisers now known as the Chicago Boys began to influence economic policy and sought to transform Chile's economy along neoliberal (free market) lines.[2]

In the first few years the reformers focused on macroeconomic policy, particularly stabilization, trade liberalization, and some privatization. But they also laid the groundwork for sweeping social reforms. Even though the private social security system did not begin until 1980, for example, it was an objective of many of the economists as early as 1975, and initial measures such as building a fiscal surplus were taken beginning in 1977.[3] The concept of targeting public social expenditures only on those who could not afford private alternatives was introduced by the economist Miguel Kast and institutionalized by his students through the Oficina de Planificación Nacional (ODEPLAN), the state planning agency. The targeting was first applied to social welfare and safety net expenditures designed to provide protection against the extreme recession of the mid-1970s. These actions included special employment programs, school meals, and mother and child health care programs. Yet the approach also began to be used in the mainstream social programs: social security, health care, and education.[4]

The introduction of market incentives into the public service sector was highly controversial in Chile, which had been one of the first countries in Latin America to develop an extensive public social welfare infrastructure. The Labor Code was introduced in 1924 and a preventive health care system for workers' families in 1938. From 1920 to 1972, social welfare spending grew ten  times faster than national income, providing extensive coverage by the state's health, education, and social security systems.[5] Thus not surprisingly, the 1980 social security reform was disliked not only by those opposed to the government but by the military, social security experts, and the administrators of the pension funds.[6] Opposition gradually decreased, however, and a decade later the reform was widely considered a success, both within and outside Chile. Some observers credit it with raising the national savings rate in addition to unifying a fractured and insolvent social security system and paying better pensions.[7] The resources administered by the private pension funds amount to US$25 billion, or 40 percent of GDP. Not surprisingly, the reform has attracted worldwide attention, and several countries in Latin America have created variations of Chile's plan.

Similarly, Chilean education reform was at first very controversial. The reform introduced choice through government-subsidized vouchers that could be used at either public or state-subsidized private schools.[8] It became even more unpopular as the value of the vouchers eroded during the 1980s. Yet the reform survived the transition to democracy, and education policies since then have left the basic model intact. Reforms have focused on improving quality and resources in the poorest schools and on extending the hours of the school day. The value of vouchers, meanwhile, has been increased along with the post-transition increases in social expenditure.[9]

This does not mean that there are no criticisms of both the education and social security systems. However, what was initially seen as a radical and unacceptable change in social welfare policy has become widely accepted in Chile and attracted substantial attention from abroad. In part the gradual transformation of public opinion about the social welfare reform mirrors economic trends. Although at first the neoliberal economic model was extremely controversial, with opposition increasing strongly after the 1982 collapse of the financial sector and the subsequent recession, support gradually increased as growth recovered and unemployment decreased. And with the 1990 transition to democracy, it became possible to separate criticism of the regime from criticism of the economic model, which also tempered opposition and ultimately consolidated support for the economic reform.[10] A coalition of Christian Democrats and Socialists, the Concertacion, defeated the pro-Pinochet forces in the 1989 presidential elections and was reelected in 1993. The Concertacion governments have endorsed and even deepened Chile's free market model and its major social welfare reforms while making extensive efforts to improve equity within the orthodox economic framework.

Before I discuss in detail Chile's reforms in social welfare, a brief description of economic and poverty trends is necessary to understand changes in public opinion about social welfare. Chile suffered an extreme recession in the early 1980s in which GDP fell by 14 percent and unemployment rose to almost 30 percent. After economic reforms were instituted in the mid-1980s, growth returned and has maintained an average rate of more than 6 percent since 1990. Unemployment has remained at less than 6 percent for several years. Poverty, which claimed 45 percent of the population in 1986, fell to 40 percent in 1990, to 28 percent in 1994, and is projected to fall to 17 percent by 2000 if the economy strong.[11]

ined economic growth and effective targeted social poliesponsible for this impressive reduction of poverty and show how social expenditures can be far more effective in reducing poverty when they are targeted. Reductions in unemployment are credited with approximately 70 percent of the reduction in poverty, while social policies are responsible for about 30 percent.[12] In addition, the economic and social welfare reforms were implemented in a highly developed institutional framework. During the crisis and reform years the government was able to rely on an extensive network of mother and child nutrition programs and focus them on the poorest people. Public works employment programs were also targeted by keeping wages well below the minimum. Public social services were restructured to benefit the poor, and private alternatives were introduced for those who could afford them. Although per capita social expenditures decreased during the crisis years, they increased for the poorest groups.[13] Throughout the crisis, welfare indicators such as infant mortality not only continued to improve but accelerated in their rate of improvement.

Chile's extensive social welfare system and its relatively efficient public sector institutions clearly facilitated reform. Yet the political context was also important: a democratic government might face greater obstacles than the Pinochet regime did in reorienting expenditures to the poorest at the expense of the middle class. With the transition to a democratic regime, the focus of the military government was maintained while social expenditure was increased almost 10 percent a year, financed by a new tax on business profits.[14] Because the demand of upper- and middle-income groups for social services is now mostly in the private sector, government increases were able to benefit the poor disproportionately and were highly effective in reducing poverty.

Chile's record on income distribution is less clear. Although average income increased across the board—average per capita income was 24 percent higher in 1994 than in 1990—improving distribution has proved more difficult.[15] In fact, except for the Pinochet years when there was a sharp worsening of the distribution and an exceptionally high concentration of income in the wealthiest quintile, the distribution has remained remarkably stable from the 1959–64 Alessandri government through the 1990–94 Aylwin government, with the ratio of the fifth quintile

Table 2-1. *Income Distribution in Chile, 1959–93*
Percent

| Quintile | Alessandri government, 1959–64 | Frei government, 1965–70 | Allende government, 1971–73 | Pinochet regime, 1974–89 | Aylwin government, 1990–93 |
|---|---|---|---|---|---|
| Quintile 1 | 3.2 | 3.2 | 3.1 | 2.7 | 3.4 |
| Quintile 2 | 7.5 | 7.1 | 7.5 | 6.4 | 6.7 |
| Bottom 40 percent | 10.7 | 10.3 | 10.6 | 9.1 | 10.01 |
| Quintile 3 | 11.9 | 11.4 | 12.5 | 10.6 | 10.5 |
| Quintile 4 | 20.1 | 19.7 | 21.5 | 18.3 | 17.9 |
| Middle 40 percent | 32.0 | 31.1 | 34.0 | 28.9 | 28.4 |
| Quintile 5 | 57.9 | 58.6 | 55.4 | 62.0 | 61.5 |
| Ratio of 5th quintile to 1st quantile | 18.1 | 19.5 | 17.9 | 23.0 | 18.1 |

Source: "Survey of Household Incomes," Department of Economics, University of Chile, cited in Marcel and Solimano, "Distribution of Income and Economic Adjustment," in Barry Bosworth, Rudiger Dornbusch, and Raul Leban, eds., *The Chilean Economy* (Brookings, 1994), p. 219.

over the first ranging from 17.9 to 19.5 percent.[16] The primary losers during the Pinochet years were the middle 40 percent of the distribution, and they have not yet recovered their losses, although the income shares of the poorest quintiles have improved (table 2-1). Given the much greater fluctuations in poverty and employment levels in this period, these trends confirm that income distribution in Chile is determined by structural factors that are not easily altered by short-term economic trends.[17]

Although Chile's income distribution seems very unequal by international standards, two important comments are in order. First, the measure of income matters. Studies that use household income rather than individual income are likely to display greater equality because poor households tend to include a larger number of people than do wealthy ones.[18] Second, another important element, which affects Chile's distribution positively but does not show up in international comparative data, is that public social expenditure and income transfers are very progressive and unparalleled in the region. In 1992, for example, one-third of all income transfers went to the poorest quintile and added 5,249 pesos, or 7.7 percent, to the average income in that quintile (table 2-2). And in 1991, while 70 percent of the real increase in the con-

Table 2–2. *Average Monthly Household Income in Chile, 1994*
Percent

| Type of income | Quintile 1 | Quintile 2 | Quintile 3 | Quintile 4 | Quintile 5 | Ratio of 5th quintile to 1st quintile |
|---|---|---|---|---|---|---|
| Independent income | 4.3 | 8.2 | 12.0 | 18.3 | 57.3 | 13.3 |
| Monetary subsidy | 33.4 | 27.8 | 19.6 | 13.1 | 6.1 | 0.2 |
| Total monthly income | 4.5 | 8.3 | 12.1 | 18.2 | 56.9 | 12.6 |
| Social programs | 39.1 | 28.3 | 20.0 | 10.4 | 2.2 | 0.1 |
| Health | 49.3 | 33.4 | 23.5 | 4.1 | –10.3 | –0.2 |
| Education | 34.8 | 26.2 | 18.5 | 13.1 | 7.5 | 0.2 |
| Total income | 6.3 | 9.4 | 12.5 | 17.8 | 54.0 | 8.6 |
| Total income, 1990 | 5.9 | 9.8 | 13.2 | 18.6 | 52.5 | 8.9 |
| Total income, 1992 | 6.4 | 9.9 | 13.2 | 18.3 | 52.1 | 8.1 |
| Total income, 1994 | 6.3 | 9.4 | 12.5 | 17.8 | 54.0 | 8.6 |

Source: "Integracion al Desarrollo—Balance de la Politica Social 1990–1993, MIDEPLAN, Encuesta CASEN 1994; and Ministerio de Hacienda, "Estadisticas de las Finanzas Publicas 1990–94," as cited in Kevin Cowan and Jose de Gregorio, "Distribuicon y Pobreza en Chile: Estamos Mal? Ha Habido Progreso? Hemos Retrocedido?" paper prepared for the Ministry of Finance/Inter-American Development Bank Workshop on Inequality and Growth, Santiago, July 1996, table 4.

sumption of the poor was due to income earnings, 30 percent was attributed to increases in social expenditure and transfers.[19]

Social policy in Chile also entails a less measurable resource transfer that is likely to improve distribution in the future. Chilean social expenditures are distributed very progressively: 80 percent of public health expenditures and 60 percent of education expenditures go to the poorest 40 percent of the population. Thirty-five percent of education expenditures go to the poorest 20 percent and are designated primarily for programs to improve the quality of schools in poor rural areas. The share of expenditures going to higher education actually decreased from 18 percent of total education expenditures in 1991 to 14 percent in 1995. This is remarkable in a new democracy because interest groups in higher education tend to be more politically organized than those in the basic levels.[20] Since poorer families spend a larger proportion of their incomes on health care and education than do wealthy ones, these transfers have an additional progressive effect. Although incomes in the 5th quintile are 13 times those in the first quintile, if they are adjusted for social expenditures, they are only 8.6 times greater.[21]

Finally, another indicator of the effectiveness of targeted expenditures in reducing poverty is that the *rate* of poverty reduction increased after the absolute amounts of targeted expenditures were raised. From 1987 to 1990, for each additional percentage point of growth, poverty was reduced by 0.5 percent. For 1990–92 this figure was 1.0 percent and for 1992–94 it was 1.2 percent. As with all investments, eventually there will be diminishing marginal returns, and the margin for increasing the rate of poverty reduction will eventually shrink as the total poverty ratio falls. It is illustrative that less progress has been made since 1990 in reducing the rate of indigence—extreme poverty—than in reducing the overall poverty rate. Indeed, as the total poverty rate goes down in Chile, a higher proportion of the poor display traits other than income poverty, such as drug addiction, delinquency, or social exclusion, that are more typical of poverty in developed economies.[22]

Not surprising in light of these trends, a 1996 survey found that overall perceptions of economic progress and of personal advancement within the more general economy remain better in Chile than in most countries in the region with the exception of Peru, where they are in part linked to the boom in economic growth there in 1993–94.[23] This stands in contrast to most of the people surveyed in the region, half of whom believed that the situation in their country is bad and 60 percent believe that there has been no progress in the past few years.[24]

An important and less well documented part of this story is the effect of Chile's social welfare reforms on equity and perceptions of equity and on the creation of new stakeholders in the market. The education and social security reforms stand out both because of their extent and the way they have given most of the population stakes in the reformed systems. Health care reform, however, has resulted in more stratification between public and private systems and was accorded far less popular approval.[25] Finally, popular capitalism, a more direct attempt to create new stakeholders in privatization, will be described briefly after the education and social security reforms because it was linked to the government's objective of increasing worker participation in the private pension funds and it serves as a point of reference, since many other countries in the study have adopted similar strategies to increase participation in the privatization of state-owned enterprises and to increase support for market-based strategies more generally.

## Chile's Social Security Revolution

In November 1980 the Chilean government announced a dramatic reform of its social security system. The pay-as-you-go defined-benefit system was performing poorly. By the mid-1970s Chile had thirty-two pension funds covering 60 percent of the labor force. With a payroll tax of 51.1 percent in the main public social security fund, the Social Security Service, in 1975 and 64.7 percent in the private employees' fund, contribution rates were among the highest in the region.[26] Weak control over contributions, extremely low returns on invested funds, and high administrative costs resulted in delays of more than a year for a worker to draw a pension at retirement and small pensions that varied with occupation and fund. Because workers could not leave the funds they were in, fund managers had little incentive to improve performance. Each occupational category had its own benefits and retirement age, with white collar workers often able to retire far earlier than manual laborers. There was no redistribution from the wealthiest category of workers to the poorest. Instead of being indexed, benefits were adjusted periodically by the legislature, a process that was highly politicized.

The system was becoming increasingly insolvent: the government subsidized 25 percent of pension fund revenues from 1973 to 1980, a fiscal burden equivalent to 18.1 percent of GDP. And the burden was projected to increase as demographic trends resulted in an increased ratio of retired persons to workers. Despite the extensive subsidies, 70 percent of retirees received pensions equal to or less than the minimum old age pension of $30 a month.[27]

The reform had five objectives: to introduce uniformity into the social security system, provide better incentives for workers to contribute by creating individual retirement accounts, allow workers to choose their own pension fund managers, introduce greater efficiency through competition, and use government subsidies to help the poorest workers. The program has four main features. Each worker finances his pension from an individual capitalization account fed by an obligatory 10 percent levy on his monthly wage. Neither the government nor employers contribute to the workers' accounts, but the state guarantees a minimum return on the accumulated savings and underwrites the capital sum itself. Workers in the system have to contribute for at least five years before they are eligible to retire. Upon reaching retirement age, or having contributed enough to earn a pension that is 70 percent of his or her average salary, a worker can purchase a lifetime annuity from a life insurance company or choose a programmed withdrawal of funds based on his or her life expectancy, or combine the options.[28] Half the workers are eligible to retire early and most do. About 90 percent choose the low-risk annuity, while most of the rest take the programmed withdrawal because they have not contributed enough to afford an annuity, which is at least 120 percent of the minimum pension. Only a very small percentage, those with high incomes, take the third and higher-risk option of delaying the purchase of the annuity in the hopes that returns on the invested funds will have a higher yield in the short term.[29]

The second feature of the reform is that workers' accounts are managed by profit-maximizing private pension funds (Administradora de Fondos de Pensiones, AFPs), which earn income from the commission and administrative charges on the accounts. The AFPs' capital must remain separate from that of the retirement accounts. The state regulates the funds heavily through an independent superintendency and sets maximum limits on the proportion of funds that can be held in each of seven asset categories. Initially, AFPs were not allowed to invest funds abroad. As of 1992 they could invest 3 percent of their assets abroad, and in 1995 the limit was increased to 9 percent.[30] They have to hold minimum reserves and are forbidden to invest funds in each other's shares or in life insurance companies or mutual funds. Workers are allowed to choose among AFPs and to switch between funds.[31] The system also provides for the payment of disability and survivor pensions by life insurance companies, a service for which workers contribute an additional 3.4 percent of their wages.

Finally, the state guarantees a minimum pension for those at retirement age who have contributed to the system for at least twenty years but do not meet the minimum pension level. The minimum, at 85 percent of the minimum wage or 40 percent of the average wage, seems high by international standards, but is low given minimum wage levels of about $170 a month.[32] Persons who have contributed for less than twenty years or are not affiliated with any pension program are eligible for the government's assistance pension (PASIS), introduced in 1961, which is about half the level of the minimum. Just under 10 percent of all people younger than age 65 are eligible for the PASIS.[33] There is a waiting list, however, that is limited to 300,000 people.[34]

The new system was made mandatory for first-time entrants to the formal labor force, while those in the old system were allowed to choose between programs. People can switch to the new program at any time and are issued a "recognition bond" (bono de reconocimiento) for their contributions to the old system that is then deposited in the worker's account in the AFP he or she chooses. The bond earns an inflation-adjusted return of 4 percent a year and upon the worker's retirement is used to create an annuity separate from the contribution-based annuity. Those remaining in the old system received the same level of benefits established under the old regime, but eligibility rules were standardized and the separate funds consolidated. Although contribution rates were reduced, the employers' contribution was passed to the workers in 1981 (whose salaries were raised to account for the difference). Thus there was a major financial incentive to switch: AFP members had to pay 13.4 percent of their salaries, while those remaining in the old system had to pay 20 percent. The deficits of the old system, including the recognition bonds, were paid by asset sales and a contribution from the state as well as by the savings in administrative costs that came from consolidating the large number of funds.[35]

The initial costs of the reform were high—4 percent of GDP in 1986—but will go down as the number of workers in the old system decreases and the fund closes around 2030 (when the last state pensioner dies). At that point the state's obligations will be limited to paying the pension supplements to workers earning less than the minimum and meeting any defaults by AFPs or insurance companies. Up to 50 percent of workers in the system may be eligible for some sort of minimum supplement (other estimates are as low as 15 to 20 percent). The fiscal burden this signifies will be determined by the number of workers below the minimum, the size of the gap between accumulated contributions and the minimum (most workers are 50 percent below the minimum at worst), their life expectancy, and the rate of return on funds, which has been high, an annual average of 14.2 percent until the mid-1990s. In 1996 the return was an unusually low 3.5 percent. Although that rate recovered somewhat in 1997, the fall prompted debate over the competitiveness of the AFPs and whether they should be allowed more flexibility in making investments.[36]

The new system grew rapidly. In the first month 500,000 workers, or 25 percent of the labor force with the option to switch, moved to the new system; 70 percent of all insured had moved by 1982. By May 1994 the system had twenty-two AFPs with 4.8 million contributors. The pensions paid by the new system are, on average, 40 percent higher than those in the old system. Eighty-six percent of the labor force was covered by 1991. (Many of those who are covered by an AFP account, however, do not contribute consistently.) The funds invested in the AFPs amounted to 1 percent of GDP in 1981 and grew to 40 percent ($25 billion) by 1995.[37] Without a doubt the AFP system has made a major contribution to the development of capital markets in Chile.

The system has had other benefits. It may have increased the national savings rate, although it is difficult to determine the extent to which "new" savings in the AFPs were actually additional savings or merely crowded out other savings.[38] Even critics of the system recognize that it makes a contribution to savings by raising individual workers' consciousness of the need to save. The new system also facilitates labor mobility by unlinking pension funds from particular occupational categories and linking them to individual workers instead.[39] Another benefit has been the removal of a potential disincentive to employment: the high payroll tax contributions for employers. Although unemployment decreased dramatically in Chile in the late 1980s, the decrease

was primarily caused by the rapid and sustained economic recovery, and thus the incentive effects of eliminating the employer's contribution are difficult to measure.[40]

One of the more complex matters to resolve is the equity implications of Chile's transition from a defined-benefit system to a
funded, defined-contribution system. Pay-as-you-go (PAYGO)
plans constitute a distributional contract between generations in
which the first generation sets the rules and tends to receive the
highest benefits. By the time the private system was instituted in
Chile, the old system had become a redistribution of income from
younger workers to retirees who, for the most part, had contributed at much lower rates for most of their careers. Second, under
PAYGO systems wealthier people, who tend to live longer than
poor ones, receive greater net benefits. Third, most professionals received credit for their years of study under the old system,
which was a regressive transfer of resources from less educated
workers to more educated ones with higher earnings potential.
Related to the third point, pensions were indexed to wages in
the final years before retirement, producing a higher return on
contributions from higher-income workers. In addition, a host
of inequities had been created by special funds and retirement
criteria for particular workers such as miners and civil servants.
Finally, a ceiling on taxable earnings makes PAYGO systems regressive.[41]

But while correcting for these inequities, defined contribution plans introduce new equity issues and trade-offs. First, by
using individual accounts, defined-contribution plans eliminate
the solidarity in PAYGO, in which, at least in theory, there is substantial redistribution among current worker cohorts (although
not always from rich to poor, as was noted earlier). Second, the
AFPs charge a flat commission (approximately 3 percent) even
though the sizes of workers' accounts vary greatly; high-income
workers thus benefit disprportionately. In the Chilean program
both the PASIS and the minimum pension provide some modest
redistribution to the poorest workers, but this comes from general revenues, not from the social security system itself: there is
no explicit redistributive tax on individual workers' accounts.

The redistributive component varies greatly among defined-
contribution plans. The Chilean system emphasizes protection of

the poorest workers, while lower middle income workers, who may contribute for years and earn meager pensions just above the minimum, receive no redistribution. In Argentina, in contrast, middle-class workers who contribute for a long time do well because all workers who contribute for thirty years or more receive a flat benefit.[42] Workers who are poor—and a disproportionate number of women—who contribute for less than thirty years receive no benefits. In Peru there is no minimum pension or any other redistributive element for a variety of reasons, including justified concerns about fiscal sustainability given the large number of very low income workers.

The new system introduces other equity problems germane to most of the stakeholders strategies discussed in this study in that the poorest are often the least equipped to take advantage of approaches that hinge on choice or voice. The least educated workers are likely to make poorly informed decisions when choosing a fund. They are also less likely to contest management decisions to encourage all workers to join the same pension fund to reduce administrative costs, as has occurred in many firms in both Chile and Peru. And because the poor tend to be risk averse, they are much less likely to take a riskier option that has the potential to earn a higher return. This is demonstrated by the small number of Chilean workers, all of them at the top of the income scale, who have postponed purchasing annuities in an attempt to benefit from higher rates of return in the future.

On balance, however, the new system has resolved more inequities than it has introduced, particularly because it provides for the poorest workers through the minimum pension guarantee. In Peru, Argentina, and other countries that have copied the Chilean system but without providing the same redistributive choices, poor workers have fared far worse. Finally, when considering the reform's effects on equity, it is important to remember that it spurs economic growth and reduces the state's future fiscal liabilities. Faster growth and a smaller obligation to pensioners will allow Chile an increased margin for essential expenditures on health care and education, which are progressively targeted and have proven essential in reducing poverty.

Two efficiency drawbacks have characterized Chile's social security system. The first is excessive switching between pension funds. Because the designers of the reform sought to emphasize choice, switching between schemes is free of cost and without limitation. The number of salespeople increased from 3,500 in 1990 to 20,000 in 1997. And while 300,000 workers changed their afiliation in 1990, some 2 million did so in 1996.[43] Switching is not caused by fund performance, which is fairly uniform among the major AFPs, but by commercial incentives ranging from free tennis shoes to financial remuneration that are offered by the plans. Most people switching are on the lower end of the income scale. In 1996 the AFPs lost more than $200 million due to switching.[44] Other countries that have copied Chile's system have attempted to place some limits on excessive switching. In part because of the switching and in part the lack of economies of scale in managing large numbers of very small accounts, administrative costs in the system are high, much higher than they would be in a well-managed, financially viable defined-benefit program.[45]

The second element of inefficiency is that AFPs' investment performances vary little because strict regulation makes them risk averse and limits investment options. The primary difference among them is the provision of accessible information and the courtesy of the service. This seems to have more effect on workers' choice of AFPs in small towns than it does in cities, but the influence remains marginal, in part because of the average worker's limited access to information. Not surprisingly, therefore, the largest AFPs and the ones with the greatest name recognition, such as Habitat, Summa, Santa Maria, and Provida, are the ones ranked best by workers.[46]

Most supporters argue that high administrative costs are a small price to pay for a system whose benefits include improving the development of the capital market, encouraging private savings, and making political interference in pension funds very difficult. One of the major problems with PAYGO, and one that has characterized social security programs in Latin America, is that the system provides incumbent governments with a large potential source of revenue to spend or borrow against. Those that stand to lose most from poor investment decisions or the erosion of those funds—future generations of retirees—are not well organized to pose political opposition, nor is it likely that they are aware of how the funds are being managed or spent.

It is important to note that social security reform is complex and country specific. One model may not be able to be perfectly replicated in other contexts. The different equity decisions made in Peru and Argentina, for example, demonstrate the extent to which a country's political economy will affect such choices in social security reform as whether to protect the poorest workers or favor those at the middle of the income scale. Another major factor is the context in which reforms are implemented: the coverage of the existing system, state of capital markets, level of poverty, and size of the informal sector.

In Argentina and Uruguay, for example, because the existing system had wider coverage and the population was older than Chile's, shifting entirely to a private system would have had much higher fiscal liabilities for the state than it did in Chile.[47] But in Peru and Bolivia, because coverage was very limited, reforms were far less expensive. However, because the average income of workers is very low in Peru and Bolivia, neither system could afford to incorporate a minimum pension: too many workers would be eligible for the minimum to make the reform fiscally sustainable. In Bolivia an innovative mechanism uses the proceeds from privatization as a temporary minimum pension in the form of an annual payment issued to all Bolivians older than age 65, but it remained outside the individual capitalization plan. In Peru the lack of a minimum pension served as a disincentive for poor workers deciding whether to switch to the new private system. Thus although Chile's system certainly has provided an important model for social security reform in other countries, the costs of reform and the equity outcomes will vary depending on the country.

## The Politics of Pension Reform

Selling the pension reform to the public was not easy, given that Chile was the first country in the world to privatize its social security system. In addition, the reform was proposed by an unpopular authoritarian regime. When it was introduced, people across the political spectrum, including certain groups who supported the Pinochet regime, opposed it. Some of the opposition stemmed from general political opposition to the authoritarian regime. Some came from those also opposed to the regime and directly harmed by the reforms: workers and labor unions. Yet their ability to voice opposition was severely limited because public sector unions were banned and most others had limited freedom. The managers of the particular pension funds, which ranged from unions to bankers' associations, were also strongly opposed because reform threatened their control over significant amounts of money. Professionals with expertise in the social security matters opposed the reform on technical grounds. Finally, the military was opposed because the reform was very radical at a time that the regime faced an important political test: the 1980 constitutional referendum. It also threatened the military's special pension fund. In the end, after the regime fared well in the referendum (65.71 percent voted for the regime's constitution and 30.19 percent against), key members of the military agreed to support the reform on the condition that the military's fund remain outside the new system.[48]

Important to the reform's acceptance was a campaign of public information launched by Minister of Labor and Social Security Jose Piñera in the six months before the privatization was introduced. Piñera contends that building grassroots support was instrumental in the new systen's acceptance among elites within the regime.[49] In a series of three-minute television spots between May and November 1980, he attempted to explain different aspects of the reform to the public. Spots focused on themes ranging from "you are the owner," which was emphasized visually with his constant waving of an individual savings passbook, to safety and regulation issues, to a minimum pension for all, to an explanation of the transition.

Selling social security reform to the public was easier than expected.[50] Worker confidence in the old system was very weak, delays in getting pensions were long, and the inequities were blatant. In addition, switching to the new system was voluntary. Thus there was very little lasting worker opposition to the reform, particularly with the strong material incentives to switch. Even the labor unions soon supported it, and some even formed union-managed AFPs.[51] By the time of the democratic transition in 1990, there was virtually no talk of reversing the reform. At the technocratic level, meanwhile, opposition dwindled when it became clear that the system was performing well and yielding high returns, and as it attracted increasing international attention. Although the reform was severely criticized by technocrats in universities in the early 1980s, a decade later most major universities offered courses on social security reform based on Chile's model.[52] After the reform had been in place for a few years, some affiliates began making voluntary contributions to their AFP accounts, another important indicator of confidence.[53]

An important element in the political viability of the reform was that it did not cause any major curtailments in public consumption in other areas because there was a fiscal surplus to fund the pension deficit. Beginning in 1977 the economics team began to accrue a fiscal surplus to cover the costs of the reform. The government began the new system with a surplus of 5.5 percent of GDP. The costs of the reform, which are primarily composed of the deficit of the old system plus the value of the recognition bonds that come due each year, were 1.48 percent of GDP in 1981, 4.73 percent in 1988, 3.87 percent in 1990, and projected at 0.95 percent for 2015 as the number of people remaining in the old system gradually decreases.

Also important in laying the political groundwork was raising and unifying the retirement age in the late 1970s to age 65 for men and 60 for women and ensuring uniform indexing of all pensions.[54] Although these measures may not have been popular, they were presented to the public before the more general reform.

Another important element in building support was the requirement that the AFPs invest their funds domestically. This may have unduly limited portfolio options, but the plans were instrumental in ensuring Chile's renewed growth and they received very high rates of return as a result. This had an important political benefit because the reform was seen as contributing to *domestic* capital markets, growth, and employment. Although countries such as Bolivia that have smaller markets need more foreign investment, the Chilean market was large enough for the AFPs to develop.

Equally important to the political success of the reform were the extensive and effective regulatory mechanisms created in conjunction with the AFPs. Because the reform had not been tried elsewhere, it would have been particularly vulnerable to a crisis of confidence if there were any kind of scandal or widespread failure on the part of the AFPs. Creating public confidence in their ability to manage the nation's retirement assets was critical, particularly in the aftermath of the damaging banking crisis of 1982. While some critics contend that the Chilean system is over-regulated, there was a compelling rationale both for the extent of regulation and for limiting most of the investments to the domestic market, at least in the short term.

The failure to regulate privatization sufficiently in the late 1970s was at the root of the financial sector collapse of 1982 and resulted in government bailouts and reprivatization of many of the resulting state-owned enterprises under extensive regulation and broader shareholder participation.[55] Building an effective regulatory system was possible in part because of Chile's strong administrative capacity, which has traditionally stood out in the region. In countries such as Bolivia, establishing effective regulatory mechanisms is more challenging but is equally critical to maintaining public confidence in and therefore political support for the shift to privately managed plans.

The social security reform created broad support from people with direct stakes in the new system.[56] Yet there is still some distrust of the AFPs as institutions. Fifty-nine percent of those interviewed countrywide in 1996 expressed little or no confidence in them. They expressed a similar lack of confidence in the central Confederacion de Trabajadores (CUT), the central labor confederation. Forty-two percent had little confidence in the banks. Faith in the new private health preparedness institutions, ISAPRES, was even lower: 66 percent of those surveyed had no confidence. The level of support for AFPs was slightly higher among those who were their affiliates. When public opinion is examined further, confidence in the four biggest and best known AFPs was much higher than for the rest.[57]

All this suggests that understanding of the system remains weak among average workers, while support for it remains strong among higher-income, better-educated workers, as well as those directly involved in or employed by the industry.[58] To some extent this reflects the extent to which genuine choice is limited by lack of information and the absence of significant differences among the AFPs. Yet it also reflects the relative newness of the system and the few pensions it has yet paid: the average worker who is expecting to retire in the next ten or twenty years has not yet received any tangible benefit.[59] As the number of workers who receive pensions increases, and particularly as their pensions are calculated more fairly and paid in a more timely manner than they were under the old system (under the previous system it took a year to retire; with the new one, retirement is possible in one month), confidence in the system should increase markedly.[60] In addition, as a response to the low confidence levels in the AFPs, the superintendency of pensions introduced a policy of providing preretirement workers with a list of options before they selected an annuity.[61]

Future support for reform will also hinge on the balance between the new equity trade-offs it introduced and those it resolved. It eliminated many blatant inequities, such as the discrimination among categories of workers, and made the system much more uniform. Other benefits, such as resolving intergenerational trade-offs, are much less likely to be understood and appreciated by the average worker. Thus whether average middle-income workers will perceive themselves to be better off as pensioners in the new system remains to be seen. Clearly, the minimum pension will guarantee the approval of the lowest-income workers, and the high returns in the system will generate support from those with higher earnings. On balance, it is likely that the stakes of these groups will outweigh the potential opposition of lower-middle-income workers who contribute enough so that they cannot qualify for a government-supported minimum pension but retire on very modest pensions. And most workers, regardless of their incomes, had limited confidence in the previous system.

Finally, whether the system can continue to generate high returns will be critical to political support for it and the public's perceived stakes in it. Some variation in rates of return is inevitable: in 1994, for example, pensioners retired at 80 percent of their earnings, but in 1996 they retired at 70 percent. Wider variations could undermine support for the system and introduce significant new concerns about equity. Given the strength of Chile's economy, however, this is unlikely for the foreseeable future. On balance, the dynamics of political economy are likely to generate more rather than less support.

## Voucher-Based Education Reform

Chile's reform of its educational system, as revolutionary as its social security reform, was also based on new market incentives and individual choice. Initiated in 1980, the education reform introduced choice into a very centralized and bureaucratic system that had been based on the French model. The reform gave people the choice of private or public school education by issuing government-subsidized vouchers that gave them the chance to exit the public system. Private schools could receive government subsidies in exchange for giving up the right to charge fees. Allocation of state funding for both private and public schools was shifted to a per-pupil basis. Another objective of the reform was decentralization, and responsibility for management of primary and secondary schools was transferred to municipalities. By 1982 responsibility for approximately 85 percent of state schools had been transferred. The reform also reduced the size and power of the Education Ministry.

A major if implicit objective of the reform was to diminish the power of the teachers' union, which had increased its influence substantially in conjunction with the rise to prominence of the Radical party at midcentury.[62] With the reform and the transfer of responsibility, teachers lost their status as civil servants and became private sector employees, a change they strongly opposed and one that was ultimately reversed after the 1990 transition to democracy. Another objective, in accordance with the regime's philosophy of focusing on social expenditures, was to transfer resources from higher education, which benefits the wealthy in most developing countries, to basic education, which benefits lower-income groups. While total education expenditures as a percentage of GDP fell from 5.2 percent to 3.2 percent in 1992, expenditures on the poorest quintiles increased (table 2-3).[63] The change in emphasis is particularly notable given that in most other Latin American countries cutbacks in social services result-

Table 2–3. *Distribution of Public Education Expenditures in Chile, Selected Years, 1974–86*
Percent

| | Education level | | | |
|---|---|---|---|---|
| Year | Preschool | Primary | Secondary | University |
| 1974 | 1.0 | 37.6 | 14.0 | 47.4 |
| 1980 | 2.6 | 45.7 | 18.1 | 33.6 |
| 1983 | 3.8 | 50.2 | 16.4 | 29.6 |
| 1986 | 6.3 | 51.1 | 18.8 | 23.8 |

| | Income group | | |
|---|---|---|---|
| Year | *30 percent poorest* | *30 percent middle income* | *40 percent wealthiest* |
| 1974 | 28.6 | 24.1 | 47.3 |
| 1980 | 33.1 | 26.4 | 40.5 |
| 1983 | 34.8 | 26.8 | 38.4 |
| 1986 | 37.5 | 28.0 | 34.5 |

Source: Tarsicio Castañeda, *Para Combatir La Pobreza (Santiago: Instituto de Estudios Publicos, 1990), p. 97.*

ing from the 1980s economic crisis disproportionately hurt primary education.[64]

It is difficult to measure the impact of the reforms. In part this is because the financial crisis of 1982–83 led to a sharp decline of the real value of the vouchers: it fell by 32 percent from 1981 to 1991. As this occurred, wealthier municipalities subsidized their schools in a variety of ways, which obviously resulted in a disadvantage for poorer municipalities.[65] Without a doubt the reform stimulated the growth of private education in Chile, and a significant proportion of the people chose to send their children to private subsidized schools. The share of preschool, primary, and secondary students attending subsidized primary schools increased from 15 percent when the reform was introduced to 33 percent by 1993. Fifty-eight percent remained in municipal schools, and 9 percent attended elite, nonsubsidized schools.[66] Repetition rates have fallen, although this cannot be directly attributed to the vouchers. And rates remain highest in the public primary schools (9.2 percent), lower in the private subsidized schools (6.5 percent), and the lowest in the private schools (1.9 percent).[67]

Compared with other countries in the region, Chile ranks fairly well in educational coverage, particularly at the primary school level, although this is not a result of the reform. Primary school coverage is fairly uniform, with an average of 96.7 percent coverage across all income groups. Secondary education coverage is more varied, with 71.4 percent of those in the lowest quintile covered and 96.2 percent of those in the highest. Preschool coverage is much more limited to wealthier groups: 33.6 percent of those children in the highest quintile and 17 percent of those in the lowest.[68] Coverage at all levels is lower in poorer neighboring countries such as Peru and lower at the secondary level in wealthier countries such as Argentina.[69]

The effects of the Chilean reform on school quality have been strongly debated. Students of subsidized private schools outperform those in public schools on the standardized Sistema de Medición de la Calidad de la Educación (SIMCE) tests.[70] Some studies find that the results differ little when socioeconomic background is considered. Others have questioned the validity of the findings, given shortcomings in the available data, particularly the level of aggregation of the test scores.[71] Still, there is 17 percent less expenditure per pupil in municipal schools with poor SIMCE results than in those with high results.[72] In addition, quality varies greatly among the new private schools. One recent study found that private schools outperformed public schools only when they enrolled students with higher income or education levels or with higher SIMCE scores. Public schools did better than private schools with students from disadvantaged backgrounds.[73]

The differences in performance between public and private schools can be explained by a number of factors. First, the parents of students in state-financed private schools are wealthier than those in municipal schools. Second, private schools tend to locate in larger urban areas, where incomes are in general higher, while municipal schools must operate in all districts, including poor ones. Most studies in and outside Chile find that private and public schools perform better when there is competition.[74] Of 334 municipalities in Chile, 203 attend to students from poor backgrounds and 91 of these, primarily rural, do not have any private schools.[75]

The impact of the reform on municipal schools was mixed. Although it may not have had much effect on increasing their quality in general, it may have improved school performance in the larger, wealthier urban areas where competition increased. At the same time, although school quality in the municipal schools in rural areas is poorer than in urban areas, it is not clear that this is a result of the reform. In the absence of evidence to the contrary, there is no reason to expect that quality in rural schools would be better had the reform not taken place. Because most students in rural areas did not have the option of attending a private school, it is unlikely that public school quality suffered because good students had transferred out. If funding levels for rural schools fell significantly as a result of the per pupil allocation, however, there might be some correlation with deteriorating quality.

In theory the reform was intended to introduce market competition into public education and provide incentives for the public schools to behave more like private ones. In practice there were obstacles to this result. First, the rules delineating the responsibilities of the ministry and those of the municipal governments were not clear, and the ministry retained an extraordinary amount of influence over important municipal personnel and curriculum matters. Second, the voucher system was intended to impose a firm budget on municipal schools and make them operate more like private ones. But as the value of the vouchers deteriorated in the 1980s, municipal schools had to rely on other kinds of transfers from the central government, a reliance that increased with the transition to democracy and more general increases in social expenditures.

Third, there was no clear evaluation system to monitor the performance of municipal schools versus private schools. The national school achievement test in Spanish and mathematics, which is administered in the fourth and eighth grades in all schools, serves as a de facto evaluation system, but it is designed to address student rather than school performance. A breakdown of scores by individual schools is not publicly available, for example. Fourth, unlike private schools that could select the best students, municipal schools had an obligation to accept all students in their jurisdiction, an obligation all the more pressing because funding levels were determined by the number of students in attendance. Thus in large urban areas, where private and public schools competed for students and a market for schools did indeed exist, competition may have improved school performance. In smaller urban and rural areas, however, municipal school performance was not subject to competition, and in some schools with small numbers of students may have deteriorated if funding decreased.

In the end, it is difficult to distinguish or separate definitively the effects on municipal school performance of the vouchers per se from those of the inherent disadvantages public schools have in low-income areas under any system. Performance outcomes correlate with socioeconomic levels in various kinds of education systems, including that of the United States. In the United States, students are assigned public schools via the neighborhoods that they live in, so choice of schools requires choice of neighborhood. There is a great deal of variation in school quality that is directly correlated with socioeconomic and other related neighborhood traits.[76]

Another issue is that private schools existed before the reform, and there was already a certain stratification in terms of which groups attended which schools. In the absence of system-wide panel data, it is very difficult to determine the extent to which the voucher system increased stratification or ameliorated it. Given the growth in the attendance of subsidized private schools and the larger proportion of those from middle-income families attending these schools, a plausible assumption is that the reform provided new opportunities to reduce stratification between middle- and upper-income groups, but was not able to do so for the poorest families. Thus the stratification between the poorest and the rest increased, not necessarily because they were worse off in absolute terms, but because they were worse off in relative ones. Even critics of the reform note that the basic principles are sound, but that the primary problem has been carrying out the reforms in a highly stratified socioeconomic context.[77]

The reforms were also based in principle on the introduction of exit and voice options. Vouchers should increase users' ability to exert pressure on the public system because people would have a new option to exit and schools would risk losing attendance-related funds. The reforms were also intended to increase parental and community participation in managing schools. Yet parents seem to have been limited in exercising more voice. First, administration of education may have been decentralized to the municipal level but political power remained concentrated in Santiago (mayors, for example, were appointed by the central government). The authoritarian political regime also discouraged active participation in civil society. And the reform itself limited the function of the parents' association because the regime was worried about the politicization that had occurred in such civil associations during the Allende years.[78] Second, Chile is a traditional society, and class differences between university-educated teachers, administrators, and mayors, and middle- and lower-income parents discouraged more active parental participation. Third, teachers, who already had their status undermined by the reform, were not receptive to parents' evaluating their performance or exercising any other management function. Finally, because SIMCE scores aggregated at the level of the school are not available to the public, and private schools have strong incentives to inflate grades, it is difficult for parents to evaluate individual schools.[79]

Finally, because funding was tied to student attendance and not to performance, neither mayors nor school directors had incentives to seek out additional parental participation. In most large urban areas, meanwhile, there are also few political incentives for seeking out parental participation, even under democracy, since many parents send their children to school outside the *comunas* in which they live and vote.[80] The contact that Education Ministry officials have with parents is also limited, in part because of the time constraints that come from dealing with vocal and directly involved teachers and school directors and because of the school-oriented focus of the reforms themselves. Thus community involvement in Chile has for the most part been limited to situations in which particularly motivated teachers have sought it out. This stands in sharp contrast to countries such as El Salvador that have incorporated active parental and community involvement into the design of education reforms. Some observers suggest that effective community involvement in decisionmaking and in the management of schools can have effects on efficiency similar to those achieved by the incorporation of market incentives.[81]

The use of the exit option was clearly correlated with socioeconomic class: lower-income parents disproportionately remained in the public system (table 2-4). The findings of a 1994 survey in greater Santiago suggest that one reason is inadequate access to information. Poor parents were far less likely to be informed about what the alternative schooling options were: 39.1 percent of parents using private subsidized schools could name two high-quality schools in greater Santiago while only 27.2 percent of those using public schools could name the top school in their municipality. (High-quality schools are defined as those with average school test scores in the upper third for their region.)[82] Middle-class families have had a traditional affiliation with private or religious schools for decades.

Because of differences in education and access to information, parents of public school children evaluate schools differently than parents of private school children do. Anecdotal evidence suggests that parents of private school students are more likely to exert additional demands on school administrators and to worry about quality-related matters such as the availability of libraries. Lower-income parents of municipal school children worry more about what the locale looks like and see improvements as a favor from the municipality rather than part of their rights as clients.[83] An additional factor is that teachers' unions oppose providing information about schools to parents. This opposition was particularly apparent in the case of low-income parents because they disproportionately choose municipal rather than private schools.[84]

Another reason children of lower-income families do not transfer is transaction costs. Although the vouchers theoretically provide cost-free access to private education, costs of transportation, uniforms, or extra time commitments have often precluded the participation of poorer children.[85] Of the households surveyed, parents of children in high-quality schools traveled farther to reach schools and spent more time selecting them.

A final reason for the failure to exercise choice is expectations. Parents of students in private paid schools and in high-

Table 2-4. *School Enrollment in Chile, by Family Income, 1996*
Percent

| Quintile | Municipal | Subsidized private | Paid private |
|---|---|---|---|
| 1 | 73.7 | 25.4 | 0.9 |
| 2 | 67.3 | 30.8 | 1.9 |
| 3 | 53.8 | 42.6 | 3.6 |
| 4 | 44.9 | 45.8 | 9.3 |
| 5 | 24.3 | 31.4 | 44.3 |

Source: Oswaldo Larrañaga, "Chile: A Hybrid Approach," in Elaine Zuckerman and Emmanuel de Kadt, *The Public-Private Mix in Social Services* (Washington: Inter-American Development Bank, 1997), p. 25.

quality schools were much more concerned about their right to choose a school for their children. While 93.3 percent of parents of students surveyed in private paid and 71.4 percent of those in high-quality schools answered that they would be "very angry or upset" if they lost the right to choose schools for their children, only 53 percent of those in middle- and lower-quality schools did. Values attached to quality of education were also higher among parents of children in private paid and high-quality schools. Regardless of these differences in valuations, there is a widespread perception that there is fair access, because there are free schools and free school lunches. Only for university education is there a barrier to access because for the most part it is not publicly provided. Yet due to class and social barriers, poor rural parents rarely consider trying to send their children to better urban schools (obviously access to information plays a role in this as well).[86]

These trends are strengthened by the behavior of the private schools (and in areas where competition exists, some of the municipal schools), most of which have admissions criteria and at least implicitly seek out children from "stable" families. *Stability* is usually defined as a two-parent family with a father who has a full-time job and a mother who stays at home with the children.[87] This is hardly typical of the working poor.

Although these findings are typical of the obstacles to the poor's participation in exit and voice strategies, the extent to which the behavior of low-income parents fits the patterns in a country that has been progressing economically as rapidly as Chile is somewhat surprising. It also suggests the difficulties of applying the Chilean education model to societies with a greater proportion of poor people and more extreme poverty, as Peru's experience with education reform suggests.

## Education Policies since 1990

With the transition to democracy the voucher system remained intact, and efforts to improve the education system have not challenged the voucher model. This is not surprising, given the large number of citizens with stakes in the new private education system. Instead, two major objectives have dominated the posttransition reform agenda: improving the quality of the municipal schools, particularly in poor rural areas, and reducing the opposition of the teachers' union to the reformed system.

The first objective has primarily been achieved by the Programa de Mejoramienta de la Calidad y Equidad de la Educación Básica (MECE) and Programa de Mejoramienta de la Calidad de las Escuelas Básicas de Sectores Pobres (P900) programs.[88] Both have sought to supplement the per student funding system with new resources. The P900 program, introduced soon after the 1990 transition, targeted the poorest 10 percent of schools and is funded primarily by grants from external donors. The program, which was eventually extended from 900 to 1,500 schools, aims to improve reading skills, increase teacher training, increase the supply of educational materials, and improve school infrastructure. Although I will not discuss it in detail here, it is important to note that 56 percent of the schools in the P900 program had SIMCE scores that were better than the average for schools in their region, and many schools have been able to graduate from the program. However, 110 schools have been in the program since its inception and have shown no improvement, suggesting the difficulties of making educational improvements in the context of severe poverty.[89]

MECE is a broader and more diverse program of interrelated projects to improve the quality of primary education. Funded by a loan from the World Bank, the program began in 1992 and is scheduled to end in 1998. Its goals are to improve the physical and educational conditions of students and teachers in primary schools by upgrading infrastructure in 47 percent of municipal schools, establishing small libraries in each classroom in grades 1 through 4, requiring teachers to screen the health of their students, and increasing teacher training. These goals are broader than those of P900, but it has the same targeting principles. While it is too early to evaluate the academic results of the MECE, it has achieved its numerical goals. In addition, the program has elicited the cooperation of teachers in teacher training efforts and the participation of parents and communities, which has apparently fostered school autonomy in the areas where it is in place.[90] Both programs seem to have improved the quality of education in the poorest schools: the gap in SIMCE scores between the worst and best performing schools has narrowed significantly (table 2-5).

In another reform, which was introduced by the 1994–98 Frei government to complement the MECE and P900 programs, the school day has been extended from six to eight hours, which introduces more flexibility into the curriculum. The reform will cost $1.4 billion during the five years from 1996 to 2001 and will be funded by maintaining the value-added tax at its relatively high 18 percent rather than reducing it by a percentage point as was originally scheduled for January 1998.[91] The reform is costly because it will eliminate the double-shift system that many municipal schools use to make ends meet and facilities stretch, and to gain the cooperation of the teachers it will require augmenting their salaries as well as incorporating new performance incentives. The reform aims to improve the quality of schools and increase students' ability to use computers and the Internet.[92]

Funding for the MECE program has been maintained as part of this broader reform effort, but the P900 program had its budget cut in half by Congress in 1996. The lack of support for the P900 program, even in a country with a track record of targeted policies, suggests the difficulties many countries face in maintaining support for programs tightly targeted on the poorest people. The MECE, which benefits a broader cross-section of the population, seems to have had more success in maintaining political support.[93]

One criticism of these reforms is that they emanate from Santiago and increase tensions among the ministry, the municipali-

Table 2-5. *Differences in SIMCE Scores in Chile, 1990, 1992, 1994*

| Test group | 1990 | 1992 | 1994 |
|---|---|---|---|
| 5 percent of schools with best scores | 80.9 | 87.6 | 86.8 |
| 5 percent of schools with worst scores | 40.5 | 46.5 | 49.1 |
| Difference | 40.4 | 41.1 | 37.7 |

Souce: Larrañaga, "Chile: A Hybrid Approach," p. 25.

ties, and the schools by creating new incentives for schools and municipalities to seek financial support from the center. Because 90 percent of school resources go to personnel costs and additional resources come from the center for the MECE program, the role of vouchers in giving school directors autonomy is limited.[94] A telling example is that even though measures have been introduced to encourage flexibility in curricula, only 400 of 2,822 state-subsidized private schools and only a small number of the 6,422 municipal schools elaborate their own curricula, while 400 of the 1,058 paid private schools do.[95]

The second post-transition reform objective was perhaps more difficult to achieve than addressing quality problems in the poorest schools, and the outcome has been far more controversial. In 1990 the Estatute Docente (ED), or Teachers' Law, was passed, which returned civil service status to the teachers and again made the Education Ministry responsible for contracting with teachers in municipal schools. The law prohibits municipalities from firing teachers, even when school enrollment decreases.[96] Because municipalities are no longer responsible for hiring teachers, and the Finance Ministry pays their salaries, municipal schools have more teachers per student, yet they have weaker performance records.[97] Not surprisingly, teachers in municipal schools have resisted efforts to reform spending. Private subsidized schools are far more cost effective than municipal schools. They have student-teacher ratios of 31 to 1 versus 21 to 1 in municipal schools and lower teacher salaries, yet generate better student performance.[98] The recentralizing tendency of the law also runs against the logic of the labor market reforms introduced in the early 1990s that sought to direct collective bargaining from the national level to that of the individual company.[99]

Although the ED makes little sense for increasing efficiency and undermines the logic of the earlier reforms, the law was an essential political compromise for the first post-transition government. Teachers had been treated poorly by the Pinochet government, and as many as 10,000 were dismissed by the municipalities when they lost civil servant status. Many were fired for political reasons. Teachers were an important source of political backing for the Concertacion during the transition and remain a very important source of support for the Concertacion parties at the local level, where they wield considerable influence. According to Ricardo Lagos, the first Concertacion government's education minister, the government needed the cooperation of the teachers if it was to launch a major effort to improve school quality.[100] Ultimately, the need to make the costly concessions is a result of the Pinochet government's excluding teachers from the reform process. In some other reforms the government made attempts to create stakeholders among the beneficiary population, but in education reform the exclusion of teachers has weakened the political sustainability of the original reform.

The new law is likely to make it more difficult to introduce incentives to improve teacher performance. Under the current system, when municipalities have problems with teachers, they go directly to the Ministry of Education rather than attempt to negotiate. Indeed, municipalities find it easier to go the Finance Ministry to ask for more money to pay teachers than to attempt to fire them, so that there are more teachers per students now than there were before the reform.[101] An example of the incentives problems generated by the ED is that in negotiations between the government and teachers in late 1996 the teachers' union was able to defeat a government proposal to differentiate salaries according to type of teacher rather than length of service. (Teachers' salaries overall remain relatively low: an average of $460 a month plus bonuses for a thirty-hour week).[102] Meanwhile, there have been some minor attempts to introduce more flexibility and autonomy at the municipal and school level, and there are some provisions for firing workers at the municipal level.[103]

Another major rigidity in education reform was generated by the political right. A proposal to introduce open elections and five-year terms for school directors, who are at present appointed for life, was blocked by the right in Congress because many school directors were appointed by the Pinochet regime and are affiliated with parties of the right.[104] Although this obviously had the political objective of countering the restored political power of the teachers, it strengthened another top-down element of the education system.

Finally, another change has been a 1994 law allowing subsidized private schools to charge supplemental tuition even though in theory they are not allowed to discriminate against parents who cannot pay. Thus far, the system has not compromised equity. The average monthly fee charged at schools with shared funding has been estimated as Ch$2,858, or approximately US$7. Paying this fee for two children would represent 3 to 4 percent of the average income for a middle-income family. These fees represent 36 percent of the resources of subsidized private schools and 10 percent of those for municipal schools.

The fee policy appears not to have compromised equity, in part because the vouchers still give schools incentives to maximize enrollment. Surveys of Santiago schools have found that most schools with shared funding follow a flexible fee policy based on either a flexible fee structure or the granting of scholarships. The amount charged is relatively low, and the enrollment at schools joining the system has risen.[105] But it may be difficult to maintain and enforce these equity-enhancing practices, particularly because private schools already often practice "parental selection." Although shared funding may be necessary to maintain and improve school quality in the private schools and to make the transition to a longer school day affordable, it may result in sharper socioeconomic distinctions between students attending private and public schools.

## A Market in Education?

Chile's voucher system is one of the most far-reaching attempts yet to introduce choice and market incentives into a national education system. Yet it has not created a genuine and equitable market model in education. First, private schools can skim off students from more privileged backgrounds, both directly through the admissions process and indirectly by locating in more prosperous areas. Most municipal schools, meanwhile, have had to accept all students that applied. Second, although the reform introduced competition in larger urban areas, which may have improved the quality of municipal schools there, it did not result in competition in poor and rural areas where there were few incentives to establish private schools. This may not have compromised the quality of municipal schools in these areas, but it certainly did not improve it.

The decline in the real value of the vouchers in the 1980s impaired school quality and gave an advantage to schools in wealthier areas that could generate alternative sources of funding. And although some of the policies introduced since 1990 have been effective in improving the quality of the poorest schools, many have resulted in a recentralization of school management and most critically personnel selection, which makes it difficult for municipal schools to operate according to market incentives. The balance of responsibilities between the Ministry of Education and the municipalities was not fully worked out before 1990 and has been made more complex by some of the recentralizing measures.[106]

Finally, the voucher system has done nothing to change the behavior of the potential beneficiaries of the reform, the parents. Their behavior has been sharply segmented by socioeconomic status, demonstrating the poverty-related limitations such as unequal access to information and inability to pay even marginal transaction costs that low-income groups may face in responding to market incentives. Although this is not a flaw in the basic design of the reform, it does suggest that government must more actively help the poor to participate in the market-based provision of public services. In Chile the government could have carried out a more effective public education campaign and considered income supplements such as free bus fares for those low-income parents who did choose private schools. The Chilean experience suggests that the difficulties in introducing a market-based approach to providing essential public services in societies with much higher poverty ratios than Chile's and where a larger proportion of the population would be excluded would be much more difficult.

Chile's education reform introduced or made worse some equity trade-offs in education programs. At the same time, the growth of subsidized private schools, their improvements in performance, and the retention of the voucher system after the democratic transition demonstrate the benefits that incorporating market incentives and voice and choice can have on public service delivery and the creation of a permanent base of stakeholders. The 1994 law allowing private schools to charge supplemental fees is a good example of the kind of political influence that stakeholders can exercise. In Chile, the voucher system is there to stay. In addition, a number of promising options have emerged from or adapted to the reforms, such as competitive municipal schools in urban areas and religious schools and other private schools that use innovative teaching methods and cater to the needs of the poor.[107]

Still, there is a great deal of room for reforms at the municipal level, and the challenge remains finding a balance between providing better public education and providing new incentives for the poor to participate in the increasing variety of private sector alternatives, as well as encouraging more active community participation in both public and private schools.[108] Recent research shows the importance of improving the quality of education, even if it impinges on access, as well as the importance of involving teachers and parents in introducing reform if change is to work. Meanwhile, the success of choice-based strategies depends on the availability of information and parents' ability to use it. Thus, not surprisingly, disadvantaged students are likely to fare worse in a system that offers choice.[109] In Chile these matters need to be resolved regardless of whether public or private sectors predominate in providing education services. Finally, while improving equity was not an explicit objective of the voucher reform, the failure to explicitly address poverty and inequality, which are among the most difficult challenges in education in Chile, have severely limited its potential.

## Popular Capitalism: New Stakeholders in Privatized Enterprises

Chile set an example in another area of stakeholders-based reform: mass-based privatization. Although a full-scale discussion of this experience is beyond the scope of this chapter, the subject is worthy of mention because the privatization programs of Peru, Bolivia, and the Czech Republic that are discussed in detail in this study picked up elements of Chile's approach.

From 1974 to 1979 Chile's government privatized 550 state-owned enterprises. By June 1979 domestic capital markets had been liberalized, nominal tariffs reduced to 10 percent, and the exchange rate fixed. This, coupled with capital inflows, contributed to a significant increase in the trade deficit. Total foreign debt, most of it contracted with private banks at variable rates, increased greatly. During 1980–81 total debt represented 50 percent of GDP. Because the bulk of the debt was private, however, neither domestic authorities nor international financial institutions intervened.[110] Although growth had been consistently between 5 and 10 percent from 1977 to 1981, in 1982 a global recession and the devaluation of the overvalued peso led to a GDP collapse of 14 percent. Unemployment grew to 22 percent. The financial sector entered a major crisis, and in January 1983 the government took over 70 percent of it, a bailout that cost 3 percent of GDP.[111] The government also bought back approximately 50 of the 550 enterprises that had been privatized in the 1970s and thus regained control of the nation's largest industries, insurance companies, mutual fund administrators, AFPs, and trading companies.[112]

After the crisis of 1982–83 the economic management team changed, most notably with the entrance of Hernan Buchi as finance minister in 1985.[113] From 1984 on the government introduced policies to encourage structural change to favor exports, savings, and investment, as well as provide a more active regulatory framework. Privatization was a crucial instrument for accelerating growth. The gross investment rate, which was 23.9 percent of GDP in 1981, had fallen 10 percentage points by 1985. Increasing this rate required eliminating constraints on investments by both state-owned enterprises and the state-managed "odd-sector" companies.[114] This second round of privatization had three components: the reprivatization of the banks and pension funds in which the government had intervened, privatization of the state-managed odd-sector companies, and privatization of the traditional state-run firms, among them the large public service and infrastructure companies. The 1984–85 divestiture of the fifty enterprises that had been repurchased in 1983 marked the beginning of the second round. If maximizing revenues was an objective of the first round, distributing ownership was the objective in the second.[115] By 1989, when privatization was complete, the government had transferred 14 percent of GDP to the private sector.[116]

Throughout this period most government subsidies went to the private sector despite increasing popular and labor protest against economic trends and the regime. Yet in a significant departure from past policy, the second round of privatizations was undertaken with specific mechanisms to incorporate popular participation in the process and to avoid the concentration of ownership and heavy indebtedness that resulted from the first round. Through efforts that fall broadly under the rubric of "popular capitalism," the Chilean government encouraged workers to purchase shares in privatized state-owned enterprises either directly or indirectly through their AFPs. By the end of 1988 more than 169,000 people had become direct shareholders of privatized enterprises, through labor, popular capitalism, and direct bidding at auction. Another 3 million (out of a labor force of 4.8 million) became indirect shareholders through the AFPs.[117] The accumulation of shares in former state-owned enterprises was worth approximately 2.2 percent of GDP.[118]

"Both institutional investors and the vast array of small stockholders helped to facilitate the transformation of Chile's marketplace from an arena limited to participation of the elite few to a broadly based market catalyst."[119] There were various creative mechanisms to achieve this objective, and strategies differed slightly among the three areas of privatization. In the bank reprivatization, very favorable credit conditions were provided for small shareholders as long as they were active or retired contributors to the pension funds, while still allowing for a single

Table 2-6. *Ownership of Selected Large Privatized Companies in Chile, 1985–88*

Percent

| Company | Pension funds | Workers | Others |
|---|---|---|---|
| Compania de Acero del Pacifico (CAP) | . . . | 34 | 66 |
| Compania Chilena de Generacion Electrica (CHILGENER) | 14 | 6 | 80 |
| Compania Chilena de Electricidad Metropolitana (CHILMETRO) | 24 | 31 | 45 |
| CHILECTRICA Quinta Region (CHILQUINTA) | 17 | 9 | 74 |
| Empresa Electrica de Aysen (ECOM) | 0 | 100 | 0 |
| Empresa Electrica Coquimbo S.A. (EMEC) | 0 | 0 | 100 |
| Empresa Electrica de Melipilla, Colchoque, y Maule S.A. (EMEL) | 0 | 100 | 0 |
| Empresa Electrica Atacama (EMELAT) | 0 | 0 | 100 |
| Sociedad Quimica y Minera de Chile (SOQUIMICH) | 23 | 18 | 59 |

Source: Christan Larroulet, "Impact of Privatization on Welfare," in William Glade, ed., *Bigger Economies, Smaller Governments: Privatization in Latin America* (Boulder, Colo.: Westview Press, 1996), p. 383.

controlling stockholder. Nearly 14,000 popular-capitalism stockholders participated in these privatizations. In the odd-sector companies, where the priority was rapid economic recovery, share packages were sold off in the stock market under normal rather than special conditions. The principal participants were local businessmen, many of whom later entered into investment agreements with foreign businesses.[120]

The direct sale of shares to employees was an important component in the privatization of traditional state-owned enterprises. This occurred through shares with guarantees or shares granted as bonuses in collective bargaining agreements. Employees were often allowed to use advances from their severance pay reserves to buy shares and, in the case of merger companies, employees were allowed to use their severance pay to acquire shares. For those processes requiring large blocs of capital, employees and small stockholders were given the option of making payments in installments, a practice later used in the Peruvian citizen participation program.[121] Workers were able to acquire shares in a number of the seventeen state-owned enterprises that

Table 2-7. *Income Distribution in Chile, 1985, 1990*
Percent

|  | Decile | 1985 | 1990 |
|---|---|---|---|
| Poorest | 1 | 1.55 | 1.59 |
|  | 2 | 2.89 | 3.22 |
|  | 3 | 3.99 | 4.16 |
|  | 4 | 4.74 | 5.05 |
|  | 5 | 5.90 | 6.00 |
|  | 6 | 6.99 | 7.25 |
|  | 7 | 8.68 | 8.70 |
|  | 8 | 11.23 | 10.51 |
|  | 9 | 16.66 | 15.07 |
| Wealthiest | 10 | 37.37 | 38.46 |

Source: Larroulet, "Impact of Privatization," p. 384.

had been fully privatized by 1990–91, and three of them are 100 percent worker owned. The government also made a special effort to disseminate information about the economic performance and capabilities of the enterprises, both through the specialized communications media and by offering small packets of shares on the stock market. Table 2-6 shows the extent to which labor was an important participant in this component of privatization. Table 2-7 shows the improvements in income distribution that occurred between 1985 and 1990. Because social expenditures did not increase during this period except for the very poorest people, it is likely that this asset transfer improved income distribution, particular for lower-middle-income workers (deciles 3–6).[122]

The privatization of the mid- and late 1980s and the tangible stakes acquired by workers stand in sharp contrast to the first round of privatization, when reform concentrated ownership and benefits. This concentration ultimately resulted in a costly bailout of wealthy entrepreneurs at a time that unemployment was at record levels. At the height of the employment crisis in 1982, for example, when the government spent vast amounts bailing out the failing banking sector and provided subsidies totaling 3 percent of GDP to fewer than 2,000 debtors, only 1.5 percent of GDP was allocated for unemployment subsidies for about 600,000 workers, while another 600,000 unemployed received nothing.[123]

The second round of privatization, in conjunction with other reforms that greatly increased the number of stakeholders in economic reform and then in a major and sustained growth recovery, undoubtedly helped build a broader and more permanent consensus in support of orthodox, market-oriented economic policies by the late 1980s. This consensus, which was also influenced by the collapse of heterodox economic experiments in Peru and Argentina, developed at a critical time. After years of authoritarian rule, democratic elections were held in 1989, and the opposition endorsed the market model in the elections.[124]

Although many issues determined the outcome of the 1989 elections in Chile, including constitutional reform and the future role of the armed forces, the state of the economy was the focus. It was evident to the opposition that campaigning against the economic model would be a dangerous electoral strategy. Not only did the military regime consider the market model a crucial part of its legacy, but the model also had broad public support. Although the platform of the opposition—the Concertacion of Christian Democrats and Socialists—noted the need to improve income distribution, any action was presented as having to be "in line with the possibilities of the economy."[125] Indeed, the opposition's platform was more conservative and favorable to market reforms than that of the Pinochet government's candidate.[126]

This does not mean that there was no opposition to the model, particularly its effects on income distribution. There were harsh criticisms, especially from teachers, who had fared poorly with the Pinochet reforms. Still, there was an underlying consensus, among elites and most of the rest of the people, that the market economy was there to stay and changes would be limited to tinkering rather than overhauling the fundamental principles or reversing privatization and the social security and education reforms. The results of the elections, and elections since then, have demonstrated broad popular support for and permanent stakes in the market model.

## Conclusion

Several issues emerge from Chile's experience in using private markets to provide public goods and creating new stakeholders in reform. First, new market incentives and the increased competition from new choices can improve the performance of both public and private sector institutions. Introducing market incentives into the public sector can be as efficient as privatization in some instances, and increasingly the distinction between public and private sectors is being blurred. But there are also instances in which the public sector is different and is hampered from competing as effectively as the private sector because of its mandate to provide services to all users. A case in point is the experience of municipal schools in poor rural areas in Chile. In these instances special measures such as the P900 and MECE programs may be required. But although the programs are important for improving equity, they can also distort the functioning of market models. In Chile, for example, the importance of vouchers in determining school choice and encouraging competition has diminished, at least in the public schools. In such circumstances it may be impossible to avoid trade-offs between efficiency and equity improvements.

Increasing market incentives and broadening individual choice also raise equity issues because the most disadvantaged people are likely to fare worse than others. These effects may be more difficult to resolve in societies that endure greater poverty and inequality than Chile does, as other chapters in this study demonstrate. Although a minimum pension and the P900 programs were affordable corrective measures in Chile, their scale would have to be far greater and might well be unaffordable in much poorer societies, as in Peru, which could not guarantee minimum pensions. Solidarity financing—contributions from wealthier workers to poorer ones—cross-subsidies, and user fees can at times correct for inequities, but they are not always easy to initiate and, if carried out poorly, can create greater inequality. The provision for charging fees in the subsidized private schools in Chile, for example, has functioned well but may introduce inequities if schools increasingly select the children of parents who can afford the fees.

The political sustainability of reform can be improved if there are large numbers of new stakeholders. But soliciting or incorporating the participation of all key actors (individuals and communities) is necessary for success. For pension system reform and the second round of privatizations in Chile, the government actively sought the participation of workers to create a base of stakeholders that made reforms virtually irreversible. In contrast, in reforming education neither parents nor teachers were fully consulted. As a result, low-income parents in particular have not exercised their choices, limiting the reach of the reform and the support for it among low-income groups. Teachers, meanwhile, have remained opposed to reform, and the need to secure their cooperation and political support has resulted in a compromise that runs against the logic of the reform and is yielding inferior performance in municipal schools.

Adequate regulation and information are also necessary for private market approaches to work. Inadequate regulation in the first round of privatization resulted in financial crisis and state bailouts. In contrast, extensive regulation of the private pension funds was critical to generating confidence in a revolutionary approach to social security. Administrative capacity is an important consideration here: many countries that are poorer than Chile do not have the capacity to regulate adequately, which can result in systemic failures that undermine support for reforms. Related to effective regulation and transparency is the provision of adequate information about new reforms, which also requires some degree of administrative capacity. In the Chilean education reform, lack of adequate information significantly precluded the poor's participation. In social security reform, however, an active information campaign persuaded the majority of workers to switch to the new system. In Peru, much less effective dissemination of public information was a factor in low-income workers' failure to participate in a new private social security system (see chapter 3). As do many political economy models, market approaches tend to assume perfect information among participants.[127] The Chilean experience shows that even with a market model in which *all* participants are accorded new choices and opportunities, lack of access to information prevents the poor from taking advantage of the opportunities.

Also critical to at least a minimum of success for all the reforms in Chile was an extensive and effective social welfare system that made it possible to focus public expenditures on the poorest people while allowing those who could afford them to choose new private delivery systems. The social security program, for example, would be far less successful without the minimum pension guarantee. The education reform, while far from perfect, still can rely on an extensive system of municipal schools to provide services in poor areas where the private sector does not choose to go. And in other areas the public schools have been able to adapt and compete with private schools.

An effective social welfare system brings up the role of the state. Although opinion on its appropriate role in market economies varies widely, there is a consensus that it is irreplaceable in providing and enforcing the laws necessary for societies and markets to function and providing protection or safety nets for disadvantaged groups. Societies differ strongly about the extent to which the state should correct for inequitable market outcomes, who should be eligible for assistance, and how much assistance they should receive. These issues remain unresolved in many societies, particularly those in which the state has a very weak administrative capacity or a tradition of poor performance.[128] In such contexts, there are often costly and destabilizing conflicts about income distribution that may be either made worse or resolved by the introduction of market reforms.[129] Although a full-scale discussion of these issues is well beyond the scope of this study, it is important to note that inequities created by the introduction of market incentives in supplying public goods are likely to be both greater and more difficult to resolve when the state is weak. Chile, with its tradition of effective social welfare policy and good public administration, is the exception rather than the rule in the developing world.

Expectations and other behavioral traits related to poverty, traits that may take much longer to change than the time it takes to carry out public policies, can affect the ability or willingness of particular social groups to become stakeholders in market-oriented delivery of services. Relative poverty levels, as well as more endogenous traits affecting social mobility rates in particular countries, will determine how important these elements are in the success or failure of market incentives in the delivery of public goods, as well as the extent of equity-related constraints.

Finally, no reform model is set in stone. With time and experience, reforms can be adapted to the situations in particular countries. The Chilean model demonstrates that a certain amount of adapting is necessary for success. At the same time, it shows that introducing market incentives based on individual choice can have revolutionary effects on the way public services are delivered. The implications for equity are less clear. On the one hand, new incentives can eliminate some inequities, such as income barriers to private school access. On the other, they may introduce new inequities. Some are inherent in the logic of the reforms themselves, such as that lower-income workers who earn less contribute less and therefore receive smaller pensions in private social security systems. Other inequities stem from poverty-related constraints such as inadequate access to information or a tendency toward risk aversion that prevent the poor from benefiting from increased choice.

Chapter 3

# Social Services, Social Security, and Privatization in Peru

THIS CHAPTER describes several attempts to create new stakeholders in market reform in Peru.[1] It explores the extent to which introducing market incentives can serve as a basis for reform of public sector institutions and the different effects of this approach across sectors and income groups.[2] The chapter focuses on reforms in three kinds of public institutions. The first is those that provide education and health care services, goods considered fully public and essential in most countries. The second, institutions that provide social security, are also usually part of the public social welfare system in most countries. Yet in Peru pensions are much less important to social policy than education and health are because only a few workers are covered by the social security system, a situation typical of many developing economies. The third kind of institutional reform is privatization of state-owned enterprises through a program to encourage popular participation in share buying. Because the goods produced by these enterprises are privately delivering in most market economies, this is obviously the least public of the sectors covered. The contrasting record of the three reforms provides lessons about the use of market incentives in providing different kinds of public goods and the potential for delivering stakeholders in the process. It also sheds light on the differences in the political feasibility of reforms across institutional sectors.

As in the other chapters in this study, political sustainability is defined in two ways. The first is simple: how people vote (that is, in favor of continuing reforms by selecting a proreform candidate, who may or may not be of the same party as the government that initiated the reforms) and how politicians campaign—are the majority of candidates running on a proreform platform, and do any candidates who propose reversing reforms pose a realistic challenge? Recent evidence from Peru suggests that government efforts to reform the public sector and related expenditure patterns, particularly in critical areas such as education, can have a direct impact on voter behavior.[3]

The second definition is a much broader concept that hinges on attaining a balance between achieving the objectives of market reform and achieving a socially sustainable allocation of the benefits of reform.[4] The first objective—achieving economic stability and stable growth and ensuring basic service delivery—involves changing the incentive structures in both the macroeconomy and in the delivery of public social services, creating new stakeholders in the market process. The second objective depends to a large extent on the capacity of particular societies to respond to new market incentives. Such a capacity can be severely constrained by a high rate of poverty and related structural obstacles—lack of education, social or cultural marginalization or both, limited access to information, and inability to pay transaction costs—to the poor's ability to respond to new incentives. The analysis of several attempts to create new stakeholders in reform in Peru will help clarify this broader concept of sustainability. Altering the incentive structure can improve the operations of public sector institutions and also involve the active participation of the beneficiaries of services. Yet the analysis also demonstrates how pervasive poverty can limit the capacity of significant parts of society from responding to new incentives.[5]

## The Political Economy of Reforming
## Public Institutions

Reforming public sector institutions has been attempted several times in Peru without success, and the social unrest and hyperinflation of the late 1980s was in a way a culmination of these failures. Since 1990 the government of Alberto Fujimori has been able to resolve the economic problems of that crisis, an achievement that has translated into very strong political support. Yet the problems in the public sector have yet to be resolved: it remains virtually nonfunctional, and political power and administrative responsibility are highly concentrated in the executive branch.

The current political context gives the government unusual freedom from political constraint in implementing institutional reform; at the same time this makes executive commitment to reform a particularly important variable, as the fate of the various reforms under study will demonstrate. In 1995 the president was reelected with a strong popular mandate and a majority in the Congress. Public sector unions and other organized interest groups are the weakest they have been in decades because of the severity and the nature of the economic crisis and the reforms that it necessitated and of the concentration of power that has persisted in the executive branch. Meanwhile, the deteriorating coverage and quality of public services and the consequent decrease in public reliance on them has reduced the influence of such groups and created an increased public receptiveness to new alternatives. Political parties, which in the past might have provided an effective voice for some of these interest groups, have been discredited and have played only a marginal role in the recent elections.

Finally, the government, which took office during a period of hyperinflation and GDP collapse, has successfully stabilized the economy and initiated an impressive number of structural reforms. The result has been strong economic growth since 1993. Both investment and savings rates have increased markedly since 1990, which should result in more sustainable growth in the future.[6] One indicator of the fundamental strength of the economy was the limited adverse effects suffered from spillover during the Mexican peso crisis as well as from a preelectoral economic overheating in the first half of 1995. The government made a necessary adjustment but was able to engineer a soft landing: although growth slowed in 1996, it remained positive, at 2.3 percent, and was projected at over 5 percent for 1997. This stands in contrast with the much sharper economic contractions in Mexico and Argentina.

There is a fairly broad consensus that what remains on Peru's agenda is reform of the public sector institutions that deliver basic services such as health care and education. These reforms are also central in the agendas of the international financial institutions that provide support to Peru. The reforms are needed to reduce poverty and improve the average Peruvian's capacity to participate in market-oriented growth.

Although there has been some progress in reforming public sector operations, it has primarily been through the creation of agencies outside the mainstream public sector. A tax reform, for example, was initiated by setting up a new agency, the Superintendencia de Administracion Tributaria (SUNAT), to replace the Direccion General de Contribuciones (DGC), which was part of the Ministry of Economics and Finance (MEF). SUNAT was able to reduce the DGC's staff by more than 2,000 employees and to increase the tax base from 4.1 percent of GDP in 1990 to 14.3 percent in 1996.[7] Crucial to SUNAT's success was a small and skilled team of twelve, most of whom had worked at the Central Bank, with the support of some international advisors. Also important was the introduction of new market incentives: the agency is allowed to keep 2 percent of the resources it generates (the DGC relied completely on the public treasury). Salaries in SUNAT are as much as ten times higher than they were in the DGC. Integral to new agency's ability to broaden the tax base, meanwhile, was an aggressive public relations campaign designed to provide information and to motivate and coerce at the same time.[8] Analogous reforms were the introduction of INDECOPI, the Instituto Nacional de Defensa de la Competencia y de la Proteccion de la Propiedad Intelectual, an agency designed to facilitate registering intellectual property rights and enforce consumer protection, and the creation of the Comision de Promocion de la Inversion Privada (COPRI), the umbrella committee for privatization. Both agencies respond directly to the president, generate some of their own proceeds, have small and skilled staffs, and have been successful at meeting their objectives.

None of these agencies operates within the normal public sector nor has to adhere to public sector personnel regulations. In addition, the reforms they carried out shared some significant characteristics: the reforms helped important political constituencies, the agencies received generous funding from the government, and the agencies were very small compared with the mainstream public agencies such as health and education. Indeed, at the core of the success of these reforms is precisely what makes them easily reversible: there are no institutional constraints such as a strong judiciary or significant participation by beneficiaries of reform in decisionmaking about reversal.[9]

The fostering of specialized agencies has been accompanied by the retrenchment of personnel in the traditional public institutions, but not by efforts to reform their operations or incentives structures. What remains unresolved is the role of the line ministries and their incentives structures and resolving relations between central and local governments in the delivery of basic social services. Although there has been a great deal of discussion about decentralization as a potential solution, it is not clear what the implications would be nor that there is a genuine executive commitment to devolve power from the center. Indeed, most of the successful cases of reform have entailed concentrating power at the executive level.

A recent evaluation of Peru's extrainstitutional reforms cited conditions for success. These were a precise diagnosis of the problems and of objectives of reform; decisive actions in initiating reform in order to establish credibility; placing more emphasis on the reforms than on keeping the institution running; a need to overcome the problems inherent in a weak public sector (such as the slow bureaucracy and poor information flows); making the changes related to reform (such as of legal structures) on time; the importance of having a reform team *within* the institution and with a stake in the reforms; the need for an effective public relations campaign that clearly identifies the winners and the losers and either coopts them or fends them off; a need to get political and legislative support for reforms; and, finally, although participation is important, clear leadership and centrally led decisionmaking are more essential.[10] Most of these conditions would also apply to reform of public sector institutions in the event the government launched a serious effort. In the case of the extrainstitutional reforms, there was sufficient executive commitment to generate these conditions. In contrast, such commitment was absent in the attempted reforms of mainstream public sector institutions, as the example of education reform will demonstrate.

For a variety of reasons, ranging from the inadequacy of representative institutions and poor public expectations of the state's performance to the president's distrust of institutions and his reluctance to decentralize political power, the underlying approach to the mainstream institutions has been to allow them to atrophy, perhaps with the hope that they will eventually disappear in the face of private alternatives, rather than to attempt reform efforts similar to those in the new and autonomous agencies. This approach has had diverse effects in creating stakeholders: where reforms have proceeded and new incentives have been introduced, a significant number of new stakeholders has been created, which may provide some permanence to the reforms, even though they have been carried out primarily by temporary institutions. But in the line ministries, with the exception of a few instances, such as the Committees for Local Social Administration (CLAS), a pilot program to involve local communities in administering health centers, there has been no attempt to reach out to those groups.

## Poverty, Public Expectations, and Reform

The government may not see reform of public sector institutions as politically urgent because the public has few expectations of the state. After a prolonged crisis, severe impoverishment, the virtual disappearance of traditional representative institutions, and the deterioration of public services, followed by a growth boom resulting from a shift to market-oriented economic management, public attitudes about the state have changed markedly. Individualism and faith in the market surged and support deteriorated for traditional forms of social or political organization, a development that provided support for Fujimori, both in the electoral campaign and in government. "Given the collapse of the state's capacity to deliver public services in the late 1980s, the urban masses were increasingly inclined to pursue individual rather than collective channels for advancement, and they were drawn to Fujimori's message of hard work, self-reliance, and efficiency."[11]

Yet concurrent with these trends, poverty remains deep and severe, and growth is concentrated in a few industry sectors.[12] GDP grew a remarkable 19 percent between 1990 and 1994 and had the highest growth rate in Latin America from 1992 to 1995, averaging 8.9 percent. Yet by 1995 real GDP per capita had recovered only to its 1968 level. The poverty ratio fell from 53.6 percent of the population in 1991 to a still-high 45.8 percent in 1994. The ratio rose slightly to 49.0 percent in 1996, in large part due to a 1995–96 adjustment. Extreme poverty, meanwhile, remained the same in 1994 and 1996, at 16.6 percent, which is much lower than the one-third of the population that was in extreme poverty when the government took office in 1990.[13] Still, a significant part of society remains marginalized from the activities of both state and market. How the traditional obstacles posed by severe poverty affect the ability of these people to respond to new market incentives and become stakeholders both in economic activity and social welfare will be explored later in this chapter.

Meanwhile political parties have declined dramatically.[14] This not only means that Fujimori faces little if any organized political opposition but that public faith in the effectiveness of traditional organizations has deteriorated. A recent survey found that political parties were the last of the institutions that the Peruvian public trusts, with just 2.3 percent of respondents in Lima and 3.6 percent in the rest of the country citing parties as worthy of trust. Meanwhile, only 13.4 percent of people trust unions, and 9.8 percent of those in Lima do. Only 3 percent of workers nationwide were in unions; less than 1 percent in Lima were. The Church fared the best, with 58.3 percent nationwide and 61.1 percent of those in Lima citing trust. Neighborhood organizations such as communal kitchens and Vaso de Leche committees were second after the Church, with the trust of 32.4 percent of those in Lima (these organizations are far less prevalent outside the capital, particularly in rural areas). Although local organizations remain relatively strong in Lima, at least among the poor, there are no national organizations that effectively channel local demands into national ones and exert pressure on the central state. Confidence in other state organizations is also very low: 85 percent nationwide had no confidence in the legislature, and 51.7 percent had no confidence in the judiciary.[15] The attitudes and organizational behavior of youth are particularly striking. In Lima 56.3 percent of respondents aged 18–24 believed that those who fought alone had a better chance in life. In the rest of the country, 61.2 percent of the same age group did not belong to any sort of social organization, including art or sports clubs. This is particularly striking in a country known for its strong community organizations.[16] It is also notable in light of Robert Putnam's recent findings on the role of "civicness" in improving economic development.[17]

The rise of individualism and the decline of faith in state institutions is reflected in public attitudes and political behavior. According to a prominent newspaper editor, "political news just doesn't sell papers anymore; everyone is interested in becoming a capitalist."[18] A similar observation was that "Peruvians' previously strong faith in the state is giving away to a pragmatic individualism: from poorest to richest, Peruvians now talk of 'haciendo empresa' [forming a business]."[19] These attitudes are also in keeping with the significance of the informal sector and self-employment activities in Peru. At least 36 percent of the economically active population is self-employed, while over 50 percent works in small and medium-sized enterprises. This new faith in the market and in entrepreneurship has even begun to blur racial divisions. Although 87.4 percent of respondents believe that people are not treated equally in Peru, only 12.8 percent attribute this to race. "Ahora en el Peru la plata blanquea."[20] This faith in the market is so strong that Peru stood out in a recent eight-nation Latin American survey as the country where the largest share (79.4 percent) of those interviewed thought their country was making progress, trusted private companies to be instrumental in development (70 percent), and thought that foreign investment was beneficial (83.2 percent).[21]

These changes in attitude have altered people's expectations of the state, as has the dismal and worsening performance of state institutions. The quantity and quality of state services deteriorated sharply in the 1980s. Education expenditures were 19.2 percent of the national budget in 1986 but only 5.45 percent in 1991. Health care expenditures fell from 7.90 to 4.07 percent. In Lima

49.3 percent of those interviewed believed that the state's role was to provide education and that a secondary responsibility was to support the poor. In the rest of the country 57 percent said that the state should support the poor, while 53.1 percent said that its primary role was to provide education. Low expecations of the state reflect its dismal performance, but they also provide a political opportunity for reform, since people are likely to be more receptive to change when discontent is great. And the remarkable faith in the market suggests that it is an opportune time to initiate reforms based on creating stakeholders in response to new market incentives. The strong public response to the Citizen Participation Program in privatization (discussed later) is a case in point.

Attitudes about the state, in part a response to economic trends and shrinking public sector services, vary according to the prevalence of poverty. Economic recovery has been strongest in Lima and slowest in the rural sierra. Although extreme poverty was reduced from 10.0 percent in 1991 to 3.9 percent in 1994, in the rural areas it fell from 47.1 percent to 44.4 percent.[22] In contrast to the promarket attitudes of those in the capital, 43.9 percent of those outside Lima said the state's role was to promote the economic development in the country.[23]

Regions vary in their levels of poverty. The poor, as opposed to the extremely poor, have relatively good access to public services. The highest concentrations of extreme poverty are among the indigenous people in the rural sierra and selva. In Lima, migrants and female-headed households are disproportionately poor. The poor are most likely to be in two occupational categories: private sector workers and the self-employed. The main problem facing them (as opposed to problems facing the extremely poor) is lack of employment. The highest open unemployment rate, 14.3 percent, is in the city of Arequipa, while the highest underemployment rate is in the city of Iquitos, with 84.1 percent. Lima has 8.8 percent unemployment and 74.3 percent underemployment. The national average for underemployment is roughly 75 percent. Both phenomena are more severe among youth.[24]

These trends suggest that there are vast differences among the poor and that while some are reasonably positioned to take advantage of new incentives and new opportunities should they arise, many are marginalized by region, race, gender, and extremely low incomes. Providing these latter with access to basic public services of reasonable quality is critical to overcoming their marginalization and increasing their capacity to respond to new incentives and participate in market growth. Public education services, for example, vary tremendously in quality and are particularly poor in rural areas. Access to health care varies accordingly. Until the structural obstacles are addressed, the poorest people are unlikely to benefit from growth or even participate in programs specifically designed to increase that participation. Reform of the mainstream public institutions, in particular health care and education, will be essential.

## Social Policy

The government has continued to address social welfare concerns through autonomous agencies outside the mainstream ministries. This approach to public sector reform has had some impressive achievements, but it has been at the expense of efforts to improve the performance of the ministries. The extrainstitutional nature of the approach has also raised questions about its sustainability and its susceptibility to political intervention.[25]

By 1990 public social expenditure had fallen to 2 percent of GDP, or $12 a person, a historic low. By 1993 it had increased to 3 percent of GDP, or $58 a person, and by 1995, after a major improvement in the fiscal balance and a surplus of 2.9 percent of GDP that was largely due to privatization proceeds, expenditure reached 7 percent of GDP, or $176 a person. Social expenditures rose to 40.6 percent of the budget for 1996. The relative shares within this allocation are telling: health care and education received 6.17 percent and 7.86 percent, respectively, for 1996, but the Ministry of the Presidency received 22.61, up from 9.8 percent in 1995.[26] The Ministry of the Presidency was the only public agency that received an increase in 1996. Its total budget was 5,033 million soles (US$2.5 billion). Of this, slightly over half went to transfers to cover administrative costs and wages for the regional governments, some of which was for education and health personnel. The rest was shared among a variety of discretionary government programs: 9.13 percent for the social fund Fondo Nacional de Compensacion y Desarrollo Social (FONCODES), 4.05 percent for the school infrastructure building agency (INFES), and 11.43 percent for the National Development Institute. Cooperacion Popular and Prona, a government food support program, received 0.96 percent and 3.8 percent, respectively.[27]

The budget of the government's program to improve the efficiency of social expenditure within the ministries was one-hundredth the size of the budget of the Ministry of the Presidency. The program aims to improve the operations of schools and health posts in poor areas.[28] Despite well-developed plans for implementation, the program seems to have had very mixed results because of limited capacity within the ministries and the absence of an evaluation system to measure the program's effects.[29]

In addition, substantial evidence indicates that expenditures in the discretionary programs in the Ministry of the Presidency were often allocated according to political criteria. INFES expenditures, for example, had very little correlation with illiteracy rates and income levels nationwide and were heavily concentrated in Lima. In 1993 Fujimori had reallocated the municipal funds to favor smaller towns after he fared poorly in rural areas in the 1993 referendum. Although this reallocation had progressive effects, it was no coincidence that it dramatically reduced the access to funds by Ricardo Belmont, the popular mayor of Lima and a political rival. School building, meanwhile, was popular and a means for Fujimori to replace the municipal funds in Lima with an expenditure that he controlled.[30] Expenditures on FONCODES, a demand-based fund for improving social infrastructure, while usually having some correlation with overall poverty levels, also had some major "outlier" departments such as Madre de Dios, in which expenditures were up to ten times the national average despite relatively high per capita income levels. There were also significant spending increases in poor departments such as Cuzco and Puno where Fujimori fared poorly in the 1993 referendum.[31] In Cuzco and Puno, Fujimori was by 1995 able to increase his electoral support significantly. In this light, and given that he almost lost the 1993 referendum over the issue of education system reform, it should come as no surprise that he does not see a comprehensive effort to reform the public sector as politically desirable, and that he chooses to rely instead on a spending strategy that is politically effective and effective in reducing poverty, at least in the short term.

It is relevant in this light to review the record of FONCODES, the highly visible social fund that started in 1991 but only reached full-scale operations by 1993, a delay due primarily to political factors.[32] By the end of 1995 the fund had financed 17,000 projects at a cost of $650 million.[33] Most involve improvements to social infrastructure. An evaluation of the agency found that 80 percent of those interviewed were familiar with it and considered its work to have improved their quality of life. Eighty percent also believed that the agency reached poor people, and most thought that its priorities corresponded with theirs. As with all such programs, there are trade-offs between demand-based allocation and reaching the poorest sectors. The program received $250 million each from the World Bank and the Inter-American Development Bank in 1994–95 (it had previously relied on domestic funds). The program has offices in all thirteen regions of the country and attempts to focus on the poorest groups.[34]

The program has clearly improved many poor and remote communities by reaching them with government benefits for the first time.[35] For example, the school breakfast program funded by FONCODES reaches 300,000 primary school students in marginalized urban and rural communities. Communities must organize themselves to request the program, arrive at a monthly distribution center to pick up the food, and then arrange the delivery through the local schools. An independent nutrition research institute supervises the administration of the program, and the food is delivered to the distribution point by the private sector. Recent evaluations demonstrate that the program is improving the attention levels and memories of nutritionally at-risk children.[36] What is most striking about the program is that despite initial concerns that demand would be weak in the poorest rural communities because of their lack of organizational capacity and the substantial transport costs they must incur to participate, demand has been greater than the program's potential to respond.[37] The strong community participation suggests that the experience of actively participating in the program and attaining a positive government response has resulted in a significant number of people with a strong stake in the continuation of this way of delivering public services.

Another FONCODES success story is PREDES, the Programa de Acciones de Emergencia y Desarrollo, which also attempts to link private and public initiatives with local governments and community organizations. The program aims to address the structural causes of poverty as well as the costs of crisis and adjustment, and begins by requiring coordination between local authorities, business groups, nongovernmental organizations, and community organizations in district level coordinating committees (CDDs). The program is conducted in fifty very poor districts and has special funds for women and those displaced by terrorism, as well as for education and microenterprises.[38]

FONCODES is not without flaws. In several instances the rigid centralized operating structure has undermined local NGOs and even the efforts of institutions cooperating with the fund.[39] And there are clearly instances in which FONCODES funds have been allocated for political reasons. Finally, and perhaps most important, is how sustainable the program is and what its relation is to the line ministries. Given the support the program has from both the government and international financial institutions, it is not going to fade out soon. Yet it has no long-term institutional position, and only recently, with the second stage (post-1995) of the program, have some efforts been made to improve its coordination with the line ministries, such as making sure that the Education Ministry can provide teachers for schools that FONCODES builds.[40] There seems to be no coherent vision of coordination between the Ministry of the Presidency, which manages FONCODES, and the line ministries. The focus of government attention, meanwhile, is the Ministry of the Presidency because it can demonstrate results that are beneficial in reducing poverty and are politically visible, yet poses few of the political challenges that reform of the ministries would.

Finally, the Ministry of the Presidency, with a new and relatively lean administrative structure, can avoid personnel disputes and the high recurrent costs that the line ministries face and also remain within executive control in a way that a reformed and decentralized Health or Education Ministry would not.[41] Indeed, one reason for the government's seeming unwill-ingness to tackle social reform is fear of the political conse-quences of decentralization, a fear that was heightened by the public debate over the decentralization of education in 1993. Yet some resolution of the as yet undefined relations between central and local level governments in delivering social services will be critical to reforming public sector institutions in Peru, as well as to any attempt to create stakeholders at the local level.

## Decentralization, Stakeholders, and Public Sector Reform

There have been many studies of the potential merits and de-merits of decentralization and the reasons for initiating the pro-cess. In the 1960s a primary objective of many decentralization programs was to strengthen democracy. In the 1990s, with the worldwide turn to market economics, those objectives now tend to be to ease the financial burden on the central government, in-crease efficiency and effectiveness, and redistribute political power. Redistribution is consistent with the stakeholder ap-proach and may be a means to strengthen the voices of groups in society who stand to benefit from a government's reform poli-cies, such as the parents of primary school children, vis-à-vis those at the center who oppose the reforms, such as teachers' un-ions.[42]

Decentralization is not always able to meet these objectives. For example, it may not be more efficient because local govern-ments often suffer from a shortage of skilled personnel. Local of-ficials, meanwhile, may be more subject than central officials to the power of special interests.[43] This is further complicated in Peru by a history of discrimination against indigenous groups, particularly in the poorest parts of the sierra.[44] Competition be-tween regions, meanwhile, may be beneficial in some cases but harmful in others. With some services, such as law enforcement and education, local governments may be more efficient provid-ers, and competition may serve to increase standards across the board. But with such services as environmental protection or the provision of social safety nets, regions may simply compete for the lowest tax rates or the fewest regulations.

Finally, decentralization can make it more difficult for central governments to maintain fiscal stability.[45] And the redistribution of political power may not always favor reform. In Peru the central forces opposed to education reform were very weak, yet there was a great deal of suspicion and misunderstanding about proposed reforms at the local level because of the government's failure to adequately explain and build support for them, as well as genuine opposition to the proposed Chilean-style voucher system.

Another genuine concern about decentralization, especially in a country as poor as Peru, is its implications for equity, as the fate of the education proposal demonstrates. Advocates of decentralization argue that it increases public choice. When market incentives are introduced into the provision of government services, consumers have new alternatives to exercise voice and choose school officials, have a say in how resources are allocated, or choose to exit the public system for new private alternatives. Critics of decentralization highlight the constraints to consumers, particularly poor people, in exercising these choices.[46] There are often transaction costs to both exit and voice strategies, such as new transportation costs that accompany exiting or the opportunity costs of time given to participating in voice strategies.[47] These costs raise two kinds of equity concerns. The first is horizontal equity: the idea that people should be treated equally with respect to services such as education. With decentralization, communities are clearly differentiated on the basis of income and administrative capacity, so that very different kinds of schools are supplied. The second is vertical equity, the relationship between expenditures on public services on the one hand and family, community, and regional income on the other, a relationship that with decentralization will clearly produce differential outcomes.[48]

These equity concerns are clearly relevant to a society such as Peru's, which has vast rural-urban differences as well as differences among regions. Taking into account the equity implications of decentralization is perhaps most important in the delivery of basic social services because it is precisely these services that are crucial to reducing poverty and it is the poorest communities that will have the least capacity to administer and finance the services adequately. Yet many of these equity issues could be resolved in a decentralized context with government regulation, appropriate incentives, adequate information, and some redistributive taxation (for example, from rich to poor municipalities). Ultimately, resolving these concerns will place some limits on public choice.[49] The first education reform attempted by the Fujimori government, for example, placed complete emphasis on public choice and none on equity. This approach was ultimately voted down by poorer Peruvians. Whatever model of reform finally does emerge will have to place more emphasis on achieving equity.

Despite all these considerations, and in particular those pertaining to equity and administrative capacity, in Peru there is a clear need to redefine the relationship between local governments and the center and to increase the capacity of local institutions. Peru's government is overly centralized for such a large and regionally diverse country, and the public sector has proven inefficient and ineffective at delivering basic public services. Lima has 30 percent of the nation's population but produces 50 percent of the goods and services and represents 85 percent of the tax base. The central government generates 96 percent of public resources.[50] The relations and functions of the central, regional, and local governments lack definition. For the most part, municipal organizations lack capacity to carry out greater responsibilities.[51] It is significant that the CLAS health program chose to bypass the weak municipal governments in order to work directly with the traditionally strong community organizations.

To date, the impromptu nature of the decentralization and regionalization processes in Peru has led to a worsening of relations between regional and central governments, and the social services have been the most harmed. Dissatisfaction with the budgeting process is pervasive, as is a sense that regional governments have shunned social responsibilities. And there are genuine problems of coordination. Centrally gathered statistics, for example, are lost in the shifting of power and responsibility from the center to the regions.[52] Resolving problems in intragovernment relations will be crucial to improving the performance of public institutions.

After rhetoric about decentralization early in the Fujimori administration, there is now a seeming reluctance to address the issue. This stems largely from the government's poor showing in the 1993 referendum, which reflected strong public opposition to its education proposal. The opposition was particularly great outside Lima because poor and remote regions believed that they would lose resources and the capacity to administer their schools. Fujimori may have won the referendum nationwide, but he did not attain a majority in many of the poor rural departments of the country and fared particularly badly in small towns in those departments. After the referendum, the mechanism for allocating funds to municipalities was altered to benefit small and poor towns. Lima's share shrank from 54 percent to 17 percent of total municipal allocations.[53] But there has been little serious discussion of pursuing decentralization further. Indeed, many of the president's senior advisors have stated privately that he does not believe in decentralization and cite his distrust of local institutions and their potential to divert political loyalties. The implicit plan within government circles is to implement gradual or pilot decentralization and privatization policies that then take on lives of their own and sell the concept to the president through their success. As a first step, officials cite their ability to succeed with the reallocation of municipal funds despite public criticism.[54] If this strategy begins to create new stakeholders at the local level, it may give important impetus to broader reform.

Resistance from the ministries is not a concern in promoting decentralization; they are too weak to raise effective opposition. The primary obstacle seems to be the president himself.

Other ministries [than education] are drifting just as badly, abandoned by a president who spends three or four days a week travelling the country, armed with a Toshiba 4400 laptop with which to micromanage infrastructure projects. Part of the problem—part of almost all the problems facing the country—is that having destroyed Peru's old institutions, Mr. Fujimori has put nothing in their place except himself. His is the most centralised and personalised regime in Latin America.[55]

There are clear contradictions between this very centralized government and the viability of a decentralized approach to reform of public institutions. Along with Fujimori's style is the strongly centralized manner in which the new institutions such as the SUNAT and Foncodes are run.[56] This does not augur well for a comprehensive effort to reform the nation's institutions by creating new stakeholders. There has been substantial progress in some matters such as pension reform. Yet for various structural reasons, the reforms cannot reach the very poor. Progress in the areas that most directly affect them, the social programs, continues to lag because of the greater complexity of reforming these programs and the government's reluctance to address the weakness of public sector institutions and the uneasy relationship between different levels of government.

## Education Reforms

As with public sector reform, there have been several attempts to reform education in Peru, most notably under the military government in the mid-1970s.[57] Yet from that point on, education and public sector reform lost out to efforts to stem Peru's economic and sociopolitical crisis. Education reform returned to the national agenda only in 1992–93, when the Fujimori regime proposed to create a comprehensive reform of the education system based on Chile's municipal administration policy and voucher-based subsidizing of both public and private schools. The proposed reforms almost cost Fujimori the October 1993 referendum. Thereafter the government backed away from any comprehensive reform effort—certainly from any proposals to decentralize or privatize education. There has been a rapid turnover of education ministers, and most attempts at reform have been piecemeal, despite some interest and effort on the part of international financial institutions. The fate of education reform in Peru demonstrates some of the political difficulties encountered in the complex process of social reform, where organized providers often have strong stakes in the status quo and beneficiaries, while numerous, are diffuse and poorly organized. This in part explains why the government has chosen to avoid these difficulties and focus its efforts on social reforms implemented outside the ministries.

Despite the lack of progress, education reform is essential both to market reform and to social integration and poverty reduction in Peru. A recent study found that 78.7 percent of those interviewed in the provinces and 49 percent of those in Lima believed that education was the most important means to achieve integration and social progress.[58] Even during the adjustment shock, higher educational attainment correlated with lower unemployment and higher income.[59] Comparative studies have found clear correlations between public investment in education, particularly basic education, and economic growth.[60] Quality of education, meanwhile, is important in determining student performance and attendance, particularly among the poor.[61]

Educational coverage in Peru is virtually universal at the primary level and high at the secondary level.[62] The main problem in the education system is quality. And divergences in quality among schools are directly correlated with differences in income and average educational attainment within and among the regions. Rural schools are a particular concern. Expenditure per student is lowest in departments that are the poorest and most rural. Equity in expenditure is also a concern. Thirteen percent of public university students are from the highest income quintile and only 9.5 percent from the lowest. The government annually spends eight times more on each university student ($514) than on each primary student ($62). Still, expenditure on primary education disproportionately benefits the poor. Of those enrolled in public primary schools, 38.2 percent are from the lowest quintile and only 5.1 percent from the highest (table 3-1). Peru has a larger percentage of low-income primary education students as a share of all primary education students than many other countries in the region (table 3-2). Yet even though expenditure on primary education is progressive, the sharp decline in spending since 1988 fell equally on primary and university education and on rural as well as urban schools, thus hurting the poor most.[63]

While public education received generous public funding in the 1960s and 1970s, overall funding levels declined dramatically

Table 3-1. *Distribution of Public Education Enrollment, Peru, 1995*

| Quintiles[a] | Primary | Secondary | Postsecondary | Total |
|---|---|---|---|---|
| 1 | 38.2 | 29.0 | 9.5 | 31.0 |
| 2 | 27.2 | 27.0 | 23.6 | 26.7 |
| 3 | 18.5 | 19.9 | 26.1 | 20.0 |
| 4 | 10.9 | 16.6 | 27.9 | 15.3 |
| 5 | 5.1 | 7.5 | 12.9 | 7.0 |

Source: Based on ENNIV household survey data as cited in Pedro Franke Ballve, "La Educacion Publica Basica y Los Pobres," *Revista Tarea*, no. 35 (June 1995), p. 6.
a. The quintiles are of total households, based on distribution of per capita expenditure.

along with all public and social expenditures in the 1980s. While the Education Ministry's budget was 25.1 percent of the total budget in 1965, it was 13.43 percent in 1990 and 6.27 percent in 1993. This total went up to 7.86 for 1996.[64] When one considers that even at the height of expenditures the ministry did not have the capacity to respond to national educational needs, it is not difficult to imagine the harm done by these expenditure trends. And despite the various attempts at reform, most education spending still goes to recurrent costs (wages and pensions for teachers), while only 7 percent goes to capital expenditures. Schools, meanwhile, have no say in hiring or firing decisions. These are controlled by the regional organizations (USEs), which have very little if any evaluation capacity. Statistics are generated at the national level, in very large numbers, and with very low credibility.[65]

The results are evident. While primary school coverage is almost universal, 495 out of every 1,000 children do not complete primary school, and repetition rates are among the highest in the region.[66] More than 50 percent of the teachers have no professional certificate, and teachers' salaries are the lowest of any occupation that requires superior education. In real terms salaries are half of what they were in 1986.

The reforms introduced by the Fujimori government began in November 1991 with Decree Law 699, which stressed the importance of communities' involvement in securing education services at all levels, giving them the authority to administer schools and raise funds for education. Although the law was met with enthusiasm from the private schools, much of the opposition

Table 3-2. *Primary Education Enrollment, by Income Level, Selected Countries, 1992, and Peru, 1995*

| Country | 40% poorest | 40% mid-income | 20% wealthiest |
|---|---|---|---|
| Argentina | 57 | 32 | 11 |
| Brazil | 15 | 80 | 5 |
| Chile | 59 | 32 | |
| Costa Rica | 57 | 35 | 98 |
| Dominican Republic | 59 | 37 | 4 |
| Venezuela | 45 | 39 | 16 |
| Peru | 65 | 30 | 5 |

Source: CEPAL, 1992. For Peru, estimates are based on 1991 household survey by ENNIV as cited in Ballve, "Educacion Publica," p. 7.

criticized it for its privatizing direction. Most political parties opposed it in Congress, and education reform was among several other issues souring relations between the executive branch and the legislature before the April 1992 coup.[67] The next round of reforms was decreed in three laws at the end of 1992, during the period when Congress was closed. They had three objectives. The first was to transfer administrative responsibility to the municipalities through new community education councils (COMUNEDs), which were placed in charge of hiring and firing personnel but were not provided clear performance evaluation criteria. The second objective was, Chile-style via the COMUNEDs, to tie funding to the number of students. The third was to open the possibility for public subsidies for private schools. The communities were supposed to have more control over the curriculum, the Ministry of Education was to act as a regulatory body, and the Ministry of the Economy and Finance would have primary financial responsibility.

But the government did not carry out the reforms. First, it became concerned about the potential political power that opposition mayors could accrue as managers of the COMUNEDs.[68] Ultimately the government was reluctant to devolve power to new local stakeholders because it feared they would support the political opposition. Second, in widespread debating before the October 1993 referendum, the opposition conducted a nationwide effort to inform people about the potentially regressive effects the reforms could have, citing evidence from Chile. Their position was that Peru's reforms were more radical than Chile's voucher system because they proposed to privatize a greater proportion of public schools and give more weight to counterpart financing: schools were to charge fees *and* receive state vouchers, which was not the case in Chile.

The opposition also charged that both the Ministry of Education and the municipalities in Chile were much better able to fill their new roles than were Peru's.[69] In a 1995 speech Chile's education minister agreed, saying that Chile's reforms succeeded because of traditionally strong administrative capacity, well-trained teachers, and a clear decentralization policy.[70] These conditions did not exist in Peru.

Given the underlying conditions in Peru, it is likely that Chile-style reforms would have made inequities in the education system far worse and would have encountered strong administrative obstacles. However, some elements of the Chilean approach could certainly be adopted in the Peruvian system and yield good effects. For example, Peruvian parents already contribute a great deal to their children's education, with the poorest spending up to 50 percent of their consumption costs on education.[71] Studies in other countries have found that schools with higher levels of local financing tend to be more efficient. In part this is because teachers have to consider the effects of greater spending on the people they live with and thus they have greater incentives to cut costs. And, too, parents have a larger stake in the efficient allocation of expenditures.[72] One can thus posit that formalizing the financial contributions that parents are already making would give them credit for their efforts and increase their influence in how their children's schools are managed.

The reforms raised other issues for debate and resulted in some alterations to the proposed new Constitution. These included government recognition of teachers as public rather than private sector employees (a clause the opposition wanted); the removal of a clause guaranteeing that 20 percent of the budget would go to education; the inclusion of a clause that allows public subsidizing of private education; the removal of a clause that all teachers should be paid "adequately"; the removal of the guarantee of free university education for those who could not pay for it; and inclusion of a provision making secondary education mandatory.[73] Yet these matters remained controversial, as was demonstrated by the results of the 1993 referendum. The laws were then suspended. The reforms did lead to some de facto privatizations of public schools, as in Arequipa in 1993, which resulted in both public and union protests against them.[74] The experience with education reform, meanwhile, seems to have steered the government away from the reform of public sector institutions and decentralization in general.

The government's subsequent strategy for education avoided addressing the problems in the ministry or at the local government level. Instead there was an almost hundredfold increase in the discretionary school infrastructure fund, INFES (Instituto para la Infrastructura Escolar). The INFES budget was $32,000 in 1990 and school construction accounted for 82 percent. By 1994 it was $112 million and construction accounted for 99 percent. Expenditures were disproportionately allocated to Lima, which received the largest number of schools per million population, 42.58, while some of the poorest districts with the highest levels of illiteracy, such as Apurimac and Ayacucho, received 7.48 and 23.48 respectively.[75] As one observer noted, Fujimori quickly realized that building schools yielded a lot more political capital than did privatization or decentralization. And it was no coincidence that the woman who was the head of INFES for Lima ran on the government's platform for vice mayor of the city in the November 1995 elections.[76] Opinion polls taken in 1994 cited school construction as one of the most important achievements of the government.[77] Yet in many instances schools were built in areas where there were no teachers, or computers were donated in zones with no electricity, hardly a systematic approach to reform of the education system or to raising the stakes that beneficiaries have in the process.

Another unresolved problem is excess administrative personnel, whose numbers have fluctuated dramatically. From the 1960s to the mid-1980s the administrative bureaucracy was approximately 2,400 people nationwide, including the regions. During the 1985–90 APRA government the number grew to 30,000. This increase favored the center and the regional governments and USE (Unidad de Servicio Educativo, or Education Service Unit) at the expense of the schools, many of which are still short of personnel. Under the Fujimori government the number of personnel at the center fell from 2,100 in 1985 to 450 in 1993. The thinning of the ministry resulted in the departure of many of the most talented people.[78] Personnel relations, meanwhile, particularly with SUTEP, the teachers' union, focus only on salary issues, no surprise given the low overall salary levels.[79]

Although the proposed reforms addressed administrative issues, they neglected the critical matter of quality of education and the relevance of other countries' experience, including Chile's. Recognizing the harmful effects of its decentralization strategies for the poorest areas, the Chilean government initiated the P900 program to improve quality in the poorest schools. The Peruvian reforms made no provision for such areas, which were unlikely to fare very well with the decentralization.[80]

After 1993, education reform entered a less defined stage, with an implicit government acceptance of responsibility for the majority of schools on the one hand but the intention to liberalize the regulation of private schools and introduce the concept of management autonomy on the other.[81] At the same time, the strategy is to increase public social expenditures from their unrealistically low levels. Yet there is no coherent vision of reform. There were eight education ministers in Fujimori's first five-year term. Once broader reform plans were scrapped, the Ministry of Education shifted its emphasis to increased teacher training. While useful, this will hardly address the major problems of the system, especially given the mixed record of teacher training programs in other countries. A crucial matter is that the ministry has refused to include SUTEP in discussions about the training program because it alleges that the union is still infiltrated by those sympathetic to the Sendero Luminoso (Shining Path).[82] An additional proposal for reform was to devolve much more authority for school management to the school principals, without any involvement on the part of teachers or the community. Principals are appointed by the Ministry of the Presidency but have very little real authority. For example, if they fire teachers, they do not have the resources to hire new ones.[83] The explicit exclusion of crucial stakeholders—teachers and the community—seems counterproductive.

Major problems in the overall administrative structure still need to be addressed. For example, the USE, the regional administrative branches, and the ADEs (areas de desarrollo educativo, or education development areas), the regional pedagogical branches created in 1993, have no clear delineation of responsibilities or coordinating mechanisms. The center sets uniform costs and curricula and makes other administrative decisions applicable to schools across the country without taking into account the heterogeneity of regions.[84]

Another important matter is the role of SUTEP. In the late 1970s and early 1980s the union had a great deal of political power and indeed was one of the forces responsible for the demise of the military government. But the severity of the economic crisis of the 1980s coupled with the authoritarian interlude of the Fujimori government have crippled it.[85] It is weak, internally divided, and lacks a vision or strategy other than the negotiation of salary levels. Yet it remains the only organization that represents the 200,000 school teachers in Peru, and its monopoly over wage negotiations gives it influence over teachers. SUTEP also controls who gets hired. And it is still very difficult to fire teachers, even though there is a surplus due to the Ley de Profesores, or Teacher's Law, passed in the 1980s. Ninety percent of school principals who want to fire teachers cannot. Meanwhile, because of the political prominence of the law, Fujimori has not attempted to rescind it.[86] As in Chile, the existence of a rigid law governing personnel management makes increasing the autonomy of individual schools very difficult.

SUTEP was, not surprisingly, strongly opposed to the 1992 education reforms, particularly the proposal to make teachers private sector employees. Thus the 1993 Constitution continues to assert that teachers are public sector employees. The government, meanwhile, has made little effort to pursuade the union to support its reforms. Similarly, the issue of the COMUNEDs was mishandled. When the COMUNEDs were announced, there were rumors that the teachers' pensions would be transferred along with the other resources to be administered by the COMUNEDs. The government made little effort to dispel these rumors or explain the reforms to the union. Teachers considered the transfer as privatization of their pensions, which significantly increased their opposition to the reforms.[87] The union leaders, meanwhile, seem aware of their limitations and their political isolation and for the first time are attempting to broaden the discussion from a radical Maoist philosophy phrased in working-class terms.[88] This suggests that a change in government approach could involve the union productively in the discussion of reform and develop a union stake in achieving it.[89]

Others with interests in Peruvian education are the Asociaciones de Padres de Familia, the parent associations. The APAFAs control parental contributions to the schools and are vital in guaranteeing chalk, books, and other school supplies. They are also important supervisors of school performance. Yet their role is informal and varies a great deal across schools and communities. At times the associations have severe clashes with the school directors, which paralyzes the management of the schools because the associations control the only resources to which the directors have access. The associations are not organized beyond the community level, so their involvement in broader debate on school quality is limited.[90] The proposed pilot reform program for increasing the autonomy of local school management would have given more authority and resources to school directors but also formalized the role of the APAFAs. Clearly any reform of school management and administration should take these associations into account. They are an obvious means to incorporate the participation of parents, who are perhaps the principal stakeholders in education reform, yet whose interests are rarely well articulated or organized.

Despite the government's lack of progress in comprehensive reform of the education system, there has been some achievement, much of it spurred by nongovernmental organizations involved in education. First, most NGOs and the government agree that responsibilities need to be transferred to the schools and that they should manage their own budgets.[91] In addition, for the past few years there has been a continuing discussion involving NGOs and academic observers, and at times the Ministry of Education, through the Foro Educativo, a voluntary association of researchers and NGOs involved with education issues. And while the idea of universal free primary education is still explosive, as the 1993 debate demonstrated, there is a widespread willingness to pay for education services, a willingness that could be formalized and better regulated: at present the poorest parents pay proportionately the most for it.[92] These trends suggest that a stakeholders approach to reform could be effective if there were a central commitment to it.

A comprehensive government effort to reform the education system seems unlikely, both because the government is focusing on the semiautonomous agencies such as the Ministry of the Presidency rather than the line ministries and because of the earlier failed attempts at reform. Some de facto progress is being made, but without a strong executive commitment, neither education nor any other reform of the permanent institutions of the public sector is likely to occur. Yet it is precisely these institutions that deliver the public services indispensable to reducing poverty, services that will eventually give the poor stakes in market-oriented growth.

## New Stakeholders in the Management of Health Services

An exception to the current approach to the reform of mainstream institutions has been the creation of local committees to administer primary health centers and posts, the CLAS, in some of the poorest areas. The program, which was developed in spite of rather than with the cooperation of the Ministry of Health staff, combines the efforts of community members, local health personnel, and local representatives of the ministry to improve the quality and coverage of primary health care.[93] The CLAS have legal and financial responsibility for administering the health posts in their jurisdiction and are provided with public resources to pay for existing personnel to work more hours or to contract with additional personnel (on a private basis) to keep the posts open longer hours. In addition, any revenues generated from fees for drugs or services are kept and administered by the CLAS, rather than sent back to the regional authorities, as they were under the previous system.[94] The program drew on substantial experience with community involvement in providing health services in

Peru as well as the Bamoako initiative, which promotes local involvement and cost sharing in providing primary health care services in Africa.

CLAS committees are composed of three representatives elected by the community, three community representatives chosen by the director of the local health center, and the director himself.[95] The Ministry of Health issues guidelines and regulations for the services to be provided. The revenues generated by the CLAS are used to improve the local health facilities and provide drugs and health care for those who are unable to pay. The total resources provided by the public sector, $200–$2,000 a month per CLAS, are far less than what is typically generated locally.[96] Together these resources have allowed the facilities to stay open from eight to twelve hours a day rather than six and to contract with additional doctors and nurses.

The increased service, in conjunction with strong outreach efforts by the CLAS, has resulted in an effective and widely popular program that, after a brief pilot stage, was legalized in April 1994.[97] There are currently 451 CLAS accounting for about 10 percent of primary health care provided in the country. An additional 400 communities have expressed a desire to form CLAS, but are waiting for a government response. These include remote rural communities, suggesting that the program has been successful in communicating its approach and results to the public. In addition to the outreach efforts, the program has made a major effort to train the community members who were taking on new administrative reponsibilities. Another important key to CLAS success has been transparency in the management of resources. This and efficiency in handling resources seems to be far more important than who actually manages the resources: one of the most successful CLAS actually subcontracted out accounting responsibilities.[98] The record of the CLAS also reflects the strong community organizational capacity that exists throughout Peru and contributes to the potential effectiveness of the approach.[99]

Some CLAS have already had demonstrable results in the form of lower rates of infant mortality and communicable disease. In some communities where CLAS programs have been evaluated, infant mortality rates have fallen 25 to 30 percent, although perhaps in part because the CLAS health surveys are more accurate. Reliance on local expertise to provide health care services and conduct surveys has resulted in a greater capacity to identify at-risk groups. In addition, the CLAS have provided information about health care services to such groups. Infant mortality rates, for example, can vary dramatically within departments, but because Health Ministry surveys are carried out at the department level, some groups or areas that are very much more at risk than others may remain undetected. In Junin, for example, CLAS delivered two to three times the amount of health care services programmed by the ministry, indicating that the program was attending to previously unmet demands for health care.[100] Meanwhile, national surveys covering access to public services have found that the share of people using public health posts increased from 39 percent in 1994 to 45 percent in 1996. While this increase is not exclusively due to the efforts of CLAS, the program is likely to have influenced the behavior of the lowest-income groups.[101]

One of the primary concerns of CLAS evaluations is that the very poorest communities are least equipped with the personnel and the organizational capacity to effectively administer the health centers and generate the necessary resources, a situation that confronts most attempts at reform based on local-level stakeholders. The administrators of the CLAS believe they must first achieve universal coverage of primary health care and then address equity issues. Yet one way they have dealt with equity is to provide financial incentives for doctors and nurses to work in remote poor regions. Although the main public system does not have differential scales, the CLAS pays up 40 percent more to public health personnel in remote regions.[102] Another concern is that patients who are unable to pay have been turned away in some CLAS posts. It is not clear if or to what extent this occurs, and to what extent it occurs in some of the regular public health care posts. Thus it is important to note that CLAS posts often charge less for health services than do those in the regular public system and still maintain a budget surplus.[103]

The regional health authorities, the UTES, are strongly opposed to the CLAS. The UTES are administrative units that rely on the resources generated by the local service providers; they have no budget of their own. Thus the CLAS reduces their control over substantial resources. Ironically, the CLAS has been criticized on the one hand as a form of hidden communism and on the other by the public sector health union as a means for the government to privatize and to get rid of public health personnel. The health union is hardly justified, given that public sector workers have not been fired due to the CLAS, and indeed many have been able to earn better pay and extend their working hours in the public health posts, rather than having to seek income supplements elsewhere. CLAS hiring under private sector contracts, meanwhile, erodes the monopoly that the unions had over employment and therefore reduces their political power. It is telling that within the unions the older workers are the most opposed, while younger workers, who are most likely to be comfortable with the new private sector approaches, are more favorable and see the CLAS as a good means to earn more without seeking alternative employment.[104] In early 1996 the minister of economics endorsed the program as an important component of the health system, which purportedly created more support for the CLAS in the Ministry of Health. This endorsement may allow the program to expand and to receive sufficient public resources to do so.[105]

The problems that have arisen with the CLAS, such as initial tensions between regional authorities, public sector workers, and the CLAS centers, could probably have been avoided with a better effort on the part of the ministry to clarify program objectives and regulations. Yet the presentation and implementation of the program were more ad hoc than usual, in part because it was not a ministry priority. Once the CLAS centers were established and the benefits to health personnel became clear, tensions with public sector workers usually decreased markedly.[106] They are still strong at the regional level, however, no doubt due to the UTES' loss of control over significant resources. These tensions have led regional authorities to make accusations of mismanagement of CLAS resources. However, transparency in financial management has been a central component of CLAS success, and it is unlikely that communities will squander resources they themselves have generated. In contrast, the regional authorities have a strong stake in regaining control of the resources. To maintain the credibility of the program, it is important that all allegations of resource mismanagement be publicly investigated.[107]

The CLAS experience demonstrates both the vitality of community initiative in Peru and the strong potential for creating local-level stakeholders in reform. At the same time it shows the difficulties of reforming central public institutions, particularly when reform entails their relinquishing some power. It also demonstrates that cooperation between public and private sectors, and the introduction of market incentives combined with effective regulation and communication with beneficiaries, can successfully affect the delivery of public services. Comments by community members active in the CLAS have been along the lines of "with CLAS the government listens to the people."[108] Yet because the CLAS committees have no point of entry into the larger public health system, their influence is limited to the local level.[109] This might be different if the program were part of a broader effort to decentralize government responsibilities. This is far from the case. In fact the original CLAS plans to work with the municipalities were replaced with the current model of working with community organizations because program adminstrators found the municipalities too administratively weak to manage health services. This illustrates the extent to which strongly centralized government and public institutions in Peru coexist with weak local government and vibrant local private sector and community initiatives.

## Reform of the Social Security System

About the same time that the education reforms were attempted, the government also initiated a reform of the social security system, the Instituto Peruano de Seguridad Social (IPSS). As in the case of education, the reform was based on the provision of private alternatives. But unlike the education reform, the pension reform was largely successful, or at least it was put in place. One reason for the contrast is that the pension system covered only 2 million workers, a small part of the total work force, rather than the entire population. Another is that although the president was not completely committed to the reform, he was at least sufficiently convinced to ensure its commencement. Meanwhile, the potential opponent of the reform, organized labor, was extremely weak and represented only a small minority of workers: less than 1 percent of Lima's population is in a labor union. Finally, with the formation of the AFPs (the private pension funds) the reform yielded fairly fast and visible results. This meant that a new constituency with stakes in the reform developed quickly and could serve as a counterweight to the opposition in pushing for further reform. First the government and then the AFPs were active in selling the reforms to the public. The government launched a major television campaign in favor of the reform, then the AFPs began a propaganda campaign, which included a door-to-door marketing effort to get workers to join.[110] Finally, also in contrast to the education reform, the pension reform was relatively simple administratively and certainly did not entail the cooperation of several levels of government.

The point of departure for the reforms was that the public, pay-as-you-go IPSS was bankrupt by the early 1990s because of demographic changes and poor management. This was widely known and created a consensus in favor of reform. By 1990 the image of the IPSS was that it was the most badly managed of the state industries, a record made even worse by a huge increase in personnel under the APRA government.[111] "Constant strikes of the administrative and medical personnel (45,000 workers) . . . images of pensioners and IPSS workers ripping up their checks in front of TV cameras because they could not cash them. Hospital patients without linens or food."[112] There were all kinds of pension categories, some allowing retirement after five years, and pensions were indexed to inflation and to public sector salary scales even during the years of hyperinflation. While the number of pensioners increased by 39 percent from 1986 to 1990, contributions fell from 2 percent of GDP to 0.7 percent. Finally, the state had often "borrowed" from the IPSS, further eroding its precarious financial situation.[113]

Most people in the public system had low expectations of the state's abilities to follow through on its pension obligations. The objectives of the reform were twofold: to increase the national savings capacity and to take care of retired workers.[114] The initial debate on the reforms was relatively contentious, with organized labor and the workers of IPSS, in particular, in strong opposition. Yet the proponents of reform had some distinct advantages.

People generally agreed on the disastrous state of the public system, and there were no real alternatives to the government's proposal. Organized labor, particularly public sector workers, were in an exceptionally weak position because of the economic crisis and the government's policy of shrinking the public sector. Finally, and most important, Fujimori closed down the Congress in April 1992, which precluded any further legislative debate on the issue. The reform law was passed in late 1992. After the private funds were set up, political debate over the reforms ceased and most discussion focused on concerns about design and administration. There now seems little disagreement across the political spectrum that the reform was necessary and its general direction appropriate.[115]

Although there were fewer obstacles to implementing the pension plan in Peru than in other countries, there were some caused by design flaws and politics. The primary proponent of the pension reform, Finance Minister Carlos Boloña, resigned from the government in late 1993, which left the program without an influential proponent. As he said, "what was missing was a political leader willing to push the reform through."[116] Yet even if he had stayed or there was someone else who could assume his role, Fujimori was not completely committed to the program, in part because of concerns over the initial political opposition to the plan. Thus when it was clear that there were distortions in rates and that the private plan could not afford to subsidize the public one, the president was apparently reluctant to eliminate the subsidy. Also, although in Chile new entrants to the public plan were prohibited after the reform began, Fujimori did not approve the closing of the public system until the June 1995 law had passed. Finally, even though the opposition was generally weak, there was a strong base in the IPSS, whose numbers had ballooned under the APRA government. In conjunction with the CGTP (General Confederation of Peruvian Workers) the union launched a relatively effective opposition campaign that discouraged new entrants and seems to have convinced the president that it was better to move slowly with the reforms.[117]

Eight AFPs were initially set up, and six are still in operation. Two of the smaller funds were unable to compete once contribution rates were lowered, particularly because some of the AFPs had spent a great deal on advertising in an effort to attract members.[118] The AFPs hold assets of just over $600 million, which is equal to half of total pension assets, and 55 percent of their investments are in the financial sector, although the promulgation of special investment regimes has since allowed the plans to diversify and invest in the communal shares of the Banco de Credito, the newly privatized national telephone company, and several other industrial enterprises. The real rate of return of the AFPs was 8.58 percent in 1994; the rate since they were set up was 9.02 percent (the AFPs in Chile had a 14 percent rate of return until 1996).[119]

As for design flaws, under the 1992 law the financial incentives for joining the private system were insufficient to attract most low-income workers. Of approximately 2 million workers originally in the public plan, half switched to the private plans; those who switched tended to be younger and with higher incomes. (These age-related differences mirrored those of public sector health workers). In addition, the Ministry of Economics was understandably concerned about the costs of a minimum pension system, so, unlike Chile, Peru provided for no minimum. Given that 35 percent of Chile's workers earn the minimum because they cannot contribute enough on their own, the proportion would undoubtedly be higher in Peru, considering the much lower average wage levels.[120]

Contribution rates were significantly higher in the private plan, in part because of high costs of administering the funds for workers with low salaries and low average contributions, a small pool of potential contributors, and (purportedly) excessive investments in advertising campaigns. In addition, the lack of a minimum pension dissuaded low-income (and older) workers from joining the plan because most correctly perceived that they would be unable to contribute enough to accumulate a decent pension. Other reasons for the lack of acceptance that had less to do with design than with structural obstacles were inadequate savings capacity (very low average salary levels result in higher opportunity costs in giving up current consumption for future security) and lack of experience with and confidence in any sort of savings scheme.[121] Many workers lacked access to information. Finally, there was a general lack of faith in government that eroded the credibility of the commitment to pay recognition bonds for those workers who would switch to the private funds when they reach retirement age, because for many workers this implied a government commitment a decade or two in the future. This situation was made worse by the government's failure to pay any of the recognition bonds until more than two years after the private system was running.[122] The first bonds were not issued until October 1995; in part the delay was due to the IPSS's lack of adequate accounts of workers' contributions.[123] But it was also due to fiscal concerns in the Ministry of Economics and Finance.

In June 1995 a revision law was passed with the active lobbying of the private pension funds superintendency, a new stakeholder in the reform process, that was intended to reduce the disincentives to switching to the private scheme. In particular, it narrowed the differences in contribution rates between the private and public plans and established the legal basis for a minimum pension. Yet by late 1995 no minimum rate had been set nor were the mechanisms for its administration and financing specified, suggesting that the government's commitment was far from complete and thereby undermining the credibility of the new legislation.[124] The absence of a minimum plan continued to dissuade poorer workers from switching to the private funds. Yet since the new law has been passed, there has been a significant increase in new entrants to the private plan, with enrollment rates increasing from 3,000 a month to 26,000 and the average growth rate of the private system increasing from 0.36 percent in the first six months of 1995 to 2.38 percent from July to December 1995.[125]

In early 1996, meanwhile, the government introduced a proposal to cap pension levels in the public system. Under the so-called *cedula viva*, public sector workers are indexed to payment scales in whatever wage category they retire. Thus there are huge distortions in the public plan, with public sector workers often retiring well before the mandatory fifteen-year contribution period and earning pensions as high as $7,000 a month, while private sector workers in the public plan often retire after thirty years and receive pensions as low as $45 a month. Although the cap will affect only a small number of privileged public workers, it signals the government's increased unwillingness to bear the fiscal burden of a severely distorted public program and may

Table 3-3. *Workers Switching to Private Pension Plan, by Age Group,*
*1994*

| Age group | Number of affiliates | Percent of total |
|---|---|---|
| Younger than 21 | 32,285 | 3.0 |
| 21–25 | 168,198 | 18.0 |
| 26–30 | 214,063 | 22.5 |
| 31–35 | 189,820 | 20.0 |
| 36–40 | 148,942 | 16.0 |
| 41–45 | 99,197 | 10.0 |
| 46–50 | 59,584 | 6.0 |
| 51–55 | 30,219 | 3.0 |
| 56–60 | 13,384 | 1.0 |
| 61–65 | 3,223 | 0.3 |
| Older than 65 | 1,455 | 0.2 |
| Total | 961,370 | 100.0 |

Source: Superintendency of the Administrators of the Private Pension Funds, *Annual Report 1994*, table 6.

provide additional incentives for workers to switch to the private plan.[126]

There were previously 2 million workers insured by IPSS and 300,000 pensioners. By the end of 1994, some 961,000 workers had switched from the public to the private plan. By March 1996, seven months after the passage of the new law, there were 1,182,654 workers in the new plan.[127] Eighty-five percent of these workers are employed by firms and 15 percent are independent. Switching seems to have been correlated with workers' income levels, with the poorest workers remaining in the public plan. It is primarily younger and wealthier workers who have moved. The average income of those that switch is more than $450 a month. The largest category of workers that switched were 26–30 years old, followed by those 31–35, then those 21–25. The smallest group were those between 61 and 65 (table 3-3). Fifty-four percent of those in the new system are in Lima-Callao, while the interior departments that have the most workers are Piura, La Libertad, and Arequipa, with 5.6 percent, 5.1 percent, and 4.6 percent respectively. Not surprisingly, these are all relatively wealthy departments. The representation by departments seems clearly related to poverty levels, although there are some outlier depart-

Table 3-4. *Peruvian Workers in Private Pension Plans,
by Department, 1994*

| Departments | Number of workers | Ratio of department GDP per capita to national GDP per capita |
|---|---|---|
| Lima | 468,387 | 134.42 |
| Piura | 54,006 | 94.81 |
| Callao | 49,616 | n.a. |
| La Libertad | 49,062 | 100.00 |
| Arequipa | 44,057 | 125.97 |
| Lambayeque | 31,058 | 109.09 |
| Loreto | 29,571 | 196.10 |
| Junin | 29,240 | 80.52 |
| Ica | 28,938 | 94.81 |
| Ancash | 27,493 | 50.00 |
| Cusco | 25,684 | 53.90 |
| Puno | 16,761 | 41.56 |
| Tacna | 15,594 | 137.66 |
| Cajamarca | 14,664 | 40.26 |
| Ucayali | 10,121 | 86.36 |
| Moquegu[a] | 9,783 | 370.78 |
| San Martin | 9,391 | 63.64 |
| Huanuco | 9,036 | 51.95 |
| Ayacucho | 8,006 | 29.87 |
| Pasco | 6,230 | 106.49 |
| Tumbes | 6,014 | 92.86 |
| Huancavelica | 5,067 | 52.60 |
| Apurimac | 4,519 | 26.62 |
| Por Asignar | 3,661 | n.a |
| Amazonas | 3,197 | 66.88 |
| Madre de Dios | 2,214 | 148.70 |
| Total | 961,370 | . . . |

Source: Superintendency of the Administrators of the Private Pension Funds, *Annual Report 1994*, p. 71; and Carol Graham and Cheikh Kane, "Opportunistic Government or Sustaining Reform: Electoral Trends and Public Expenditure Patterns in Peru, 1990–95," *Latin American Research Review*, vol. 33, no. 1 (1998), pp. 71–111.
n.a. Not available.

ments, such as Ancash, Junin, and Cusco, all poor departments with more than 25,000 workers joining the private scheme (table 3-4). Of the total that switched, 0.4 percent, or 3,751 workers, withdrew. Most of those returned to the public system while it was still legally possible; the rest either failed to pay, had multiple affiliations, or died. An August 1995 law allowed switching

Table 3-5. *Worker and Employer Contribution Rates in Public Pension System, Peru, 1995*

| Plan | Previous | | Current | |
|------|----------|------|---------|------|
|  | Workers | Employers | Workers | Employers |
| FONAVI | 3 | 6 | 0 | 9 |
| IPSS-health | 3 | 6 | 0 | 9 |
| ONP-pensions | 3 | 6 | 11 | 0 |
| Total | 9 | 18 | 11 | 18 |

Source: *Actualidad Economica*, no. 165 (July 1995).

between the AFPs for the first time as long as a person had contributed to another AFP for at least six months.[128]

The two major reasons workers stayed in the public system were the higher contribution rates in the private system and the lack of guarantee of a minimum pension. Lack of information about and understanding of the new system was also important.[129] Among those that stayed, while the promises of a decent public pension were questionable, the risk of not earning a sufficient pension in the private system, coupled with the higher contribution rates, were major disincentives to switching. For many, the difference in the contribution rates was sufficient, given their already low incomes. Initially, the contribution rate in the IPSS was 9 percent; it was 15 percent in the AFPs. With the change in the law in 1995 the rate in the public system rose to 11 percent and to 13 percent in 1997. The AFPs' rate was lowered by eliminating some of their payments from the VAT and eliminating a solidarity bond to the IPSS. The rate was 11.4 percent in 1995 and increased to 13.4 percent in 1997 (tables 3-5 and 3-6).[130] The June 1995 law also declared the public pension system bankrupt and prohibited new entrants. If the provisions are enforced, they are likely to raise the rates even further for those remaining in the public system.[131] Initially workers who joined the private system could continue to receive health insurance from the IPSS, but at a higher cost and with the requirement that they pay an additional fee after retirement, which was another disincentive. With the June 1995 law, employers cover workers' contributions to both IPSS and Fondo Nacional de Vivienda (FONAVI).[132] Even with these changes, costs in the private plan are still an obstacle for

Table 3-6. *AFP and Public System Worker Contributions to Pensions, 1997*

|  | Before | | 1995 | | 1997 | |
| --- | --- | --- | --- | --- | --- | --- |
| Plan | Public system | AFP | Public system | AFP | Public system | AFP |
| Contribution | 3.0 | 10.0 | 11.0 | 8.0 | 13.0 | 10.0 |
| AFP Commission | . . . | 2.0 | . . . | 2.0 | . . . | 2.0 |
| IPSS/FONAVI/Solidarity | 6.0 | 1.0 | . . . | 0 | . . . | 0 |
| Survivors Pension | . . . | 1.6 | . . . | 1.4 | . . . | 1.4 |
| Total | 9.0 | 14.6 | 11.0 | 11.4 | 13.0 | 13.4 |

Source: *Actualidad Economica*, no. 165 (July 1995).

poorer workers and will continue to be until commissions fall substantially.[133] A related matter is that there was some misinformation in the initial AFP propaganda campaign. Workers often joined AFPs at one rate; contribution rates then increased, and they were unable to switch their funds. Although this has since been corrected and workers can switch AFPs after six months, the early experiences generated worker distrust.

Despite the changes, significant numbers of workers remain in the public system. One problem still seems to be access to information.[134] Another is that enterprises have tended to encourage all their workers to join the new system or all to stay in the public one because having workers in both systems increased the businesses' administrative costs. And although there was an initial one-time 15 percent salary increase for those who joined the private plans, some enterprises gave all their workers the raise to reduce administrative complexity.[135] Finally, because of the debt crisis and the hyperinflation years, there is still a general distrust of saving as well as a distrust of private savings plans that was fostered by the collapse of CLAE market.

A survey conducted for AFP Horizonte by the respected private polling firm APOYO of workers affilated with both private and public plans confirms that these attitudes are prevalent among low-income workers.[136] Most workers in either plan doubted that they would ever earn a pension sufficient to subsist on, and most also saw owning a small business as key to earning sufficient income after retirement. Those who were members of an AFP believed the advantages were having life insurance, being able to contribute to one's own retirement, and being able to retire earlier than the official age. Others who switched to the private system did so because they knew the promoter or had a friend who had joined. Some expected they would use their funds from the AFP to start their own business after retirement, while others believed that they would get sufficient payments to receive a decent pension. Yet those in the private system still had doubts about the future and saw AFPs as enterprises that could crack. There was a strong preference for those that were backed by large and presumably solid businesses, such as AFP Union. Lack of information was obvious from the interviews; it was also cited as a concern by the workers themselves. Not one of them knew that there was a superintendency to administer the private funds.

Among those not affiliated with the private plans, most wished to avoid decisions about their retirement. Many were pessimistic about living long enough to retire, given trends in living standards in the past decade. Those that remain in the public plan expected to have to earn extra income to supplement whatever pension they received. Yet they had no intention of switching plans: they had no trust in private enterprises managing workers' funds; they thought the contribution rates were too high; they had a general perception that the system was for rich workers and had very little genuine information about it; they cited the loss of access to IPSS services; and finally they believed that the laws concerning AFPs would be changed arbitrarily. Many of the concerns of poorer workers—for example, lack of awareness of the superintendency administering the AFPs and of the improvements in the June 1995 law—could be alleviated with better communication. As with attempts to create stakeholders among other groups, it is the poorest that have the least access to information and are the least prepared to participate. An active government effort to explain reforms is crucial to broadening participation.

Another problem remains the approximately 70 percent of the work force in the informal sector that remains outside either system. Thus far the reform has been reasonably successful at attracting workers from one forced saving plan to another. Although workers in the informal sector are allowed to join the private system, they make up less than 10 percent of the affiliates. For a variety of reasons, which include low incomes and limited capacity to save now to have security in the future, lack of adequate information, fear of regulation and tax burden, and lack of experience with formal savings plans, they have not participated in the new private system.[137]

Thus the benefits of the reform have been limited to the million or so workers that shifted from the public to the private system. This suggests certain limits to the potential of social reforms that rely primarily on market incentives to achieve the widespread participation of the poor, because the reforms do not, or cannot, address some of the nonmarket obstacles to their participation.[138] For reasons ranging from lack of purchasing power to weak access to information, the acceptance of services on the part of the poor is likely to be disproportionately lower than that of other socioeconomic groups. To reach the poor, design, presentation, and incentives may have to be tailored specifically for them. Yet economic constraints and the size of the informal sector suggest significant barriers to such a strategy's being adopted through pension reform in Peru.[139]

The pension experience also demonstrates the extent to which strong executive commitment is essential to the success of such reforms, in particular in soliciting the contribution and participation of the intended beneficiary groups. This is particularly true in Peru, where political power is highly concentrated in the president, and a wavering commitment to the reform as well as lack of adequate information seems to have undermined an already weak confidence in the new system, particularly among poorer and less educated workers.

Although the reform was at least started, which is no small achievement, many problems remain unresolved. Neither system pays a decent pension unless workers are on the upper end of the salary scale. Even the administrators of the private system admit that it is a segmented one that benefits middle- and upperclass workers. Ownership of the AFPs is concentrated in the main economic power holders in the country: the bankers. This may give some impetus to capital markets, but observers also admit that it is not an adequate social insurance system.[140] There is still no resolution to the minimum pension problem. And workers' general lack of confidence in private savings plans has not been addressed. Indeed, constant changes in the law and in contribution rates have probably eroded confidence even further. The inequities introduced by the new system as well as its coverage of only a small minority of the work force remain major matters for further reform. Resolving these problems completely may not be possible, but some progress in that direction will be crucial to incorporating the marginalized majority as stakeholders in the reform process.

### The Citizen Participation Program

An interesting program that aims to create new stakeholders in reform among lower-income groups and has links with the new pension system is the Programa de Participacion Ciudadana (PPC). The program, modeled on similar programs in the United Kingdom, Spain, and Chile, among others, seeks to facilitate the participation of small-scale investors in privatization. The plan was first a pilot project with three stages of sales and 18,500 participants. The relative success of the pilot led the government to plan a substantial expansion. The program was featured prominently in both the president's and the prime minister's inaugural addresses in 1995.[141] In June 1996, about 270,000 people applied to buy shares in the privatization of the telephone company, and in November more than 50,000 bought shares in the privatization of Luz del Sur, an electricity distributor.[142] The government aims to reach half a million people by 2000.

The program is occurring at an opportune time. In the past few years Peru has privatized fifty-one state companies for a total of $3.6 billion. The purchasers have committed themselves to $4.1 billion in new investments, and the remaining government holdings are scheduled for sale by 2000.[143] The sales have generated more revenue than expected, especially a $2 billion surplus from the sale of the national telephone company. Like most of the successful public sector reforms in Peru, the privatizations were handled by a semiautonomous agency, COPRI, which has a small, skilled staff, many of whose members came from the Central Bank. The first stage of the privatization, beginning in 1992, was to devolve state ownership and find strategic operating investors for the firms on offer. The next stage, announced in June 1994, was to diversify ownership of the solid and profitable enterprises, with the aim of broadening participation in privatization. The program now also has international support, receiving a $1 million grant from the Inter-American Development Bank's multilateral investment fund in May 1995.[144]

The PPC program is run out of COPRI. Like COPRI, the program counts on a few well-trained technocrats who were at the core of the COPRI team and the services of APOYO, S.A., one of the most respected public opinion and survey firms in the country. The team has the support of the influential former presidents of COPRI, Daniel Hokama and Carlos Montoya. The program was envisioned early on in the privatization, and the team spent time studying other countries' experiences. They focused on privatizations in which shares had to be purchased instead of being given away, and a crucial element of the program is that it is not a giveaway scheme. This obviously sets limits on the participation of the very poor, but is important in terms of providing lessons about savings and entrepreneurship.[145] The program's aim was to strengthen local capital markets but also to build support for the economic model and reinforce it by creating a larger base of owners and investors.[146] And because privatization has largely been dominated by foreigners, the program seeks to encourage local entrepreneurship. The team also had the tacit support of the Ministry of Economics and Finance because the program did not cost the ministry anything, there was very little risk to the rate guarantees offered, and it was an easy way to get political support for the economic program.[147] The program's initial success seems to have given it firm executive backing as well. The pilot program, which was implemented in three stages in 1994–95 and attracted more than 18,000 small investors, was crucial to the launching of the participation plan.

The team faced several problems. One was the low-income base of the population. Another was similar to that faced by the private pension system: the lack of public confidence in such programs because of the inexperience with intangibles and the collapse of CLAE. Finally, after years of terrorism, most companies were not accustomed to opening their books to the public or even to publishing the list of directors, yet transparency was key to the success of such a plan.

The participation program has been designed with a clear view to reaching lower-income investors, if not the very poorest (on an economic scale of 1 to 4, with 4 being the poorest, the program aims for 3, whose members have an average income of $500 a month). The purchasable shares are inexpensive (the minimum purchase was 515 soles, or US$234, and the maximum was 3,090 soles, or US$1,404), and purchasing entails enough small bureaucratic steps to prevent wealthier investors from finding participation attractive (for example, having to physically go to respective program offices to pick up shares; they are not transferred automatically by mail or wire). Shares can be purchased in three-year installments, at a relatively low interest rate (12 percent, calculated on the expected inflation rate), and the government guarantees the share prices for the three-year payment period. The promoters that market the program are trained to aim for lower-income participation. A significant effort is made to encourage investors in provinces outside Lima, and approximately 35 percent of the participants do come from outside Lima. Finally, a major objective of the program is to generate public confidence in privatization, and thus a highly profitable and attractive public company, Cementos Norte Pacasamayo, was chosen for the pilot.

Several mechanisms were identified for distributing shares: sales in installment payments, cashing in of recognition bonds in the pension system for shares, the exchange of workers' time-for-service bonuses (CTS) as shares, sales to public sector workers, sales to enterprise workers, and mutual funds.[148] The installment payment system was the only one used in the pilot because it had several obvious advantages. It gave people the option to buy over the long term with very small payments. Payments spread over three years also gave the managers a chance to educate the participants in the program about their shares. Finally, the installment plan also has a very small margin for speculators.[149]

The enterprise that was chosen for the pilot, Cementos Norte, was a low-risk venture with stable profits. It was based in the north rather than in Lima, which was good for encouraging participation in the provinces, and it was already registered in the bolsa (the stock exchange). Fifty-one percent of the company was sold off to an operating investor; the state owned the remaining 49 percent. The participation program was authorized to sell 20 percent of what the state owned. Operative support for the sales was obtained from the Banco Continental. The program was launched with a broad public information campaign using leaflets, videos, and promoters hired to market door-to-door. In general these were the same people that had been hired to market the private pension funds. The program also worked with local opinion leaders to explore marketing tactics. The target groups were workers in the enterprise and low-income workers and professionals such as teachers.[150]

The attention to design and providing information paid off. The first auction, which was held in November 1994 and which the program organizers thought would last 30 days, lasted 3 hours and 40 minutes. More than 3,000 people bought shares, and many were left wanting to buy after the shares ran out. For the second and third campaigns, share sizes were made even smaller to try and avoid this disappointment. In the third campaign, to attract a broader range of people, investors were allowed to reserve shares by telephone. Four thousand people participated in the second campaign, which sold out in 45 minutes. By the end of the third campaign, which was held shortly after the 1995 national elections, 18,500 people had purchased shares.[151]

The pilot program managed to reach a broad range of people. Follow-up surveys showed that 88 percent of the purchasers had never bought shares before. More than 5,000 purchasers were from outside Lima. Newspaper interviews at the time of the sales indicated that even street vendors participated. In the words of one vendor who bought shares: "To tell the truth, it is not impossible. Now . . . all Peruvians, no matter if we are street vendors, housewives, executives, lower or upper class . . . have the opportunity to transform ourselves into 'investors in enterprises with great potential.'"[152] Another participant, a housewife, noted, "Because it is an enterprise that is progressing, one has confidence in buying shares," while a public employee said, "it is a new alternative for investing the little bit one has."[153] A survey of participants found that 64 percent bought shares as a way to provide for their future, 27 percent because of expected profitability, 6 percent because they had been advised to by an acquaintance, and 3 percent because of publicity. More than half did not know how to check for share values on the stock exchange in the newspaper or elsewhere.[154] The program was widely perceived to be reaching the average person because the papers were filled with interviews of street salesmen and people of other low-income professions. There were headlines such as "Privatization Stays Open for Cholos [people of mixed race]," "Cement for All," and "With Only One Hundred Soles One Can Become a Shareholder in Cementos Norte."[155]

One indicator of the program's success is the extent to which participants viewed their shares as long-term investments and participated in the follow-up training provided by the program. Of those who bought shares, 97 percent have kept them as savings, while only 3 percent have sold them. When workshops were offered in the provinces, 60 percent of those who had bought shares attended. And only 2.5 percent of those who bought shares in the pilot failed to pay their quotas in the first year. That rate later increased to 7–8 percent.[156] The desertion rate of those that reserved shares in the auction was 17 percent if they applied by telephone (a remarkably low rate if one considers that there was no commitment attached to the telephone reservations), and 13 percent if they reserved through the promoters. (The latter rate is lower in part because the promoters had a major incentive to follow up and secure the reservations as actual purchases.)[157] Finally, share prices in Cementos Norte rose after the auctions: they originally sold at 5 soles per share and a few months later were trading on an international level at 5.60 soles.[158]

The program is not without flaws, and some mistakes were made during the pilot stage, although they were of marginal importance given the overall success. First, the timing of the third campaign has been an issue. Although it was actually held after the elections in June, it was announced the week before. At the same time, it was announced that between 10 and 15 percent of the shares of Edelnor and Luz del Sur, aiming for 100,000 investors, would be sold soon after the third campaign. Critics could easily have contended that this was blatant use of the program for political reasons, but given that national attention was much more focused on the campaign, the criticism did not occur.[159] Second, there were problems in implementation, such as the limited reach of the banking system. Shares were offered through the national Banco Continental, which does not have branches in all the departments. People in Ayacucho, for example, had to go all the way to Ica to get to a bank branch. A third problem was difficulty in predicting the extent of response. On several occasions, including the first pilot and the Telefonica sale in June 1997, demand for shares was far greater than the program personnel were prepared for, both in administrative terms and in numbers of shares.

Another problem, which was criticized strongly by the newspaper *Expreso* after the third campaign, was the perceived privileged access of the door-to-door promoters. The third campaign was divided into telephone and promoter reservations. Hundreds of people were left waiting to reserve by telephone by the end of the campaign, but all of those who reserved through promoters were able to buy shares. Although the explanation was that the telephone mechanism was new and untested and demand was again higher than expected, it raised accusations of insider trading. The head of COPRI, Carlos Montoya, then issued a public listing identifying the promoters, who were primarily former salesmen from the AFPs, to alleviate public suspicions. Ultimately the matter received little public attention, and even the critics in *Expreso* admit they were looking for something to criticize about the popular and well-publicized program.[160] Yet the situation highlights the need for complete transparency and adequate public information, something that the program has tried to achieve.

After the pilot phase the program sought to participate in the privatization of many of the large enterprises remaining in state hands. The enterprises next slotted for participation in the core program were the remaining shares in the public telephone company (Telefonica) and Luz del Sur, a major electricity distributor. Like Cementos Norte, these were high-earning, low-risk firms. Telefonica was sold first, in June 1997, and approximately 29 percent of the shares, valued at $1.4 billion, remained for purchase.[161]

In the Telefonica sale the program aimed for 100,00 to 200,000 investors. A massive public relations campaign was carried out in three stages. The first sought to educate people about the Citizen Participation Program, the second to educate them about Telefonica; and the third to encourage them to buy shares. The program organizers maintained that they preferred to reach 100,000 educated investors rather than 200,000 that would not keep their shares or would fail to make payments. Thus an addition to the pilot was a fidelity bond for people who keep their shares more than eighteen months: they receive one free share for every twenty held. Although the pilot sale had been conducted through the state-owned Banco Continental, all private banks participated in the Telefonica sale, with one, Banco de Credito, selected in public bidding as overall coordinator. What remained of the $1.4 billion that was not auctioned by the program was to be auctioned internationally, at a share price 5 percent higher, and marketed by J. P. Morgan and Merrill Lynch.[162]

While Telefonica was better known to the Peruvian public than was Cementos Norte, there were still some obstacles to expanding the program on such a large scale. The banking system, for example, remained weak; Peruvians' incomes remained low; and public confidence in the reform program had been shaken by disappointing economic trends in the first quarter of 1996.

Regardless, demand for Telefonica shares far outpaced what the program organizers expected as 270,000 Peruvians applied for shares. At the same time, the government also received stronger-than-expected demand for shares from international investors: demand exceeded supply by five times, raising the share price by 10 percent the first day the stock was offered. As a response to the higher price the government decided to halve the local allocation and sell more shares internationally. Of the total $1.4 billion, $1.1 billion was ultimately sold abroad. The change in the allocation surprised the PPC organizers and eroded the program's and the government's credibility. The program handled the cuts by favoring smaller investors: all those that applied for share packages of $400 or less received them, while those requesting more were subject to pro rata cuts. Ultimately, this resulted in a large amount of unfavorable publicity for the government, which, to satisfy the demands of domestic investors, then issued shares for an additional 1 percent of the 5 percent of the company that it had kept.[163]

Thirty percent of the shares in Luz del Sur, worth $200 million, were sold in November 1996. Approximately $120 million of the offering was reserved for the PPC, and more than 50,000 people applied to buy packages of shares whose values ranged from $200 to $8,000 and required a 10 percent down payment and an eighteen-month installment period for the rest. Having learned from the Telefonica experience, the program limited the amount that single investors could purchase. In addition, the government made a more explicit commitment to maintaining the percentage of shares that were reserved for local purchase.[164]

Cutting back on local share allocations in the Telefonica sale certainly eroded the government's credibility in its attempts to create a strong domestic base of shareholders and also injured the credibility of the program. The PPC's response—putting small investors first and then issuing additional shares—helped ameliorate some of the damage, as did proceeding in a different manner with subsequent sales, as in the case of Luz del Sur. And regardless of its flaws, the program obviously stimulated a great deal of interest, as well as continued participation, by small investors, both in and outside Lima. Sixty-six percent of investors in the Telefonica sale were from Lima, while 34 percent were from the provinces. Public awareness and understanding also increased, in part as a response to the active information campaign undertaken by the PPC. In March 1996, about 42 percent of the population interviewed knew of the PPC mechanism for share buying. After the pre-Telefonica public relations campaign, 82 percent knew of the program.[165]

Potential candidates for the PPC in the future include Mantaro, Centromin, PetroPeru, and the Banco Continental, which together are worth approximately $3 billion.[166] The pace at which the program can proceed depends on the pace of the economic reform and privatization programs, both of which received an unprecedented amount of public criticism in early 1996. Although the criticism was due in part to a slight slowing of growth and increase in inflation in the first quarter of 1996, much was due to

the controversy over the proposed sale of the national oil industry, PetroPeru.[167] The PPC could be a useful means for building
public support for the sale of the company, which many consider
a strategic national asset.[168]

The goals of the program are to broaden the base of participation, particularly low-income investors, and to use other sale
methods, such as the cashing in of government recognition
bonds. Although the program team has no illusions of reaching
income class 4, members do want to increase the participation of
the 3 level. At present, with the aid of APOYO, they are conducting market surveys and trying to develop better incentives for the
lowest-income investors.[169] Market surveys indicate, for example,
that low-income groups care more about the state of the enterprise that is being sold and the opportunity to pay in installments
than they do about the interest rate. In addition, they were un-
comfortable committing for a period of longer than eighteen
months because they were uncertain about their economic and
employment status beyond the near future.[170]

There is also a proposed plan that will allow workers to
trade in their recognition bonds from the public pension plan
for shares in the PPC, which can then be invested in AFPs. The
success of this idea will depend in part on cooperation from officials in the National Pension Office and in the Ministry of Economics and Finance, who are currently responsible for the recognition bonds. This mechanism gives the program a potential
million-person base to tap into, and about 200,000 shares have
been allocated to it. There are some unresolved matters, including some delays in the issuing of recognition bonds and the
need for Congress to pass a law to verify the procedure. There is
no reason to expect much opposition in the government-
dominated Congress or from the Ministry of Economics because
this would free the ministry from having to pay the bonds. It
should also be feasible to get the AFPs' support for the process
since it gives them a cost-free means to participate in the privatization.[171]

Another option, developed in 1997 and announced in the
president's annual Independence Day address, was that of mutual funds, which aim to reduce the risk of investing for low-
income workers by offering shares in even smaller amounts than

in the direct auctions. A particular target of this option was low-income workers in the public sector (those in income level 3) to give them an increased stake in reform.[172] A related mechanism, which has both been influenced by the PPC and which the program plans to support, is the sale of shares to workers in the privatized enterprises. This has already occurred to some extent; in May 1995, for example, $36.98 million worth of shares in fifteen enterprises were sold to enterprise workers. In addition, some enterprises allowed their workers to cash in their time-for-service bonuses and other social benefits for shares, while others allowed financing in installment plans.[173]

There are several lessons from the relative success of the Citizen Participation Program. First, the success has depended on executive commitment that has allowed the program sufficient resources to attract a good technical team and hire outside advisors and divert some of the proceeds of privatization to the program. The president and prime minister have also given the program important publicity in speeches. Unfortunately, the program's credibility was eroded when the executive cut its share allocation during the Telefonica sale, a measure that was particularly surprising given the popularity of the project. The lack of any kind of organized opposition to the program made it a highly desirable reform from a political point of view. And unlike most reforms, it has no adverse effect on any particular social group. One potentially disgruntled group might be those who were left waiting to buy shares after the three pilot auctions and then in the Telefonica sale. Yet this seems to have been corrected with the sale of Luz del Sur. Another potential problem is those who are too poor to participate yet believe they should get some benefit from the sale of public companies. But as with most other issues, their voice tends to be less politically effective than that of more organized groups, they have poor access to information, and their potential (and unlikely) opposition is not much of a concern for the government. Unlike the pension and education reforms, both of which aroused varying degrees of political opposition, the PPC is a potential win-win proposition for the government. The program implicitly addresses the problem of lack of faith in state promises by providing the average citizen the opportunity to purchase private shares in traditionally profitable public companies.

There are important contrasts between the PPC and the pension reform that are inherent but also stem from program design and implementation. The PPC's success highlights the importance of adequate public information and education. The program overcame a general lack of experience with saving by using aggressive advertising and promotion campaigns as well as follow-up information for participants that has improved public understanding of investing. In contrast, the promotion campaign for the AFPs was far less transparent, and false promises by some funds ultimately undermined public confidence in them. Pension reform was, at least initially, far more politically sensitive, and an active opposition emphasized the risks in the new private system. In addition, there is an obvious difference between purchasing shares in companies whose operations are visible and yield dividends in the immediate term than in participating in a savings scheme that offers less visible benefits much further in the future. This difference gives the PPC an advantage over the AFPs in reaching or attracting new lower-income participants and in creating tangible stakes in the reform.

Overall, the PPC is an obvious means to improve the participation of a broader section of society in reform and to create tangible stakes in its continuation. As with all such attempts, reaching a balance between equity considerations (reaching low-income workers) and those of economic sustainability will continue to be a concern. In Peru, where many reforms have yet to yield tangible results for lower-income people (other than the obvious effects of macroeconomic stabilization), the equity implications are of particular concern, and whatever progress can be made in creating new stakeholders among them through the PPC will be at least a first step toward strengthening the long-term sustainability of market reforms.

## Conclusion

The contrasting experiences of the three reform efforts highlight the challenges to reforming public institutions in Peru and also present some relevant lessons for other countries. There are more than 1 million workers in the new private pension system, while the PPC will reach another half million out of a total population of more than 24 million. Both programs make significant contributions to the political sustainability of reform by increasing the number of stakeholders in the reforms, encouraging savings and investment, and providing valuable experience with participation in newly emerging capital markets. Both may also result in an improved allocation of public expenditures because resources previously going to subsidize state-owned enterprises or the public pension system can be diverted to other areas, such as education.[174]

Yet reforms of semi- or quasi-public institutions, such as state-owned enterprises, cannot substitute for reforms of institutions that deliver basic social services to the majority of the population and are of particular importance to the poor. Discretionary public expenditures, which have until now provided very visible and tangible benefits, many of which, such as new irrigation systems or new schools, are also of considerable importance, are also not a substitute for basic social services.

The contrasting experiences also highlight the greater political and administrative complexities involved in social reforms. The pension reform was more politically controversial than the popular capitalism program. Education reform was far more administratively complex and politically difficult than pension reform. Until now, with the exception of a few isolated attempts, the government has avoided comprehensive attempts at such reforms out of fears about political opposition (even though it is much less formidable in Peru than it is in countries with strong public sector unions or legislative opposition) and out of unwillingness to devolve authority to local levels. Without executive initiative in these matters, progress is likely to be ad hoc or too cautiously sought and is unlikely to address the underlying problems and skewed incentives structures in the most important institutions. Yet given the current political context, the success and demonstration effects of small or ad hoc attempts at reform of social service delivery, such as the CLAS health reform and related attempts at decentralization, will be the only basis for broader reform efforts.

The contrasting experience of the different reforms also shows the importance of executive commitment and of a reform team within the sector being reformed. These two factors were crucial to the success of the PPC. Pension reform suffered from a lack of complete executive commitment and of a strong reform team. Its strongest proponent, Carlos Boloña, was in the Finance Ministry and then left the government. Only when the AFPs were in place did people with strong technical skills and the incentive to push further reforms emerge in the newly set up superintendency. That team then had some influence in improving the reform, such as through the passage of the June 1995 law. For education reform, there is clearly no coherent guidance within the ministry, a situation that has frustrated many well-intentioned efforts by the international financial institutions and others. And while President Fujimori initially attempted education reform, the political controversy it created undermined whatever commitment he had.

The experiences also expose the trade-offs between temporary, extrainstitutional efforts and those within the mainstream public institutions. The efforts outside institutions are clearly the easiest and demonstrate rapid and visible results. They may indeed be necessary at critical political moments to generate crucial support for reform. And they may also yield important public benefits, such as some of the infrastructure created by Foncodes or the distribution of shares in public companies through the PPC. They may also have beneficial demonstration effects for the operations of mainstream institutions. Yet these reforms are short term. Foncodes could be dissolved tomorrow by executive decree. The PPC will last only as long as there are unsold shares in public companies. And neither program addresses broad societal needs, especially the needs of the poor, in the same way that a reform of education or health care services would. Pension reform has provided a private alternative attractive to higher-income workers, but has failed to solicit the participation of poorer workers, who remain in the increasingly bankrupt public program. Nor is the reform likely to give poorer workers in the informal sector access to social insurance. Neither are simple tasks, and it is unclear that they are viable in the short term. Yet the effects of income in determining participation in these two reforms point to the need for public institutions that can address the needs of those who face poverty-related limitations to responding to market incentives, particularly in social services.

As the discussion of decentralization suggests, and the experiences in Peru and other countries in this study show, there are often unavoidable trade-offs between the objectives of improving institutional performance through increased voice and choice and improving equity. Increasing choice is often a necessary and effective means to improve the performance of public institutions. Yet the poorest people are often at a disadvantage in responding to new voice and choice strategies because they have the least information, the weakest administrative capacity, and often the lowest expectations. Although they may benefit in the long run from improved institutional performance, either directly or indirectly through demonstration effects, in the short run the effects on equity may be harmful. Thus it is not surprising that the rural poor in Peru were opposed to choice-based education reform, once they were made aware of its potential effects by the political opposition. Participation in the private pension system and in the share-purchasing plan for low-income investors was much greater in urban areas, particularly in the capital, than in poor rural ones. Again this suggests the need for special provisions to facilitate the poor's participation in new stakeholders strategies, particularly when they are applied to the delivery of essential public goods. The impressive results of the CLAS health program in soliciting increased participation from the poor suggests that effective training and public education can be very important in overcoming poverty-related constraints.

A final matter is the extent to which significant parts of society have a stake in the particular reforms and how or if those stakes can be increased. Although education is where the largest numbers stand to benefit from reform, there is no effective articulation of the public's interests or particular stakes in reform. Pension reform, meanwhile, may have created new stakeholders in the private system who have helped deepen the reforms, but these people are a relatively small and privileged minority. The popular capitalism program demonstrated that there was far more demand—and at lower levels of income—to participate in privatization, but again demand was limited by income constraints. An important factor in the success of the PPC in getting as much participation as it has was an active campaign to educate people so they could make informed decisions. This contrasts sharply with the pension reform, for which public information was insufficient and at times inaccurate, and with education reform, for which the government made no attempt to involve either the public or teachers in the proposed changes while the opposition waged an effective campaign to educate the public about the risks of the proposals. The importance of effective communication in the success of stakeholders strategies is a theme common to virtually all the illustrations in this study.

Reform of public institutions is difficult to carry out in any country and certainly in one as poor as Peru. The successes that have been achieved in Peru are indeed worthy of note, and much of those successes has stemmed from incorporating market incentives and creating new stakeholders. Yet there are legitimate concerns about the ability of the poor to respond to those incentives and participate in the benefits of reform, as well as about the sustainability of the government's extrainstitutional approach. What remains urgently on the agenda is reform of the public institutions that provide the basic services critical to reducing poverty. In the short term the kinds of programs that have been started can contribute to the political sustainability of reform and may even influence voting patterns. The records of the programs also suggest that new market incentives can improve the performance of public institutions. Yet crucial to the longer-term sustainability of market-led growth is incorporating these incentives into broader institutional reform efforts in health care and education, reforms that improve the capacity of the poor to respond to new market incentives and to participate in growth as genuine stakeholders.

Chapter 4

# The Capitalization and Popular Participation Programs in Bolivia

S OME OF THE MOST innovative efforts to broaden the base of stakeholders in market reforms have begun in South America's poorest country, Bolivia.[1] The 1993–97 government of Gonzalo Sanchez de Lozada introduced a novel approach to privatization termed *capitalization* that has invested 50 percent of the shares in privatized public enterprises in a new social security system. This provides a new institutionality for increasing savings and economic growth and distributes the dividends in the form of annual payments to all Bolivians older than age 65. At the same time, through the Popular Participation program the government initiated a major redistribution of public resources to benefit poor rural areas and to allocate and deliver social services by devolving responsibility to communities. These reforms, in conjunction with a major education reform, make up the Sanchez de Lozada government's Plan de Todos (Plan for All), an attempt to involve the majority of Bolivians as direct stakeholders in reform.

## The Political Economy of the Plan de Todos Reforms

It is no surprise that Sanchez de Lozada was the driving force behind initiatives to improve the sustainability of market reforms. In 1985 Bolivia was the first country in the region to stabilize high inflation and begin structural reforms under democratic auspices. As minister of economics and planning during the 1985–89 Paz Estenssoro government, Sanchez de Lozada was the architect of the macroeconomic reform package widely known as the New Economic Policy (NEP). The main features of the package, which stabilized one of the world's highest hyperinflations and achieved positive rates of growth, were market liberalization and price decontrol, the opening of the economy to foreign trade and investment, and liberalization of the labor market. The NEP also dismantled much of Bolivia's state-owned tin mining sector. Although the Bolivian economy relied heavily on tin exports for foreign exchange, the industry had become one of the highest-cost producers in the world. And by the mid-1980s the world price of tin had virtually collapsed. In 1986, in part out of concern for the plight of the unemployed miners, the same government created an innovative safety net program, the Emergency Social Fund, that by demand of the beneficiary population introduced market principles into the allocation of benefits. The idea has since been adopted by dozens of countries.[2] And unlike many countries where social funds have been temporary policy tools, in Bolivia they have been incorporated permanently into the public sector's operations via the Social Investment Fund (FIS), which is responsible for financing health and education infrastructure.[3]

By the mid-1990s all the major political parties in Bolivia were committed to a continuation of the NEP, and all had run on a proreform platform in the 1989 and 1993 national elections. Although Sanchez de Lozada's Nationalist Revolutionary Movement (MNR) party was out of office from 1989 to 1993, the governing coalition of the Leftist Revolutionary Movement (MIR) and the Nationalist Democratic Action (ADN) parties maintained the NEP reforms and deepened them in some areas.

Despite the consensus among the major political parties, there is a more pressing need to broaden the base of support for reform in Bolivia than in most countries in the region. First, it has the highest poverty rate in South America. It is also unlikely to achieve the boom levels of growth that have helped build broad support for reform in Peru and other poor countries. In addition, Bolivia has a vocal and highly ideological union movement, which while not by itself capable of reversing the course of economic policy, can mobilize opposition to reforms and create social unrest. Although the union movement was significantly weakened by the dismantling of much of the state-owned tin mining industry, the Confederation of Bolivian Workers (Central Obrera Boliviana, or COB) retains influence and monopoly control over certain critical services such as education. It remains strongly tied to the statist, nationalist ideology of the 1952 revolution. The COB refers to the Plan de Todos reform laws as the "tres leyes malditas," or the three "accursed" laws.[4]

There is also a strong populist current in Bolivian politics that is outside the realm of the three major parties. This movement has been most evident in La Paz, where it is embodied in support for the (recently deceased) antireformist politician, Compadre Carlos Palenque Aviles and his Conscience of the Fatherland (Conciencia de Patria, or CONDEPA) movement. CONDEPA and other populist movements do not have sufficient support to supersede the influence of the major parties, but they are vocal reminders of the high levels of poverty and the extent to which the poor have not benefited from the reforms except for the immediate benefits achieved by the halting of inflation.[5]

Adding to this was the public perception that the macroeconomic reforms had been imposed by elite technocrats who were concerned solely with efficiency. "Indeed, because the path of structural reforms was shaped 'on the go,' they were generally justified on the basis of engineering values of efficiency and rationality at the expense of the ingrained values of solidarity and expectations of greater equality."[6] The ESF (Emergency Social Fund), for example, was a highly visible safety net program that provided income relief and infrastructure improvements for poor, if not the poorest, groups. It was therefore efficient in reducing poverty and may have even built support for reform among previously marginalized groups. Yet it received little support among the direct "losers" in the process: the lower and middle classes and organized labor, who for the most part would not work for ESF wage levels, which were at or near the unofficial minimum.[7]

Finally, of all the structural reforms, privatization of state-owned enterprises was politically the most difficult to initiate, even though many of them were incurring major losses. The governing MNR party had made its political fortune through the 1952 revolution, in which the country's major industries—tin mining, natural gas, electricity, and railroads, many of which were foreign-owned—were nationalized. The union movement had its origins in the revolution, particularly in the mining and oil industries. For a small, poor, racially divided, landlocked country with great income inequality and a history of foreign economic domination, the 1952 revolution had far-reaching political implications. The prospect of returning the nation's natural resources to private hands caused an explosive political debate, even as many other countries in the region, which started their macroeconomic reforms much later than Bolivia, initiated far-reaching privatization programs. The MIR-ADN government made only minor progress in privatization, and more often than not maintained enterprises under public ownership while introducing intermediate reforms such as performance contracting, which links the budgetary allocations of the enterprises to improvements in their performance.[8] The six major state-owned enterprises, which accounted for 12.5 percent of GDP, remained untouched.

Given this context, the Sanchez de Lozada government had at times conflicting objectives in the Plan de Todos reforms: providing immediate benefits from reform for the average poor Bolivian and increasing national savings and investment to generate higher growth rates.[9] The most controversial of the reforms was the capitalization plan. Capitalization has two major objectives. The first is to make privatization more palatable politically by keeping 50 percent of the shares of the enterprises in Bolivian hands and distributing the dividends among all Bolivians. The second is to increase savings and investment in the Bolivian economy by requiring the buyers of the enterprises to pay for their shares through new investments in the enterprises and by creating a new private pension program in which most dividends are initially invested.

The Popular Participation program, which was introduced before capitalization, doubled the amount of tax revenue designated to local governments and changed the expenditure allocation from one based on the legal residences of taxpayers to a per capita basis. As a result, many poor rural areas received signifi-cant increases in resources and more than 200 new municipalities needed to be formed.

A third component of the Plan de Todos is education reform that increases local responsibility for managing and financing schools, introduces competition among schools and new require-ments for teachers as well as new curricula and texts, and pro-motes diversity of cultures and languages in education—a critical matter in a society as racially heterogeneous as Bolivia's. Yet be-cause similar reforms have been introduced elsewhere and because the success of education reform hinges in large part on the success of the participation program, I will focus on the more novel capitalization and participation programs, particularly their objective of increasing the number of stakeholders in reform.

## The Evolution of Political Consensus

The most notable aspect of Bolivia's political economy is the extent to which the political parties have agreed on the irreversi-bility of the economic reform program. This is surprising in a country whose political landscape before 1985 was marked by fragmented and polarized party politics and repeated military in-terventions. The consensus stems partly from the severity of the economic crisis and the instability that threatened Bolivia's frag-ile new democracy in 1985. As in many countries that have expe-rienced extreme economic instability and hyperinflation, resolv-ing the crisis required developing a domestic political consensus. Such agreement often is an important source of political stability and support for continued economic reform after the crisis is re-solved.[10] Economic and political reforms can then complement one another because each requires predictable rules and a state that is capable of serving as a neutral guarantor of the rules rather than a provider of favors for competing interest groups. The structural reforms that were introduced in Bolivia sought to re-orient the state into one capable of taking such a role.[11] Finally, the economic changes that the NEP introduced and the collapse in the international price of tin dramatically reduced the power of the radical left and of the labor movement.

While not a sufficient condition for democratic development, macroeconomic stability was certainly necessary in Bolivia. Inflation fell from 25,000 percent in 1985 to 3 percent two years later. GDP, which fell between 1978 and 1985, grew 2.7 percent in 1987 and 3 percent in 1989. The national budget deficit, equal to more than 25 percent of GDP in 1984 fell to 3 percent by 1988. Exports, which fell to $500 million in 1985 increased to $813 million by 1989, despite negative trends in the terms of trade. In the 1990s, the pace of growth and investment gradually picked up, in part as a response to the Sanchez de Lozada government's capitalization program. Growth was 3.7 percent in 1995, 3.7 percent in 1996, and is projected to average at 5.4 percent annually from 1997 to 2005.[12] Tax receipts were 12.3 percent of GDP in 1994 and 13.5 percent in 1995.[13] Public and private investment increased 5 points in 1996 to 19 percent of GDP, with the bulk of the increase in private investment.[14] Other important reforms included the establishment of an independent Central Bank, with the president holding a seven-year term, and the passage of the SAFCO (System of Administration and Control of Public Accounts) law, which makes all public servants responsible for their decisions and accountable for the resources they spend.[15]

The gradual development of consensus and the need for coalition building seems to parallel, and has perhaps contributed to, the development of a more moderate, less fragmented multiparty system. "This has been possible because interparty competition, once channeled into confrontation, now tends to express itself in the form of bargaining and coalition formation. . . . The availability of a space at the center of the governmental system that could be filled by bargaining increased the incentive to bargain, and bargaining induced parties to become more centrist."[16] Between 1979 and 1993 the number of parties legally registered with the Electoral Court fell from seventy-one to sixteen. The most significant of the new ones are ADN, MBL, UCS, and CONDEPA. Although no single party has majority status, the creation of a majority is possible with the center dominated by MNR, ADN, and MIR, whose total share in the past three general elections was between 63 and 65 percent.[17] Article 90 of the Constitution calls for a congressional vote for president among the top three candidates if none is able to achieve a clear majority. The president is then elected for a fixed term of five years, with no consecutive reelection. Since the resumption of legitimate elections in 1979, no candidate has attained a majority in the first round.

Thus there have been a number of likely—and unlikely—electoral coalitions or pacts. In 1989, for example, a coalition between the moderately left-wing MIR, led by Jaime Paz Zamora, and the center-right ADN elected Paz Zamora to the presidency, even though Sanchez de Lozada and the MNR had attained a plurality of the national electoral votes. Despite the unlikeliness of the alliance, the Paz Zamora government was both stable and committed to continuing the economic reform program. In 1993 the MNR again won a plurality but not a majority (table 4-1). The MNR allied with the MBL (the Free Bolivia Movement) and a splinter faction of the UCS (Civic Solidarity Movement) of the (deceased) populist leader, Max Fernandez, to achieve a governing majority in Congress.[18]

Despite this consensus among the major parties, a strong populist current dominates the discourse of some of the newer parties, such as the UCS and CONDEPA. Some of the discourse is antireformist, particularly CONDEPA's, but most of it is anti-institutionalist, emphasizing the charisma of its leaders. The fates of UCS and CONDEPA are therefore unclear because their leaders have died.[19] Thus although populist opposition to reforms is a political concern, it remains at the margin of a fairly strong base of support for reforms among the three major parties.[20] Finally, a constitutional reform that aims to make the electoral system more representative—and thus reduce the appeal of populists—was passed in 1994. The reform added to the electoral system based on party lists by introducing first-past-the-post voting in single-member districts for 50 percent of the 130 congressional seats.[21]

Consensus on maintaining the market model, as well as coalition politics and the same alternating set of parties, again dominated in the June 1997 national elections. Hugo Banzer and the ADN took 22 percent, a plurality of the vote, followed by Juan Carlos Duran of the MNR with 18 percent (Sanchez de Lozada, as incumbent president, was prohibited from running again by the Constitution), and Jaime Paz Zamora of the MIR with 17 percent. Banzer, who campaigned on promises to fight poverty and improve health and education services as well as to continue free

Table 4-1. *Presidential Election Results, Bolivia, 1985, 1989, 1993, 1997*

| Candidate (party) | Percent of the popular vote |
|---|---|
| 1997 election | |
| Hugo Banzer (ADN) | 22 |
| Juan Carlos Duran (MNR) | 18 |
| Jaime Paz Zamora (MIR) | 17 |
| Ivo Kuljis (UCS) | 16 |
| Remedios Loza (CONDEPA) | 16 |
| 1993 election | |
| Gonzalo Sanchez de Lozada (MNR) | 33.8 |
| Hugo Banzer (ADN) | 20.0 |
| Carlos Paenque Aviles (CONDEPA) | 13.6 |
| Max Fernandez (USC) | 13.1 |
| Antonio Aranibar Quirogo (MBL) | 5.1 |
| 1989 election | |
| Gonzalo Sanchez de Lozada (MNR) | 23.1 |
| Hugo Banzer (ADN) | 22.7 |
| Jaime Paz Zamora (MIR) | 19.6 |
| 1985 election | |
| Hugo Banzer (ADN) | 28 |
| Paz Estenssoro (MNR) | 26 |
| Jaime Paz Zamora (MIR) | 9 |

Sources: 1997: "Bolivia Names Ex-Dictator President," *New York Times*, August 6, 1997, p. A8; 1993: http://194.151.8.68/users/derksen/election/bolivia.htm; 1989: James Painter, "The Paragon of Polls Falls from Grace," *Christian Science Monitor*, June 2, 1989, p. 5; and 1985: Carol Graham, *Safety Nets, Politics, and the Poor* (Brookings 1994), p. 56.

market economic policies and the reforms implemented by the Sanchez de Lozada government, then allied with the MIR in Congress to obtain the votes necessary to form a government. Although independent and populist candidates were again present—CONDEPA's Remedios Loza and the UCS's Ivo Kuljis each received 16 percent of the vote—they made little headway in eroding the traditional three-way split of the vote held by the MNR, the ADN, and the MIR (table 4-2).[22]

There are still major political challenges ahead. The internal structures of most political parties, with the exception of the MNR, which had an internal reform in the early 1990s, are far from democratic. Insufficient and inadequate voter registration also remains a problem, in part because of the remoteness of some regions of the country. The judicial system is obsolete, cor-

Table 4-2. *Congressional Election Results, by Party, Bolivia, 1993*

| Political party | Percent of popular vote | Number of deputy seats | Number of senator seats |
|---|---|---|---|
| Nationalist Revolutionary Movement (MNR) | 35.1 | 51 | 17 |
| National Democratic Alliance (ADN)[a] | | | 8 |
| Movement of Revolutionary Left (MIR)[a] | 21.2 | 36 | |
| Citizens' Unity Solidarity (UCS) | 13.3 | 19 | 1 |
| Conscience of the Fatherland (CONDEPA) | 12.5 | 13 | 1 |
| Movement Free Bolivia (MBL) | 5.3 | 7 | 1 |

Source: Informatieblad Bolivia; see http://194.151.8.68:80/users/derksen/election/bolivia.htm.
a. ADN/MIR election results represent the parties' combined total.

rupt, and subordinate to the executive. The union movement, despite its reduction in size since 1985, remains strongly opposed to neoliberal economic policies and is capable of launching damaging work stoppages in critical productive sectors, such as petroleum, as well as in education. In April 1995, for example, the government had to call a six-week state of siege after 70,000 teachers went on indefinite strike, which led to violent protest.[23] In March 1996 tens of thousands of state workers took to the streets as part of a national strike to demand higher wages and protest the planned capitalization of the national oil industry. The COB-led strike, which began with a hunger strike and the shutdown of public schools and universities, was joined by public health workers, miners, and some employees of the state petroleum industry.[24] But although the strikes were disruptive, they did not achieve their objective of reversing the reforms, nor did they generate a broader political opposition movement. This reflects the extent to which the union movement's stance is primarily a defensive one that seeks to protect its position in the public sector. In any event, establishing a new trust between the traditional organizations of the state and those of civil society will be important to consolidating democracy and maintaining broad support for market reforms.

*Poverty and Equity Issues*

Foremost among the challenges facing policymakers and critical to the sustainability of both economic reforms and democratic institutions is reducing Bolivia's poverty and inequality. Approximately 60 percent of the Bolivian population lives below the poverty line, with some estimates as high as 70 percent.[25] GDP per capita, at $876, is by far the lowest in South America. Income distribution is also highly unequal: the richest quintile of the population receives approximately 50 percent of total income, the poorest only 6 percent. The infant mortality rate, at 73 deaths per 1,000 live births, is the highest in South America, and is twice as high in rural areas. Population growth is 2.3 percent, making it difficult to reduce poverty at average economic growth rates of 2 to 3 percent. Life expectancy is 61 years, the lowest in South America, and is ten years lower in rural areas. Although 74 percent of the urban population has access to safe drinking water, only 33 percent of the rural population does (slightly over 50 percent of the population is urban). And only 17.5 percent of the rural population has access to basic health care services. Adult illiteracy is 23 percent; in Peru it is 15 percent.[26]

Resources available for social expenditures are distributed unequally. Until the education reform was begun, the government spent $600 a year on each university student versus $70 a year on each primary education student. Ninety-eight percent of the total budget for health and education goes to payroll expenditures.[27] Total expenditures, at 3 percent of GDP, have recovered from their pre-1985 crisis levels, but they are still far below the reform objectives of 6 percent.[28] Recent research highlights the urgency of improving the quality of and access to education services. Differences in educational attainment explain more of Bolivia's income inequality than all other factors combined, and an additional year of education increases a worker's salary by 10 percent.[29]

Not surprisingly, social policy issues are a central concern for the Sanchez de Lozada government. Two of its three major reforms, education reform and Popular Participation, involve social policy. The major education reform launched in July 1994 increased the responsibility of municipal governments for financing and managing schools through locally constituted *nucleos escolares* (school nuclei), which include school board representatives, the mayor, and the school directors. The reform also introduced standard evaluation processes for teachers, introduced new textbooks and curricula, and encouraged diversity of culture and language in education. By the end of 1996 the new system had been applied to 351 school nuclei, which accounted for 2,200 schools and 16 percent of enrolled students. The system was to be extended to 500 additional nuclei and 3,250 schools by the end of 1997, covering approximately half the country's student population.[30] Popular support for the reform gradually increased. Although 39 percent of the population supported it in March 1994, 60 percent did in March 1996.[31] Yet the reform was met with widespread opposition from the teachers' union and resulted in the April 1995 national strike and state of siege.

In part because of the opposition from organized workers in the public sector, the education reform has been managed largely by the FIS (Fondo de Inversion Social, or Social Investment Fund), the successor to the Emergency Social Fund that has taken the leading role in innovations in social policy in Bolivia in recent years. The FIS, for example, was the first social policy institution to incorporate poverty criteria into its allocation decisions.[32] Although this is a result of the agency's strength and efficiency, it also suggests that much more needs to be done before the reform is institutionalized in the public sector and reflects the difficulties that most countries face in reforming public sector agencies.[33] The education reform clearly did not have a leader or driving force. It is telling that there were four ministers of human development and three ministers of education during the four-year term of the government.[34]

The Plan de Todos reforms attempt to address some of the underlying causes of poverty, but they also raise important equity issues. They are intended to benefit all Bolivians, and all benefits are allocated per capita. This immediately improved equity because there are far more poor Bolivians than wealthy ones. Before the reforms the poor for the most part received fewer net benefits from public expenditures. Yet one could also make a strong case for a more progressive allocation—or at the least for limiting the benefits going to wealthy groups—when there is such a shortage of resources for basic social services for the poorest groups and such an inequitable distribution of income. The very poorest municipalities could certainly benefit from a share greater than per capita because their administrative capacity is weak and their ability to generate matching resources is much less than that of wealthier municipalities.

Another important choice affecting equity was to invest the proceeds from capitalization in the pension system. Critics—including the major opposition parties—argue that many of Bolivia's social needs are far more pressing than social security.[35] The transfer may well be regressive because the wealthy are more likely than the poor to live beyond age 65. Yet there are many sound reasons for the government's decision. First, the high infant mortality rate skews life expectancy figures downward, and the average person that lives beyond 1 year of age also lives beyond 61 years. Second, because immediate social needs are so great, and certainly well beyond any available resources, it would be difficult to invest any of the capitalization resources in future growth if they were directed at the social services, where there is virtually unlimited demand. Investments in human capital make significant contributions to growth and poverty reduction, but higher savings and investment rates in Bolivia are necessary if not sufficient conditions for achieving those objectives.[36]

In all countries there are trade-offs between making politically popular investments in immediate consumption and investing in longer-term growth. They are particularly difficult when the gap between available resources and legitimate demands for those resources is very large. These trade-offs are even more difficult to accept in the context of economic reform, which affects differentially the living standards of particular groups, who are usually not the most poor and vulnerable and are usually vocal and organized.[37] Given these trade-offs and the very clear need for increased investments in Bolivia, the Sanchez de Lozada government's decision to direct the revenues from privatization to investment while at the same time reallocating existing fiscal revenues to poor rural areas is bold and forward-looking. In addition, it would make little sense to increase resources for health care and education significantly before fully implementing reforms in those services. The implementation record will ultimately determine the extent to which they increase both efficiency and equity as well as generate support by creating new stakeholders, who themselves will help determine the level of resources allocated to the social services.

## The Capitalization Program

Bolivia's capitalization program is an exceptionally innovative initiative that combines three objectives: privatization, social security reform, and broadening the base of stakeholders in the market process. The program was an explicit part of the 1993 electoral campaign of Sanchez de Lozada and was a central objective of his government.[38] Although Bolivia implemented far-reaching economic reforms well before many countries in the region, it lagged far behind in its attempts to privatize state-owned enterprises. Privatization was a particularly contentious issue due in large part to Bolivia's economic dependence on a few mineral exports. This, coupled with limited domestic investment capacity, heightened concerns that privatization would result in a selling off of the national wealth and a return to foreign economic domination. The predominance of the mining and hydrocarbons industries also strengthened the political power of organized labor in those sectors, and unions understandably feared that they would have weaker bargaining capacity against large multinational enterprises.

The Sanchez de Lozada government introduced capitalization as a means to make privatization politically viable, keep at least a part of the wealth from natural resources in Bolivian hands, and generate vital foreign investment. Under the program the government allows a strategic investor, selected through competitive bidding, to purchase 50 percent of the shares in the privatized company. Instead of paying the government for the enterprise, the buyer agrees to invest the amount in the enterprise within a fixed period of time. The other 50 percent of the shares are turned over to the Bolivian population and deposited in the collective capitalization fund of the new private pension plan. The dividends from the shares, called bonosols or solidarity bonds, are invested by two new pension fund managers, the Invesco Argentaria consortium and Banco Bilbao Viscaya, and are distributed annually to all Bolivians older than 65 in payments of about $200 a person, regardless of whether they contribute to the new pension plan. All workers who were contributing to the public pension plan at the time of the reform received recognition bonds for their past contributions, and their retirement accounts are transferred to a new private pension system, which is managed by the new pension funds and regulated by the state.

Capitalization was a Bolivian initiative.[39] Major international agencies such as the World Bank and the International Monetary Fund were initially opposed to the program, but they eventually lent their support (in varying degrees) as the first capitalization, that of ENDE, the state electricity company, made it clear that the program was feasible.[40] Bolivia then received a $50 million IDA (International Development Association) credit and a $70 million loan from the Inter-American Development Bank to support the capitalization process.[41] The government had considered a voucher scheme like the Czech Republic's, in which all citizens are given shares in state enterprises. Yet in a context like Bolivia's, where most of the population is below the poverty line, there was a legitimate fear that people would sell off their shares for immediate income. Even in the Czech Republic, the majority of those at or near the poverty line immediately sold their shares (see chapter 5).

## Capitalizing the Enterprises

The six major state-owned enterprises, accounting for 12.5 percent of GDP, were included in the capitalization program. These were ENDE (National Electricity Company), ENTEL (National Telecommunications Company), LAB (Lloyd Bolivian Airlines), YPFB (Bolivian Petroleum Company), and EMV (Vinto Smelting Company). The capitalization law, passed in 1994, transformed these enterprises into mixed-capital corporations that could issue shares for purchase. By mid-1997 five of the six had been capitalized with new investments of $2.5 billion (table 4-3). The program was completed in June 1997. It was managed by the Ministry of Capitalization, an independent ministry with-

Table 4-3. *Capitalization of Enterprises, Bolivia, 1990s*

U.S. dollars

| Enterprise | Strategic investor | Book value | Capitalized value (50 percent) | New value |
|---|---|---|---|---|
| Total ENDE | | 99,060,000 | 139,848,400 | 238,908,400 |
| Corani (ENDE) | Dominion Energy | 33,030,000 | 58,796,300 | 91,826,000 |
| Guaracachi (ENDE) | Energy Initiatives | 35,280,000 | 47,131,000 | 82,411,000 |
| Valle Hermoso (ENDE) | Constellation Energy | 30,750,000 | 33,921,100 | 64,671,000 |
| Total ENTEL | ETI Euro Telecom (STET) | 130,000,000 | 610,000,000 | 740,000,000 |
| Total LAB | VASP | 24,000,000 | 47,475,000 | 71,475,000 |
| Red Andina (ENFE) | Cruz Blanca | 29,000,000 | 13,251,000 | 42,251,000 |
| Red Oriental (ENFE) | Cruz Blanca | 24,000,000 | 25,853,099 | 49,853,099 |
| Total ENFE | | 53,000,000 | 39,104,099 | 92,104,099 |
| Empresa Petrolera Andina (YPFB) | YPF-Perez Compano-Pluspetrol Bolivia | 129,980,000 | 264,778,000 | 394,758,000 |
| Transredes (YPFB) | Enron Transportation (Bolivia)- Shell Overseas | 97,180,000 | 263,500,000 | 360,680,000 |
| Total YPFB | | 382,860,000 | 834,948,000 | 1,217,808,000 |
| Total | | 1,124,780,000 | 2,545,427,598 | 3,670,207,598 |

Source: Ministerio de Capitalizacion, presentation at World Bank, June 23, 1997.

out porfolio, responsible directly to the president and with a mandate to dissolve itself once the capitalizations were completed.

In addition, a new regulatory framework was set up. The framework had three components. SIRESE was the system of sectoral regulation and has a mandate to oversee the electricity, telecommunications, transport, hydrocarbons, and water sectors. SIREFI, the system of financial regulation, oversees the pensions, banking and other financial services, and insurance systems. SIRENAFE, the system of regulation of renewable resources, oversees forestry and agriculture. The entire program, which is overseen by a general superintendent who is independent of any of the sectors, is supposed to act as the guarantor of the rights of the state, the private operators, and consumers. The superintendents for each of the components were selected by Congress, with presidential approval, in March 1997 for terms of five years. The system was based on several countries' experience and is a hybrid of both autonomous and multisectoral regulatory models. The superintendents have an independent budget, for example, which comes from fees levied in each sector, and thus are not financially dependent on the national budget.[42] The ability of these institutions to maintain their independence and integrity will be critical to the success of the capitalization. One hopes that the establishment of central bank independence and the encouragement of greater accountability in the public sector through the passage of the SAFCO law will serve as a reinforcing influence.

For the most part the revenues generated by the program exceeded the government's expectations. The capitalizations began with the sale in August 1995 of ENDE, a profitable company with a straightforward sales strategy that the reform team knew could yield immediate and beneficial results.[43] The company had a book value of $99 million, but the 50 percent share was sold at $139 million, increasing its book value to $238 million. It was split into three generating companies, Empresa Electrica Corani, Empresa Valle Hermosa, and Empresa Electrica Guaracachi, that were sold to three strategic investors, Dominion Energy, Energy Initiatives, and Constellation Energy Consortium, all from the United States.

The next capitalization was ENTEL, again a sale that the team knew would yield good results. Yet the sale exceeded even those expecations. Although ENTEL's book value was $130 million, STET International, an Italian company, bid $610 million, committing itself to invest that amount in Bolivia's telecommunications network in six years. STET agreed to invest a certain percentage in rural telephone service, which is nearly nonexistent in Bolivia, as well as to meet targets for providing public telephones, new installations, and new equipment. In exchange it received exclusive rights for long-distance telephone calls for six years. In November 1995 STET deposited $610 million in ENTEL's account to achieve all the obligations. The net worth of the company is now $742 million.[44]

LAB's book value was $24 million and the 50 percent share in it was bought for $47 million by a Brazilian company, Viacao Aerea Sao Paolo (VASP), an agreement that included VASP's supplying some new airplanes and allowing use of some of its air routes. ENFE, the state railroad company, was valued at $52 million, and the controlling share was bought for $39 million by Empresa Cruz Blanca, a Chilean company. In exchange for exclusive rights for forty years, the company agreed to provide a certain level of service in addition to the investment in the company.[45] Although ENFE was probably the least profitable of the state-owned industries, it was one of the most contentious capitalizations because it was bought by a Chilean company. Bolivia's access to the sea was lost in the nineteenth-century war of the Pacific with Chile, and there was political opposition to the national railroad's being bought by Chileans.

The most politically difficult capitalization was YPFB, which was sold near the end of the capitalization. The hydrocarbons law was passed in April 1996 and authorizes YPFB to enter into joint venture contracts. By mid-1997 part of the enterprise was capitalized in three separate branches, while the state retained ownership of the extraction part, which was the largest with the strongest union and the most workers. Enron-Shell purchased Transredes, the transportation sector of YPFB, a purchase that included an agreement to invest in the completion of a planned natural gas pipeline to Brazil. The two exploration units, Empresa Petrolera Andina and Empresa Petrolera Chaco, were sold to YFB-Perez Compano–Pluspetrol Bolivia and Amoco Petroleum, respectively. The three capitalized sectors of YPFB had a joint book value of nearly $383 million, and the strategic shares were sold for $835 million, raising the total value to more than $1.2 billion. Each of these three sectors has about 400 workers, while the extraction sector retains 3,500 workers, many of whom are redundant.[46]

An important objective of the reform team was to obtain the support of the enterprise workers early in the process. This was not simple in a country where shares were not traded openly on the market and where public understanding of capitalization was weak. Thus workers were given the option to purchase $20 worth of shares at book value, with another option to buy more shares at the same price once the results of the capitalization were clear. They could buy shares with a 5 percent down payment and installments during the next twenty-four months.[47] They could buy shares in an amount equivalent to the value of their social benefits (such as pension contributions and disability insurance). For the most part this was a highly profitable venture, and participation ranged from 95 percent of ENTEL workers to 59.63 percent of LAB workers. Although LAB was one of the least profitable capitalizations, its workers received $42.24 per share, or 105 percent over book value. In the first twelve months of the program, more than 15,000 workers participated in the program by purchasing shares in their companies, thereby creating a substantial number of new stakeholders in privatization.[48] And given the limited number of channels for trading or selling shares, it is likely that a significant percentage has held on to them, although these data are not yet available. The reform team agreed that concerted efforts to keep the process transparent and to provide information to the workers were crucial to achieving the high levels of participation.[49]

### Social Security Reform

There were two primary reasons for including social security reform in the capitalization plan. First, one of the central objectives of capitalization was to increase the growth potential of the economy. An immediate distribution of the proceeds in a country as poor as Bolivia would have resulted in a significant increase in consumption but little new investment. At the same time, there was no investment channel for the resources being transferred from the state-owned enterprises that would yield universal benefits. The new pension system could serve as such a channel and had the potential to develop capital markets as well. Second, the public social security program was on the brink of bankruptcy, covered few workers, and had a very low contribution rate even among the affiliated population.

The public social security program covered 314,437 of 2.8 million employed workers in the labor force, about 10.8 percent, and 10.4 percent of the economically active population. The dependency ratio of 3 to 1 was to become financially unsustainable in the near future. In addition to the primary public fund were thirty-six industry- or sector-specific complementary pension funds to which workers and employers made additional contributions. The complementary funds were for the most part riddled with corruption and administrative inefficiencies, and more than twenty of them had less than one year's reserves.[50]

Social security reforms are politically difficult to achieve in most contexts. Thus the reform was not initiated until the capitalization of enterprises was well under way and yielding favorable results. The reform set up two types of funds. The Individual Capitalization Fund (FCI) collects all individual contributions from workers. The Collective Capitalization Fund (FCC) is built from the shares that Bolivians own in the capitalized enterprises and uses the dividends from the shares to pay annual dividends of approximately $200 to all Bolivians 65 and older. The fiscal cost of the reform in 1997 dollars was an estimated $3.395 million, while the implicit debt of the existing pension system was $2.219 million.[51]

The reform eliminated the complementary funds and established a single (and lower) contribution formula for all workers: 10 percent for pensions, 2.5 percent for life insurance, and 0.5 percent in commission to the AFPs (the private pension fund administrators), a total of 13 percent of salaries. Under the previous system the average contribution rate was 14.82 percent. Employers no longer contribute, but they are required to raise individual salaries to account for the 4.5 percent that they contributed under the old system.[52] Two private pension funds were established through competitive bidding, Banco Invesco Argentaria and Banco Bilbao Viscaya. The government chose the reduced risk of relying on internationally recognized firms rather than developing domestic firms in a context that was, at least for the short term, a small and risky market with limited opportunities for profit. For the short term, each AFP was given exclusive rights in half the rural areas in the country because the rural market is considered too small and costly to reach to establish competition from the start. In the urban areas the pension funds are allowed to compete, although workers are initially assigned to one or the other.[53] Urban workers are allowed to switch from one to the other, but only once a year. This is intended to avoid the excess switching that occurred in Chile, resulting in high expenditures on advertising and higher commission costs.

The Bolivians found innovative solutions to two social security system problems that have proven politically contentious in many countries. The first was the retirement age. Under the old system, the retirement age had been 55 for men and 50 for women.[54] Rather than set a retirement age or enter into political difficulties over raising it, the new Bolivian system allows all workers to retire when they have contributed enough to accumulate a pension that is based on 70 percent of their average salary. If they have not done so by the time they are 65, they are allowed to retire and draw on whatever pension they have accumulated. Critics pointed to the life expectancy of 60 years, which meant that the average person would not live until a retirement age of 65. However, as was pointed out earlier, life expectancy in Bolivia is very much influenced by the high infant mortality rate, and most of those that do live beyond their first year live longer than 60 years. Life expectancy for those who retire at 65 is an additional 13 years.[55]

The second issue was that of a minimum pension. As in other poor countries like Peru, establishing a minimum pension was not feasible in the short term because too many retired persons would require a government-subsidized minimum. Another potential problem in the two countries was that the existence of a minimum pension guarantee would encourage independent workers to underdeclare income and make very small contributions to their pension accounts in order to qualify for the minimum.[56] Yet a major difference in Bolivia is that the bonosol serves as an effective minimum pension for the first cohort of workers in the new system. If the system develops well, increases its number of contributors, and has high returns, and if wage levels gradually rise, it may be more feasible to introduce some sort of minimum by the time the postbonosol generation retires. (All Bolivians 21 years or older by the end of 1995 are eligible for bonosol, and the last bono is expected to be issued on or around 2055).

An explicit aim of the new pension system is to increase revenues from contributions. In the previous system the contribution rate was very low among enrolled workers, in part because of the incentives for evasion created by the large number of complementary funds. It is likely that simplifying the system and introducing better incentives (slightly lower payroll taxes, higher returns, and individual savings accounts) will raise the contribution rate among enrolled workers. Attracting informal sector and rural workers to the scheme will be more difficult, as it would be in any country. Low-income workers are unlikely to voluntarily join a forced saving scheme. Yet the absence of adequate alternative savings mechanisms for the poor in Bolivia suggests that the system might have appeal for some independent workers, particularly in rural areas where banks are few.[57]

Upon retirement, workers have two options, which resemble those in the Chilean system. The first is to purchase an annuity from a life insurance company. The second is to purchase an annuity from an AFP, which functions like a group insurance plan and spreads out the funds over the expected life span of the pensioner in variable amounts. Those workers who have not contributed enough to earn a pension that is 70 percent of their salary by the time they are 65 cannot exercise either of these two options but instead will make monthly withdrawals from their accounts. The amounts allowed for withdrawal will be determined by a formula set by the AFPs and the pension superintendency that accounts for life expectancy and number of dependents.

The reform of the social security system initially met some opposition, even though it was publicly known that the complementary funds were bankrupt and that the state system was increasingly vulnerable. The strongest opposition came from the administrators of the complementary funds. Given the widespread allegations of corruption in their management, they feared the consequences of audits as well as losing access to rents. Another vocal force was the association of retired persons within the COB. The COB called a twenty-four-hour strike in November 1996 in an attempt to stop the reform, but was unable to muster sufficient popular support to alter or delay it.[58] This ineffectiveness in part resulted from the COB's mixed position toward the complementary funds: some in the COB leadership initially had opposed their being set up as industry-specific, independent units and wanted to control their management and resources.

Another explanation for limited opposition was that workers were poorly treated under the previous system and had little reason to oppose change. They were often forced to pay administrators bribes to obtain the documentation necessary to begin to withdraw their pensions, for example. Meanwhile, opposition from the fund managers gradually subsided because of an explicit government policy to find the workers in the fund administration places in the new system where possible.[59] The need to identify and issue identity cards for all Bolivians older than 65, many of whom did not have them, created new demand for administrative skills, as did the private pension system and its regulatory wing.

A problem that was evident throughout the transition was lack of sufficient information about the new system, both for individual workers and for adminstrators in the old system.[60] Although the difficulty of providing adequate information is unique neither to Bolivia nor to pension reform, it makes reforms more vulnerable to irresponsible accusations from the opposition, such as the warnings in Bolivia that social security was being eliminated altogether.

The new AFPs, meanwhile, clearly were entering uncharted territory. A major problem was time pressure. The social security reform law was passed in November 1996, and the bidding to authorize the operations of the AFPs was finished in January. Yet the government wanted to complete the capitalization by the end of its tenure in June 1997 and to have the AFPs operational. In particular, it wanted to issue the bonosol in May, just before the June elections. But this schedule created enormous pressure on the AFPs to become operational quickly, and in a situation where they had very poor information about the existing system, including the identity of individual workers and the level of contributions. This obviously posed a challenge to issuing adequate recognition bonds, as well as hiring the necessary personnel.

Another unresolved issue was the amount the AFPs would be allowed to invest abroad. The law stipulated that this should be between 10 and 50 percent of AFP funds, the exact percentage to be determined by the president of the Central Bank. This range is high compared with the percentages allowed Chilean AFPs, which initially were prohibited from investing abroad and now are allowed to invest slightly under 10 percent of their funds. Yet given the small size of the Bolivian market, diversifying portfolios and reducing risk by allowing a greater percentage of funds to go abroad makes sense, even if there are trade-offs in terms of Bolivia's domestic capital market development. Domestic political pressure, meanwhile, was more likely to agree to keeping a higher percentage of funds abroad.[61]

A potential problem for the AFPs was that the initial calculations for bonosol payments—$200 a person annually—may have been too generous. With at least 240,000 beneficiaries, the AFPs had to pay out slightly over $59 million a year in their first year of operations. At least initially they are dependent on the dividends from capitalization for 95 percent of their working capital. There is an obvious risk for them if the capitalized enterprises do not earn a sufficient return. According to the law, the fund itself is supposed to grow for the first thirty years, then its capital begins to be distributed and must be consumed with the death of the last bonosol recipient.[62]

Another risk for the AFPs was political opposition to the entire reform. Most observers predicted an opposition victory by the ADN candidate, Hugo Banzer (and his much more dynamic running mate Jorge Quiroga), in the June 1997 elections. The ADN's campaign platform explicitly stated that the dividends from capitalization should go to health care and education rather than to pensions. Although it is unlikely that once in power the ADN will risk damaging the country's reputation in the international community by reversing the reform, its comments as opposition clearly created a sense of uncertainty. Once in power, Banzer stated that he did not oppose the capitalization reform; he would review, not rescind, the contracts with international investors.[63] Even talk of reviewing contracts was probably more likely a face-saving measure than a genuine threat: attempting after the fact to change the terms of the most prominent investment contracts in the country would jeopardize all foreign investment.

Finally, because by law the AFPs have to invest current workers' contributions and also have to pay current retirees, they are unlikely to generate profits in the short term. Current retirees will receive their rents from the national treasury. AFPs, meanwhile, are contractually obligated to buy bonds issued by the national treasury for that purpose and for other fiscal costs relating to the reform in an amount that cannot exceed $180 million a year. This requirement spreads the fiscal costs of the reform into the future. In theory the bonds will come due when the system is running smoothly and the government has few, if any, liabilities to retirees still in the public plan. The AFPs' main opportunity for profit in the short term is to enlist new subscribers in the system and in the life insurance market, which is underdeveloped in Bolivia. Given the small size of the market, their investment would be minimal and marketing costs very low because each fund has exclusive rights in much of the country.[64]

The government clearly wanted to complete the capitalization program before it left office. Yet the pressure also posed a risk that the AFPs would be set up too hastily. In addition, investors in some of the capitalized enterprises saw the electoral pressure as a sign of future instability. In March 1997, for example, ENTEL, the capitalized telecommunications firm, threatened to reduce the overall amount of its investments from $170 million to $120 million for 1997 because of the uncertainty created by the opposition's threat to renege on the government's commitment to grant the company exclusive rights to the telecommunications market for six years.[65]

As with all major structural reforms, there were obstacles in implementation, which were complicated by the timing of the elections and the extent and complexity of the reforms. But the reforms' potential to transform the savings profile in Bolivia and generate growth in the long term is impressive. Although some observers argue that the savings in new pension funds merely crowds out alternative forms of saving, this seems unlikely in a country with so few alternatives for saving, alternatives that are particularly scarce for the poor. In addition, if the investments in the capitalized enterprises generate new employment and better salaries, savings could also increase.[66] In considering the relevance of the capitalization model for other countries it is important to emphasize that the reform could not have been implemented in a context of high fiscal deficits because the government would have needed the revenues from privatization to reduce deficits. Capitalization was implemented at a time that the macroeconomy was in balance and the fiscal situation well under control.[67]

The reform should also immediately increase growth, given the size of the new investments relative to the size of the economy. Some observers predict increases of 6 to 8 percent a year by 2000 (versus the projected 4 percent). At the least, as Laurence Whitehead has noted, an investment of more than $2 billion by efficient international corporations into an economy of $6.4 billion *should* improve growth. And the projected $60 million annual pension payout is a significant consumption boost in an economy with a total personal consumption of $4 billion a year (and is equivalent to about 10 percent of fiscal revenues).[68] The capitalization could also increase the national savings rate: given the extent to which workers formally enrolled in the old pension system were not contributing, the margin for increasing savings is high. Domestic saving was less than 2 percent of GDP in 1992–94, which is extremely low by international standards. If the AFPs accumulate dividends of $200 million to $300 million a year, as is projected, the national savings rate would increase to 5 percent of GDP.[69]

## Equity Issues

By relieving the government of having to support state-owned enterprises that were losing money, the reform makes more revenues available for essential social expenditures. The government budget was 6.4 percent lower in 1996 than it was in 1995, yet spending on health care, education, and sanitation was three times greater than spending on state-owned enterprises. In contrast, in 1994 the enterprises received more than all social expenditures combined.[70] The beneficial effects from this revenue substitution, combined with the country's desperate need for savings and investment to generate growth, make a strong case for the equity choices the government made. Investing the proceeds from the sales of the SOEs immediately in health and education would clearly have provided a dividend in human capital, but there would have been no improvement in savings and investment. And concurrent with capitalization, the government was investing resources and political capital in the social sectors. Although there is no doubt that both efforts could benefit from increased resources, it may well be more effective to wait until the reforms are operational before deciding the level of additional resources necessary and how they should be allocated.

The bonosol, meanwhile, will serve as a major income increase for rural families. Most elderly in Bolivia, particularly in rural areas, do not live alone, which suggests that the bonos will be redistributed within poor households and serve as an important income supplement. One of the aims of the program was to increase respect for the elderly in Bolivia because a great many live in poverty.[71] In addition, if the 4.1 million Bolivians living below the poverty line benefit more from the transfer than the 3 million that are not poor, the transfer will be progressive, although to some extent this outcome depends on the unresolved matter of determining the life expectancy of the poor. The wealthy are likely to live longer than the poor, and thus a valid criticism is that wealthy Bolivians will receive bonosol transfers for a longer time than poor ones. Yet the data to prove this are far from complete. And it is difficult to gauge whether the costs, political and administrative, of attempting to target the bonos to the 70 percent or so of Bolivians that are poor, as opposed to making the program a universal transfer, would outweigh the benefits. Targeting is most viable when the poor are a small and easily identifiable group, which is clearly not the case in Bolivia. Finally there was a political rationale for distributing the assets of the state-owned enterprises to all Bolivians. Still, there may be both equity and efficiency gains from some targeting of the benefits, given Bolivia's skewed income distribution.

## The Politics of the Capitalization Program

Regardless of all its merits, the capitalization program was not particularly popular. Many observers have commented on how much more popular the program is outside Bolivia than inside. Initial support was limited to the governing party, its allied parties in the government, and the business sector. The major opposition parties, the MIR and ADN, which had supported the genesis of the program when they were in power, became vocal opponents when it was implemented. The ADN's position was that a traditional privatization with the revenues invested in health care and education would have been more efficient. The MIR, meanwhile, criticized the selling of the national wealth, as did other parties of the more radical left and the populist CONDEPA. Organized labor strongly opposed on ideological grounds the individual capitalization of state assets.[72] As the president said, "The political cost has been almost immeasurable for the party and the president. . . . The only thing left is credibility. People think we are going to get it done."[73] This is in sharp contrast to the participation program, which despite some initial reservations on the part of the opposition, soon became widely popular.

There are several explanations for the capitalization program's lack of political appeal. The first is its sheer complexity. The average person does not understand the concept of capitalization, which is no surprise given the average education level in Bolivia. Even some international investors had difficulty understanding it.[74] The lack of public understanding was made worse by the government's failure to adequately explain the program, a failure that is recognized by the government. The publicity campaign, which was limited to short and sporadic announcements on television, was too technical to convince the average citizen, much less to generate active support. Publicists relied on Chilean advisers for the campaign, and the glitzy logos they used failed to appeal to the average Bolivian. Instead it reinforced the program's public image as concerned with efficiency and with capital markets at the expense of the poor.[75] And thirty-second television slots were just too short to explain the reform.[76] The government was unable to adequately respond to the disinformation campaign that the unions launched, for example. The unions relied on scare tactics, telling workers that they were going to lose social security altogether. Some of the public's failure to understand will be resolved with time as the system delivers benefits and public familiarity and confidence in it increase. Yet there will be a continued need for better public education about the system for this to occur and to maximize the potential positive effects.[77]

Second, it would be difficult to make any program that forgoes immediate consumption in favor of long-term investment popular in a country with so much poverty and so much immediate need. The opposition argued that resources going to pensions in a country with hunger and illiteracy made little sense. Third, implementing the program involved challenging powerful labor unions in hydrocarbons and mining that were for the most part united in their opposition to both the capitalization and education reforms. Their slogans, such as private pensions eroding national solidarity in the social security system, were politically catchy if factually incorrect.

Still, there were limits to the unity of the opposition of the organized labor movement. The radical and often intransigent stance of the COB on many issues was increasingly perceived as against the interests of individual workers by the workers themselves. This was demonstrated by their response when shares in the newly capitalized enterprises were issued: while the COB strongly opposed the action, individual workers realized that they had a strong material interest in buying shares, and most did so.[78] And despite strong opposition from the unions and administrative personnel in the enterprises, workers in some of the capitalized enterprises were also receptive to new differentiations in pay scales based on quality and output.[79] Meanwhile, the umbrella power of the enterprisewide unions was eroded as the enterprises were split up for sale and branch-level negotiations took on much more importance. There were wide variations among the positions at this level. Unions in the more efficient, less political, and quickly capitalized enterprises such as ENDE tended to have more of a stake in being cooperative, while those in less efficient operations such as the extraction branch of YPFB—where there was also more corruption—accurately perceived that they had more to lose from capitalization and posed more formidable opposition.[80]

Regardless of strong initial opposition to the program, it is likely that the longer-run evaluations will be more favorable. Not surprisingly, the opposition won the June 1997 elections, continuing the rotation of parties in government since 1985. The MNR, which took second place, fared poorly because Sanchez de Lozada's successor lacked appeal as a candidate for president and the benefits of the capitalization reforms were far from clear to the average voter. Yet the program is likely to be a wise investment in Sanchez de Lozada's political stakes in 2002. Once the bonosol system operates for a few years, popular evaluations of the program will likely improve. The first bonos were issued in May 1997, and those people who did not have their identity cards were given a five-year grace period to obtain them, with the bonos for those years issued retroactively.[81] The popular response to the issuing was far more rapid and extensive than the government expected and at first overwhelmed the distribution system. More than 200,000 people out of an eligible population of 300,000 received bonos in May alone. Recipients expressed incredulity at actually receiving the promised amount, and many said they intended to vote for the MNR.[82] This may have boosted the MNR's electoral performance because some exit polls expected support for Duran to be well below 18 percent.

In the long term the success of the program depends on political stability and therefore ultimately on broad support for the program. Although most investors, both in the capitalized enterprises and the AFPs, have been fairly confident in stable economic and political trends for the foreseeable future, many still fear the effects of highly partisan politics and strong populist political sentiment as potential threats to the program.[83] ENTEL's uncertainty about proceeding with its planned investments because of the campaign rhetoric, for example, highlights the extent to which building broad-based political support for capitalization will be the key to its success.

Finally, any political evaluation of the effects of the capitalization program should take into account the policy context, particularly the Popular Participation program. While capitalization may have been politically unpopular because it sacrificed immediate consumption for long-term investment, participation provided immediate and substantial reallocation of resources to the local level and had revolutionary effects on the way social services were delivered.

## The Popular Participation Program

Popular Participation is Latin America's most dramatic experiment in decentralization because the devolution of resources and responsibility to the local level has been the most extensive. Although the results thus far are mixed, mistakes have been made, and there is a tremendous amount of learning by doing, the program has improved equity and created a broad base of new stakeholders among poor Bolivians, who now have much more voice and choice in how their public services are allocated than they ever had in the past.

The Popular Participation Law (PPL) was passed in April 1994 and important accompanying legislation, the Administrative Decentralization Law, in January 1996. Before its passage, provincial and department capitals were the only municipal governments, and general tax revenues were allocated to them based on the distribution of taxpayers. As a result, most expenditures for municipal governments were concentrated in urban areas, particularly the nine department capitals. After passage of the PPL the general tax revenues going from the central to the local level increased from 10 percent to 20 percent (approximately $21 a person). The law stipulates that 85 percent of coparticipation revenues must go to investments rather than to operating expenditures.[84] In addition, the expenditures are allocated on a per capita basis. This has resulted in the formation of 250 new municipal governments, raising the national total from 61 to 311 functioning municipalities. Before the law, many municipalities had governments in name only because they had no operating budgets. The law also gives municipal governments increased facilities for generating local revenues. It devolves all nonpayroll responsibilities of the health and education ministries to the department level. And for the first time prefectoral governments are advised by, and financially accountable to, elected representative councils. Finally, for the first time in Bolivia's recent history the law recognizes local grassroots organizations such as indigenous, community, and nongovernmental organizations, which are called *organizaciones territoriales de base* (OTBs). It gives them a formal role in planning municipal government investments through locally elected vigilance committees (VCs).[85]

The Popular Participation Law emerged from the coordinated efforts of two groups of intellectuals: foreign-trained technocrats in the Sanchez de Lozada government, who are concerned with the sustainability of market-oriented reforms, and reform-minded intellectuals, who are influenced by their exposure to various indigenous movements, as well as the Katarista peasant union movement, and are affiliated with a number of local nongovernental organizations. Both groups are loyal to the president rather than to his party and are part of a movement known as *Gonismo*. Meanwhile, the president himself was apparently influenced by his experience with New England town councils. The law was a product of a discussion between these groups that excluded the political parties, and it was done in confidential discussions in which the president was directly involved.[86] Although this approach was effective in circumventing a potentially explosive political discussion and getting the law passed quickly, this "reformism by stealth" contributed to an initial lack of understanding of the program and to the prevalence of disinformation that still plagues the implementation of the law. It also brought on a negative attitude toward the reform on the part of the opposition parties. This suspicion was driven by a political context characterized by a great deal of confrontation between the government and the unions over other policies such as the education reform.[87]

### Results

The immediate results of the law were impressive and fairly quickly eroded most political opposition. In addition to the new municipalities, approximately 19,000 community or grassroots organizations received legal recognition, and vigilance committees were formed in most municipalities. Fewer than 100 of these organizations had legal recognition before the passage of the law.

Table 4-4. *Popular Participation Statistics and Major Policy Challenges, Bolivia, 1996*

| Main socioeconomic change | Before the law | After the law |
|---|---|---|
| Legal recognition and representation of naturally occurring peasant and indigenous communities (who have veto power over budget) | Less than 100 communities | 19,000 communities |
| Number of municipios receiving funds from tax coparticipation | 61 | 311 |
| Percentage of tax revenues subject to municipal coparticipation[a] | 10 percent | 20 percent |
| Amount of tax revenues subject to municipal coparticipation[a] | 0.8 percent of GDP in 1993 (US$45 million) | 2.4 percent of GDP in 1995 (US$140 million) |
| Mechanism for distribution of funds | Based on legal residences of taxpayers | Based solely on population (per capita) |
| Effect of funds distribution | 3 largest capital cities received 90 percent | Capital cities, rural areas receive 50 percent |
| Municipal share of total public investment | 11 percent | 39 percent |
| Social investment has doubled | 1.72 percent of GDP in 1993 (US $90 million) | 3.62 percent of GDP in 1995 (US$180 million) |
| Investment in education has tripled | US $10 million in 1993 | US$30 million in 1995 |

Source: George Gray Molina, "Social Investments under Popular Participation in Bolivia: Explaining Municipal Investment Choices," UDAPSO/HIID, La Paz, November 1996.
    a. Twenty percent of total tax revenue is earmarked for per capita block grants—about $21 a person.

The amount of tax revenues transferred to the municipalities as coparticipation revenue increased from 0.8 percent of GDP in 1993 (US$45 million) to 2.4 percent in 1995 (US$140 million), and the municipal share of public investment increased from 11 percent to 39 percent. Social investment (which includes central government transfers and municipal coparticipation investments) doubled from 1993 to 1995; investment in education tripled (table 4-4). Before the law passed, the three largest capital cities received 90 percent of tax revenues. Since then, capital cities receive 50 percent and rural areas 50 percent.[88] Legally, administratively, and politically, the Popular Participation Law is nothing short of a revolution.

The procedure for participation in municipal investment decisions has three stages. The first is to create a municipal development plan (PDM). This is the most participatory stage, in which grassroots organizations such as unions, indigenous organizations, mothers' clubs, and other local groups hold community meetings to discuss local needs and formulate them into investment projects. Communities often receive assistance in elaborating the development plan from regional nongovernmental organizations, the Catholic Church, and other local groups. The second phase is the formulation of the annual operating plan (PAO), which is the yearly investment plan and entails fewer participants. These include the mayor, the municipal council, and the vigilance committee. The prefectural municipal development units and the Secretariat of Popular Participation provide technical assistance for this stage. The operating plan must be approved by the vigilance committees and the Finance Ministry (for technical approval) and is then included in the national budget, which is approved by the Senate. The vigilance committees are also supposed to enforce the rule that no more than 10 percent of the municipal budget is allocated to current expenditures. The final phase is the elaboration of municipal budgets, which is usually done by officials from the municipalities.[89]

Not surprisingly, this process filters community demands, amending or excluding initial proposals. This is particularly common in rural municipalities, where agricultural, transportation, and irrigation needs tend to dominate at the PDM phase, but social sector investments dominate the final budget phase.[90] To a large extent this pattern reflects the strong influence of matching grant funds on investment decisions in cash-strapped rural municipalities. Large urban municipalities (capital cities) rely equally on own-generated resources (30 percent) and central government coparticipation resources (29 percent), but rural municipalities rely on coparticipation transfers for 64 percent of their funds and on donations for another 18 percent.[91] The influence of matching grants was strengthened by a January 1996 presidential decree that requires municipalities to allocate at least 30 percent of their budgets for health care, education, water, and sanitation and at least 25 percent to economic development (rural roads, electrification, communication, tourism, industrial development, and agriculture) to be eligible to receive national development funds and grants.[92]

There are also major differences in the kinds of investments made by urban and rural municipalities. Urban municipalities invest 68 percent of their resources in urban infrastructure (plazas, streets, markets, and parks), and only 6 percent in education and 2 percent in health care. Rural municipalities invest most of their resources in the social sectors: 30 percent in education, 20 percent in sanitation, and 6 percent in health care versus 23 percent in urban infrastructure.[93] There are several explanations for this. First, the matching grants, which have strings attached, have greater influence in small poor municipalities with less capacity to generate their own resources. Preliminary results (still subject to revision) of regressions of the variables influencing investment decisions show per capita transfers from the FIS to be the most important variable influencing investments in the social sectors. It is important to note that the effects of FIS matching grants were to "crowd in" rather than crowd out investments in the social sectors. For each additional dollar of FIS transfers, municipalities invested an average of $0.55 per capita in social resources.[94]

The second reason is politics: investments in urban infrastructure are more likely to yield political payoffs in concentrated urban areas, while those in schools and health posts are more likely to have an impact in rural areas where there are shortages of such services and constituents are more dispersed. The number of grassroots organizations is also a significant variable affecting investment decisions. For each additional OTB, communities spent on average an additional $0.86 per person on social investments and $0.74 on education. Although these groups have a formal role only in the first stage of decisionmaking, their lobbying power in the later stages seems to increase where they are greater in number and possibly in political strength. Another political factor affecting investment decisions is party affiliation. Municipalities governed by mayors from opposition parties are much more likely to invest in social sectors than are those of the ruling party. One explanation is multicollinearity: the MNR did better in large cities than in small rural towns in 1995, and urbanism predominates in the investment portfolios of the nine large capital cities.[95] Another may be that the political mandates of the smaller opposition parties tended to be more tenuous and derived from a number of constituencies, all of whom have competing demands for investments, and small investments in schools and health posts are more easily divided among a number of constituencies.

Putting the Popular Participation Law into practice has been far from simple, and the results have been mixed. One problem has been a poor, or at least mixed, project implementation record, at least in the first year of investments. Although municipalities made ambitious public investment plans for 1995, less than half were implemented. And while urban development projects had a 365 percent completion rate, education and health care projects had respective rates of 40 percent and 47 percent. A major reason for the lower rates was bottlenecks and delays in the receipt of matching grants from the central government investment funds.[96] Delays of six months to a year in obtaining matching grants also resulted in popular disillusionment with the program after expectations had been raised by the participatory nature of the planning process.[97]

Perhaps the most obvious reason for the diverse outcomes in the program is the diversity of the communities themselves. Some are relatively homogeneous and coherent; others are much more heterogeneous, with various indigenous groups and competing and sometimes conflicting priorities. Resources allocated per capita may constitute a significant amount in a community that is fairly homogeneous and can agree on priorities. But the amount will seem far smaller in a more diverse one with competing demands for how funds should be allocated. In addition, communities vary in their organizational capacity.[98] In some, unions or other traditional institutions take the lead and have links with grassroots organizations; in others there is conflict between the two. In north Potosi, for example, where rural unions are strong and feared that their influence would be undermined by the OTBs, there were widespread protests against the law. Elsewhere, unions launched damaging disinformation campaigns that slowed the legal recognition of grassroots groups. In still other communities there is very little tradition of local organization, and local politics, to the extent that it exists, is dominated by one or a few powerful interests such as owners of large farms.[99] In addition, the nature of indigenous communities them-selves—their hierarchies, approach to cooperating with outside groups, view of leadership—all affect the way participation func-tions.[100]

A related reason for variations in implementation is that small municipalities, because they are much less able to generate autonomous resources, depend much more on central govern-ment transfers and on matching grants from the FIS, and thus their expenditure decisions are very much influenced by external requirements. The FIS, for example, primarily funds education and health care infrastructure. In general, the municipalities that can generate their own resources invest in sanitation and urban infrastructure rather than in social seervices. In very poor mu-nicipalities the top-down decisionmaking of intergovernment transfers often overwhelms the bottom-up grassroots lobbying mechanisms established by Popular Participation. Although matching grants are essential for correcting equity imbalances between resource-rich and resource-poor municipalities, the lat-ter have much less freedom in making investment decisions be-cause of their dependence on the grants.[101]

There are often major asymmetries between the power of the mayor and that of the vigilance committees. Mayors and munici-pal council members are paid elected officials and, since the onset of Popular Participation, have unprecedented resources to spend. Vigilance committee members are not paid and are often at a sub-stantial disadvantage, particularly when they come from remote rural areas and have to deal with more experienced urban politi-cians. There have been some instances in which mayors have at-tempted to influence VC members through financial cooptation and even physical threats and intimidation. And overriding the mayor and soliciting a rapid response from the central govern-ment is far from easy for VC members, for whom lack of re-sources, transportation, and information can all pose significant obstacles to making effective demands.[102]

Particularly where indigenous organizational capacity is weak, VCs were formed almost by command of the mayor and are not genuinely representative. There are also legitimate fears that the new forms of organization are undermining some traditional ones.[103] Nevertheless, the VCs have exercised their right of control to a surprising extent. They are able to appeal to the central Secretariat of Participation, and ultimately to Congress, when municipalities do not respond to their demands or misuse funds. In the program's first two years of operation, Congress froze the funds of twenty-three municipalities because of misuse, and five mayors were investigated.[104]

A recent study has found that vigilance committees have had the most positive effects on municipal performance when they have been strong in opposition to elite municipal councils. Good performance was defined as likely to make social investments, allocating more resources to rural communities, and sponsoring more stable political coalitions. Weak VCs or municipalities in which grassroots organizations were in charge of municipal councils and the committees played a complementary role invested less in social services and were more politically unstable.[105]

Another issue is that although nongovernmental organizations are critical supporters at the local level, many are also highly politicized and have their own agendas, which have ranged from supporting particular parties at the local level to flat opposition to the reform and involvement in disinformation campaigns.[106] NGOs are more influential in rural than in urban areas because in urban areas they are less likely to have a monopoly or at least a strong influence over access to information and resources.

Political dynamics also differ significantly. When the program was first proposed, unions and opposition parties were suspicious that it was a means for the MNR to circumvent them and to increase its influence over grassroots organizations.[107] This proved not to be the case; opposition parties maintained and even increased their influence vis-à-vis the MNR in the 1995 municipal elections. Unions, meanwhile, under the umbrella of the Asamblea para la Soberania de los Pueblos (ASP) and in conjunction with parties of the left such as the MBL (Movimento Boliviano Libre, or Free Bolivia Movement), have also strengthened their political position in local politics in some areas. Indeed, their effectiveness in attaining political representation via this mechanism in many cases turned the tables as the unions went from being the primary opponents of the program to being in charge of the municipality that had to implement it.[108] And while party politics has dominated participation in some communities, in others community-based movements have been able to increase their influence.

In part this reflects developments occurring in many countries in Latin America: local elections are increasingly distinct from national ones, local leaders tend to be elected on local issues rather than according to partisan criteria, and the influence of parties is much weaker at the local than at the national level.[109] In the 1995 elections, for example, the MNR lost ground to new parties such as the MBL and the UCS (Union Civicade Solidaridad, or Civic Solidarity Union), even though it retained its position as the party with the largest number of votes. Many community and union movements, such as the ASP, ran in the elections under the party umbrella of groups such as the MBL. These parties, meanwhile, are well aware of their dependence on the grassroots movements for their political success. Some observers have referred to this process as "reverse cooptation."[110] Among other things, this trend "may reflect the growing importance of a new kind of local politician who has his or her own electoral pull based on a local reputation for honesty and getting things done."[111]

The fluidity of political power at the municipal level is also evident in the new process of censuring mayors. Beginning with the 1995 municipal elections, in cases where the mayor is not elected by a full majority and is therefore appointed by the council, the council is allowed to censure the mayor once a year and call for new elections. This occurred in one third of all municipalities in the year following the 1995 elections, and fifty actually voted in new mayors.[112] In Santa Cruz, for example, only three of forty-seven mayors were elected with a majority, and five were censured.[113] With the inception of the program, mayors lost little time exploiting opportunities for enrichment, such as using participation funds to secure kickbacks from contractors for themselves and their clients. But as a result, by the end of 1995 up to ten municipalities had their funds frozen by Congress for corruption.[114] All this implies that while there are clearly attempts by the political parties to manipulate the process, the process itself, in conjunction with changes at the civil society level, has created opportunities for new, local people to gain political influence. In this sense, Popular Participation is indeed generating a revolution, not only in how social services are allocated and delivered but in democracy at the grassroots level.

## Bottlenecks

While recognizing the important contributions that the program has made thus far, critical issues remain unresolved. First, although the program has introduced a new institutionality for the delivery of social services, it is not yet clear whether it is adequate to introduce desperately needed improvements in social services. There seem to be major bottlenecks in service delivery, as the poor record of social sector investments suggests. In addition, the devolution of responsibility did not include responsibility for hiring and firing personnel. This makes it extremely difficult for municipalities to coordinate service provision. Remote rural communities, for example, have little recourse when centrally hired health care personnel do not fulfill their responsibilities to attend rural health posts.[115]

A principal agent problem remains in the social sectors. In education, for example, the Ministry of Education guarantees norms and standards and is responsible for hiring and firing. It also deals directly with the union that has a monopoly over personnel issues. The financing for education is channeled through the prefecture level for administrative and teaching personnel, and through municipal governments, which are directly responsible for infrastructure and recurrent costs. With the implementation of education reform, locally elected school committees will have some say in the management of schools and evaluation of teachers, which should help in reducing the principal agent problem.[116] In health care a December 1996 law allowing municipalities to contract additional health care personnel alleviates the problem somewhat, although the personnel still are paid with central government resources. Directorios locales de salud (DLOS) were set up with the participation law as local boards to manage the administration of health services at the municipal level and are composed of the department health director and representatives of the mayor and the vigilance committee. Yet these organizations face the same kinds of tensions and political pressures that the VCs do, which is obviously a constraint to their operating effectively.[117]

Under the current financing structure, there is also a great deal of diversity in results in social services. The amount of resources that municipalities allocate varies greatly.[118] In education, for example, eight municipalities assigned no resources at all to social services in 1996, while in Tiraque in Cochabamba and San Joaquin in Beni, almost 100 percent of resources went to education. Absolute levels varied even more than the percentages of the budget did: Filadelfia in the department of Pando assigned $402 per student, while Poopo in Oruro invested $0.40 per student, differences that reflect variations in percentage allocations as well as levels of municipal resources and student-teacher ratios.[119] These vast differences may be reduced somewhat by the 1996 decree requiring municipalities to invest at least 30 percent of their resources in human development to be eligible for matching grants and development funds, although thus far the decree has been enforced loosely.[120]

Resources allocated to health care also vary considerably, with thirty-seven municipalities assigning no resources at all to health care and others up to 65 percent. Absolute amounts range from $0.17 to $49 a person. An important health program that is run from the center and is increasing health coverage for mothers and young children is the National Health Insurance for Maternity and Childhood. The program has increased the number of births attended by health professionals and the number of consultations for children younger than five with diarrheal and respiratory diseases. The response to the program has not been uniform, however, and the response rate has been higher in urban areas and the lowlands than in the Altiplano.[121]

There must be a certain level of central government involvement and coordination for the effective operation of social services in a country as poor as Bolivia. Education reform, for example, has been implemented in isolation from the program of Popular Participation.[122] Although they are two distinct reforms, there is also an important role for coordination between them. As with any reform, many of the details of how Popular Participation coordinates with the social sectors need to be worked out with time. Regardless, no decentralization is alone sufficient to resolve problems of access and quality of basic service provision, and in the short term it may even make them worse.

A second matter not resolved by the participation program is equity. The program has entailed a substantial devolution of resources to poor areas. But rich and poor municipalities are treated equally, and poorer ones are at a significant disadvantage in administrative capacity, which is likely to affect the quality of services delivered. Although diversity in outcomes is not necessarily bad, it may well be essential to incorporate some correctional criteria in the public investment formula that seeks to prevent poorer municipalities from falling into a poverty trap in which key services are markedly inferior and thus the opportunities of the poor are limited from the start.

The program has one tool to address problems of this nature: a training program to provide help in planning, administration, and finance that is run out of the municipal support units in the offices of the subprefects throughout the country and has held workshops in 280 of the 311 municipalities. Yet the training staff is young and inexperienced and hardly equipped to make up for some of the significant gaps in capacity. For example, 85 percent of OTB leaders are illiterate.[123] All of this points to a definite need for institutional strengthening at the local level and for more accessible support services from the center.

### The Future of Popular Participation

Although the participation program has demonstrated that even very poor municipal governments can make sound investment decisions, the record demonstrates that it is far more difficult to implement those decisions, particularly in key social services. Both municipal governments and the vigilance committees need support in administration and finance as well as in the management of social services. Although the FIS provides important infrastructure support, it does not address critical management issues such as personnel and curricula in social services or the quality and coverage of services. At least in the transition period, a coordinating body is needed that can identify gaps and bottlenecks in the operations of health and education services. UDAPSO, the Unit for Social Policy Analysis which was originally set up in the Planning Ministry but is now in the Ministry for Human Development, might fill this role. At present the agency is marginalized and underfunded, a situation that threatens to squander an important and rare public sector capacity for social policy analysis.

Related to this is the matter of overall expenditures. Coparticipation resources from the government were roughly $140 million for 1995, and resources from the FIS were $40 million.[124] They account for about 90 percent of all public investments in social services because most of the central expenditures go to salaries. Although these amounts are an improvement over the levels of spending of the adjustment crisis years, they are still low if one considers that $48 million will be spent by the government on bonosol transfers. Once major bottlenecks in the implementation of the Popular Participation program are identified and education reform is fully operational, an increase in expenditures will almost certainly be necessary to achieve the desired improvements in the quality and coverage of social services.

Decentralization is often used as a panacea for desperately needed institutional reforms in the public sector. But although decentralization can help make service providers more accountable and make services more appropriate to local contexts, it cannot substitute for important reforms at the center, where institutions such as the Health and Education Ministries still have irreplaceable responsibilities for setting standards, monitoring performance, and ensuring that certain essential services such as the distribution of vaccines are universally provided.[125] Such institutional reforms are far from complete in Bolivia. It is telling that the education reform is being implemented by the FIS rather than by the Education Ministry and that personnel issues within the FIS remain its predominant concern.[126] Although participation is a tremendous innovation and promises to revolutionize both local government and social service provision, without an increase in capacity of central institutions to respond to the needs of new local forces the program's potential will be extremely limited and could result in popular frustration. Education reform is an important first step, but there is a long way to go.

Popular Participation has resolved some issues but also has presented new challenges. Its greatest innovation is to allow for bottom-up solutions to problems and challenges that until now have been addressed ineffectively from the top down. At the least, the government should be commended for exercising the political will necessary to implement the reform and to convince the actors in La Paz to transfer their resources and responsibilities to the local level. And letting go at the center means being willing to accept diverse and unexpected outcomes. Herein lie both the strengths and the weaknesses of the reform. Diversity is what allows local groups to use initiative, to express preferences, to tailor policies to meet their particular demands. It also provides added incentives for them to contribute their efforts and their resources. Yet at the same time, it is the poorest and the least well organized communities that will have the most difficulty taking the initiative and providing their own resources. There is clearly a need for a strong central leadership to correct major imbalances in equity as well as to provide more general support and monitor social services. An active effort, which would play an educational as well as a surveillance role, would probably be more effective in improving the quality of social services than the existing legal provisions requiring specific budgetary allocations for human development.

Finally and more generally, the program has great potential to raise the awareness and participation of the average citizen in economic and institutional change in the country. Almost 50 percent of the population polled expressed support for reform in 1996.[127] This support is likely to increase as initial problems are corrected. The heightened awareness and expectations that have resulted from Popular Participation should complement the activities of new AFPs, for example, as they attempt to increase participation in a new savings plan and identify all the citizens who are or will be eligible for the bonosol payments.

## Conclusion

Bolivia's Popular Participation and capitalization programs are innovative reforms. Given the state of public services before reform, it would be surprising if they did not have some beneficial effects on institutional performance. The aggregate political effects are less clear, however, in part because of the very different nature of the programs. The government received high rates of approval for the participation program almost immediately after it was implemented. The political benefits of capitalization will not be evident for several years. This is not surprising because many structural reforms gain support only gradually as results become clear and beneficiaries' stake in them increases. In Bolivia, workers' acquiring stakes in the private pension plans will be gradual as they make contributions and eventually receive benefits as retirees.

Although many of the results of capitalization will become evident only years later, the direct income from the bonosols is likely to generate immediate political support among recipients: public support for capitalization seems to have increased somewhat after the first bonos were issued in May 1997. Similarly, for Czech vouchers, which are discussed in the next chapter, much of the initial popular support for the program was due to the immediate income that people realized when they sold their vouchers. In the case of the bonos, the transfer will be annual for those older than 65 and an anticipated one for those near retirement age, which together make up a significant number of people. In addition, if the program leads to new investments and increased growth and employment, it will increase the number of stakeholders in the social security system and more generally in market-oriented growth. Although it is likely that capitalization will generate more support for reform in the future than it has during its initial years, in the short term the program has generated as much opposition as it has support, and the government has demonstrated an impressive level of foresight in pressing forward with its implementation.

In contrast, the participation program was widely popular almost immediately after it began. The program provided a significant transfer of resources to poor rural areas, and, more importantly, gave previously marginalized groups a new channel for participating in local government and an increased voice in the delivery of social services. There will obviously be some transitional problems, and the poorest municipalities—where there is the most need—will remain at a disadvantage in terms of implementation capacity unless the program design is altered. Yet a significant proportion of the people have become stakeholders in the design and delivery of public services through Popular Participation, a dynamic that is likely to permanently transform local government and the way that public services operate in Bolivia. The logic of this transformation, with its basis in increasing individual choice and participation, complements that of market reform and is likely to increase the reform's political sustainability.

The Plan de Todos reforms faced a number of obstacles to improving equity that are, for the most part, similar to those faced in other countries. In general and not surprisingly, countries with greater poverty face greater constraints in administrative capacity. They also have more difficulty soliciting the poor's participation in the reforms. The poor are least able to afford transaction costs: the time required to participate or additional bus fare to attend a new school or small user fees for health posts or slight differences in social security contribution rates. Another constraint is lack of access to adequate information. Income limitations, meanwhile, often differentiate between those who participate in reforms for short-term benefit and those who become permanent stakeholders. It is difficult to get people to make long-term investments when they face immediate income constraints. It explains the low probability of getting poor independent workers to join the new private social security plan, as was also the case in Peru. And while not as prevalent, these poverty-related constraints are also present in countries with flat income distributions, as the chapter on the Czech Republic demonstrates. Thus it is no surprise that there were significant obstacles to achieving equitable outcomes in the Bolivian reforms.

In the Popular Participation Program the poorest villages, which have the least access to information and lack administrative capacity, are having the most difficulty delivering decent public services. This has also occurred in other countries in the study. In Chile, for example, schools in poor and remote municipalities were of much lower quality after the education reforms were in place, whereas in the rest of the country quality improved somewhat. In the 1990s a program to correct for quality differences in the poorest schools was begun as a response. In Zambia, which is discussed in chapter 6, the poorest half of the population was often unable to realize the benefits of the health reforms because of a lack of adequate information about user fee exemptions and a badly managed fees policy. In Peru the same approach to health reform was much more effective, even among the poorest people, due to extensive training and outreach efforts by those responsible for the program.

The Bolivian experience and the experiences of other countries in this study suggest that reforms that rely on increasing voice and choice may introduce new equity issues and challenges at the same time that they attempt to improve the capacity of institutions to deliver essential public services. Adverse poverty and equity outcomes often can be corrected by government policy, and the generalized benefits of improved institutional performance eventually outweigh the short-term equity costs, as the Chilean experience suggests. Yet such policies require resources and administrative capacity and are likely to take time in a country with poverty levels as high as Bolivia's. In Bolivia, achieving equity objectives will also require further government efforts to educate people about the reforms. They need to better understand new means of participation as well as the importance of investing in human capital to reduce poverty if they are to make appropriate decisions about resource allocations for social services.

A final equity-related lesson from Bolivia is that longer-term investments in growth will ultimately be more productive and equity enhancing than will short-term giveaway or handout schemes. The Bolivian program is unusual in investing the bulk of proceeds from capitalization and distributing only the dividends. It stands in sharp contrast to the experience in most countries. In Peru, for example, President Fujimori used millions of dollars in revenues from privatization to build schools and other public works just before his 1995 reelection campaign. Although these expenditures were politically popular and redistributed some resources to poor rural areas, many were also unproductive. Schools were built in areas where there were no teachers to staff them, for example. And the larger matter of education reform was bypassed by the government.[128]

The capitalization program will almost certainly increase economic growth. It is also likely, although less certainly, to improve the savings rate, which could also increase growth. In addition, by freeing resources that previously went to support state-owned enterprises, the program will allow more essential expenditures in social services, investments in human capital that should improve equity as well as growth. The transition from an increasingly insolvent pay-as-you-go social security program, while entailing some short-term costs, will reduce the state's liabilities to future pensioners; lower the contribution rate for workers and encourage more consistent contributions; eliminate the contribution for employers, removing a potential disincentive to formal employment; and (presumably) pay better pensions and encourage new entrants to the program. Finally, until the last eligible recipient of bonosol dies in the middle of the next century, the program will transfer a significant amount of income to elderly Bolivians, most of whom are poor. It is also likely that the families of the recipients will benefit. It is difficult to argue that the program will not have significant and positive effects on equity.

That does not mean that the program is free of flaws or that all of the equity choices that were made were for the best. Wealthy Bolivians probably live longer than poor ones, and therefore will receive more transfers per capita than their poorer counterparts. Yet there are more poor Bolivians than wealthy ones, and in net terms the poor will probably receive more. Making the benefits universal may be politically appealing and is in keeping with the government's overarching political slogan for its reforms, the Plan de Todos. Yet in the future it may be worth considering eliminating benefits for Bolivians with incomes above a certain level, particularly if dividends from the capitalized enterprises are less than expected and the program has difficulty retaining the current level of transfers. Alternatively, the bonosol resources designated to nonpoor Bolivians might be redirected to social services once the reforms there are fully implemented.

The Popular Participation program is also not a replacement for providing social services and reducing poverty. Without a doubt, the program provides a substantial transfer of resources to poor areas and gives a vital impetus to local government. It has also created an important new base of stakeholders in the reformed system and will have far-reaching effects on social service provision, although these are far from straightforward. Clearly, giving responsibility for service provision to the local level and incorporating the opinions of users in the management of services has considerable potential and has proven successful in many countries. And public services were in very poor shape in Bolivia, leaving a great deal of room for improvement.

However, many new municipalities lack sufficient capacity to fulfill their unaccustomed responsibilities, creating bottlenecks in providing services that are crucial to the welfare and productive potential of the poor. The participation program's per capita resource allocation, while clearly an improvement from the previous taxpayer-based allocation, does not provide enough resources for communities that are particularly poor or heterogeneous, which creates conflicting demands for a small pool of funds. In these cases, additional transfers from the center seem vital to the success of the program, and training and administrative assistance may be far more important than money in improving the access to and quality of key public services.

Finally, the program has had an effect on and been affected by partisan politics. It has certainly supported the trend toward more independent and performance-based voting at the local level by giving local governments and organizations independent access to resources, freeing them of dependence on the governing party at the center. And to the extent that the participatory mechanisms of the program support independent decisionmaking and influence, they are clearly helpful. Yet there are also instances in which the program and the local decisionmaking bodies it has created are coopted by party politicians or debilitated by partisan rivalries. It is difficult to correct for such trends: in the end, politics is politics. However, the mechanisms that local groups have available for recourse in such instances need to be strengthened so that such disputes do not discredit the entire process and, more importantly, so that the delivery of services is not jeopardized.

All of the Plan de Todos programs, including education reform, have altered the face of Bolivian politics and vastly increased the potential for improving the quality and coverage of the social investments crucial to growth and poverty reduction. They have also created a significant number of stakeholders with a strong interest in maintaining the new reforms, reforms that will be important to future economic growth and poverty reduction. The political success of the reforms will not be judged by who voted for the MNR in 1997 but rather by the performance of the new social security system and the development and vitality of the new participatory mechanisms. Ultimately, it is through these mechanisms and increased rates of economic growth that permanent stakes in a reformed, market-oriented economic system will be generated in Bolivia.

Chapter 5

# Voucher Privatization in the Czech Republic

IN 1992 vouchers that could be traded for shares in state-owned enterprises slated for privatization were made available to all adult citizens of the Czech Republic.[1] The voucher program was a mass invitation for Czech citizens to participate in a new market. The government had two principal objectives: to transfer a large part of state-owned assets into private hands as quickly as possible and to generate broad public support for privatization and for market-oriented economic reforms more generally.

Like the other chapters in the study, the analysis of the Czech voucher program focuses on political sustainability and equity. First the chapter explores the extent to which the voucher program contributed to the political sustainability of privatization. Then it examines the extent to which the program was able to create a broad base of new stakeholders. Finally, it examines the effects of the program on institutional performance, that is, to what extent did introducing new market incentives and expanding ownership in stocks result in better performance by the former state-owned enterprises?[2]

It is difficult to measure the political sustainability of reform in any definitive, much less quantitative, manner. As in the other cases in the study, sustainability is defined here in two ways. The first, which is relatively easy to measure, is delineated by how people vote and by how politicians campaign. Are voters in favor

188

of continuing reforms by selecting a proreform candidate who may or may not be of the same party as the government that initiated the reforms? Are most candidates running on a proreform platform? Do any candidates proposing to reverse reforms pose a realistic challenge? Using these guidelines, there is wide agreement that the voucher program was a critical factor in the election of the reformist government of Vaclav Klaus in May 1992 and that it also helped generate public consensus in favor of privatization and other market-oriented reforms, at least in the short and medium term.

The second definition of political sustainability hinges on the balance between the objectives of market reform and achieving a socially sustainable allocation of the benefits of reform.[3] Achieving the first objective—macroeconomic stability, stable growth, and functional provision of basic social services—involves changing the incentive structures in the macroeconomy and in the delivery of public services. The second objective depends to a large extent on the capacity of individuals to respond to the new incentives. In some societies, as in Peru and Zambia in this study, such a capacity can be severely impeded by widespread poverty and such related obstacles as unequal access to information and inability to pay transaction costs. In transition economies such as the Czech Republic, where few people had experience with markets, it seems likely that social groups will have different capacities to respond to new market incentives.

Because the distribution of income before market reforms was very equal in such transition societies, one would expect poverty-related impediments to be less important and other factors, such as type of employment and educational attainment, to be more significant in determining individuals' capacity to respond to new market incentives. What the experience of the Czech voucher program demonstrates, however, is that both types of constraints apply. The ability of the government to create genuine stakeholders in privatization was affected by limitations unique to the socioeconomic profile of postcommunist societies, as well as those typical of poverty in other cases in this study. This is surprising, given that income distribution in the Czech Republic was the most equal of all the transition economies and the country had the least poverty of any country studied here.

In the Czech Republic, as in other countries in the study, altering the incentive structure aided the reform of public sector institutions, in this case state-owned enterprises. It also resulted in a large number of new participants in the market. Yet, as in the other countries there were substantial obstacles to some groups becoming genuine stakeholders. The voucher program clearly was important in facilitating rapid privatization, and, more arguably, in creating capital markets and resolving some initial concerns about corporate governance. But it was less successful at creating a broad base of permanent, active shareholders. Even though most citizens received some benefits from the program, half the shares were ultimately concentrated among a small group of banks and investment funds. Those people who kept their shares, meanwhile, tended to be wealthier, more educated, and more supportive of reform than those who sold them.

In this light it is important to note the extent to which the benefits from the program were public goods.[4] Education or social security, for example, are widely considered public goods, even if they can be privately delivered. In contrast, most of the enterprises that were privatized in the Czech Republic, such as steel and manufacturing, would have been outside the realm of the state in most market economies. Thus differences in investment behavior resulted in differences in income gains, but not in any income losses and increases in poverty. This contrasts with major differences in individual responses to the privatization of more public goods such as education, a development in which the poorest people can lose access to crucial services. Still, an explicit objective of the program was to broaden participation in new markets. The outcome suggests that achieving that objective entails some equity trade-offs, at least for the poorest groups. These trade-offs apply to the private delivery of public goods in most market economies, regardless of their income levels and degree of inequality.

## The Political Economy of the Transition

Of all the former communist countries of central and eastern Europe at the time of transition, the Czech Republic (Czechoslovakia at the time) was the most dominated by orthodox, Soviet-style rule.[5] Unlike Poland and Hungary, which had experimented with political liberalization and market reforms, the Czech economy remained completely state run, with less than 5 percent of property in private hands. The transition was a clean break with past policies and was carried out by technocrats led by Finance Minister Vaclav Klaus, who were committed to rapid, market-oriented reforms. By the time the stabilization program began in January 1991, one year after the November 1989 "Velvet Revolution," the broad outline of the program—stabilization, liberalization, voucher privatization, and social protection—was "clear to any citizen who opened a newspaper."[6]

Relatively high per capita income, little poverty, rapid and extensive reforms, and quick growth in response to the reforms has led to what is widely known as the "Czech exception." By the mid-1990s the Czech Republic had the highest per capita income of any of the postcommunist countries ($7,550 in 1996), the lowest unemployment rate (3 percent in 1996), the lowest poverty ratio (less than 1 percent of all households), and was the only nation in the region to receive an "A" rating by international investors.[7] Attitudes are more favorable toward reform than in other countries in the region, economic growth since 1992 has been steady and strong at 4.8 percent in 1995 and 4.4 percent in 1996, approximately 75 percent of the economy has been privatized, and foreign investment has been substantial, although less so than in Hungary and Poland (table 5-1).[8] And despite a prolonged authoritarian interlude, Czech political culture and entrepreneurial behavior since 1989 reflect the collective memory of the prewar period, in which markets and democracy flourished.

The Czech Republic is also unique in terms of its relatively stable political party system. Vaclav Havel's original Civic Forum movement, which instigated the Velvet Revolution, developed into several organized, broad-based political parties—Klaus's Civic Democratic Party (ODS), and the allied Civic Democratic Alliance (ODA) on the right, and a mixture of small parties and the Social Democrats on the left. The small parties of the moderate left were gradually absorbed into the Social Demo-

Table 5-1. *Economic Indicators, Czech Republic, 1993–97*

Percent

| Indicator | 1993 | 1994 | 1995 | 1996 | 1997[a] |
|---|---|---|---|---|---|
| GDP growth | –0.9 | 2.6 | 4.8 | 4.4 | 2.7 |
| CIP percent (inflation) | 20.8 | 10.0 | 9.1 | 7.5/8.5 | 7.2/7.6 |
| Unemployment | 3.5 | 3.2 | 3.0 | 3.2 | 3.5/3.9 |
| Current account to GDP ratio | 0.4 | –0.1 | –4.1 | –5.4 | –5.7 |
| General government budget balance to GDP ratio | 0.7 | 0.9 | 0.4 | 1.4 | 0.8 |
| Public expenditures to GDP ratio | n.a. | 47.7 | 47.3 | 44.7 | 42.5 |

Source: "Financial Times Survey," *Financial Times*, April 20, 1996, and May 14, 1997.
a. Government projections.
n.a. Not available.

cratic party (CSSD). Of all these, Klaus's ODS party developed into an organized, patronage-based party machine that guaranteed the political continuity of the reform program in elections in 1992 and in 1996.

While the Czech exception is not without some underlying problems, the country's economic record and political stability stand out among the postcommunist countries. The so-called left turn that has occurred in other countries in the region, the election of former communists or leftists campaigning on antireform (or at least slower reform) platforms has not occurred in the Czech Republic, although the governing coalition did begin to face a more credible challenge from the left opposition in 1996. Most observers attribute at least some of the credit for this record to the voucher privatization program initiated in 1992. "Key to the success of reform [has] been coupon privatization, which involves every citizen as a direct owner of property and thus makes him a supporter of the process, and a heritage of political and economic stability and precommunist democracy in Czechoslovakia."[9] Yet the effects of the voucher program must be evaluated in the context of economic and political trends since the transition, as well as the contexts of poverty, inequality, and social policy.

## The Czech Exception

Part of the reason for the success of the Czech reforms lies in favorable initial conditions. In contrast to Hungary and Poland the Czech Republic had little inflation and very little external debt. And much of the country's industrial structure had been developed before the communist takeover. But communist domination of the economy was more complete, and there was little experimentation with market reforms before 1990. A great deal of the economic success of the Czech reforms is due to the efforts of Finance Minister and then Prime Minister Vaclav Klaus, who was a strong proponent of rapid, free market reforms, yet at the same time a staunch nationalist.[10] Klaus was committed to minimal regulation, rapid liberalization and privatization, and price and wage stability. And he was a political pragmatist and a good communicator.

Klaus's policies resulted in a rapid transition to a market economy, but it was coupled with strong government regulation of wages for the first five years. The low-wage strategy was crucial to keeping unemployment low and Czech exports competitive. Although the government did not initiate radical reforms in social policy, expenditures were targeted somewhat to needier people. More important, the government avoided the explosive expenditures on social security that have crowded out other social expenditures in countries such as Poland and Hungary, precluding effective protection for the neediest groups and creating unsustainable fiscal burdens.[11]

Another reason for the success of the Czech program is proximity to Germany, which has provided a market for Czech exports and for relatively cheap labor. Unemployment rates, for example, are clearly correlated with proximity to the German border. Tourism has also been important in keeping unemployment low. Although Prague and some of the border regions have near zero unemployment and rely on guest workers from countries such as Ukraine, the unemployment rate in regions such as Northern Moravia is as high as 12 percent.[12]

Yet some of the factors credited with the success of the Czech reforms may also be liabilities. The rapid liberalization and low tariff rates, in conjunction with an overvalued exchange rate, are now blamed for a growing current account deficit. The deficit, which was close to zero in 1994, rose to 4 percent of GDP in 1995 and 7.7 percent at the end of 1996.[13] Lack of regulation of financial and capital markets, meanwhile, has led to collusion in ownership and to banking and money laundering scandals that are discouraging foreign investors and have begun to undermine popular support for the government. A dozen small banks failed in 1996. In August 1996 one of the nation's largest banks, Kreditni Bank, collapsed, with losses of $441 million and spillover effects for the entire financial sector. Another major bank, Agrobanka, had to be bailed out by the government in September 1996.[14]

Collusion between the major banks and the largest investment funds, which hold most of the shares in the newly privatized enterprises, has led to a principal agent problem in corporate governance. The funds, which are prevented by law from owning more than 20 percent of shares in enterprises have little incentive to improve enterprise management by restructuring.[15] The banks, which own shares in the funds and also directly in the companies, have provided enterprises with a continuous open line of credit that has discouraged genuine restructuring. Meanwhile, in a situation in which capital goods are expensive and bank finance and labor are relatively cheap, the enterprises, have responded by hoarding labor and limiting investments in new capital. Foreign-owned firms fire more labor and invest three to four times more in new capital.[16] This helps explain the low unemployment rate but also points to the need for substantial enterprise restructuring if the country is to maintain industrial competitiveness.

These liabilities came to a head in June 1997 when the government was forced to publicly recognize its mistakes in economic management and to call for a vote of no confidence to guarantee the political support necessary to initiate austerity measures to restore investor confidence and curtail a surging current account deficit. It won the vote 101 to 99. The measures included a 10 percent devaluation of the koruna and a 5 percent cut in government expenditures. Weak investor confidence, however, was as much due to the financial scandals in the stock market and banking system as it was to economic trends, and investor response was lukewarm.[17] Increased confidence seemed to hinge on the demonstration of a government commitment to more extensive financial sector reforms and to improving the regulatory environment. Klaus's public statements and the June 1997 vote signified a turning point.

It is not clear how or if Czech policymakers could have avoided these developments. In their own words, they had to "create markets before they could regulate them."[18] In part this was an ideological reaction of sorts to regulation, given years of strict central planning. And unlike transition countries where some market reforms preceded the transition, Czech policymakers did not have an existing domestic entrepreneurial class they could rely on as enterprise managers. Yet by the mid-1990s there was clearly a need for new policy reforms. The government seemed to have lost momentum, in part due to its loss of majority control of Parliament by a narrow margin in general elections in June 1996.

Not surprisingly, the political context has changed substantially since the postrevolution euphoria of the early 1990s. In the early months of the transition there was a debate over whether gradual or radical reform was appropriate to the Czech context, with Valtr Komarek, the deputy prime minister, in support of gradualism, and Vaclav Klaus, then finance minister, in support of fast reform. In October 1990 Klaus won a surprise victory for the presidency of the Civic Forum and attempted to turn the movement into an organized political party. Because many members of the movement, including President Havel, wanted to preserve the Forum's role as an umbrella organization representing society as a whole, Klaus formed the ODS. The Forum then broke down and two other parties emerged: the Civic Democratic Alliance (ODA), which was ideologically sympathetic to the ODS, and the Civic Movement (OH), which included many of the left-wing Prague intellectuals. Other members of the Forum joined the Czech Socal Democratic party, which has grown in size and strength in recent years.[19]

Klaus and his ODS handily won a majority of the seats in parliament in the June 1992 elections, and he became prime minister (table 5-2). He had campaigned on a strong reformist platform that clearly clashed with the vision presented by Vladimir Meciar, who won a similar majority in the same elections in Slova-

Table 5-2. *Parliamentary Elections by Party, Czech Republic,*
*1992, 1996*
Percent

| Political party[a] | 1992 | 1996 |
|---|---|---|
| ODS | 29.7 | 29.6 |
| ODA | 5.9 | 6.4 |
| KDU-CSL | 6.3 | 8.1 |
| CSSD | 6.5 | 26.4 |
| LEFT-BLOCK | 14.1 | 11.8 |
| SPR-RSC | 5.9 | 8.1 |
| LSU | 6.3 | 2.1 |
| HSD-SMS | 5.7 | 0.7 |
| Other parties | 21.3 | 7.4 |

Source: Petr Matějů and Blanka Řeháková, "Turning Left or Class Realignment? Analysis of the Changing Relationship Between Class and Party in the Czech Republic, 1992—1996," Social Trends Working Papers, Institute of Sociology, Academy of Sciences of the Czech Republic, Prague, January 1996, p. 1.

a. ODS—Civic Democratic Party; ODA—Civic Democratic Alliance; KDU-CSL—Christian Democratic Union; CSSD—Czech Social Democratic Party; LEFT-BLOCK—Communist party, Left Block, and Party of the Democratic Left; SPR-RSC—Czechosolvak Party of Republicans; LSU—Liberal and Social Union, SD-LSNS in 1996; HSD-SMS—Moravian Parties, HSMS-MNS and MNS-HSS in 1996.

kia. This precipitated the so-called velvet divorce between the two republics.[20] At the time, the voucher privatization program gave Klaus a vital political boost. The first wave of the program was completed in May 1992, just before the election, and the timing was far from coincidental. More than 79 percent of the eligible citizens of both republics participated, exercising their options for ownership of shares in $10 billion worth of equity in state enterprises slated for privatization (participation cost $35, about a week's average wage to purchase a book of vouchers).[21] Klaus had actively campaigned to solicit participation in the program, and his signature appeared on every voucher.[22] The vast majority of participants gave the program very favorable evaluations in surveys taken soon after it began.[23]

From that point on, Klaus proceeded with his economic reform program but also attempted to introduce substantial changes into Czech social policy. During the first two years of the transition, when he was finance minister, he had to share responsibility for social policy with Petr Miller, Minister of Labor and

Social Affairs. Miller represented the social democratic side of the Civic Forum and was committed to a social democratic model. Klaus was committed to social policy reforms of the type championed by Britain's Margaret Thatcher, emphasizing individual initiative and responsibility, and he gained more responsibility for social policy when he became prime minister.

In the first two years most efforts to reform social policy were aimed at protecting vulnerable groups during the transition. These included direct cash payments to all citizens to compensate for price liberalization. Additional payments were given to pensioners and women with young children, who were being given incentives to leave the labor force. Measures also included the introduction (and then reduction of) of generous unemployment benefits and aggressive job creation programs. Wages, meanwhile, were regulated and kept low to maintain export competitiveness and reduce unemployment. The government had a fair amount of room to maneuver in the wage policy. In contrast to countries such as Poland, where unions are powerful and were in the forefront of the revolution, in the Czech Republic unions were weak and widely distrusted by the public because they were largely controlled by the communists.[24]

Klaus signaled a change in direction of social policy in 1994 when he announced a new social security system based on private individual contributions, a measure strongly opposed by the labor unions. The next year he attempted to target parent and child allowances to the neediest families, although he was forced to water down his proposal signficantly because of strong political opposition.[25] Still, debate over social policy was far less contentious in the Czech Republic than in Poland, where the relative political power of pensioners seems to have been greater, and large expenditures on pensions crowded out other essential expenditures, such as on health care and social assistance. In most other transition economies, measures like the ones Klaus managed to implement, such as raising the retirement age and moderate targeting of family benefits, have proven far more difficult to carry out.[26]

Yet Klaus's attempt to move to a Thatcher-style social welfare policy in a country with a legacy of both social democratic and socialist policies was not without political costs. "The final im-

pact of Klaus's shift away from the initial social policy compromise is still not clear at present, although these events corre-
sponded with a sharp rise in popularity for the Czech Social
Democratic Party."[27] Social welfare issues, particularly health
care and housing policy, were among the most pressing popular
concerns in the June 1996 elections. The "threat" to social policy
gave the left perhaps the only issue around which it could unify,
given that there was little room for criticism of economic reform.
Although unions are generally weak in the Czech Republic, it is
telling that of the major strikes in 1995, two of the three were in
the social services: teachers and physicians (the third was railway
workers).[28]

Political developments did not depend solely on social policy. First, by June 1996 Klaus had been in control, if not directly in
charge, of the transition for six years, a long time in the political
life of any leader.[29] In addition, many observers noted that the
prime minister, already known for his strong ideological affinity
for neoliberal economics and his unwillingness to compromise,
ran a rather arrogant or at least elitist political campaign in 1996.
The leader of the Social Democrats, Milos Zeman, was seen as
much more a man of the people than Klaus. Second, corruption
scandals shook the highest levels of the ODS and affected the
campaign. The general perception was that big contributors to
the party "got away with it all," and thus that the government
was very lenient about "black money."[30]

Third, and perhaps most important in political terms, the previously fragmented noncommunist left unified to a large extent
under the umbrella of the Social Democrats (CSSD). Whereas in
1992 a number of small left-wing parties failed to garner enough
votes to qualify for seats (5 percent was the minimum necessary),
in 1996 a large part of those votes went to CSSD, whose support
grew from 6 percent to 26 percent of all voters. Klaus's ODS lost
its majority in parliament in June 1996. The result was not so
much due to a loss of followers by Klaus, whose support remained steady (29.7 percent in 1992 and 29.6 percent in 1996), but
rather to the ability of the left to unify in opposition (table 5-2).
The October elections for a new Senate, which used a first-past-
the-post rather than a proportional representation formula, also
narrowed the number of parties in the race.[31]

Yet the Social Democrats did not fare as well as expected in the Senate elections. First, serious splits in the party emerged in the fall of 1996. The most visible example of this was just before the elections. The Social Democrats had campaigned in favor of more spending on social welfare and called for a 3 percent budget deficit and debt financing of higher expenditures. Four Social Democratic deputies defied party discipline and voted with the government in favor of another balanced budget for 1997. This caused a larger split in the party, with supporters of the four deputies who defected pitted against those of the often controversial party chairman, Milos Zeman. This very public rift was a contributing factor in the decline in support for the Social Democrats in the November 1996 Senate elections. The Social Democrats captured 20.3 percent of the total vote, and only 25 of the 81 Senate seats, compared with 36.5 percent of the vote for the ODS and 52 seats.[32] The increased support for the opposition gave Klaus a much less free hand in government, as was demonstrated by his need to call the June 1997 vote of no confidence and his very narrow margin of victory in that vote.

Not surprisingly, support for the left correlates strongly with education and income and with how people fared during the transition. The left had stronger appeal in rural than urban areas, for example, as well as among lower-income groups in general. Yet the majority of pensioners (55 to 57 percent), whose incomes had been protected but are certainly not winners in the transition, voted for Klaus's coalition in 1996.[33]

The left's ability to unify significant opposition support does not imply that it was ready, or even willing, to govern, as was demonstrated by its sharp division before the 1996 Senate elections. Even if the left were to win a general election in the near future, fiscal constraints would dictate little departure from Klaus's market model. The support of some of the party for a balanced budget is illustrative. It is telling that former communists in Hungary and Poland moved well to the right of their rhetoric once elected. In the Czech Republic the existence of radical extremes in Parliament—the extreme nationalists on the right and the "non-reformed" communists, who have moved to the left in recent years—may serve as another moderating force, pushing the two major political blocs to the center.[34] Yet the Social Democrats were unlikely to push ahead further with targeting, private insurance, and other "Anglo-Saxon" style social reforms and were even debating lowering the retirement age once again, which would obviously have high fiscal costs.

Also affecting political behavior was a growing perception of inequality. Although income distribution in the Czech Republic remains equal relative to other countries, inequality has increased somewhat since 1990, particularly at the highest income levels. This, coupled with the scandals in the financial sector and the increasing political relevance of the left, served to focus much greater public attention on equity issues than in the early years of the transition. By 1996, for example, with both waves of the voucher privatization program complete and ownership of many of the shares consolidated in a number of investment funds, it was increasingly evident to the public that while most of the 6 million participants had made some profit, the big winners were investment funds and banks, many of which had cross-ownership ties. Public criticism of the privatization increased from 1992 to 1996, with fewer people agreeing that the process had been fair. Criticism was stronger from the left than from the right.[35] In addition, the 1994 indictment of one of the architects of the program for fraudulent use of insider information added to these perceptions.[36]

A major left turn, as has occurred among some other polities in the region, seems unlikely in the Czech Republic, although there has been some consolidation of political support for the left. Klaus's support has remained remarkably constant for a long time and is backed by an increasingly organized and patronage-based party machine, as evidenced by its strong showing in the Senate elections.[37] There is no strong union opposition to major tenets of the reform program, as in Poland. Nor is there a political movement against privatization, as there is in Russia, where most citizens share the perception, quite correctly, that the process has been dominated by insiders.[38] In the Czech Republic the extent to which the public was able to participate in the process has built a lasting base of support for privatization and for reform more broadly. Extensive failures in the financial sector would certainly undermine some of this support but would be unlikely to result in a widespread political backlash.

The seriousness of the left turns in several countries, meanwhile, remains a question. In Hungary and Poland, if measured by the proportion of total votes cast, there has been no major move to the left. However, there has been an increase in the number of people that vote for the left, which has affected the allocation of party seats. In the Czech Republic there has been a crystalization of left and right orientation. This has been related to a class realignment as well: by the mid-1990s the strongest predictor of voting for leftist candidates was a person's perception of his or her lack of socioeconomic mobility. And while left-right orientation did not change, the content of the debate shifted markedly from a discussion based in symbols and ideology in the early posttransition period to one of material interests in this later phase.[39] Interestingly enough, there is no direct association between macroeconomic developments and respondents' evaluations of their situations. Indeed, evaluations were more positive in 1992, when the economic situation was far worse, than in 1995. Part of this is explained by the shift from value-oriented to interest-oriented perceptions of the transition, since the post-revolution euphoria is over. People's expectations are also higher. And although those with financial problems contest the reform program with increasing intensity, the percentage of dissatisfied persons has fallen: 85 percent of those who are not in financial difficulties supported the reforms in 1995 versus 40 percent in 1990 (in 1995 these figures were 62 percent in Poland and 53 percent in Hungary).[40] How popular perceptions and voter behavior were affected by equity and social welfare issues, and by the voucher privatization program, are discussed later.

## Poverty, Equity, and Social Policy during the Transition

From an objective viewpoint there is little cause for concern about poverty and inequality in the Czech Republic. Poverty and unemployment rates are far lower and average income higher than in the transition economies of Poland and Hungary (table 5-3). Poverty and unemployment rates are lower than in most OECD countries, while per capita income is roughly comparable

Table 5-3. *Poverty, Inequality, and Unemployment in the Czech Republic, Hungary, and Poland, 1995*

| Item | Czech Republic | Hungary | Poland |
|---|---|---|---|
| Average per capita income (U.S. dollars) | 7,550 | 6,050 | 5,000 |
| Per capita income of poorest 20 percent of population (U.S. dollars) | 4,000 | 3,300 | 2,000 |
| Gini coefficient 1993–94 (based on macroeconomic income data) | .27 | .23 | .31 |
| Poverty rate (percent of population, based on macroeconomic income data)[a] | <1 | 2 | 31 |
| Unemployment rate (1995) | 2.9 | 10.3 | 14.7 |

Source: Mark Kramer, "Social Protection Policies and Safety Nets in East-Central Europe: Dilemmas of the Post-Communist Transformation," paper prepared for the National Academy of Sciences Task Forces on Social Sector Reforms in Economies in Transition, Washington, September 19–20, 1996, tables 1–3, 10–12. Based on Czech government statistics.

a. Poverty rate based on Branko Milanovic, "Income, Inequality and Poverty during the Transition," World Bank, Washington, 1995. PPP-adjusted level of $120 per month.

to that in Greece. Less than 1 percent of the population is poor, unemployment is 2.9 percent, and income is more equally distributed than in most market economies, with a Gini coefficient of .27 in 1993–94. In Poland, the other fast-growing major economy in eastern Europe, 13 percent of the population is poor, 14.7 percent is unemployed, and the Gini is .31.[41] The average Gini for OECD countries, meanwhile, is slightly higher (and therefore more unequal) than that of either Poland or the Czech Republic.[42]

Yet poverty, equity, and social policy concerns are increasingly prominent in the Czech Republic. First, income inequality has increased somewhat; the top of the distribution has seen the greatest gains, separating this quintile further from the rest. The most significant gains from the voucher privatization, for example, were eventually concentrated in the hands of a small group of investment companies and banks, particularly after the so-called third wave of privatization, in which the funds bought out the majority of small shareholders. Although public understanding of the process is far from complete, and privatization is still viewed favorably by most people, more now also believe that the gains have not been distributed fairly. In addition, as noted earlier, people's political behavior has gradually shifted from a value-oriented to an interest-oriented perspective and expectations have increased. The attempts of the Klaus government to change the manner in which social welfare benefits are distributed, if limited in their scope, certainly brought the matter of entitlements to the public eye. Surveys indicate that while Czechs are not willing to pay more taxes for entitlements, they expect the same level of benefits as in the pretransition period.[43] Finally, the growth of the left in coherence and organizational capacity has coincided with these trends and, in the absence of economic issues, social welfare policy is a logical focus of attention.

*Poverty*

It is difficult to measure and compare poverty among transition economies because of different standards of measurement and the changing weight of state transfers and benefits vis-à-vis earned income in determining living standards. Nevertheless, a number of surveys and studies have provided a fairly accurate picture of poverty and its changing nature in the transition economies.[44] In addition, recent or ongoing household surveys in the Czech Republic and in the neighboring countries of central and eastern Europe are useful in depicting subjective as well as objective trends in poverty and income distribution.[45]

In contrast to other countries undergoing the transition from a state-planned to a market economy, in the Czech Republic poverty did not increase substantially. In fact, poverty rates for households actually fell from 1988 to 1992, in part because of the introduction of slightly stricter measurement criteria (a legal subsistence minimum was introduced in November 1991). Before the transition, some poverty existed, primarily among members of the former bourgeoisie, including peasants, who were paid extremely low pensions; single mothers with children; and gypsies.[46] Since then, the situation of pensioners has improved because of a policy of protecting pensions at the bottom of the scale while not increasing those at the top (thereby flattening the distribution). The situation of single mothers with children, however, remains a concern, because family benefits have not kept up with inflation as well as pensions have. Since the transition, three other causes of poverty have emerged: new unemployment, the removal of price subsidies, and the opening of borders, which has resulted in a large number of migrants who are not covered by social welfare benefits.[47]

Regardless of new causes, the poverty rate remained the same or fell, depending on how it is measured, during the transition period. This is a remarkable achievement given that officially measured real household incomes fell by 25 percent between 1989 and 1991. It is largely attributable to comprehensive safety net policies, which combined some modest alteration of the existing benefits system with policies introduced to address transitional problems, such as new unemployment benefits. Real incomes began to recover in 1992 and by 1993 stood at 83 percent of their 1989 level.[48]

If the subsistence minimum, the living minimum, is used as a measure, 2.9 percent of households, or 3.5 percent of all persons, are poor. This rate was 4.5 percent of households before 1988 and 2.7 percent of persons. Children fared less well: 2.1 percent were poor in 1988 and 6.0 percent were in 1992. The status of pensioners improved during this period because pension benefits were valorized more rapidly than family benefits. Thus families with children fared worse in relative terms and more of them fell into poverty. In general they receive only 87 percent of average household income.[49] Not surprisingly, the determining factor of the poverty rate is the number of dependent children.[50]

Other estimates of poverty for the Czech Republic are slightly different. Branko Milanovic, using a puchasing power parity adjusted poverty line of $4 a day, or $120 a month, finds poverty in the Czech Republic to be under 1 percent.[51] Jiri Vecernik, using the European Union poverty line, finds slightly different poverty rates than the ones based on the legal minimum: from 1988 to 1992 the number of poor households fell from 6.1 percent to 2.3 percent and of poor persons from 3.1 to 2.4 percent. The share of children in poverty rose from 1.2 to 3.5 percent. The difference in the level of children's poverty comes from variations in the calculation of their equivalent income. Vecernik argues that the EU calculations underestimate the costs associated with rearing children in the Czech Republic. When this slightly higher line is used, although the number of dependent children is still a major determinant of poverty, so too is the age of the head of household.[52] This poverty line applied to the European Union finds slightly higher rates. For example, poverty rates ranged from 5 to 10 percent in Belgium, Germany, and the Netherlands.[53]

Vecernik also uses a measure of subjective poverty developed by Flemish and Dutch economists that reflects the distance from a commonly shared idea about the minimum subsistence income. Applying this to the Czech Republic, he found the rate to be 25 percent in 1992 and 30 percent in 1994. These rates are similar to Belgium's (24 percent, where objective poverty is 2.9 percent), while in the Netherlands and Luxembourg the rate is 10 to 15 percent of households. The approximately 30 percent of households in the Czech Republic that thought of themselves as poor shared certain traits, such as the number of adults in the household, as well as certain social characteristics (older, less educated). This group generally had higher expectations of the state's responsibility in reducing poverty and was more likely to contest the legitimacy of newly acquired wealth in general.[54] Unlike in Poland and Hungary, there is no correlation between subjective poverty and unemployment in the Czech Republic.

A particularly striking trait about poverty in the Czech Republic is that the poor are not socially excluded: distributional poverty has no consequence for subjective poverty thus far. Nor is the intensity of political life significantly less. And poor households are relatively well equipped: almost 40 percent have a car, for example. The variance among households in terms of financial problems, meanwhile, is hardly explained by standard sociodemographic and socioeconomic characteristics, with the exception of elementary-school versus university-educated people.[55] The socially marginalized tend to be Gypsies and migrant workers rather than the poor in income. More recent data, however, show increasing differences between poor and non-poor households and an increasing link between income and family wealth, both of which suggest that poverty may take on a more enduring character in the future. Regardless, so far poverty in the Czech Republic is primarily an income phenomenon.[56]

Another interesting trend is that since 1993, as real incomes have begun to recover, people have begun to save more. Given negative real interest rates and an increase in consumer goods, this suggests that there is substantial underreporting of income. Savings by wealthy pensioners have decreased, which may reflect the flattening of pension benefits. In general, the increases in savings are coming from the top of the income distribution, while the poor are dissaving.

## Income Inequality

Income inequality in the Czech Republic has increased since the transition, and official statistics may underestimate actual trends because there is a rather large grey economy as well as substantial underreporting. The Gini coefficient for individual earnings was .19 in 1988 and had risen to .27 in 1993.[57] Although the change is significant, Czech incomes are slightly more equal than those in Poland and Hungary, and much more equal than those of most OECD countries, particularly if household income adjusted for transfers is used as a measure (table 5-4). If one uses adjusted income, the Czech Republic, with a Gini of .24, would correspond to the Ginis of the low-inequality Scandinavian countries (.20–.24); while Poland and Hungary, at .29, would belong to the third lowest group of European countries that includes France, Italy, and the United Kingdom.[58] And consumption inequality in the Czech Republic actually decreased from 1989 to 1992, reflecting the extent to which the benefits system protected the incomes of those at the bottom.[59]

Yet criticisms of inequality have increased more than the increase of inequality itself. In 1991, 40 percent of respondents saw inequality as "extensive." In 1989 about 55 percent evaluated ongoing changes as bringing more justice; this figure fell to 35 percent by 1993. Two trends have made changes in these perceptions turn for the worse. First, the former communist nomenklatura not only survived but successfully converted political capital into business capital, and black marketeers and speculators fared exceptionally well. Related to this, the percentage of people who thought that privatization should be continued "regardless that the property fell into improper hands" declined from 30 percent to 19 percent between mid-1992 and the end of 1993.[60] The second

Table 5-4. *Income Inequality in the Czech Republic, Hungary, Poland, and Slovakia, 1988, 1992*

| | Czech Republic | | Hungary | | Poland | | Slovakia | |
|---|---|---|---|---|---|---|---|---|
| Quintile | 1988 | 1992 | 1989 | 1992 | 1989 | 1992 | 1988 | 1992 |
| *Total household income (adjusted for transfers)* | | | | | | | | |
| 1 | 6.6 | 7.0 | 7.0 | 6.5 | 5.9 | 7.4 | 6.5 | 7.6 |
| 2 | 13.5 | 12.7 | 13.0 | 12.2 | 12.3 | 13.2 | 13.7 | 13.6 |
| 3 | 19.9 | 17.9 | 18.3 | 17.5 | 18.3 | 18.1 | 20.0 | 18.7 |
| 4 | 25.4 | 24.0 | 24.1 | 23.8 | 24.5 | 24.1 | 25.0 | 24.2 |
| 5 | 34.6 | 38.4 | 37.6 | 40.1 | 39.1 | 37.2 | 34.8 | 35.8 |
| Ratio Q5/Q1 | 5.2 | 5.5 | 5.4 | 6.2 | 6.6 | 5.0 | 5.4 | 4.7 |
| Gini coefficient | .29 | .32 | .31 | .34 | .33 | .30 | .29 | .28 |
| *Per capita income* | | | | | | | | |
| 1 | 12.0 | 11.4 | 10.9 | 10.0 | 9.1 | 8.9 | 11.9 | 11.7 |
| 2 | 15.6 | 15.3 | 14.8 | 14.0 | 13.9 | 13.7 | 15.7 | 15.6 |
| 3 | 18.4 | 17.9 | 17.8 | 7.2 | 18.0 | 17.8 | 18.6 | 18.9 |
| 4 | 22.3 | 21.5 | 22.0 | 22.0 | 22.9 | 23.1 | 22.4 | 22.4 |
| 5 | 31.8 | 33.9 | 34.5 | 36.8 | 36.2 | 36.4 | 31.5 | 31.5 |
| Ratio Q5/Q1 | 2.6 | 3.0 | 3.2 | 3.7 | 4.0 | 4.1 | 2.6 | 2.7 |
| Gini coefficient | .20 | .22 | .23 | .27 | .27 | .28 | .19 | .20 |

Source: Jiri Vecernik, "Incomes in Central Europe: Distributions, Patterns, and Perceptions," *Journal of European Social Policy*, vol. 6, no. 2 (1996), p. 108.

trend is a rising cost of living that has curbed household expenditures in the face of a dramatic increase in the availability of consumer goods.

Yet in comparison with Hungary, Poland, and Slovakia, criticisms about inequality have increased the least in the Czech Republic. Although less than 10 percent thought existing income disparities were too large in 1990, slightly over 60 percent thought they were too large in 1995. In Hungary the share increased from 20 percent to almost 90 percent, in Poland from 15 percent to 80 percent, and in Slovakia from 10 percent to 75 percent.[61] These different perceptions about inequalities also relate to broader perceptions about society. "Whereas most Poles and Hungarians regarded their societies as having a large base with a small middle and top, Czechs and Slovaks perceived the social structure as a regularly graduated pyramid, or even, Czechs especially, as a middle-class society."[62] Households in the Czech Republic reporting great financial difficulties in 1995 were

Figure 5-1. *Financial Difficulties of Households, Czech Republic, Hungary, Poland, and Slovakia, 1980, 1996*

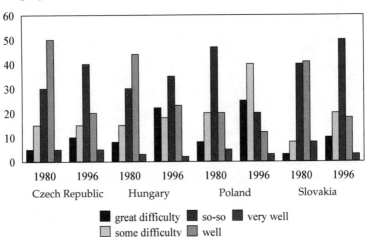

Source: Vecernik, "Incomes in Central Europe," p. 118.

5 percent as opposed to 24 percent in Hungary, 10 percent in Poland, and 10 percent in Slovakia (figure 5-1).[63] The ability of nomenklatura elites to maintain their advantageous position in the income hierarchy is striking. Peter Makeju and Nelson Lim make a distinction between transition countries where elites circulate—new people are able to enter new elite ranks created by political and market changes—and those where they are reproduced—people from the old elite take on the new positions. Higher rates of circulation before 1989 tend to create a more competent elite and less circulation after the transition. Yet in the Czech Republic, where there was very little reform before the transition, the elites were for the most part able to convert their political assets into economic capital, not only because they were well educated but also had access to social networks. A survey of 2,518 randomly selected families in 1989 and again in 1992 found that even controlling for education, those with managerial positions (cadres) before the transition fared better in income. And being a cadre increased the chances of starting a business by a factor of three. (Cadres, who held positions based on technical merit in the bureaucracy, are distinct from party members, al-

though some were also party members). The returns to education also increased with the transition. From 1989 to 1992 the returns for a university education increased by 6 percent.[64]

In comparative terms, returns to education were less important in explaining income mobility than in Hungary and Poland, for example, while firm ownership and branch activity were more important in the Czech Republic.[65] This supports the thesis that there has been more elite reproduction in the Czech Republic than in countries where there was more reform, and therefore more elite circulation, before the transition. Economic elites in all three countries, meanwhile, were primarily male (90 percent), younger than age 50, university educated (80 percent), and many were either former members of the Communist party or their fathers were. More elite reproduction occurred among the economic rather than the political elite, and directors of new private sector firms were more likely to be of elite origins (but not directly members of the Communist party) than were those in the state sector.[66]

Comparative studies of Bulgaria, Hungary, Poland, Russia, Slovakia, and the Czech Republic have found that in all countries a sense of improved social position was linked with certain social characteristics: younger age, higher level of education, profession, and independent economic activity. But the Czech Republic was where the sense of relative deprivation was weakest and the sense of improvement strongest. In terms of social and economic mobility, Czechs scored the highest in the "no change" or "improvement" categories, while Russia and Bulgaria fared the worst. This is not surprising, given that although half the populations in Hungary, Poland, and Slovakia reported experiencing a loss in relative income position within society, only 30 percent of Czechs had the same experience.[67] The Czech Republic also demonstrated the most consistent association between economic insecurity and leftist orientation. Finally, the Czech Republic was the only country where satisfaction levels with the market economy, human rights, democracy, and the overall direction of the country were converging by 1994.[68]

Thus although income inequality has increased and concern about inequality has increased even more, incomes have remained more equal than in most neighboring countries, upward mobility remains greater, and subjective evaluations of the situation more positive. And the position of those at the bottom seems to have been, for the most part, effectively protected. Given that some increases in inequality were inevitable to establish a market economy and that others, such as higher returns to education, are unquestionably beneficial, the record in poverty and inequality certainly contributes the sense that there is a Czech "exception." These trends clearly were affected by the social policy of the Klaus government.

## Social Policy

The Klaus government has made several isolated attempts at reforming social welfare policy, such as a supplementary private pensions plan, the modest targeting of family benefits, and the decentralization of health care services. The result for the most part has been the maintenance of the old system with a few innovations and alterations. Yet the government has avoided major political confrontations on social policy issues, often watering down or backing off controversial proposals, as in the case of family benefits. It has not presented a vision or introduced a broader public debate on the need for social policy reform and thus has not clearly posed the trade-offs involved to the public. People continue to want high levels of state welfare protection and economic freedom and low levels of taxation at the same time. The Social Democrats have been able to capitalize on this, focusing on the broader concerns and playing on people's expectations but avoiding specific proposals.[69]

The absence, until recently, of a public debate on social policy has several causes. First, there was no such debate for more than forty years. Second, state bureaucrats were not trained to think in terms of policy innovations or efficiency trade-offs, but rather in terms of delivering benefits. Third, the impetus for the transition was one of allowing market forces to function rather than rethinking the role of the state.[70]

In the first two years of the transition the Klaus government focused on protecting the vulnerable rather than on devising new social policy. The intent was to work through the existing bene-

Table 5-5. *Transfer Income as Percent of Total Income: Distribution by Deciles*

| | Distribution per household income | |
| --- | --- | --- |
| Decile shares | 1988 | 1992 |
| 1 (highest) | 95.0 | 90.0 |
| 2 | 68.2 | 74.4 |
| 3 | 55.2 | 69.2 |
| 4 | 40.6 | 66.0 |
| 5 | 29.5 | 40.6 |
| 6 | 23.2 | 27.6 |
| 7 | 19.1 | 20.0 |
| 8 | 16.8 | 16.7 |
| 9 | 15.2 | 14.0 |
| 10 (lowest) | 13.6 | 8.6 |
| Average | 26.2 | 28.7 |

Source: Jiri Vecernik, *Markets and People: The Czech Reform Experience in Comparative Perspective* (Aldershot: Avebury Press, 1996), p. 76.

fits system and to supplement it with safety net measures, particularly in employment. A "living minimum" was introduced in November 1991 that established a universal standard for minimum pensions, social benefits, unemployment benefits, and a minimum wage level; it is indexed to changes in the CPI and the average wage. The minimum fell 8 to 9 percent below its initial 1991 level in the first few years but has since been maintained in real terms.[71] Benefits were restructured in favor of poor pensioners in particular, while families with children fared less well.[72] In addition, subsidies on heat and housing were left untouched.[73] Other price liberalizations were compensated by direct cash payments: as an interim measure in the face of food price increases of 25 percent, all Czech citizens received a cash benefit of 4 percent of the average wage or Kcs 140 a month.[74] The percentage of transfer income (versus total income) received by poorer people increased from 1988 to 1992, except for the very poorest, and decreased for the wealthiest (table 5-5). Average levels of social transfers as a share of income remained the same, at 19 to 20 percent, from 1989 to 1993, although this may have changed marginally because benefit levels were slightly targeted in 1995.[75] Social assistance benefits in general are slightly less generous than average levels in Poland or Europe. Yet the experience of other countries, including Poland, shows that levels of assistance often matter much less than how they are targeted and administered.[76]

The Czechs introduced a new system of unemployment benefits in 1990. At first benefits were too generous: there were almost no eligibility requirements and very good compensation. People who had always been outside the work force began receiving benefits, and the offical rate of unemployment increased. In 1992 the maximum duration of benefits was cut from one year to six months, eligibility requirements tightened, and a low limit placed on compensation. These changes led to a sharp drop in the number of people seeking to qualify for benefits as well as a 33 percent drop in the share of unemployed who qualified. Benefits are now among the least generous in the region.[77] In addition, a series of employment programs was initiated that provided public employment or subsidized firms that hired unemployed workers and employed up to 200,000 workers in the first two years of the transition.[78]

There was a cumulative reduction of 640,000 workers, or 12 percent of the labor force, from 1989 to 1994. The government introduced new incentives for mothers with young children to exit the labor force, added a required year of secondary education, and restricted benefits for working pensioners.[79] More important, up to 100,000 workers left the labor force to join the informal sector, especially in services, and more than 50,000 workers departed to commute to jobs in Germany and Austria. Detailed econometric analysis of Czech employment trends finds that higher unemployment rates correlate with distance from the German and Austrian borders. The same study finds that outflows from unemployment (controlling for the number of unemployed) are correlated with higher expenditures on active employment programs in the Czech Republic but not in neighboring Slovakia, suggesting that the Czech programs were relatively effective.[80] Meanwhile, a policy of wage regulation that reflected an explicit choice to keep wages low in order to limit unemployment and boost export competitiveness complemented these labor market policies.[81] Wage regulations were lifted in June 1995.[82]

Pensions were increased for the poorest pensioners but flattened at the top end of the distribution. This served to protect the poor while avoiding the pensions explosions that affected Poland

and Hungary, crowding out other essential social expenditures and creating a major fiscal liability for the state. And given that pensioners are usually politically organized, raising pension levels is rarely a reversible policy and tends to lock in the fiscal burden, regardless of the trade-offs and costs. Expenditure on pensions increased from 8.3 percent of GDP in 1989 to 9.0 percent in 1994 in the Czech Republic versus 7.9 percent to 15.5 percent in Poland. Some of the increases are due to demographics, some to the increase in early retirement as governments tried to stem unemployment increases, and some (in Poland) to overly generous pension increases.[83]

In 1991 the Czechs were one of the first of the transition economies to raise the retirement age. Still the increase is modest: the age was 60 for men and 55 for women and is to rise two years for men and four for women by 2007. The payroll tax going to pensions (32 percent) remains high (the U.S rate is 12.4 percent and Switzerland's is 9.6 percent).[84] While pension levels have kept up and thus far kept pensioners out of poverty, pensions are still small: while the average wage has doubled or tripled since the 1990 transition, pension levels have only increased 1.8 times.[85] Still, the Czechs spend a higher percentage of their GDP on pensions than do any of the Baltic countries or Russia, for example.[86] The Czech social security system could certainly benefit from a more comprehensive reform.

After Klaus became prime minister in 1992, the government attempted to change some of the fundamentals underlying the delivery of social services. A tax reform was carried out in 1993. A value-added tax replaced the turnover tax, and income and corporate taxes were restructured to bring them in line with western European systems.[87] The reform also introduced separate payroll taxes for pension and sickness insurance, unemployment insurance, and health insurance, which is a marked departure from most transition economies in which these tend to be lumped into one (usually insolvent) fund. The health insurance fund, in particular, was separated from the general budget where it was vulnerable to cuts, allowing for public and private choice. This was important in avoiding problems such as Poland's, where the deficit-ridden social insurance fund is increasingly draining what public resources there are for health care. A great deal of responsibility for health care provision has been decentralized, meanwhile, with mixed results. Debate about the final state of the health care system is continuing and was a major subject in the 1996 elections.

The Klaus government also wanted to create a separate pension fund, which would have opened the door to private choice, but gave in to union opposition on this issue. Still, the social insurance fund is currently in surplus, which goes to finance social assistance. In addition, employee contributions were introduced into the social security fund; they were intended to increase the transparency of the fund and introduce a sense of individual responsibility. "Reformers believed that employee contributions would make citizens realize the full costs of the social safety net and therefore reduce demands on the paternalistic provision of the state. The tax reform emphasized the principle of insurance, rather than universal free provision from general funds for pensions and health."[88]

While steering clear of a full-blown social security reform, which was advocated by some advisers, the government introduced a new supplementary pension plan in 1995 as an attempt to boost private savings.[89] Individuals are allowed to make monthly payments into capitalized pension accounts managed by private funds and are rewarded with matching payments by the state. Employers contribute on a voluntary basis. Unions strongly opposed the scheme because they wanted to participate in the management of enterprise-based pension funds, and they launched a twenty-four-hour protest strike. Yet they were unable to stop the reform, which reflects, among other things, their relative weakness.[90] The reform is not without flaws. For example, the state is now subsidizing wealthy retirees, the sole contributors to the plan, and several of the funds have been singled out as corrupt. Ten to fifteen funds have been set up, most of which have links to the banks. Contributions thus far have been minimal, averaging Kcs 300 to Kcs 400 a month (average salaries are Kcs 9,000 to Kcs 10,000 a month). One problem with the plan, which would certainly apply if a more thorough reform were considered, is that its success hinges on the record of capital markets, which are coming under increasing criticism for corruption and lack of adequate regulation.[91]

Also in 1995 the Klaus government attempted to target family benefits. The original proposal would have reduced the benefit to those families living at more than 1.25 times the minimum. The measure was criticized for being at the expense of those slightly above that level, who also lived very poorly. After substantial opposition, a compromise staggered benefits for people living at one to two times the minimum, with those at the lowest levels receiving more benefits. This means that all except the wealthiest 5 percent of families receive some sort of family benefit.[92] Although the reform was watered down, one could argue that merely introducing the philosophy of targeting was a political coup and a rare achievement in the context of a transition economy, with most people firmly tied to the concept of universal entitlements. Some observers note that the debate over child benefits in 1995 was a spark that kindled the debate on social issues because it was the first time these concerns received so much concentrated attention.[93] Unions striking over a supplementary pension system were unable to capture public attention sufficiently to alter the government's course of reform, but the challenge to an entitlement that affected all families raised far more fundamental issues about the sustainability of universal entitlements.

Many observers argue that Klaus missed his opportunity on social policy reform. If he had pushed for changes such as social security reform early in his government, he would have had much more success. Indeed, measures that were introduced earlier, such as raising the retirement age, met with surprisingly little public opposition.[94] By 1995–96, however, the opposition had had time to coalesce, and the postrevolution honeymoon was over. And because the policy framework was established and stable, people were far less willing to consider, much less accept, dramatic change.

This is certainly in keeping with other countries' experiences. Those that have moved quickly in social policy matters have been able to implement sweeping reforms under democratic auspices. A number of countries in Latin America, for example, have carried out dramatic social security reforms. A context of sharp macroeconomic change, meanwhile, tends to undermine the position of established interest groups, at least in the short term. Thus it is possible that Klaus could have pushed through more far-reaching social policy reforms with far less opposition and far less political cost had he done so early. Yet given the government's already overwhelming agenda in the early years of the transition, which included rapid, massive privatization, it is not clear that other major reforms would have been administratively feasible. Unlike Poland and Hungary, where there was a cadre of bureaucrats with some experience with reform and an organized opposition movement, civil society had been much more repressed in Czechoslovakia. Klaus had no one he could rely on except the existing party-based bureaucracy.[95] And later in the first term, the government probably calculated that more thorough reforms in social welfare would jeopardize its chances of getting reelected in 1996.[96] In any event, by the mid-1990s social policy had become one of the primary reasons for the political stalemate affecting the Klaus goverment's second term.

The bits and pieces of reform that were established can serve as building blocks for future reforms and did introduce certain changes in philosophy. Whether that philosophy is politically acceptable to a society accustomed to universal entitlements is less clear. It seems to be changing gradually, as increasing concern about inequality and the consolidation of support for the Social Democrats indicates. Yet it is unclear what alternative—and affordable—model the left would actually propose if in power.[97] The Senate elections gave a clearer electoral mandate to Klaus, which may have some effects. Meanwhile, attitudes are also crystalizing along class and ideological lines: according to several sociological surveys, by the mid-1990s, attitudes in favor of the free market and those favoring stronger social protection correlated closely with general political inclinations and employment prospects.[98]

One concern that will surface as the debate on social policy becomes more coherent is the extent to which maintaining the status quo will compromise future growth. Although the Czech Republic has made more progress than many neighboring countries, social spending takes up 20.5 percent of GDP and total government spending 50 to 51 percent. While this is equivalent to Poland's ratio and less than Hungary's 60-plus percent for government spending, it is much greater than the 20 percent average maintained by most of the fast-growing emerging market economies: the East Asian tigers and Chile.[99] Income from government transfers remains a high percentage of total income for more than half the population (table 5-5). Similarly, pension-related payroll taxes in the Czech Republic are much higher than those in most European Union countries and also dictate trade-offs in terms of employment. This will become more of an issue if wage levels begin to increase and Czech workers lose their comparative advantage in attracting subsidiaries of foreign companies.

## The Voucher Program

One matter that will clearly influence the debate over equity and social policy, and economic reform more generally, is the changing public perceptions about the voucher privatization program. It is impossible to discuss the Czech transition, particularly its political economy, without considering the voucher program. The program had direct immediate effects on the political sustainability of reform. These effects also changed somewhat as the benefits became concentrated in fewer hands. The program also changed the way a large part of the economy, previously state controlled, is managed and had very clear effects on corporate governance. Finally, it had strong implications for equity: there were big winners, some losers, and a wide variety of outcomes for average citizens. As these became more evident in the years following the initial auction of shares, they also affected public attitudes toward privatization and market reforms more generally. Not surprisingly, how people fared as well as their perceptions of privatization tend to mirror the distribution of the population along income, education, and ideological lines.

Few processes of privatization have received as much attention as the Czech voucher program, and with good reason. In mid-1992 in a country in which less than 5 percent of the economy was in private hands two years before, more than 6 million people in an adult population of 7.4 million purchased vouchers that allowed them to bid on $10 billion worth of shares in state-owned enterprises.[100] The voucher system, conceived by Finance

Minister Klaus and a few close advisors, was part of a three-pronged privatization strategy. The first phase was to restore thousands of small businesses and companies confiscated after February 1948 to their previous owners and to establish a system of compensation for those that had been destroyed or absorbed by large industrial properties. Tens of thousands of owner-managed businesses quickly began to operate and provided an important impetus to the economy early in the transition. The second phase was known as small privatization and involved the sale of perhaps 100,000 shops, enterprises, and small industries. Small privatization was accomplished by public auction, with minimum sale value during the first round set at one-half the book value of the property. Foreign investor participation was allowed only after the first round. As with restitution, this process was rapid and largely successful.[101]

The third and most ambitious phase was large privatization, the sale or denationalization of 3,000 large and medium-sized enterprises. It occurred in two waves, the second of which took place after the breakup of Czechoslovakia, and primarily in the Czech Republic. The companies chosen for the first wave were in general more profitable, or at least likely to succeed in a market economy. In the Czech Republic 988 companies were put up for sale in the first wave, with approximately 61 percent of the shares available for vouchers. The second wave entailed 676 companies, plus shares of 185 companies that had also had shares auctioned in the first wave. The firms that participated in the second wave were in general larger and had a smaller percentage of shares available for vouchers. In some the state maintained its influence by keeping a "golden" share, or veto power, over management decisions. There were also 32 enterprises (mainly water-line companies) in which more than 50 percent of the shares were transferred free of cost to municipalities.[102]

The Ministry of Privatization was the ultimate decisionmaking body in the process, although proposals had to go through the "founding" ministries, the interim owners of the companies to be privatized, who determined the restructuring needs of the companies. In most cases this was the Ministry of Industry. Methods of large privatization were varied. The most common approach was for Czech companies to form joint stock corporations, the shares of which were then sold during the privatization. Most direct sales were to foreign companies, who were well-known leaders in their industries—VW (which purchased Skoda), Philip Morris, Procter and Gamble, General Motors. Because of the lack of domestic capital, the government took a favorable view of such foreign investment as long as the potential partners demonstrated a long-term commitment to the companies and their employees. Yet the government was also determined not to let foreign capital dominate privatization, which was one of the reasons for the development of the voucher program.[103]

The voucher program had several objectives: preventing foreign domination of privatization; preventing the nomenklatura or insiders from dominating it; valorizing the companies' shares through the auction mechanism; and building public support for privatization and reform in general. The government's initial vision, although not the ultimate outcome, was to mimic the Thatcher government's attempts to turn unions into stakeholders in privatized firms.[104] Every Czech and Slovak citizen over the age of 18 (about 11 million people) was eligible to buy a voucher booklet for Kcs 1,000 or $35, equivalent to a week's average salary, a fee that covered administrative costs of the program. The vouchers could then be used to bid on shares designated for voucher privatization, the bidding for which took place in several rounds. Although it was estimated that the book value of stocks that each voucher could purchase would be thirty times its nominal value, the government avoided denominating the vouchers in a currency amount, thereby heightening expectations. In addition, rather than promising great profits, the government used slogans such as "distributing responsibilities in a bankrupt economy."[105]

In the first few months of the program in early 1992, only 25 percent of the population expressed an interest in participating. About one month before the auctions were to be held, however, the Harvard Fund (no relation to the university), the brainchild of young entrepreneur Victor Kozeny, offered to manage the portfolios of voucher holders for one year, after which it would give them the option of signing over their shares to the fund in exchange for Kcs 10,000 (ten times purchase value). Hundreds of other funds followed Harvard's suit, offering similar or better deals, including collateral loans based on vouchers. The funds launched an advertising and marketing blitz, and by August 1992 an estimated 8.5 million people in the two republics had purchased vouchers to bid on $10 billion in equity. In the Czech Republic, almost 6 million people participated in the first wave and 6.1 million in the second, which occurred in 1994.[106]

An unforeseen development was the extent to which the funds dominated the process. In the first wave, investment funds received 71.8 percent of all vouchers in circulation and in the second wave 63 percent. A smaller percentage of people purchased shares through funds in the second wave: their image was tarnished because some did not follow through on their promises in a timely manner. The funds, meanwhile, succeeded in their gamble; only 7 to 15 percent of investors chose to redeem their shares for cash.[107] The ten largest funds gained control over 51 percent of all investment points, and the thirteen largest controlled 62.5 percent. And 55 percent of all the funds are owned by fourteen investment groups, most of which are banks.[108] This translated into control over enterprise shares. The funds (IPFs) have more than a 50 percent share in 334 companies. Individual investors have a more than 50 percent share in 272 companies. The National Property Fund has more than a 50 percent stake in 23 and more than a 20 percent stake in 118. Foreign investors control 19 and direct domestic investors control 16.[109] This outcome is particularly notable given that one of the primary concerns about the program was that ownership would be too diffuse, creating a problem of corporate governance. It is telling that management has more influence on the boards of the companies controlled by individual investors, and that the funds, and the banks that own many of them, have more influence on the boards of the companies that they dominate.[110]

Czech banks were important participants in this program. They proved willing to lend for risky, highly leveraged acquisitions, a willingness in part explained by the extent to which the banks are directly involved through the setting up of their own funds and therefore taking part in the management decisions of most of the companies to which they lend. The financial institutions emerged from the first wave as majority owners of the equity of the newly privatized companies. No one entity was allowed to purchase more than 20 percent of equity in the voucher program; thus many companies have three or more majority equity owners, most of which are funds owned by banks.[111] In a so-called third wave of the program in 1994, banks and firms further consolidated their positions, buying out substantial numbers of individual investors.

Despite this consolidation the program concluded with relative share prices that have shown considerable consistency on the stock market, and stock market prices are also positively correlated with the net assets and profitability of the company as well as the presence of a foreign investor.[112] This suggests that the program was successful in establishing a functional share price mechanism and a means of corporate governance that functions, even if not ideally.

The program has been criticized for lack of sufficient regulation. The attitude of the Ministry of Finance was to combine a "largely laissez-faire attitude toward substantive regulation with close administrative oversight for fraud, insolvency, or embezzlement."[113] The ministry developed a software program that allowed it to monitor the points acquired by each fund and later to monitor its portfolio. It also required the IPFs to disclose information about the financial promises they made and the number of points they acquired through those promises. The implicit threat behind this was that if the ministry disclosed that a fund had insufficient liquidity to meet its promises, a run on it would be likely. The regulators were relatively lax. First, concerns about runs on funds were tempered by the fact that vouchers sold for an arbitrarily low price of $35 while the book value of the property that the average Czech citizen acquired was $2,000. So the fund's offer of $350 for that amount of property was still well below its total value and thus theoretically would have been payable even if many more people had cashed in their funds. In reality only 7 to 15 percent did so. Second, ideological considerations were significant. Both Klaus and his advisor Dusan Triska believed strongly in free markets, open access, and minimal regulation.[114] As Triska noted, "In our context, we had to build markets before we could regulate them."[115]

A third reason for government tolerance is that it needed the funds and the banks as much as they needed it. The advertising campaign launched by the funds was crucial to creating the large-scale public interest in a program that was critical to the government's political and economic success. But while there is no doubt that the funds' role was important, it should not be overblown. Early registration is rare for almost any transaction that requires putting money up front. In the second wave, in which the funds participated from the start, there was also very little registration until close to the deadline. Thus although the funds clearly increased interest in the program in the last month of the campaign, they may not be responsible for the entire increase in registration.[116]

One of the significant concerns in any privatization, and one that distinguishes the Czech experience from others in the region, is the extent to which insider dominance of the process was limited. This stands in sharp contrast to the Russian privatization program, for example, where insiders dominated to such an extent that the program was discredited in the minds of the public. The rules were altered to facilitate worker buyouts, and three-quarters of the firms took the option of selling 51 percent to management and workers. The Russian Property Fund typically kept another 20 percent. This usually left only 29 percent of shares available for the voucher auction. There was little incentive for management to sell shares for vouchers because they would only lose control to outsiders, and the management of many firms actually bought out their workers' vouchers. In Russia, management controls an average 65 percent of stakes in privatized firms; in the Czech Republic management controls 4.4 percent. And the privatization program has proven a major political liability in Russia, undermining support for economic reform more generally.[117] In addition, unlike the Czechs, the Russians had no national-level monitoring system, and there was a great deal of manipulation by regional elites. Finally, the Russian vouchers were worth only $10 to $20, but they were worth on average $350 to $500 in the Czech Republic (for those who cashed out to funds after one year; many shares were worth much more), so there was far less incentive to participate.[118]

In the Czech Republic there were 23,607 buyout proposals made to the Ministry of Privatization for the 4,338 companies offered in the two waves. Twenty-one percent of the proposals were from top management, while others came from lower-level management, local governments, consulting firms, and claims for restitution. The most numerous group of people were prospective buyers, yet they were far less successful in receiving approval than managers (62 percent of management proposals were approved as opposed to 18.3 percent of all others). In many cases there was no competition for a company. Outsiders tended to concentrate their attention on the most profitable firms, and thus there was also more competition among proposals, which explains the lower approval rate. In many instances in which management proposals were approved, they were the only bids, and the privatization authorities gave tacit approval to management's strategy of "picking the raisins" (selecting and bidding for the most profitable parts of large companies).[119] Yet managers did not completely dominate the process as in other countries, nor did they dominate among the most profitable firms.

Although it is still too early to tell what the long-term economic effects of the Czech privatization will be, in the short term it has clearly been successful. First, a lot of the worst fears were never realized: there was no run on funds, there was not too much dispersion of ownership (indeed, one could argue that the opposite occurred), and there is no indication that firms privatized by vouchers exhibit perverse behavior. Second, the program transferred billions of dollars of state property into private hands and in the process set up a functioning stock market with the prices established in the voucher trades generally reflecting market values. Third, the program had important effects on politics: more than 75 percent of the eligible population participated, and even if they sold off their shares quickly, they made some profit. Approval ratings of the program were extremely high in the years immediately preceding and following its implementation, a development that contrasts sharply with the experiences of other countries such as Russia, where privatization undermined support for market reforms.[120] In the Czech Republic, the voucher program, which was, not coincidentally, implemented just before the June 1992 parliamentary elections, helped give the ODS and Finance Minister Klaus four years in government with a strong electoral mandate.

## Corporate Governance Issues

Since the completion of the second wave of privatization there has been a consolidation of ownership and control by the largest investment funds and banks that has been christened the third wave of privatization. By the time of the second wave some investment companies controlled several funds that were each tailored to specific kinds of investors: low-income, professionals, or investors with an interest in a particular region. Many observers, including Tomas Jenek, the head of the National Property Fund during the first wave, and now the chairman of the Prague stock exchange, believe that this consolidation has been at the expense of good corporate governance and, equally important, at the expense of the interests of many small shareholders. And as a result of the consolidation a series of major bank failures and government bailouts took place in 1996.[121] The third wave has been referred to as a struggle between the "lights on," western-oriented economists, who wanted to regulate the process, and the "lights off Wild East economists."[122]

There has been some debate over whether the Czech industrial structure is evolving toward the German model of consolidated ownership, with some observers noting that a model closer to the more dispersed ownership and more active shareholder participation, as in the United States, might be more appropriate. In the German or Treuhand model the banks that control the firms they bought out also have control over equity. Thus they have a strong stake in how the company is managed. In the Czech system the banks have de facto control over the investment funds that for the most part dominate the enterprise boards, but they do not have direct equity in the companies. And because no single entity is allowed to have a share of more than 20 percent, none of the funds has a majority stake, which would increase their incentives to improve corporate management and restructure the companies. Thus there is control without ownership and a close relation with the banks, which provide a virtually open line of credit. Because most of the shares in the companies are sold as closed-end funds, there is also no incentive to make the company more marketable or profitable in order to issue new shares. It is significant that most of the profits the funds make come from trading shares (96 percent) rather than from company dividends (4 percent). A recent survey of new enterprise owners found that they have limited interest in improving the management of the firms and much more in consolidating shares.[123] Thus there are few built-in incentives for improving profitability or restructuring inefficient managements.

Some critics have referred to this management structure as a "Czech sandwich" in which owners and management, each organized as a limited liability society, squeeze the company.[124] Two-thirds of Czech companies are undercapitalized and rely on short-term credit, which the banks have a government mandate to extend. There have been scandals in which loans have been made to companies that were empty shells, and the loans were never repaid. Equally important, the management structure also has resulted in very limited corporate restructuring. This in part explains the low level of unemployment. Given the current management and credit structures and limited availability of new capital (one disadvantage of the voucher model is that it did not bring in substantial amounts of new foreign capital), hoarding existing labor and capital is a rational survival strategy for many Czech companies.[125] In the long term, however, the combination of relatively inefficient industries and a collusive corporate ownership structure may deter foreign investors and undermine the competitiveness of Czech exports.

Incentive for reform of the current structure is limited by a principal agent problem. The funds are in a position of being part lender and part owner, so cutting companies' credit is not in their interest. Many of the banks, meanwhile, have shares not only in the funds but in insurance companies that would be liable if massive loan defaults occurred. And the government has been wary of rocking the boat: a major shake-up of firm management, which would undoubtedly entail some bankruptcies and increases in unemployment, would compromise the government politically and cause the country's international investment rating to fall.

What is most ironic, given the original fears that ownership would be too dispersed, is the extent to which the current structure is not benefiting the average shareholder. Because for the most part companies do not issue dividends, and in many cases have means of transferring profits out, some shares are becoming worthless. Small shareholders have the least capacity to protect themselves, and certainly less access to information than do most funds: they are therefore very vulnerable. This means that the people who chose to invest their shares individually rather than go through the funds are likely have the least influence. This group has tended to be the strongest Klaus supporters: middle-class, relatively well educated people who followed the government's advice to do their own investing rather than go into a fund. But the average investor does not understand or have access to information about corporate governance problems and tends to blame his or her own investment decision rather than the system if shares do poorly.[126]

Another criticism is that there are too many publicly traded companies with too little government regulation and too little information for individual investors. There are 1,700 publicly traded companies in the Czech Republic, while France, a country of comparable economic size, has only 400.[127] Investors can invest through the Prague Stock Exchange (PSE) or through the more popular RM system (RMS), which has local offices throughout the country and is geared toward small investors. Although the PSE has all the membership requirements of a typical stock exchange, the RMS is open to anyone for a small commission. But despite the number of public companies and easy access to the stock markets, very few individual investors actually trade their shares. Most either sell or keep them.[128] Approximately 50 percent of participants in the voucher program still have their shares, although lack of publicly available information makes it difficult to provide a precise figure.

Despite the disadvantages of concentrated ownership by the funds, they may have actually improved company performance. A recent study found that companies managed by funds outperform those with dispersed ownership. This is not surprising, given that managers have more influence on the boards of companies with dispersed ownership than those managed by funds. In addition, the price of a fund's share on the market is influenced by the extent of the stakes it has in diverse companies and its management strategies. The market clearly prefers funds that attempt to manage the companies rather than those that are passive board members. The power of funds in managing companies is directly related to the size of their stakes: large funds have an advantage because they can hold large stakes in companies and still diversify their portfolios. These funds also have an advantage in attracting investors: the funds that ran the biggest advertising campaigns were the ones that attracted the most voucher points.[129]

Despite all the criticisms and potential problems, the Czech voucher program was still remarkably successful. It achieved its primary objective of rapidly privatizing the corporate structure: 65 to 90 percent of all assets in the Czech Republic are privately owned; in 1990 about 4.5 percent were privately owned. Meeting this objective was important to proceeding with the market transition. The country has the lowest inflation and unemployment rates in the region and strong political support for the market system, to which the voucher program contributed. Its market has been capitalized at $12 billion and has received $2.7 billion in foreign direct investment since 1990.[130]

That the ownership structure did not remain diverse may not be detrimental to the system. In the United Kingdom, for example, where the "popular capitalism" program increased the number of shareholders from 3 million to 8.5 million in eight years, there was considerable buying out of small shareholders by larger investors, and despite some active participation by small shareholders in annual meetings, most power remains in the hands of major financial institutions. In terms of company performance, promoting competition had a greater effect on improving performance than did the transfer of ownership from public to private hands.[131] Ultimately, vouchers seem better suited to meeting the objective of transfer of ownership than to resolving corporate governance problems. "Voucher privatization may come to be remembered as a better mechanism for mobilizing the necessary popular support to permit a timely transfer of ownership than as a mechanism whose implications for ownership, and consequently for economic performance, are optimal."[132]

Attaining broad-based ownership is challenging; sustaining it is even more so. "One clear lesson emerges from worldwide experience: if participants *can* access their shares and liquidate them, many of them *will*, including pocketing any incentive used to encourage their ownership, a phenomenon common to privatizations in the UK."[133] Although 23 percent of the people in the United Kingdom are shareholders and only 5 percent are in Germany, approximately 50 percent are in the Czech Republic.[134] When considered in this light, the record of the Czech Republic looks good.

## The Politics of the Voucher Program

The voucher program was a main part of Finance Minister and then Prime Minister Klaus's main political message to the Czech public: your future is now in your own hands, and what is necessary in the transition economy is direct access and free entry for private enterprise. Klaus and his administration put a great deal of effort into building support for the program; he traveled to virtually every town in the country to explain the program, and his signature was on every voucher. The aim of the program was, without a doubt, as political as it was economic.[135]

Yet getting a high rate of participation was far from easy, which is not surprising given political and economic conditions in the Czech Republic and the novelty of the market. In polls taken soon after the program was launched, 25 percent of respondents said they would participate, 25 percent said they never would, and 50 percent said they might. Very little happened in the first two months of the program, but millions of people registered in the last month after the entrance of the funds and their aggressive marketing campaign.

Funds hired people ranging from professionals to mothers on maternity leave to market the program and even went into nursing homes to encourage participation. In the end, 75 percent of the eligible population registered, with 30 to 40 percent doing so because of the bandwagon effect.[136] Those who did not register were prevented by severe income constraints (the vouchers cost a week's worth of the average wage, which some people may not have been able to part with) or lack of understanding (people needed at least minimal understanding of the market to participate). There were also those such as the members of the Communist party and some Social Democrats (including the present leader, Milos Zeman) who did not participate for ideological reasons.[137] And of those who participated, it is likely that as many did so for the promise of a short-term profit as for the opportunity to become shareholders.[138] Regardless of the reasons for participating, surveys conducted several years after the program began found that participation, especially continued ownership of shares, was associated with support for economic reform.[139]

Even those that participated but cashed out immediately earned ten times their original investment. This certainly boosted faith in the potential of the market and provided some level of education, even if it was to learn that the shares increased further in value after they were sold. But even the smallest profit—ten weeks of average wage—was not a negligible income transfer at a time when most people had suffered recent drops in income. Few transition governments can claim to have made such a transfer at a difficult economic time, and it would be surprising if it did not have some effects on voting.[140]

That individual shareholders were marginal participants in the program is hardly unique to the Czech Republic: it is not clear that such shareholders are any more active in the United States or Britain, for example. And the 50 percent of Czechs who are still shareholders is a greater proportion than in most countries. Surveys have found that those who kept their shares were much more likely than others to appraise past reform efforts favorably, expect a good future, oppose state intervention in the economy, hold democratic values, and cast votes for the government coalition.[141] The process was clearly important in breaching a political or psychological barrier to reform.[142]

From a political standpoint the voucher program had some valuable elements. It was implemented quickly and yielded rapid results. It was broad and very democratic: everyone could participate. It kept foreigners from dominating the country's businesses and buying up the "national wealth," a common public criticism of privatization programs. It also secured the support of company managers, who felt much less threatened by dispersed public ownership than by a foreign buyout or highly concentrated ownership. Although ownership is more concentrated than expected, managers have maintained more control in the companies where individual investors rather than the banks and funds dominate. And even under such direction, there has been far less restructuring than in foreign companies.[143]

At the same time, as ownership became more concentrated and the profits of some of the biggest shareholders became more evident, public evaluations of privatization became less favorable and perceptions of insider advantage increased: "Not human capital and competence but previous positions, contacts and information or simply belonging to closed networks are what really matters when privatization projects requiring a detailed knowledge of the organization are submitted."[144] In December 1990 about 60 percent of the population agreed that all state firms should be privatized; by January 1993 this had fallen to 50 percent. And while in 1990 almost 60 percent approved of unlimited freedom for foreign firms, by 1993 less than 40 percent approved and by 1996 about 30 percent.[145]

Despite the concentration of ownership, significant interest groups with a stake in privatization were created. This contributed to the irreversibility of economic reform. That, above and beyond the proceeds of privatization, has an inherent value to society. The dismal economic performance and the harsh prices paid by the poor in the many societies in the region where reforms have been stalled or abandoned provide sufficient evidence of the costs of such reversals.[146]

It is also important not to overestimate the effects of market reforms. Many people still do not understand capital markets and stock markets—and here the Czech Republic is really no different from many developed market economies, although a higher percentage of the average citizenry is involved in the stock market. And since the privatization, other concerns have come to dominate the public debate: health care, housing, and transportation (since the transition and curbing of some public services, small towns have lost access to continuous free public transportation, for example).[147]

## Winners and Losers in the Voucher Program

After an initial widespread favorable response, the public has begun to sort out the winners and losers and to evaluate the success of the voucher program. People's perceptions have crystalized along lines of their political inclination or ideology, educational attainment, job prospects, and whether or not they sold shares for immediate profit.

Investors' behavior was determined to a remarkable extent by socioeconomic factors and political inclinations. Although this seems plausible in less equal market societies such as the United States or even Peru (see chapter 3), one would expect less clear delineations in behavior in a society as egalitarian and homogeneous as Czech society in 1992. The Czech Institute of Sociology's Economic Expectations and Attitudes Survey, which has been conducted annually since May 1990 and covers 1,500 respondents older than 18, incorporated questions about shareholder behavior in its 1995 surveys. Fifty-three percent had kept all their shares, and 19 percent had sold all their shares. Twenty-eight percent invested none of their shares in funds in the first wave; in the second wave 39 percent invested in the funds. Fifty-seven percent invested all their shares in funds in the first wave and 46 percent in the second (table 5-6). This decrease reflects the drop in confidence in funds when some did not meet their promises after the first wave. Harvard Fund, for example, which was late in its payments after the first wave, dropped from receiving 500,000 investors to receiving 300,000 in the second wave.[148]

Table 5-6. *Fund Participation and Share Selling, Czech Republic, 1995–96*

| | Percent of voucher points invested in funds | | | Percent of total |
|---|---|---|---|---|
| Shares (percent) | First wave | Second wave | Shares sold (percent) | investors having sold shares |
| Zero | 28 | 39 | None | 53 |
| Less than 50 | 3 | 4 | Less than half | 7 |
| About 50 | 9 | 8 | About half | 16 |
| More than 50 | 3 | 3 | More than half | 5 |
| 100 | 57 | 46 | All | 19 |

Source: Večernik, "Economic Expectations and Attitudes Survey."

Table 5-7. *Investors Selling Shares in Privatized Enterprises, by Party Preference, 1995–96*[a]

Percent

| Question | LEFT-BLOCK | SPR-RSC | CSSD | KDU-CSL | ODA | ODS |
|---|---|---|---|---|---|---|
| *Did you benefit from privatization?* | | | | | | |
| Definitely | 14 | 20 | 16 | 21 | 23 | 27 |
| For the most part | 26 | 35 | 39 | 42 | 46 | 41 |
| Not really | 22 | 13 | 26 | 15 | 17 | 19 |
| Absolutely not | 38 | 32 | 19 | 22 | 14 | 13 |
| *Have you sold off shares in either firms or funds?* | | | | | | |
| Sold none | 39 | 38 | 49 | 59 | 55 | 60 |
| Sold some | 24 | 28 | 30 | 23 | 33 | 27 |

Source: Večernik, "Economic Expectations and Attitudes Survey."

a. ODS—Civic Democratic Party; ODA—Civic Democratic Alliance; KDU-CSL—Christian Democratic Union; CSSD—Czech Social Democratic Party; LEFT-BLOCK—Communist party, Left Block, and Party of the Democratic Left; SPR-RSC—Czechosolvak Party of Republicans.

These percentages shift when party preferences are incorporated (controlling for education): 37 percent of those who voted for the Communists sold all their shares, 21 percent of Social Democrat voters sold all shares, but only 13 percent of ODS supporters sold all their shares (table 5-7). And people's perceptions about how they fared in the privatization also reflected party preferences, income, and education levels, with wealthier, more educated people, who also tended to support ODS, giving much more favorable evaluations of the program. The surveys found that the strongest predictor of a favorable evaluation was education, followed by wealth and then relative youth. For example, although 62.7 percent of those with only an elementary education sold their shares, just 39.3 percent of people with university education did (table 5-8). And far fewer people with university educations invested in funds than did people with less education. Those who held individual shares also tended to be younger than those who bought shares in the funds. Other variables in the subjective evaluations of gain from privatization were social ties and business instincts.[149] Again, these are factors that one would expect in most market societies, but that they are so important in a society as equal as that of the Czech Republic is a bit of a surprise.

Table 5-8. *Investors Selling Shares in Privatized Enterprises, by Education Level, 1995–96*

| | Points passed to IPF | | Percent of total shares sold |
|---|---|---|---|
| Activity | First wave | Second wave | |
| Participation | 81.7 | 81.4 | |
| *Passed or sold the shares* | | | |
| No | 27.5 | 38.7 | 52.8 |
| Less than half | 3.3 | 4.4 | 7.1 |
| About half | 9.5 | 8.3 | 16.2 |
| More than half | 2.9 | 2.8 | 4.7 |
| All | 56.8 | 45.8 | 19.3 |
| *Those saying no, according to education (education category = 100 percent)* | | | |
| Elementary | 13.0 | 15.8 | . . . |
| Vocational | 19.3 | 26.3 | . . . |
| Secondary | 27.1 | 41.0 | . . . |
| University | 38.7 | 53.6 | . . . |

Source: Vecernik, "Economic Expectations and Attitudes Survey."

Opinions about privatization to some extent reflect the same social divisions that explained people's willingness to participate before the program began: 25 percent said that they would never participate, and roughly the same percentage sold off all their shares. Yet the program clearly did have some impact. For example, what is remarkable is not so much that 37 percent of Communists sold their shares, but rather that 63 percent kept at least some. In addition, 40 percent of those who voted for the Communists answered yes or "rather yes" when asked if they benefited from privatization (68 percent of those that voted for the ODS answered this way).[150] It is difficult to imagine 40 percent of Communists in Russia rating the privatization program favorably.[151]

Individual investors tended to be more educated and wealthier, but some of these people put their money in funds because they had neither the time nor the interest to manage their own portfolios or they thought the funds were a better way to invest, although this consideration was tempered by the poor performance of some funds after the first wave. And it is also not clear that individual investors fared better. Many small enterprises that looked good in the beginning later performed poorly. In addition, as many less educated people sold off their shares immediately for a profit, share prices were driven down in some companies. And as was noted earlier, small shareholders have little influence in companies. As a group they are usually minority owners compared with the funds, and where they are majority owners, management dominates company boards. Unlike in the United States and Britain, in the Czech Republic shareholders do not attend annual meetings.

The program had different effects on different income and education groups. For the least wealthy and educated, it was primarily a means to earn a short-term profit. Indeed, the funds, with their promises of immediate profits, encouraged such behavior, particularly among the less educated. In the second wave Expandia Fund, for example, had an explicit strategy aimed at low-income groups, and offered a Kcs 3,000 (US$105) loan with the voucher points as collateral. Most people took the Kcs 2,000 ($70) profit and forfeited the points to the fund. Spotetana Bank, meanwhile, offered a similar, but larger loan of Kcs 10,000 for up to 950,000 people; again many forfeited their shares instead of paying back the loan after one year.[152]

For wealthier and more educated people the program did indeed provide an important learning experience, given that most had never participated in the stock market. People could read the newspapers and see how their investments did in comparison with other companies or with investments in other funds. Since the privatization, 40 percent of the population reads the stock exchange news, which is high by most countries' standards.[153] This group was much more aware of the potential market value of their shares and was far less likely to sell them off for an immediate profit of a few thousand korunas. The drop in support for funds in general, as well as varying levels of support for different funds in the second wave in response to their performance in the first, is significant. Of the 5,977,466 people who participated in the first wave, 4,351,595 went through the funds; of 6,160,503 participants in the second wave, only 3,911,815 went through funds.[154] A lot of attention was also given to the few instant millionaires who emerged from the first wave, which encouraged more people to believe that investing individually might be more profitable.[155]

The funds did better in urban areas, especially Prague, while the banks did better in rural areas where they were already known as local institutions. Investments in funds actually yielded higher returns than share points invested individually. For each voucher point invested, funds received an average return of Kcs 11,250, while individuals received Kcs 8,913.[156] The funds also fared better because they could invest all their vouchers as shares, leaving very few unused points, whereas in each wave about 2,000 people came out of the bidding with points uninvested. "The bidding process was clearly too complicated for some to follow."[157] Still, according to survey research, the feeling of gain from privatization was greater among those who purchased shares individually than among those who bought shares through the funds (although only by a small margin).[158]

With the concentration of share holdings in the third wave, more individual investors have sold off their shares. At least 24 percent of the individual shareholder accounts at the National Property Fund are now empty.[159] And as more and more people sell, overall share prices drop and individual investors fare less well. Clearly, the third wave did not benefit individual investors. It is relevant to note, however, that differences in education levels continue to be a determining factor in who sells shares.

There are various assessments of who won and who lost in the voucher program. One is that it provided an important learning experience for many Czechs, as well as a significant income boost for those who did not participate as active shareholders and sold their shares for a small but quick profit. This result is not much different from experiences with mass-based privatizations in other countries. In both the British and French privatizations, most people sold for short-term profit. In France, for example, until May 1997 the capital gain accumulated disproportionately to wealthier households: only 2 percent of low-income households bought shares, but the proportion among top income groups was 30 percent. In the United Kingdom, popular capitalism was a major part of the 1982 electoral campaign, and the program nearly tripled the number of shareholders by 1987. The government sold shares at reduced prices to encourage the participation of small investors, but as in the Czech Republic, this encouraged larger investors to buy out smaller ones by capitalizing on the discount. Still, shareowners increased from 2 percent to 23 percent of the population.[160]

Other assessments are not as generous. They focus on the extent to which large profits were made by a few and the potential profit that was forfeited by small investors. "In a way, the brilliance of voucher privatization was to provide a distraction for millions of citizens in the early days of the transition, while powerful moneyed interests divided up the economy behind the scenes—always careful to give something to the public through vouchers."[161] Yet the less educated said they were content to receive "at least something." Certainly a minimum profit of ten times the original investment of $35 is not bad by any country's standards and probably raised people's expections of their prospects in the market economy.[162]

What is clear is that those who profited most were those with education, time, and some insider information. What is less clear is how lower-income or less educated groups would have fared had they had better access to information. First, all investments are risks, and one could argue that no one really had information in advance of the share auctions. Thus, those in a better position to take risks, the wealthier and and better educated, had an inherent advantage but not necessarily insider information. As in all market outcomes, such groups tend to have an advantage, but it is not clear what more the government can do to level the playing field. What is surprising, though, given the equality in Czech society, the importance of government transfers in equalizing income, and the very flat income distribution, is the extent to which the typical inequalities in markets applied in the Czech experience.

There were constant allegations about unequal access to information, whether well founded or not.[163] And certainly the marketing campaigns run by some of the funds were designed to take advantage of ignorance and the need for immediate income among some groups. Perhaps more could have been done to educate the average investor about the equity market, as some critics contend.[164] And even to be eligible for immediate profit, one had to have some market understanding and some available cash, particularly in the first wave when the registration fee was worth a week's salary (by the second wave it was only worth half that amount). Yet given the starting point for the government, it is also important to recognize how much was done so quickly.

## Conclusion

Despite the Czech Republic's exceptional economic record and low unemployment in comparison with other transition economies, social welfare concerns have become increasingly important in the political debate in recent years. In part this reflects certain measurable trends: income distribution has become less equal since the transition, although it remains much more equal than in the average OECD country. The incidence of poverty has not increased and may even have decreased, depending on the measure one uses. Yet in political terms perceptions are as important as objective trends, and they have been affected by rising expectations, dwindling postrevolutionary euphoria, and the visibility of large profits made by some of the winners in the transition. Concern about social welfare also reflects continuing economic changes and the increasingly evident need for further business restructuring. The June 1997 austerity measures, for example, are likely to bring social welfare concerns further to the fore of the political agenda. How these issues are resolved will be important to Czech politics in the future and therefore to the course that economic reform takes.

The voucher program has helped shape these perceptions. Without a doubt the initial effects were instrumental in sustaining economic reform. However, as the benefits of the program became more concentrated and winners and losers became apparent, the effects of the program were more mixed. The winners were, on average, wealthier, more educated, and right-leaning than were the losers. Surveys indicate that a tendency to keep shares rather than sell them almost directly mirrored a tendency to support the Klaus government. Among this group of people, it is likely that support for the program and for reform generally remained strong well after the end of the program. Among the group that sold shares, trends are more mixed, and among some, initial support for the program turned into harsh criticism.

The concentration of benefits of the voucher program, coupled with the exposure of instances of corruption or collusion in the banking system, contributed to criticism about increasing inequality and of winners unfairly profiting from reforms. Better regulation of the process might have avoided some of the funds' excesses as they sought to buy up shares and might have controlled the concentration of benefits, which ultimately undermined support for the program.

Some of the same obstacles to the poor's responding to new market incentives in other countries were also evident in establishing the voucher program. Despite very flat income distribution and little poverty, people's response to the program was still very much determined by income and education levels. Access to information was crucial, as it has been in other countries. The need for immediate income also conditioned responses, particularly since the first wave of the program took place when incomes were falling. For the poorest people, an immediate return of 100 percent was more attractive than an unknown return on a longer-term investment. Not surprisingly, the small percentage of eligible adults who did not participate in the program tended to be poor and at the margin of society. Poor people were also more likely to sell their vouchers to funds for a short-term profit, and some funds even tailored advertising campaigns to buy up these shares. This occurrence emphasizes the need for adequate information and public education to ensure broader participation by lower-income people, a challenge generic to most countries. In other cases in this study—education vouchers in Chile, social security reform in Peru, health care reform in Zambia—inadequate information and poor people's limited incomes were also obstacles to their responding to new market incentives.

The difficulties of creating permanent shareholders when there is an option for immediate profit are not unique to the Czech Republic. Indeed, one could argue that an exceptionally large percentage of Czechs held on to their shares, which demonstrated unusual interest in and support for the new market economy. The fact that shareholding corresponds with political support for the Klaus government supports this observation. However, it also suggests that the program might have been more effective at soliciting the participation of those who would have been less skeptical of the voucher program if they had better understood the potential gains from holding on to their shares.

Regardless of its flaws, the voucher program still contributed to the political sustainability of reform and provided a financial benefit to most Czech citizens at a time of economic uncertainty. The program also helped educate a population unaccustomed to markets. It created a significant base of shareholders in a country with a nascent market economy. The program's contribution to equity, however, is far less clear, as is its contribution to better management of formerly state-owned enterprises. Still, the Czech experience with vouchers serves as an important example of the kinds of tools governments can use to improve equity and increase political support for reform, while at the same time increasing the numbers of people with a permanent stake in the market process.

Chapter 6

# Adjustment and Reform of Social Services in Zambia

THIS CHAPTER examines macroeconomic reforms and the introduction of private markets in the provision of public goods in Zambia, one of the poorest countries in Southern Africa and by far the poorest country in this study.[1] Like the other countries, Zambia incorporated a stakeholders approach in its reform efforts. Yet the country's deep poverty and weak administrative capacity limited the potential of the approach more than in any of the others and posed significant equity trade-offs. At the same time, the dysfunctional state of the country's public institutions suggests that the potential gains from improving institutional performance could be much greater—for growth and for poverty reduction—than in most other settings.

In late 1991 Zambia underwent a transition to a democratic regime and at the same time embarked on extensive structural economic reform. The October election of Frederick Chiluba and his Movement for Multiparty Democracy (MMD) brought dramatic political change and open debate for the first time in more than a decade. Democratization seems to have improved the prospects for economic reform. The previous regime of Kenneth Kaunda, like many of the authoritarian regimes in Africa, depended heavily on maintaining patronage-based networks in the public sector, which was hardly conducive to the introduction of economic reform. Democratization increased government accountability through the introduction of political opposition and a free press. Public administration was delegated to technocrats and to the permanent bureaucracy to a much greater extent than in the past, when it was completely subordinate to the interests of the governing party. In addition, at least initially the legitimacy of both the government and its reforms was improved by a more open and inclusive debate about economic policies.[2] At the same time, the interest groups that would typically pose effective opposition to economic reform in most democratic countries, such as unions and those elements of the private sector that depend on state support, remained weak or poorly organized.

Substantial obstacles remain to achieving sustainable economic reform in Zambia, however. Policymakers are severely limited by lack of institutional capacity, fragile political parties, and a weak judiciary. For reform to be sustainable, particularly in the context of regular elections, the institutions responsible for carrying out the necessary policies must be strengthened and the base of support for reform extended to more of civil society.[3] Given the limited resource endowments and administrative capacity in Zambia, as in much of Africa, the challenges are even more formidable than those in most other regions.

This chapter, like the others in this study, focuses on the effects of the stakeholders strategies in market reform. It is not coincidental that these strategies were first used by some of the more successful economic reformers, such as Chile and the Czech Republic, and are now being copied by other reforming countries, including very poor ones such as Zambia. Given the poverty and poor education of the majority in most African societies, the reforms likely to have the most far-reaching effects across all social groups, and therefore the broadest implications for political sustainability and for equity, are those of basic service delivery systems for education and health care. Other reforms discussed in this book, such as changes to social security and voucher privatization, would be unlikely to reach most of the population in Africa. Not coincidentally, countries such as Zambia and Malawi have launched comprehensive attempts to reform social service delivery systems in conjunction with macroeconomic reforms. In part this occurred because these systems had deteriorated to the point that they became major foci of more general public dissatisfaction with prereform political and economic systems. Yet the trend also reflects the democratic reformers' political need to deliver tangible social benefits during difficult stabilization and adjustment efforts. Because of ideological trends and fiscal and administrative realities, most of these reforms have incorporated decentralized service delivery as well as a new reliance on local participation and contribution.

Zambia was selected for this study for several reasons. First, the government began a far-reaching reform of the health care system soon after launching macroeconomic reform, and progress has been remarkable. Health care reform was a focus of the MMD campaign platform and is very much internally driven, although it has strong and coordinated support from donors. The philosophy behind the reforms builds on the government's perceived need to change people's attititudes about public services by incorporating their participation and contribution. The reform has devolved resources and management responsibility to the local and hospital levels and has introduced user fees for most services. An additional factor that makes Zambia interesting is that progress in reforming health care contrasts sharply with the lack of progress in education, where there is no internal leadership for reform, nor is there political momentum for change. The reasons behind this contrast are primarily political, and highlight the difficulties entailed in carrying out reforms of the public sector, as well as how creating new stakeholders can facilitate the process.

The health care reforms have improved supplies of drugs and clean linens in hospitals and health posts and actively involved district and local personnel in the management and delivery of health services. Once the changed incentives and new management structure were introduced, involving myriad local providers and other participants, reform took on a momentum of its own. The reforms have also revitalized morale and vision among personnel in the Ministry of Health, a rare development in public sectors in the developing world. However, the programs have also been victims of weak administrative capacity in the public sector and the underdevelopment of new democratic institutions. Because of perceived political urgency, user fees and prepayment plans were introduced in a haphazard and untimely manner and without adequate guidelines for implementation.

The effects on the use of health services were both harmful and regressive.

The Zambian experience with adjustment and health care reforms demonstrates both the potential the stakeholders approach has to spur institutional reform and its limitations, in particular the adverse effects on equity it can have if it is poorly carried out or inappropriate to the context. The importance of adequate planning, administrative capacity, and government communication in introducing such dramatic changes in the delivery of basic services is clear from Zambia's experience and the experiences of other countries in the study. While both the macroeconomic reform program and the health care reforms may ultimately succeed, the human cost could have been far smaller had reform measures been introduced in a more organized fashion and with adequate guidelines, and had the public been better informed about their rationale and content. The Zambian experience also provides some insights into which stakeholding models are appropriate in a particular context. Where the vast majority of the population is impoverished, exit options based on people's ability to pay or on the development of private alternatives are likely to have regressive effects.[4] Private alternatives, given demand and supply constraints, are likely to serve only upper-income urban groups.[5] Voice options, however, which require at the community level the contribution of time rather than fees, do seem to work in impoverished areas and have a good track record in Zambia, both in health care and in safety net programs.[6] This suggests that they are more appropriate where the poverty ratio is extremely high, or at the least that considerable caution is necessary before introducing cost recovery mechanisms for essential services.

## The Politics of Reform in Zambia

Immediately after its inauguration in 1991, the government of Frederick Chiluba moved to introduce stabilization and adjustment measures. Shortly thereafter it initiated comprehensive reforms in health care. The government had substantial freedom to move rapidly with reform: it was the first freely elected regime in Zambia since the 1960s and thus had a considerable political honeymoon period as well as a strong majority position in the National Assembly.

Progress was, indeed, remarkable. The government succeeded in reducing the budget deficit from 7.4 percent of GDP in 1991 to 2.5 percent in 1993 and then generated a surplus in 1994, with consequent reduction of inflation. Crucial to these achievements were the removal of maize meal subsidies, which before the liberalization had taken up to 17 percent of the government's total budget, and the introduction of fiscal stringency as exercised through the increasingly notorious cash budget.[7] The cash budget is a visible mechanism introduced in early 1993 to enforce the government's public commitment not to spend more than it generated in revenue.[8] In addition to its administrative role, the cash budget also served an important political purpose by providing a convenient and depersonalized focus of blame for unpopular budget cuts. The introduction of the budget, coupled with the 1994 creation of the Zambian Revenue Authority (ZRA), a semiautonomous tax collection agency, had two beneficial effects that were likely to outlive the government. The first was the development of organizational structures to implement consistent budget and revenue collection rules, and the second was the creation of demand for accurate data and reporting from both within and outside the government.[9]

The government's commitment to maintain macroeconomic stability, at least on the surface, seemed strong throughout its first term in office. Although beginning in 1995 there was some slippage in maintaining the cash budget, this was as much due to external shocks and revenue shortfalls as it was to weakening commitment.[10] A test of the government's commitment to the budget was meeting the International Monetary Fund's benchmark of a 20 billion kwacha surplus (roughly US$200 million) by the end of June 1996. With national elections scheduled for November (the MMD retained its majority), the government was facing increasing pressure from members of Parliament who wanted to be seen as doing something for their constituencies.[11] The need to keep external funds flowing (primarily the IMF Enhanced Structural Adjustment Facility), however, was an important force toward resisting this pressure and keeping the fiscal recovery on track.

What the budget did not do, and what remains an obstacle to the progress of many structural reforms, was set priorities among different public expenditures. Given fiscal limitations, the government had to make choices between desperately needed increases in social services versus other expenditures like public sector salaries. Although nominal expenditures on social programs increased from 1992 on, they continued to decline in real terms, and there were arbitrary cuts in public service and capital expenditures.[12] Meanwhile little progress has been made in reducing the size of the civil service, and before the election the government capitulated to higher than expected public sector salary increases. Some structural reforms, such as the liberalization of trade and agricultural marketing, and health care reform, have progressed rapidly. Others, such as privatization of the large parastatal sector and tax and civil service reform, have proceeded far more slowly.

Despite the government's achievements in macroeconomic reform, there have been strong limitations on achieving growth, which is critical to generating sustained political support for reform. The agrarian sector was hit hard by drought in 1992–93, as well as by a poorly managed liberalization of maize marketing.[13] The contraction of consumer demand coupled with the closing of several firms that were unable to compete in the face of rapid trade liberalization led to redundancies and layoffs in Zambia's already small formal sector work force. This has been made worse by a credit squeeze, which stemmed from high real interest rates and a reduction in liquidity as banks invested in high-yielding government treasury bills. The government used the bills to make up for shortfalls in expected revenue flows from external donors. External shocks in early 1995, meanwhile, forced a devaluation of the kwacha and necessitated a government bailout of one of the major banks, Meridian Bank, to prevent failure in the already weak financial sector.[14] Not suprisingly, the response of private investors was lukewarm.[15]

Zambia remains highly dependent on the export of copper, and for the foreseeable future new investments in that sector will be essential to achieving sustained growth.[16] While some privatizations were pushed through early in other sectors, political stalemate over how to proceed with the state-owned copper enterprise, Zambian Consolidated Copper Mines (ZCCM), by far the country's main foreign exchange earner, lasted throughout the government's first term in office. There was litle consensus in the governing party over the course that privatization should take and widespread fears of returning to foreign domination of the economy.[17] The stalemate was finally resolved after the 1996 elections in which the government was returned to power. ZCCM was unbundled to prevent concentration of ownership and then scheduled for sale by the end of 1997. The initial sales have proceeded slowly. The long delay cost Zambia important foreign investment, which could have spurred a desperately needed recovery of growth.

Revenue generation remained very fragile. Despite attempts to increase tax revenue and the very public introduction of the ZRA in 1994, the results were disappointing and the government remained heavily dependent on copper for revenue. With no improvement of revenue collection and fiscal stringency the key to keeping inflation at reasonable levels, social expenditure and public sector reforms remained vulnerable to fluctuations in the macroeconomic balance. The situation was made worse by the increasing pressure for wage increases that public sector workers have placed on the government.[18] This was a Catch 22 of sorts. The lack of revenue made it very difficult for the government to move forward with the plans for civil service reform that were initiated in November 1993 because it could not afford the rather generous redundancy package that it negotiated with the unions.[19]

The situation was much more fragile for most of the population. Approximately 69 percent of Zambians lived below the poverty line in 1997; some estimates were much higher. Although the high poverty ratio is primarily the result of decades of poor policies and skewed incentives under the previous United National Independence Party (UNIP) regime, the effects of adjustment-related fiscal constraints took an additional toll on the poor. Real wages were low and continued to fall. Use of education and health care services declined notably in the 1990s because of their deteriorating quality and the formidable economic difficulties confronting the poor. Basic survival, defined as getting enough to eat each day, was the most cited concern of the majority of Zambians.[20] Household capacity to cope had been eroded by years of poor economic performance, a recent drought, and deteriorating health conditions.[21] The post-1991 economic reforms necessary to reverse decades of misguided macroeconomic management had mixed effects on the poor. The credit squeeze and high unemployment rates were disastrous, as were arbitrary cuts in public services. Yet the development of commercial farming and tourist lodges, for example, gave the rural poor new opportunities for direct employment as well as for local piecework and trading.[22] Sectoral reforms, particularly those in health care, had some good results for the poor in general, but clearly harmful ones for the poorest among them.

This situation had obvious political implications for the government, which could no longer draw support from its postelectoral honeymoon. The MMD was an eclectic coalition united by opposition to the Kaunda government, and included the private sector and much of the union movement. Fairly soon after it came to power, internal rifts weakened its political coherence. In April 1993 several of the key members of Chiluba's original MMD coalition as well as some of the most ardent supporters of reform left the government. Two of them subsequently formed a new political party, the National Party, which served as an alternative for many increasingly disillusioned with the MMD government. The remaining core of Chiluba supporters who are also strong advocates of reform was very small, and there were tensions even in this small group due to credible allegations of corruption among some of its members.[23] Political support was increasingly a concern for the president as the 1996 elections approached, which helps explain the government's backsliding on some adjustment measures, such as a late 1996 public sector wage increase. The slow investment and growth response, meanwhile, raised doubts even among some of the most committed technocrats. "As in Ghana, there is widespread concern in Zambia that the standard policy prescription has harmed agriculture, industry, and employment. To many technocrats, the problem translates into dissatisfaction with the standard framework used to set policy, which does not take into account the real effects of monetary and fiscal contraction or structural constraints to adjustment."[24]

Because democratic liberalization occurred only in 1991, the political system remained underdeveloped. Despite the introduction of considerable political freedom, mechanisms to ensure accountability, transparency, and popular participation remained as limited as they were under the UNIP regime.[25] In contrast to the Kaunda government, which relied heavily on the UNIP party apparatus for organized political support for several decades, the eclectic and transient nature of the MMD coalition was not a party apparatus that could generate sustained political support. This, coupled with the fragmenting of the governing coalition, resulted in Chiluba's relying increasingly on personalities who were capable of delivering political support but were not necessarily committed to reform. A clear example was the appointment of Michael Sata, a controversial personality with no background in social services, as minister of health in early 1994. His appointment to a ministry that was noted within and outside Zambia for its achievements in reform was a puzzle to most observers. Yet because Sata was capable of delivering substantial political support, and at the same time was considered a formidable political opponent, Chiluba may have been pressured to place him in a visible and important position despite the deleterious effects the appointment could have on the health reforms.

On a more positive note, the absence of a dominant party made policy implementation less partisan than it was under UNIP, which monopolized that as well as political decisionmaking.[26] The MMD government had to rely more on the cabinet and on the permanent civil service. However, this reliance and the absence of a strong base of party support made it even more difficult for the government to reduce the size of the public sector, which would have been politically unpopular in any event.

The political effects of fiscal austerity and weak party cohesion were made worse by two discouraging trends. The first was blatant corruption at the cabinet level. By the end of 1994, almost half the original 1991 cabinet members had either resigned or were dismissed due to corruption-related allegations. And because of the nation's new and flourishing free press, corruption was much more a public issue than it would have been under the previous regime. This is compounded in that some prominent members of the government have used intimidation and other heavy-handed tactics to suppress political opposition.[27]

The second trend was the government's failure to publicly address the issues of poverty and the social costs of adustment. Although it managed an effective drought relief program in 1992, and some safety net programs were put in place, the programs were small given the extent of the need. There were members of the government who were concerned about the effects of adjustment policies on the poor and saw the need to deliver benefits beyond the stabilization of inflation.[28] But there were obvious limitations of resources for any safety net effort. Still, the government's failure to effectively *articulate* concern for the plight of the average Zambian contributed to a bad public image. This was no doubt made worse by credible stories of cabinet ministers enriching themselves at the public's expense.

Related to these developments was increasing frustration, particularly in urban areas, with the lack of employment opportunities, a frustration that could form the basis for effective political opposition to the government. Urban poverty is relatively new in Zambia and is due in large part to the high and variable inflation of the 1980s. Only 4 percent of the urban population was poor in the 1970s; 46 percent was poor in the 1990s.[29] Urban areas, meanwhile, have traditionally been much more of a focus for political competition than have rural ones. The participation rate of registered voters, for example, tends to be much higher in urban than in rural areas.[30] The MMD's support was weakest in urban areas, and some MMD members of the National Assembly actually switched districts in urban areas to minimize their chance of losing by-elections. In other urban areas the MMD was dependent on certain personalities who had followings that were much stronger than their support for the party.[31]

Despite the many reports of increasing popular frustration with adjustment policies, there were few, if any, credible political alternatives to Chiluba's MMD government. The National Party was rife with internal squabbles. Even if it develops a more coherent leadership and platform, it is unlikely to diverge far from the reform policies of the MMD. Speculation about a Kaunda comeback, meanwhile, was fueled before the November 1996 elections by several well-attended rallies for the former president. Yet it is unclear how much of this attendance was the result of curiosity or of antigovernment sentiment rather than genuine support, given the extent to which his regime was discredited by 1991. The government, meanwhile, responded to the challenge from Kaunda in a surprisingly defensive manner. It added an amendment to the country's constitution stating that Zambians whose parents are not Zambian born cannot be presidential candidates. This was widely perceived as a challenge to the former president, whose parents were immigrants from Malawi. This sparked a wide debate about the mode of adopting alterations of the constitution, and the opposition called for Constituent Assembly rather than parliamentary ratification. The government also arrested Kaunda twice on charges of holding political rallies without authorization, a law that was, ironically, written under Kaunda's presidency.[32] In June 1996 several bilateral donors responded to Chiluba's undemocratic tactics by withholding aid, a measure that cost the government $350 million worth of annual support.[33]

Perhaps the most prominent sentiment, which dominated in the 1996 national elections, was widespread apathy. In by-elections in Chingole and Mwande in April 1995, roughly 16 percent of eligible voters actually voted, down from 50 percent in 1991.[34] Given the prevailing negative public attitudes about the government, most observers, including those within the MMD, predicted that it would lose the elections. However, it won by relatively large margins in both elections, indicating the extent to which the opposition is as yet unable to present itself as a credible alternative.[35] The apathy favored the MMD in the November 1996 elections.

In the national elections held November 18, 1996, Chiluba and the MMD were able to gain 70 percent of the vote and more than 120 of the 150 parliamentary seats. Yet the victory was tainted by a boycott of the elections by Kaunda and the UNIP party, as well as by extremely high abstention levels. Turnout was only 40 percent of those registered, who in turn accounted for less than 60 percent of those eligible to vote.[36] While this faint approval limited Chiluba's mandate, it was counterbalanced by two forces. The first was the lack of a viable political alternative, because even the challenges from Kaunda and UNIP had marginal appeal for voters. The second was continued, and essential, support for Chiluba's economic program by the major international financial institutions, despite the withdrawal of support from several bilateral donors in response to his undemocratic tactics.

While discontent with the situation was high, there was little if any talk among key economic and political people of returning to UNIP-style policies, as the November elections demonstrated. The political rejection of UNIP in the late 1980s and early 1990s was dramatic, and the major productive sectors—labor unions and the private sector—were strong participants in a movement that had widespread popular support.[37] Because of the adverse effects of the government's command economy policies in the late 1980s, a process of policy learning seems to have occurred.[38] Even strong opponents of the Chiluba government could not offer realistic alternatives to making necessary and difficult adjustments, and most criticisms of the adjustments were directed at the pace and implementation of the measures rather than at their intent. The organized interest groups that posed the most formidable opposition to reform in many countries remained very weak in Zambia. The primary issues for unions, for example, were salaries and survival, not challenging the current macroeconomic strategy. The Zambian Congress of Trade Unions (ZCTU), which enrolls 75 percent of formal sector workers and was among the strongest union federations in Africa a decade ago, saw its power decline dramatically with the economic deterioration of the 1980s. The ZCTU was also in a rather odd position vis-à-vis the government because Chiluba was the president of the federation at the height of its opposition to the Kaunda regime and retains a strong base of support. In addition, in the mid-1990s Zambia adopted the ILO convention, which prohibits the "one industry, one union" clause that ZCTU supported, and the federation became embroiled in debates over how to contend with breakaway unions.[39]

The private sector, meanwhile, most actively represented by the Zambian Association of Chambers of Commerce and Industry (ZACCI), had a much higher profile in the promarket environment of the Chiluba government than it had during the days of UNIP. Zambian business elites are notable for their homogeneity and the smallness of their group, and it is not uncommon for them to resolve problems by directly approaching ministers to whom they have links. Yet because the business community generally supported the direction of the government's policies, it was much more difficult to launch a unified opposition to any one measure. Indeed it was easier for the private sector to pose a unified front in political opposition to Kaunda's antientrepreneurial policies and ultimately to his regime than to oppose particular adjustment policies that would have different effects in each industrial sector.[40] In addition, some of the most prominent members of the MMD government, such as Finance Minister Penza and MP Enoch Kavindale, were closely associated with the private sector. Thus, there was no significant political opposition from the private sector, despite the fate of some industries in the face of liberalization and tight credit.

At the popular level, while there was very little understanding of adjustment or of the overall macroeconomic strategy, there also seemed to be a relatively widespread understanding that the government could no longer provide as much as it did before. This stemmed from the steady and visible deterioration in government services as well as from the administration's rhetoric and the direction of its policies, such as the health care reforms. There was also a visible increase in street trade. Although this was primarily the result of redundant formal sector workers entering the informal sector, it may also reflect an increase in individual initiative and a gradual change in attitudes and expectations about what the government—and indeed the formal sector—could provide.[41] In any event, until there is a significant turnaround in growth and improvement of infrastructure in the delivery of basic public services, the poor are unlikely to benefit very much from reform. Nor, however, are they likely to pose a relevant political challenge to its continuation.

In sum, it seems likely that reform will stumble on in Zambia, although not at the remarkable pace of the early Chiluba years. First, the honeymoon period is over, and while results on the fiscal side were good, disappointing growth undermined the government's confidence, although it did get a brief second wind after the November 1996 elections.[42] Second, the nature of the reforms changed. Although stabilization and fiscal reforms lend themselves to rapid action and concentrated decisionmaking, the structural and institutional reforms that remained on the agenda tend to entail a larger and more diverse number of participants, such as public sector unions, the legislature, and sectoral institutions, and the reforms also require greater implementation capacity. Several attempts at macroeconomic stabilization in the 1980s, as well as initial progress in reforming agriculture and health care, contributed to important policy learning experience in public administration and greater implementation capacity. Yet no equivalent experience has occurred in many of the areas where reforms were pending.[43] While reform of health care progressed at a remarkable pace, for example, equally important reforms in education were not yet even in the policy design phase.

Critically needed progress in privatization, meanwhile, stalled markedly during the government's first term. The government was very involved in the economy: in 1991, parastate enterprises generated 80 percent of GDP. The Zambian Privatization Authority (ZPA) was set up in July 1992 with ambitious plans to privatize 160 enterprises in five years. The process was slowed by the lack of response from private investors, which is limited by the size of the private sector and weak domestic capital markets (a stock exchange was set up only in 1994); by Zambia's remaining a risky investment for foreign investors; and perhaps most importantly by indecision at high levels of government about which industries should be privatized. Government attempts to sell the concept of privatization to the public were weak at best, and there was insufficient political support for the process. Public understanding was also weak, while fears of foreign domination of the economy, which stem from colonial days, remained strong. In addition, many of the top MMD leaders were lukewarm in their support because several had vested interests in the continuation of the rent-seeking apparatus in the parastate enterprises.[44]

The MMD also seemed reluctant to rock the boat—and its comfortable political advantage—over contentious matters such as the privatization of the ZCCM before the 1996 elections, and progress on most reform fronts was extremely slow for more than a year. Yet this also meant that the desperately needed economic growth would come much further down the road, limiting the chances for poverty reduction and improvements in social services in the short term.

Fortunately, progress in privatization picked up after the 1996 elections. As of March 1997, 60 percent of the 280 state-owned enterprises had been privatized, and the ZCCM was scheduled for sale by the end of the year. The head of the ZPA, Victor Chitalu, increasingly gained a reputation as the architect of one of Africa's most far-reaching privatization programs and was even rumored to be a possible successor to Chiluba.[45] Still, the withdrawal of aid by a number of important donors remained a concern for investors and limited the government's budgetary flexibility.

Regardless of central-level political trends and indeed remarkable, however, were the scale and scope of changes in health care provision. Reform was launched early, when political support was still strong, and took on a momentum of its own, in large part due to the groups that acquired a stake in the process through the devolution of resources and responsibility to local levels. Such an action was important to overriding the bureaucratic inertia at the center and to launching reforms quickly, and it was crucial to sustaining them as the government faced increasing political challenges.

## Social Sector Reform: Health Care

Even before the 1991 change of government there was momentum for health care reform. Additional impetus came from the Chiluba government's political need to demonstrate some visible and beneficial social results during difficult macroeconomic adjustments. The state of health care had been an issue in the 1991 campaign, and there was relatively widespread consensus on the need for change. The approach taken was based on the devolution of resources and responsibility to local providers. It also proposed using fees and prepayment plans to create a sense of individual responsibility among users and at the same time empower them by increasing their capacity to demand accountability from providers. The core proposals of this program, particularly a greater community role in financing and admini-

stration of services, was endorsed by several African governments and supported by donors in the so-called Bamako initiative in 1987. Parts of this program, particularly the devolution of
management and financial responsibility to locally appointed
boards, have been adopted in countries ranging from China to
Peru, and in many cases have clearly helped improve public
health services. The CLAS pilot program in Peru, for example,
demonstrates how such an approach can improve quality and
coverage of service and at the same time create new local stakeholders who participate in and benefit from the reform. To some
extent these newly organized stakeholders are able to counterbalance the forces within the public sector bureaucracy opposed to
reform.

Unfortunately, weak implementation capacity and widespread and extreme poverty have limited the potential of the
idea. In many poor countries, decentralization of service provision and community financing initiatives have failed from lack of
supervision and follow-up. In such contexts, "decentralization
requires carefully planned institutional and individual capacity
building efforts at the local level in order to succeed."[46] Zambia
has neither the resources nor the administrative capacity to
launch such an effort on a broad scale. Local capacity also varies
greatly, with little household capacity to respond to changing
health conditions in at least some if not all poor rural areas.[47]
More important, the focus on payment of fees as mechanisms to
increase voice was not particularly appropriate to the Zambian
context. Although the central element of the reform was to increase local participation and management capacity, the untimely introduction of fees dominated public attention and severely limited the ability of the poor to participate.

Despite these obstacles, significant progress was made in devolving management responsibility and resources, which demonstrates how creating local stakeholders can contribute to the irreversibility of reform processes. It also demonstrates how the
devolution of relatively small amounts of resources coupled with
more substantial increases in responsibility can generate local initiative and support for reforms. Yet the difficulties encountered
in creating stakeholders among the poorest groups suggest that
specific provisions for them must be made when initiating such a

program. This is particularly important with essential social services. It may be less necessary or relevant for voucher privatization or social security reforms.

The health system in Zambia had virtually broken down by the early 1990s. Infant mortality had increased from 97 per 1,000 in 1980 to 107 per 1,000 in 1992 and child mortality from 152 per 1,000 in 1978–82 to 191 per 1,000 in 1988–92. Life expectancy decreased from 51 years in 1982 to 45 in 1992.[48] AIDS was and remains a devastating problem. More than 30 percent of mothers in prenatal clinics in Zambia are HIV positive. Before the reforms, drugs were in short supply or not available, many rural health care posts lacked staff as well as supplies, and even the best urban hospitals were short of essentials such as clean linens. Many of the best doctors had left for better conditions and salaries abroad.

Health care reform activities involving a small but qualified team of technocrats had already begun within the Ministry of Health in the late 1980s, and early on received coordinated support from donors. The process was given additional impetus when a think tank for health reform was established that involved the relevant ministry personnel, nongovernment agencies, and prominent members of the opposition to the UNIP government. The UNICEF-sponsored Universal Child Immunizations initiative (UCI) had meanwhile demonstrated considerable untapped potential at the level of the district and health care center and that a modest increase in resources could have far-reaching effects on service delivery.

Because health care had been a prominent issue in the 1991 political campaign, the MMD government had both a strong political mandate for reform and a team in place with momentum, ideas, plans, and pilot programs. Its presence in the ministry and the technical and financial advantages acquired through collaborating with health care experts and with donors were crucial to its being able to override normal bureaucratic opposition to the devolution of power and responsibility from the center to the district and local levels.[49] The extent of public dissatisfaction with service delivery, meanwhile, had also eroded the strength of the bureaucratic opposition. In addition, the donors were unified in support of the program, which contrasts with usual support for independent sectoral projects, a contrast that stems at least in part from the internally driven nature of the reforms.

The strategy was to focus on universal access to a basic package of essential services, decentralization of management, cost recovery, increased accountability in relations between users and providers, and a new role for private providers. In meeting these objectives, reformers faced a basic tension between the need to deliver immediate and visible results, such as improving the supply of drugs and amounts in hospitals, and longer-term structural changes, such as increasing management and administrative capacity at the district and local levels.[50] Despite this tension, as well as administrative and financial constraints, remarkable progress was made on all fronts. There are locally run hospital and health center boards in place, and substantial resources have been devolved to the local level in the form of block grants. Initial attempts to set up insurance and prepayment systems have been made in some areas, and user fees have been widely applied. These fees and their effects have been the most controversial subject in the debate over health care reform, and indeed that debate has distracted public attention and therefore the development of a broader public understanding of the central elements of the program.

There are several reasons for the extensive debate on user fees. They were introduced suddenly, before improvements in quality of service had been achieved and without clear guidelines for exemptions and implementation, a move strongly opposed by the donors supporting the reform, in particular the World Bank, UNICEF, and the United Nations Development Program. The reform team, meanwhile, was in favor of a gradual introduction of the fees. Yet in February 1993 the Ministry of Health overrode these plans and announced the introduction of the fees nationwide. Although *Implementation Guidelines,* which called for the need for providers to explain fees to users *before* charging fees and to make adequate provisions for those who could not pay, were developed by the ministry in 1994, the guidelines were not adequately disseminated to provider institutions, and they had little impact on how fees were actually applied.[51] Thus neither users nor providers were clear about procedures. In a similarly haphazard manner, prepayment schemes were introduced in early 1994 without adequate guidelines.

As of early 1994 these trends could in part be explained by the attempts of the new minister, Michael Sata, to maintain some element of centralized control over the rapidly moving reform, as well as by his political objectives beyond the health sector. There have been various instances of his overriding the decisions of hospital boards, for example. In April 1994 he unilaterally withdrew all charges for drugs, precisely the service most people expressed willingness to pay for and the service most effective in achieving some degree of cost recovery when user fees are imposed. This also made solving one of the main problems in health care services—the lack of a reliable drug supply—even more difficult. And, in early 1995 he unilaterally rescinded recently introduced mortuary fees.[52] This was backsliding from the reform, and was done without consultation of the reform team. The mortuary fees were extremely unpopular, and Sata's move was probably driven by politics, in particular the upcoming elections, rather than by concern for health care reform.[53] The sudden introduction of fees and prepayment programs, meanwhile, was probably driven by the need to deliver rapid and visible results. Health care workers, for example, welcomed the immediate cash inflow and the new availability of drugs and supplies. Local management boards also responded well to new resources.[54]

Although evidence is patchy and contradictory, what is available suggests that the effect of the fees on the use of health care services was disastrous. In poor urban compounds, for example, the number of daily visits to health posts dropped from 30 to 5, and had yet to recover by late 1995. In a hospital in another poor urban area, visits dropped from 100–200 a day to less than 20, but then recovered somewhat. In some other areas where quality improvements clearly accompanied the introduction of fees, attendance remained roughly the same. Evidence also suggests that attendance fell less in areas where income-generating activities were available.[55] Drop-offs were the highest in precisely the services that were supposed to be exempt from fees: prenatal care, immunizations, and treatment of STDs (sexually transmitted diseases).

Because the effects of the introduction of fees were evident, and in response to pressure from donors, the government introduced exemptions for children under age 5, the elderly, and those who were unable to pay. Yet the exemptions policy was poorly publicized and is not well understood by users, particularly the poor. Implementation of the policy also varied among hospitals, districts, and health centers. Fee levels are highly variable, as is the collection process. It seems that at least in some small rural posts, patients are treated first and asked to pay later. At least there is more flexibility in the requirements for payment in most rural health posts.[56] In many larger urban centers, patients are turned away by untrained screening personnel if they are unable to pay, well before they see anyone with medical training. And in poor urban and rural areas, many poor stopped going to the health centers once fees were introduced. They are usually unaware of the exemptions policy and have assumed they would have to pay and still would receive poor service and no drugs. In contrast, there were also many instances cited in which people noted visible improvements and the availability of drugs in health centers. They also demonstrated an increased willingness to demand better service because they had to pay for it. Indeed, those health institutions that maintain a steady supply of drugs have not experienced a drop in patient attendance.[57] While a systematic evaluation of the effects of the fees has not been conducted, evidence indicates that the effects have been highly regressive.

User fees and other cost recovery mechanisms, if properly carried out, can do several important things. In the first place, they help to specify the contract between user and provider. If users understand what the contract is, and are actually contributors to it, they are more likely to demand accountability. Setting prices for health services also helps rationalize their provision and is a means to rationalize use of different services, for example, by encouraging screening at local health posts before hospital visits.[58] Yet the ability of fees to perform these actions is far more limited if they do not actually cover costs or are set nominally or arbitrarily, as has occurred in Zambia. Given the low average per capita incomes in Africa, and certainly in Zambia, community-based prepayment insurance plans may be more effective mechanisms than fees. Some prepayment mechanisms are in place in Zambia. But they were implemented ad hoc by the up-

per echelons of the ministry, despite the existence of a comprehensive financing plan within the ministry's own reform unit as
well as a pilot plan for financing health for the indigent through
the public welfare assistance system.[59]

User fees seem to affect the use of health care services differently, depending on income group. Although recent studies describe only marginal decreases in the use of services when quality
improves, the conclusion is primarily based on evaluations of
people's willingness to pay rather than on a systematic evaluation of the use of services by households and income level. The
same study notes significant drops in use when fees are introduced without improvements in quality.[60] These results do not
distinguish among users, and it is possible that the poorest reduce their use because they simply cannot afford the fees, regardless of the quality improvements (this is certainly the case in
Zambia), while the still poor but slightly less poor may increase
their use when quality improves.[61] Other studies suggest that equity is a serious concern in carrying out cost recovery programs,
particularly for rural areas. In addition to generally higher poverty ratios in these areas, the availability of cash fluctuates sea-
sonally, so that use of health facilities fluctuates accordingly once
charges are introduced. This is particularly evident where cost recovery is based on payment per visit, as in Zambia.[62] Evidence
from an extensive study in Chiwana indicates that although some
poor are willing to pay for improvements in quality, others are
just not able to, and critical health decisions are made on the basis
of a difference in 400 kwacha, less than 50 U.S. cents.[63] In addition, in some rural areas there is a great deal of resentment at having to pay fees to use facilities that the community had spent both
time and resources to maintain. Another concern for rural communities is that they have to pay what is for them a tremendous
amount for transport to the hospital (up to 6,000 kwacha), so with
the introduction of fees many believed that they had gone from
"paying once to paying twice."[64]

The government's rationale for the fees was as much ideological as fiscal, particularly since the fees are far too low to cover
a significant part of costs. In most countries in Africa, health posts
are able to generate less than 3 percent of health care funding
from fees. One of the few successful experiences with cost recov-

ery from fees has been in parts of China. There, profits are set high on drug sales and low on admissions and consultations; recovery rates have reached approximately 80 percent.[65] The opposite approach was taken in Zambia: fees were removed from drugs and maintained on consultations.

The Chiluba government says that it wants to change people's attitudes about free government services and encourage them to take more responsibility for their own fate. Despite the existence of guidelines produced by senior advisors and officials in the Ministry of Health, which called for caution in applying fees, "these concerns appear to have been overtaken by policy decisions at the top, stemming in part, perhaps, from the need for a 'big push' to get the bureaucracy moving, and in part from more political considerations—the desire to make an impact with the principle 'everyone should contribute.'"[66] The latter idea was intended to break the cycle of poor quality care and user passivity sometimes known as the "dependency syndrome."[67] This is an understandable objective in a country where such dependence has been generated by decades of patronism and free universal delivery of most social services.

Yet the introduction of cost recovery policies in a country where 70 percent of the population is living at the subsistence level was not necessarily sound conceptually and, even worse, was carried out very haphazardly. In addition, and equally damaging, the poor record of user fees and the predominance of the cost recovery issue in the health care debate has the potential to undermine the substantial achievements in care and distract attention from the challenges that remain.

There are measurable indicators of improvements in health care provision. Management boards are operating in most hospitals. District responsibility for the management of health services was increased. Management training, along with a focus on primary health care, was extended to district-level staff. User fees enabled hospitals to put a bonus system in place, which helps raise the otherwise meager salaries of health workers. Senior health workers, meanwhile, cite their ability to make decisions locally, and to set priorities and allocate newly available revenue to those priorities, as the most important change.[68] The incidence of cholera fell to 10 percent of the levels of previous years. Gender issues and AIDS awareness were addressed for the first time, but the examination remained in the initial stages and political will in the capital to address these matters was woefully inadequate.

Although there is still a great deal of variability, local management boards are operating in most districts, and progress has been made in getting block grants to the districts.[69] Observers cite the importance of the increased drug supplies and other supplies to the users of health care services. Some users do not link the improvements with the fees that they pay, while others pay fees and expect better service.[70] One survey found that people are more willing to pay fees once their rationale was explained. For example, when people have to pay for drugs they will complete the course of the prescription (for antimalarials, for example), when previously they would throw away whatever was left over as soon as they felt better. The staff in a Chiwana health post complained that people were much more demanding now that they paid for services. It is also telling of the value placed on curative rather than preventive care that most people are more willing to pay for drugs (which was occurring before the fees were introduced) than they are for consultations.[71] This supports the view that fees are more effective and do less to deter use if they are presented as payment for an entire package of care or limited to drugs, rather than levied on individual consultations.

Another important development is that the government focused first on improving the operations of small clinics instead of the large hospitals in order to get the referral system into operation. The fees at clinics are lower than those at hospitals, which has encouraged more use of the clinics. In addition, the drug supply at the clinics, provided by donors, is more steady and reliable than at the hospitals, which is provided by the government.[72]

Expenditure trends also demonstrate the government's commitment to health care reform. In 1994, expenditures of $12 per capita from donors and $7 per capita from the government were at least in theory sufficient to cover the costs of the basic package of care advocated by the Bamako initiative. Public expenditure on the health sector as a whole rose from an average of 7 percent in the 1980s to a budgeted figure of 13 percent in 1994, with nearly 20 percent of this allocated to the new district boards and

9 percent for drugs.[73] Although the amount allocated to health care does not necessarily translate into efficient use or guarantee universal access to the basic package, attaining realistic expenditure levels is important.

Despite significant achievements, major challenges remain in reforming the health care in Zambia. In particular, policies relating to personnel, drugs and supplies, and private sector participation still need review. And more emphasis needs to be placed on the core activities of the basic package: treatment of malaria, HIV, and prevention of maternal mortality. One constraint is that the returns on investments in these activities are long term, and the government was under pressure to demonstrate visible results in the short term. The implementation of reforms, meanwhile, still must rely on a public administration with extremely limited technical and financial capacity and a very centralized tradition. Decentralization of government, which has obvious implications for the decentralization of health care services, lagged far behind the health care reforms. District development committees, which coordinate the activities of district governments and the health management boards, were legalized in January 1995 and began to operate later that year.[74]

Most important, however, in light of the difficulty of launching public sector reforms in almost any country, is the seemingly irreversible momentum that the reform implementation itself generated. The incentives it has given to local professionals and practitioners, for example, more than counterbalance any opposition to reform from central bureaucrats. The national and international attention the reform brought to the Ministry of Health helped revitalize public administration. And the devolution of management responsibility to communities and local health care centers, despite problems and variability in implementation, is nothing short of a revolution in social service delivery. Given the poor record that most countries have in changing the way their public sectors, particularly their social services, operate, the Zambian experience with health care reform provides a wealth of valuable lessons. Not least of these is the local and participatory nature of the reform, which created new stakeholders. Once the process was launched, it became to a large extent irreversible, even in the face of centrally led attempts to reestablish control.

Yet the experience also illustrates the limited feasibility of creating stakeholders through cost recovery in the context of very high poverty rates. It also shows the importance of good government communication, and therefore public understanding, of the reform. In addition, the rapid pace at which health care reforms were introduced suggests the importance of initiating such reforms when political support is strong, early in the government's mandate and in conjunction with macroeconomic reforms rather than after their completion. The timing in Zambia was critical: public dissatisfaction with the previous system was at its height, and therefore there was strong receptivity to change, which limited the significance of normal bureaucratic opposition.

## Social Sector Reform: Education

At the same time that changes in health care have progressed at a record pace, almost no progress has been made in reforming the education system. Statistics in education are as dismal as they were in health. One-third of the adult population is illiterate, and only 44 percent of all Zambian children attend school.[75] An obvious question is one of political economy: why was one sector a priority and not the other? The first explanation is sheer visibility. Significant numbers of Zambians were dying because of the breakdown of the health care system. The longer-term effects of deteriorating educational attainment were much less visible and were distributed more unevenly than were the health problems. The map of poverty, female-headed households, and high illiteracy rates coincided; the deterioration in health had a more uniform impact across social groups. It was not limited to rural health care posts or poor urban compounds. The University Teaching Hospital (UTH), for example, the main teaching hospital in Zambia, had suffered dramatic declines in the quality of its care and was short of supplies, essential drugs, and staff. AIDS, meanwhile, was affecting all social groups. These developments created a more broadly based consensus for change and translated more easily into a political issue. Reform of the health care system became an electoral issue that had resonance and urgency across social groups, while education reform did not. The diver-

gent political priorities are also reflected in expenditure allocations. From 1984 to 1992, health care expenditures did not fall as
much as those for education, and indeed, had health care expenditures been allocated more efficiently, they would have been far
closer to sufficient levels than education expenditures would
have been.[76]

In contrast to health spending, in education, where reform
lags far behind, expenditure levels remain unrealistically low.
Total public spending on education has not returned to its 1980s
average of 13 percent of the budget, and stood at 7.9 to 10.8 percent from 1986 to 1994. At 2.3 percent of GNP in 1993, this is low
even by regional standards.[77] The government may recognize
that without basic reforms in education, increasing expenditures
is unlikely to translate into any kind of benefit for the poor.

The allocation of expenditures is as important as their overall
levels in achieving better service provision in both health care
and education. In Latin America, for example, Venezuela spends
an average amount per capita on education that is twice that of
neighboring Costa Rica, and four times that of Argentina, Chile,
or Jamaica. Yet illiteracy, dropout, and enrollment rates are
among the worst in the region. One reason is that Venezuela
spends more than half its education budget on higher education,
and 90 percent of the ministry's operating budget goes to personnel costs.[78] And while Zambia's education expenditures, at
2.3 percent of GNP, are low, several countries in Asia with much
better education indicators spent a comparable percentage of GNP
while doing so. Sri Lanka spent 2.8 percent of GNP in 1980, while
the rate in Korea went from 2.0 percent to 3.6 percent from 1960 to
1980, and that of Singapore from 2.8 percent to 3.4 percent.[79]

Health care expenditures also exceeded those for education
because of the relative political weights of the users of public
education services. In health care the introduction of fees was a
significant departure from previous practice. In education de
facto fees have been in place for years (for uniforms, books, and
so forth), but the quality of education has declined dramatically.
Impoverished families, particularly rural ones, are far less likely
to send their children to school as the cost increases and the returns diminish. The decline in enrollment was greatest among
the rural poor, girls in particular, who are not particularly organ-

ized or relevant in political terms. Wealthier urban groups, meanwhile, who are much more likely to be politically organized, have an exit option not available to the rural poor, and for the most part send their children to private schools. Not surprisingly, "the distribution of private schools is closely related to the disparities in urbanization and in economic influence."[80]

The difference in attention paid to health care and education has also stemmed from dynamics within the ministries. In the Health Ministry there was a small but active team of technocrats with experience and a vision of reform. This provided an internal drive that could generate donor support and take advantage of political dynamics after the MMD was elected. There was no comparable team within the Education Ministry. It is suggestive that the turnover of education ministers was higher than the turnover of health ministers during the first MMD government.

The contrasting records also result from political priorities, both outside and inside the sectors. At independence the percentage of Zambians with higher education or technical training was very low relative to that in other African countries. Thus the government strongly emphasized education in general and higher education in particular. The government's involvement, coupled with the philosophy of the one-party state, resulted in a more complete elimination of private and nongovernment education efforts than occurred in health care. The emphasis on higher education, meanwhile, created expenditure allocations that disproportionately favored university over basic levels of education. In addition, formal training in fields such as philosophy were given more emphasis than acquiring technical skills. Not only did this result in training that was inappropriate to the realities of most Zambians, but it also perpetuated a very elitist view of education.

This bias has also resulted in very rigid and not necessarily relevant rules, such as school uniform requirements in places where the cost of the uniforms precludes many families' sending their children to school. Although meeting school fees is a problem for many families, the primary constraint cited by many teachers and parents is the lack of places. Supporting this observation is the great variability in the stringency with which school fees are enforced by headmasters in rural areas, with some villages waiving fees during difficult economic times or for particular families.[81] Despite this, many rural families are unable to enroll their children in schools that are within any sort of reasonable distance. Thus many rural poor do not perceive education as relevant or critical to their children's needs and future and are far less willing, even if they are able, to incur the expenses necessary to send children, especially girls, to school.[82]

As the economy deteriorated and resources were cut in the 1980s, the primary schools suffered disproportionately. This would come as no surprise in most countries because primary school parents and teachers tend to be far less organized and vocal than university students and professors. Yet the extent of the disparities is notable: the government spends 166 times more per university student than it does per primary student, and the grants that university students receive are often more than the median wage they will be able to earn upon graduating. In addition, although 90 to 95 percent of expenditures on primary education go to salaries, primary school teachers' salaries are still considered too low to motivate them. Thus the quality of education has deteriorated and enrollments have declined: primary school enrollment was 96 percent in 1985 but 77 percent in 1994. Overall expenditures, meanwhile, are extremely low, even by regional standards.[83]

There was some vision of reform in the Education Ministry, but it was far from the implementation stage. The main focuses for reform of the system, to the extent that they have been articulated, are access, equity, and relevance. The problem of access to education is cited most by parents.[84] There are equity implications of both income and gender, with girls in poor families having the lowest enrollment rates and performance indicators. Related to gender concerns is public education about HIV, which until now has been a social taboo of sorts. Yet the extent and severity of HIV incidence is dictating the need for new kinds of action, something that the ministry is beginning to recognize. And high dropout rates indicate a problem with the relevance of education.

The MMD manifesto called for the decentralization of education and the legalization of private schools. Within the Ministry of Education, there also seemed to be a commitment to decentralized management, liberalization of service provision, and cost sharing as guiding principles. Yet there was a strong fear of moving too fast and encountering some of the problems faced by the Health Ministry. Health care reform was followed closely by the key personnel in education, and they noted the health team's failure to fully explain and communicate its policies. The Education Ministry personnel stated that as a result they were moving much more slowly and were taking care to build consensus among teachers' unions and district-level officers. They proposed to have public discussions of the proposed policies and eventually dissemination of information from teachers and heads of schools to parents.

Some caution and learning from the mistakes of others is obviously sensible. Yet in health care reform, embarking on the process—particularly, devolving responsibility to levels beyond the central ministry—was crucial to establishing momentum for change. The momentum is often difficult to establish, but once in place is difficult to reverse because so many groups are involved at the local levels and in the hospitals that decisions at the political center are likely to have a far more diffuse impact than they would otherwise. In education, reform is likely to occur slowly, because there does not seem to be the same commitment to embark fully on reform that there was in health care. Although there is a pilot decentralization program in the Copper Belt, and district officers have been informed about proposals for a broader decentralization of management, little progress has been made toward actually devolving responsibility. The improvements that have been made have concentrated on visible rather than systemic change, primarily providing desks in schools.[85] Yet in the absence of qualified teachers and sufficient places in schools, such improvements have little effect.

There are also some constraints to decentralization. In the absence of private school options, for example, local PTAs, which often reflect community social stratification, will take on a decisionmaking monopoly of sorts.[86] There may be no solution to this in the foreseeable future, but existing local hierarchies and inequities could be perpetuated and even reinforced by the devolution of authority. This was certainly a major issue in the debate over decentralization of education in Peru.

There was some political pressure to "do something" before the 1996 elections. UNICEF, for example, attempted to make reform of the education system an issue in the elections. Yet this pressure was short-lived, and the government, once reelected, was preoccupied with budget shortfalls resulting from funding support withheld by donors. Because its record on education was already weak, the government was likely to attempt to avoid the issue altogether, an outcome also similar to that in Peru. This reinforces the importance of initiating reform when the government's political momentum is strong. When and how a broader reform effort will be initiated remains to be seen.

## Communication

One very clear lesson that emerges from reform efforts in Zambia, both at the macroeconomic and sectoral levels, is the importance of good government communication. A primary criticism of many observers is the government's failure to communicate, "even when they do things right." After its initial election the government made some efforts to reach the public, as in the December 1991 liberalization of maize meal prices or the efforts of particular cabinet members such as Dipak Patel and Guy Scott to explain policies, but this was short-lived.[87] Failure to express any concern about the social costs of adjustment was especially the subject of widespread criticism. Experience demonstrates that the articulation of those concerns, even if it is not followed by the adoption of ideal policies, does have an effect on the public's perception of the government and of reform. Better public understanding of particular policies often increases their feasibility and promotes implementation. In Zambia, public understanding of reform in general and of social service issues in particular is very weak. For example, one observer noted that if the public understood the extent of corruption in ZIMCO (Zambia Industrial and Mining Corporation, a large state holding company), there would be no opposition to its privatization.[88] In health care reform, public education is potentially important in maintaining the technical quality of public and private providers and, perhaps more important, in increasing consumer demand for preventive rather than curative care.[89] Community-level communication, meanwhile, has been cited as an important factor in helping the rural poor understand and participate in the liberalization of maize marketing, since they had no experience with a free market in agriculture.[90] More generally, as long as public understanding of macroeconomic and sectoral reform is very limited, any government's capacity to generate sustainable support for the program will also be limited.

In health care Katele Kalumba, one of the leaders of the reform team and now deputy minister of health, made an effort early in the first Chiluba government to sell the need for reform through activities that included a Saturday morning phone-in program about HIV. Undoubtedly these efforts helped make health care a focus of the government's mandate. Yet communication was not incorporated into the implementation of the reforms, and some of the more unfortunate results are the direct result of lack of government communication. User fees were introduced without sufficient information and guidelines for providers. Nor did the government make any effort to explain to users that the fees were a means to improve quality of service. Equally damaging was the failure to adequately publicize the exemptions policy. As a result, those targeted for exemption, such as female-headed, low-income households in rural areas, remain uninformed and still refrain from using health services. The lack of clear communication about the fees has resulted in a great deal of variability in the actual charging of fees and exemptions policies across hospitals, districts, and regions. A community public education or relations effort, similar to that which occurred with maize liberalization, will be essential to reducing these discrepancies and ultimately to the success of the program.

The government's failure to educate the public has meant that debate has focused primarily on fees and not on the objectives and more positive elements of health care reform such as decentralization of service provision and improvements in quality and the availability of supplies. And although the government seemed to recognize the need to improve communication with the public, in part as a response to pressure from foreign advisors, its efforts were limited to newspapers and radio, which have a very limited audience, particularly among the rural

poor.[91] Involving local NGOs, for example, in the public education campaign would probably have been more effective. At a
more general policy level, the government made one attempt to
improve public understanding of the reforms by setting up a
Council of Economic Advisors in late 1993 through which ministers could explain policy measures. Yet its reach does not extend
beyond a small group of urban elites.[92]

The government's failure to communicate effectively stems
from, first, a reluctance to spark debate about its policies: both before and after the 1996 elections it had sufficient political strength
and control of the legislature to carry out most policies without
building a broad consensus. Second, the failure results from a
sheer lack of capacity: the number of skilled technocrats is limited, and their skills are in demand in all aspects of policy work.
In general the problems posed by a lack of adequate communication seem to surface after policies are put into practice and thus
are not seen as a priority. There is a lack of experience with both
reform and democratic government. It is no surprise that inadequate government communication also has compromised policy
reforms in the transition economies in eastern Europe and the
former Soviet Union. There the importance of educating the public about the market and reform has only recently been recognized by some policymakers as well as some advisors in the international financial institutions.[93] In Zambia, improving
government communication with the public could go a long way
toward correcting some of the mistakes made in health care reform, particularly by easing access to services by large numbers
of people currently excluded by ignorance about fees and exemptions. More generally, better communication and ultimately public understanding of market-oriented changes will be crucial to
building a broad and more sustainable base of support for reform.

## Decentralization and Local Capacity

Another matter important to the success of both macroeconomic and social service reforms in Zambia is the capacity of
local communities to carry out their new responsibilities. There

are several ways of supporting community organization and self-help initiatives, and they have had varied results. A recent empirical study, as well as my extensive interviewing, suggest that household coping capacity and community organizational capacity are very weak.[94] Yet some programs, particularly the World Bank's Social Recovery Project, have been successful in promoting infrastructure rehabilitation based on different forms of community contribution (usually cash in urban areas and labor in rural ones). The SRP has found that communities are equally likely to mobilize for health and education projects, although the communities that organize around local primary schools tend to be smaller and more closely knit than those surrounding health posts, which serve larger areas than do schools. Now, with several years of experience, the program is attempting to provide much more tangible assistance and training for district and community capacity building while maintaining roughly the same number of projects. The SRP is trying to coordinate more closely with the line ministries, particularly at the district levels. The objective is to get the districts involved in activities that are currently the responsibility of the SRP, such as monitoring, and thus develop their capacity to take them over once the projects are finished.

At the same time, the program continues to face difficulties in reaching the poorest and most remote communities, which are the most expensive to reach and are the least likely to present viable project proposals.[95] These are also the communities and households likely to have the weakest capacity to cope with challenges to their economic or physical well-being. This suggests that any reform effort that is based on the creation of stakeholders will probably have difficulty succeeding in a systematic manner among the poorest groups, at least in the short term.

The experience of the only government program for the incapacitated poor, the Public Welfare Assistance Scheme (PWAS), is illustrative. The program relies on communities to identify those who are unable to help themselves and should receive in-kind assistance. Although this is attractive in theory, in practice the effectiveness of the safety net program depends very much on the quality of the local PWAS committee, which varies among communities. In some there is a clear awareness of the different situations of households and an ability to carry out programs by involving people of different capacities. In others, however, there is less awareness and cohesion, and the poorest households may be left out completely.[96]

In addition to a limited capacity to reach out to the poorest, there are also political constraints. Evidence from various countries shows that when programs are politicized, they tend to undermine independent community initiative and capacity to participate in programs.[97] For example, the government's Food for Work Program (FFW) was an effective drought relief effort, but was extended beyond the duration of the crisis and has since evolved as a handout program with political objectives. When the program operated as a crisis relief effort outside the normal public administration, it was cited by many observers as exceptionally effective, particularly given the financial and administrative difficulties involved.[98] Later the FFW became a regular government program directed through permanent administrative channels. A recent evaluation concluded, "political interference was evident in most places we visited, particularly with Ward Chairmen having an undue influence on allocation of relief."[99]

At the same time, the FFW was carried out with virtually no targeting criteria or monitoring, so that rather than providing effective food security for the poorest, it served as a general and haphazard food subsidy. The program was run according to "political equity goals," that is, the same amount of food was distributed per district, regardless of differences in population, and it rarely reached the most remote communities. And the government often failed to deliver the programmed amount, which eroded the program's and the government's credibility.[100] In many communities where the FFW was made available, people were no longer willing to contribute labor voluntarily to SRP projects.[101] The effects that such handouts have on autonomous coping strategies are evident and suggest that a focus on capacity building and the creation of genuine stakeholders is a better investment, even if there are drawbacks in terms of speed, scale, and reaching the very poorest.

NGOs in Zambia vary in their administrative capacity and quality and depend heavily on external support. The lack of a tradition of cooperation between government and these organizations remains evident. "The government and NGOs are not generally cooperating or collaborating in the social safety net sector. The government wishes to control NGOs whilst NGOs remain independent and somewhat condescending about the ability of the civil service to perform."[102] While this statement is by no means intended to discount the importance of the participation of such groups, it does point to the need to develop local capacity and establish ties with relevant local organizations in conjunction with the devolution of responsibility for service provision, particularly if an objective is to raise community members' stake in the process.

A recent assessment of community-based programs noted the factors that eroded community organization and those that promoted it. Among the former were that some community members were earning money in a project in which the rest were participating voluntarily; coercion from a chief or school principal threatened to withdraw services from community members who do not participate in projects; Food for Work created the expectations that payments would always be made for community work; some community members were too busy working in income-earning activities to participate in programs; and communities resented having to pay fees to use facilities that they had contributed to building. The factors that promoted organization were the participation of capable and skilled leaders; adequate information flows; an urgently felt shared community need, such as an inadequate water supply; a relatively high level of literacy; and homogeneity among community members.[103] This assessment suggests both the potential and the limitations of participatory or stakeholders strategies in providing effective safety nets or delivering basic services. It also has implications for the equity effects of reform of service provision based on the creation of stakeholders. Although such a strategy can generate important self-help initiatives among many poor, it is not easily able to overcome the barriers that face the poorest or least cohesive communities, which have the most to gain from better social services. It also demonstrates that in certain contexts the introduction of fees can actually erode ownership. And it emphasizes the importance of information flows and communication in carrying out such a program.

Finally, a note of caution about decentralization in general in Zambia. Although decentralization in theory improves service provision, in practice it can have serious drawbacks. One criticism of the local health boards, for example, is that they have sometimes preempted existing grassroots organizations, but at the same time they are dependent on directives from the center in a way that the groups they displaced were not. Another concern is that in many villages society is still organized around the chiefs and headmen, and many programs rely on their traditional role in making allocative and other decisions. Disrupting this structure could easily compromise any program that relies on community participation, but countenancing it does demonstrate how decentralization can perpetuate local hierarchies and inequities. There is no obvious solution to these tensions, but one must pay attention to the limits of decentralization and participatory-based strategies as well as to their potential advantages.

## Conclusion

It seems that macroeconomic reform in Zambia will continue, but most likely at a slower pace than in the early Chiluba years. Although the MMD dominated the 1996 elections, in large part due to the absence of a credible challenge from the opposition, that does not discount the possibility that a populist candidate might effectively exploit latent popular discontent with declining living standards, particularly in urban areas. The high proportion of abstentions in the election no doubt reflects significant popular discontent. Still, the MMD's dominance of the executive and legislative branches was likely to make carrying out reforms, particularly second-stage reforms such as privatization and civil service and sectoral reforms, quite feasible, as the increased pace of privatization after the 1996 election suggests. This pace also suggests that the most opportune time to initiate sectoral or institutional reforms is early in an administration, when political support is strong. Once such programs are begun, they may take on a momentum of their own that can override central-level political trends. This is particularly true if the reforms have created new stakeholders at the local or sectoral level, as occurred in the health reforms and may well occur with privatization.

Reforms in the provision of social services are also likely to continue, particularly in the health care system. Health care reform seems to have a momentum of its own that has already survived attempts by one minister of health to jeopardize the process and has maintained the strong support of donors. Reform of the education system is likely to follow, but at a much slower pace. The implementation of reforms across sectors, meanwhile, has been set back because of inadequate administrative capacity, particularly by poor communication with potential beneficiaries. This is a simple and inexpensive policy mistake to correct, and at least in health care reform the government seems to have recognized the necessity of clear communication. It is less evident that the government will extend its efforts beyond health care reform or reach out out to the many Zambians that do not have access to newspapers or television. This is where the international financial institutions might play a role in stressing the importance of adequate communication in building public consensus for reform, in particular in relaying the experiences of other countries. The importance of public communication and marketing of reforms stands out in the successful voucher privatization in the Czech Republic and pension reform in Chile, for example.

Perhaps the most important lesson from the Zambian experience is that the creation of stakeholders can give momentum to reform and indeed make it virtually irreversible. For all its flaws, the progress made in reforming health care provision is notable and would be difficult to reverse. The many participants that have been given responsibility for management and resources are unlikely to give that responsibility back. At the same time, having this power means that local providers and organizations are far less vulnerable to directives from the center. The effects of the stakeholders approach in health care reform suggest that privatization might be strengthened by some attempt to create a broader base of stakeholders, as was done in the Czech Republic and is currently being attempted in Peru and Bolivia. The potential of such a strategy would be limited in Zambia, however, because of the extreme poverty of the average citizen. The Zambian experience also demonstrates that the success of such approaches depends on a willingness at the central level to devolve responsibility and resources. Such a willingness existed for health care reform, but was lacking for education reform, resulting in little progress, an outcome similar to the experience with education reform in Peru.

Finally, Zambia's experience vividly demonstrates the potential limitations of a stakeholders approach, particularly if methods are used that are inappropriate to the sector and the context. The introduction of cost recovery mechanisms without adequate guidelines for putting them into practice and before any improvements in the quality of service, and most important, in a context of widespread and severe impoverishment, threatened to damage equity and severely compromise the overall reform. Stronger focus on voice options, such as the local management boards that have begun to operate, seems more appropriate than an exit option that relies on fees or the provision of private alternatives and is likely to exclude significant numbers of the poor.[104] Yet even voice strategies face constraints in reaching the poorest groups in a country as poor as Zambia. And it is precisely these groups that are most in need of basic social services.

The incorporation of market incentives and participatory strategies can improve the performance of public institutions in the delivery of essential social services, spurring a reform process integral to reducing poverty and achieving long-term economic growth. The returns to making such improvements are particularly great in countries such as Zambia, where institutional capacity is extremely weak. Yet there are trade-offs, and the effects on equity are not always positive. Where possible, attempts to create stakeholders should be accompanied by measures to address the needs of those who are unable to respond to new incentives because of extreme poverty. And where such constraints are very large, as in Zambia, a note of caution is warranted about the potentially harmful effects of relying on market incentives and individual contribution for the allocation of essential public goods. Ultimately, these effects must be considered in light of the potential benefits that improved institutional performance would have for the poor in the long run.

Chapter 7

# Private Markets and Public Goods: Efficiency Gains and Equity Trade-offs

A S COUNTRIES WORLDWIDE turn to the market, they are also incorporating market incentives in providing public goods. In many countries the debate is no longer whether this approach is acceptable but what is the best way to integrate new incentives in a manner that improves the performance of public institutions and at the same time guarantees widespread public access and at least minimum standards for services. This study has explored experiences with private market approaches to the delivery of public goods. A common element among the programs was their reliance on exit and voice strategies to improve institutional performance and create new stakeholders in reform. An underlying assumption is that better institutional performance is critical to the economic and political sustainability of market reforms.[1] The study has explored two propositions. The first is that strategies that rely on new market incentives—in the form of greater voice and choice—can improve the performance of public institutions, particularly their ability to provide significant public goods to broad parts of the population. The second is that such strategies will strengthen the political sustainability of market reforms by increasing the direct stakes that the public has in the process.

The study has also explored the effects of market reforms on improving the availability and quality of public goods for the poor. In many countries that are carrying out macroeconomic reforms, unequal access—to education in particular—constrains economic growth and thus limits the potential of the reforms.[2] In such contexts improving the poor's access to services is essential to their participating in market growth. An underlying assumption is that increasing their economic and political participation in markets for public goods improves the potential and sustainability of growth because it will be more likely to be inclusive and broadly shared. It is also likely to enhance democratic governance.

As always, practice is more difficult or at least more variable than theory. This study has explored a number of attempts to increase the public's stakes in reform by introducing private incentives in the public goods via voice and choice, a strategy termed the stakeholders approach. The case studies have included mass-based privatization strategies in Chile, Peru, Bolivia, and the Czech Republic; social security reforms in Chile, Peru, and Bolivia; and education and health reforms in Chile, Peru, and Zambia. It has assessed the effects of these programs on the political sustainability of reform, the performance of public institutions, and equity.

The results of the experiences were rarely straightforward, and the outcomes varied across countries, sectors, and institutions. Still, some trends emerged concerning the effects of private market approaches in providing public goods. In particular it was evident that the introduction of new market incentives has a great deal of potential to improve institutional performance and can create new stakeholders in reform. When the reach of such reforms was broad, and significant parts of society participated, the specific reforms could contribute to the political sustainability of the market economic process more generally.

Yet the improvements to equity of introducing market incentives were far less consistent. In some cases poor people did not participate in reforms, or even worse, lost access to essential public services because poverty prevented them from responding to the new incentives. In other cases short-term trade-offs that compromised equity could be corrected by government policies targeted to the poor. Unfortunate effects could also be counterbalanced in the long run by improved institutional performance. A country's political economy, extent of poverty and inequality, policy design, and the administrative capacity of existing public institutions all helped determine the balance of equity outcomes. Indeed, the book has opened as many new questions as it has been able to resolve.

In almost every case the introduction of new incentives made it possible to broaden the base of people participating in reform and improve the performance of public institutions. Yet there were wide differences in the ability of the reforms to include all social groups, particularly the poorest. Often these limits could be corrected with specific policies targeted toward those who had been excluded. In a few, however, the extent and nature of poverty-related constraints were such that significant numbers could not or did not respond to new market incentives. This suggests that there are limits to the potential of the private market approach in the face of the formidable challenges in the poorest countries. Yet given the extent to which state-centered actions have failed dramatically in most of these countries, an optimal alternative is far from clear.[3]

This raises the broader matter of the role of the state. Although there is a wide range of opinion, a minimum consensus is that the state has an irreplaceable responsibility in providing and enforcing the laws necessary for societies and markets to function. It also must provide some protection or safety nets for those people who cannot provide for themselves. Merilee Grindle posits that, at least in theory, states should have *capacity* in four areas. They should have the institutional capacity to regulate economic and political interactions; the technical capacity to establish and manage macroeconomic policies; the administrative capacity to ensure the availability of basic physical infrastructure and social welfare services; and the political capacity to provide channels for making demands, representation, and conflict resolution.[4]

Yet even if there is agreement on essential government functions in market economies, there is much less agreement about the extent to which the state should correct for inequitable market outcomes, how to define who should be eligible for assistance, and how much assistance they should receive. These issues are particularly difficult to resolve in countries where governments have very weak capacity.[5] In such contexts there are often costly and destabilizing distributive conflicts, which may be either made worse or resolved by the introduction of market incentives in providing public goods.[6]

The cases in this study have shown that either outcome is possible. Often new incentives increased the capacity of public institutions to deliver essential services by increasing the role and contribution of beneficiaries through voice and choice, thereby creating consensus on a new model for public service delivery. Yet in countries with extensive poverty and weak state capacity, people were often unable to respond to new incentives. In such contexts the gap between the poor and the rest of society grew worse because the poor lacked access to essential services. This phenomenon, described as social exclusion in the introduction to this book, limits the economic potential of market reforms and jeopardizes their political sustainability.

The solution for poor countries with weak state capacity may lie in a mix between gradual improvements in the performance of public institutions in response to new market incentives and complementary policies that improve the capacity of the poorest people to respond to new incentives and alternatives. Such policies include government communication and public education efforts to encourage broad participation, cross-subsidies to help the poor cover the transaction costs of embracing new opportunities, and support in meeting the basic nutritional and educational requirements of the very poorest. Improving the performance of public institutions and their capacity to enhance equity will be more gradual in these states than in others. Although such a gradual strategy seems insufficient given the extent and urgency of the challenges facing poor countries, even incremental improvements in the capacity of public institutions, which ultimately contribute to those countries' potential for growth and reducing poverty, are likely to have higher *marginal* returns than would similar improvements in wealthier countries, in part because there is so much room for improvement and people are likely to be receptive to institutional change.

A primary objective of this study has been to contribute to an understanding of what makes public institutions perform better and how these improvements can make market-led growth more sustainable and equitable. Although the experiences described rarely yielded clear guidelines for improving institutional performance in all countries, a number of lessons emerged that are of relevance to policymakers. Some reforms are potentially better than others given particular countries' income and poverty levels. In some cases reforms that were in theory appropriate failed because of mistakes in implementation. The study suggests ways to avoid repeating these errors. The experiences reviewed also provide strategies for incorporating equity objectives in reforms from the beginning, because damaging equity can undermine the potential of reforms as well as political support for the market process. The results also point to areas where further research is necessary. One is how the approach interacts with market growth. Stakeholders strategies may not always be efficient from a pure economics perspective, but they may be necessary to make reforms politically feasible. Another area for further research is the effects of the stakeholders approach on equity.

These conclusions may not be very satisfying for those seeking concrete guidelines for reforming public institutions. Unlike macroeconomic reform, about which there is increasing agreement on the policy measures required, on the reform of public sector institutions policymakers agree on the diagnoses of problems, but lack prescriptions for solutions. "Public management is not the arena in which to find Big Answers; it is the world of settled institutions designed to allow imperfect people to use flawed procedures to cope with insoluble problems."[7] In the absence of an established theory that cuts across academic disciplines, the insights in this study may serve as a starting point for organizing further thinking and research about these problems.[8]

## Stakeholders Reforms and Institutional Performance

The many examples in this study make it clear that introducing market incentives such as competition and choice can substantially improve the performance of public institutions. They also suggest that related changes in the operations of these institutions, such as increased participation, voice, and nonfinancial performance incentives, can have equally beneficial effects.

Among other things this reflects the extent to which the lines between public and private sectors are increasingly blurred. The examples in this study provide a range of public-private mixes. At one end is the creation of exit options: the total privatization of services such as social security and of state-owned enterprises. Then there is state-subsidized competition between private and public alternatives—allowing a mix of exit, voice, and loyalty—as in education vouchers in Chile. At the other end is the continuation of primarily public provision of services, but with the incorporation of increased participation, or voice, by users in the management and delivery of services—as with social services in Bolivia and health care services in Peru and Zambia.

The move toward market incentives by no means eliminates an active role for the state in providing public goods and services. Indeed, in this study most unsuccessful reforms stemmed from government failure rather than market failures. In some, as with education reform in Chile, social security in Peru, and health care in Zambia, inadequate communication and public education restricted public participation in reforms, particularly among the poorest people. In others inadequate government regulation and monitoring of newly privatized sectors hindered performance, as with investment funds in the Czech Republic or the decentralization of social services in Bolivia and Zambia. But overregulation from the center, as with education reforms in Chile, can also limit the potential of stakeholders approaches.

Achieving the appropriate balance between central government involvement and regulation and local freedom to some extent comes from trial and error. In the Czech Republic, for example, too much regulation too early could have prevented the very novel market process from getting off the ground. Several years later, however, it became increasingly evident that the government's lax attitude toward regulation was hindering economic performance and investor confidence. In the case of popular participation in the delivery of social services in Bolivia, the entire process was driven by the unprecedented devolution of power and responsibility to local actors. Too much central government control too early might well have raised suspicion and inhibited participation, which would have limited the creation of new stakeholders. Yet in all cases, government vigilance and willingness to adapt and correct policies as errors become evident is essential to the long-term sustainability of the reforms and to ensuring some degree of equity.

Because regulation requires administrative capacity, it is no surprise that some of the poorer or less experienced countries have had more difficulty in establishing adequate regulatory mechanisms for new private market approaches. This is where multilateral institutions can participate, not only in offering financial assistance, but more importantly through technical assistance. In the capitalization reform in Bolivia, for example, such assistance was vital to establishing the complex regulatory framework required for the operations of the newly privatized companies and the private social security system.

Another fundamental role for the state, which also requires a delicate balance, is in providing financing for essential goods and services. Although the public sector obviously has a role in financing, requiring some contribution from beneficiaries through user fees or other mechanisms is often invaluable in increasing the propensity of users to demand accountability.[9] With locally administered health boards in Peru, for example, allowing local providers to charge fees and administer the resources that those fees generated resulted in increased availability and quality of health care services for the poor. In Bolivia, new community vigilance committees have demanded accountability from the center when municipal governments fail to deliver. However, user fees can preclude participation by the poor, as they did in health care reform in Zambia. There the government's failure to communicate an exemptions policy for children, preventive care, and those unable to pay fees resulted in a dramatic drop in the use of health services by the most poor and vulnerable groups. The appropriate level of the fees, sufficient public support for those unable to pay, and clear communication of the exemptions policy are determining factors in the success of fee-based programs.

Insufficient public financing, meanwhile, can undermine the potential of stakeholders reforms, or at least unlevel the playing field for those who cannot afford to supplement insufficient state financing with private funds, as was true with education vouchers in Chile. The real value of the vouchers dropped dramatically shortly after the reform was initiated. As a result, schools with the capacity to generate additional resources did so, while those in poor areas saw the quality of their schools deteriorate. The erosion of the value of the vouchers, rather than the use of vouchers per se, was largely responsible for performance differences between schools in poor and wealthy areas. However, too much money channeled from external sources can overwhelm and ultimately undermine nascent local initiatives, as has occurred with countless development projects.[10]

One of the most important factors determining the potential of stakeholders strategies to improve public sector performance is adequate government explanation of reforms to the public. Stakeholders reforms usually require a response from broad sectors of the public to new incentives and a contribution of either personal effort or resources in order to participate. In many programs discussed in this study, lack of public understanding of the reforms limited participation, particularly by the poor. This constrained the potential of the reforms to contribute to political sustainability and increased their potential for having deleterious effects on equity.

Surveys referred to in the study found that lack of adequate information was often a major reason the poor did not participate in new private market reforms, including social security in Peru, education in Chile, and investment vouchers in the Czech Republic. With health care reforms in Zambia, lack of public understanding of the fees and exemptions policy resulted in the extremely damaging drop in the use of health services by the poor. Although the government was effective in the initial selling of the reforms, it failed to provide adequate information during implementation.

In contrast, effective communication campaigns seem to have resulted in greater than expected public responses in citizen participation in privatization in Peru, voucher privatization in the Czech Republic, social security reform in Chile, and worker participation in enterprise privatization and social service reforms in Bolivia. Although communication cannot by itself make up for structural limitations such as great income inequality or for poorly designed reforms, it is a straightforward and inexpensive means to overcome one of the most widespread obstacles to the response of the poor to new market incentives: lack of adequate information.

A related issue is the role of expectations and other behavioral traits related to poverty, traits that are in part endogenous to social mobility in some countries. Attitudes and expectations can help particular social groups to become stakeholders in response to new market incentives. In the reform of Chilean education, for example, one survey of urban parents found that expectations were an important factor in their propensity to use their vouchers to send their children to new private schools. Many poor parents surveyed did not think they had the "right" to send their children to better schools, even though the distribution of vouchers was universal. Changing attitudes and expectations is likely to take much longer than initiating public policies and is likely to occur gradually as new systems begin running and people see the results. Again, active efforts to explain new reforms to the poor must be integral to the programs.

Political context may also matter. The poor may be more reluctant to participate in new incentive schemes in countries with a recent history of political repression or where systems of political representation are hierarchical and rigid. The Chilean education reforms were initially implemented in such a context, and participation by the poorest people was weak. In Bolivia's social reforms, meanwhile, the success of locally managed service delivery systems often varied according to the relative strength of autonomous local participants vis-à-vis municipal councils. Because municipal government and local political participation are novel features in Bolivia, in some places mayors and municipal councils are authoritarian and have a monopoly over resources and decisionmaking, limiting the vital participation of the community vigilance committees.

Although the potential of stakeholders reforms depends on the capacity and propensity of intended beneficiaries to respond to new incentives and exert pressure for change from the bottom up, the reforms cannot succeed without a strong central government commitment as well. Changing the way public services are delivered and giving new responsibilities to users inevitably challenges established interests in the central public institutions who have a strong stake in the status quo. These interests are usually more vocal and organized than the potential beneficiaries of reforms, particularly at the outset. Without strong central commitment to reform, it is extremely difficult to override organized opposition, as the failure of education reform in Peru demonstrates. The government failed to devolve responsibility for management of schools to the local level because it feared opposition from teachers and administrators and was reluctant to loosen its political control. Thus no structural change occurred in education. In the longer term, the weight of new local stakeholders can make reforms irreversible. The stakes that were created in the new private schools in Chile and in locally managed health care services in Peru and Zambia ultimately overrode opposition from central or regional public sectors.[11]

Stakeholders approaches work best in improving the quality and coverage of providing public goods and services in places where the public sector can serve as a default valve when private sector alternatives are inadequate or fail to reach the poor. The education reforms in Chile, for example, could rely on an extensive social welfare system as well a far-reaching system of municipal schools to provide services in disadvantaged areas where the private sector did not choose to go. This system then provided an effective channel for public programs to improve the quality of education in poor areas once the reform was in place. In poorer countries such as Zambia and Bolivia, providing the poorest with sufficient access to services remains a problem and at times can be made worse by private market approaches.

This is not a heartening conclusion, because public sector approaches also tend to work better when administrative capacity is adequate and incomes are higher. The same factors that facilitate efficient public sector operations also increase the potential of stakeholders approaches to achieve wide participation, thus leaving limited gaps in coverage that can be effectively filled by the state with corrective policies, cross-subsidies, or targeted programs. A case in point is the success of the P900 and MECE education programs in Chile, which provided new resources and technical support to improve the quality of poor rural schools. Because the problem was limited to the poorest rural schools, it was possible to correct it with government policies without creating an extreme fiscal burden or introducing perverse incentives in the overall system. In addition, Chile has the institutional and administrative capacity to carry out effective targeted policies.[12]

But in Zambia the reach of health care reform was far more limited, and the challenge for policies to ameliorate harmful effects on equity was far greater. At the same time, the potential of the state to fill the gap was much weaker.

This suggests that the poorest countries remain at a disadvantage regardless of stakeholders reforms. Yet it also suggests the critical importance of improving public sector performance and that stakeholders strategies can make important contributions in very poor countries even if the reforms are not as successful as those carrier out in wealthier countries. If stakeholders strategies succeed in improving the capacity of public institutions in poor countries, they will contribute to the sustainability of market reforms and therefore to growth and poverty reduction in the future, even if the reforms have negative or mixed effects on equity in the short term.

Equally important, stakeholders approaches give the users of public services incentives and channels for demanding greater accountability from public institutions. These pressures are particularly important where weak institutional capacity leaves a large margin for improvement in performance and central capacity to make changes is weak. But some policies have better outcomes in poor countries than in wealthier ones because there is more room for improvement and for demonstration effects and because weak institutional performance over time makes the public more receptive to changing the system. The poor may then benefit as free riders if institutional performance improves sufficiently. Considered in this light, stakeholders reforms may have greater marginal returns in poor countries than in wealthy ones. The relative value of these returns will depend on the balance between the reforms' ability to improve institutional performance and political sustainability and their negative effects on equity.

Finally, no one reform model is completely duplicable from country to country. The same reform in theory, implemented in different countries, will in practice reflect differences in political economy and levels of poverty and inequality. In Chile, for example, a minimum pension was affordable and was built into social security reform from the beginning. In Peru there is no minimum pension. It would have been an unaffordable fiscal burden for the government because very few workers in the system earn enough to cover a pension above the minimum level. In addition, there was no effective political voice for the poorer workers in the system. And because coverage is extremely limited, with the poorest workers remaining uncovered, it is not clear that subsidizing covered workers would have been the most equitable choice for public investment. Thus the reform designs reflect different political economy contexts. This limited low-income workers' participation in the new system in Peru. In Bolivia, a similar reform had very different outcomes because of the government's commitment to distribute the proceeds from privatization to all Bolivians in the form of a universal social security payment. The annually distributed solidarity bonds (bonosols) effectively served as a minimum pension, and thus the reform was better for poor workers. The same reforms may also not be politically viable in some countries. Chile-style vouchers for education, for example, proved politically unworkable in Peru.

## Stakeholders and Political Sustainability

The many experiences in this study suggest that stakeholders approaches can have substantial and beneficial effects on the political sustainability of institutional reforms and of the market process more generally. The timing and extent of these effects vary according to the countries and the nature of the reforms. The political effects of strategies to broaden participation in privatization are perhaps most straightforward in the experiences of the Czech Republic with vouchers, the Chilean share-selling program, and the Peruvian citizen participation programs. In each instance, participation was much greater than expected and most shareholders kept their shares, thus retaining stakes in the reformed systems. In the Bolivian capitalization plan, meanwhile, the government chose to invest the bulk of the proceeds in future growth through the development of a new social security system rather than to focus on distribution or selling of shares. This had less immediate beneficial political effects. But since the system is running and as greater numbers of people receive annual solidarity bond payments, public stakes in the reform will increase.

The short-term effects of social security reforms on politics, meanwhile, vary according to the initial extent and coverage of the public systems and the availability of guarantees for poor workers. In Peru, for example, because the coverage was limited, the potential for creating a large base of stakeholders was also limited. The potential of the reform was further limited by the absence of a minimum pension, so that significant numbers of workers *within* the social security system did not support the reform and the switch to the new private program. From a political perspective, the strongest stakes in social security reforms will be formed in the future, when new private systems begin to pay pensions to large numbers of people. Even with "successful" social security reform in Chile, the average worker does not express direct political support for private pension funds, given that most workers in the new private system are far from reaching retirement age and therefore from receiving tangible benefits.

The political effects of reforms in social services are the most variable. Stakeholders reforms can create substantial bases of support for new systems among users, but they often also entail challenging groups who are politically organized against change in the old systems. In many countries the education and health ministries are the largest employers in the country.[13] If this substantial number of stakeholders is excluded from the process of reform rather than included or coopted, the political sustainability of the reform can be jeopardized.

In Chile the exclusion of the teachers when reform was initiated created several problems. A clear line of responsibility for personnel was not established between local and central governments. The problem became worse with the 1990 Teachers' Law, which returned responsibility for personnel in municipal schools to the Ministry of Education, while it remained at the school level in the private system. In Peru, local public health workers were initially opposed to the CLAS pilot health reform and the setting up of local management boards because they feared their jobs would be jeopardized. When they realized that they could benefit from the program by working additional hours and earning more income, they became strong stakeholders. Still, the opposition of people at the center coupled with an absence of executive commitment to the program prevented the reform from spreading beyond the pilot project phase.[14]

In Zambia and Bolivia, however, the genuine devolution of responsibility and resources to local levels ultimately created strong and irreversible political support for reforms that outweighed opposition from the center. In Zambia a new minister attempted to recentralize responsibility for health care services, but local groups refused to give up their newly gained autonomy. In Bolivia the number, vibrancy, and popularity of new municipalities and community organizations is unprecedented in the region, and it is difficult to imagine how a government could recentralize such widely dispersed authority.

The political feasibility of reforms is also affected by the public's attitudes about the relation between markets and equity. Although private market initiatives are acceptable in some countries, particularly those where policy is in flux or where the state has performed extremely poorly, in others, strongly held public views about equity and the role of the state in providing such services as education and health care make the introduction of market mechanisms far more difficult politically. In the Czech Republic, although the voucher privatization program was politically very popular, in no small part because it provided material rewards, even limited debate about market incentives in social services proved far more difficult and was ultimately politically damaging for the Klaus government. In Peru, where the state had virtually abandoned its role in public health care for years and where user fees were the norm, there was more public demand for the CLAS pilot health program than the government was willing to satisfy, because meeting the demand would have entailed devolving even more power and responsibility to the local level. Yet in Peru also there was little public support for introducing market incentives in education, in which the state did have a strong, nationwide presence.

## Private Markets and Equity

Perhaps the most complex problem in evaluating stakeholders reforms is how they affect equity. First, in virtually all countries the poorest people are least equipped to take advantage of voice and choice alternatives and usually make the least informed choices. They also tend to be risk averse, which limits their willingness to try new alternatives and generally results in their choosing those with the lowest return, as, for example, when choosing retirement alternatives.[15] Some of these effects can be corrected for through government policy, such as public education or cross-subsidies. Yet the constraints of the poorest people participating are surprisingly pervasive, even in contexts of very little poverty and inequality. In the Czech Republic, for example, the poorest people did not participate in the voucher program—or quickly sold their shares—for the same reasons that the poor do not participate in much poorer countries: inadequate access to information, transaction costs, and wary expectations and attitudes.

Second, the effects of stakeholders reforms will vary among countries, particularly according to levels of poverty and inequality. Government policy is essential to helping the poor overcome poverty-related obstacles. Public sector capacity also tends to be weaker precisely where poverty and inequality are greatest, making the challenges more formidable. Yet because the institutional framework is weak, the benefits of improving the performance of public sector institutions may have greater value added. In addition, stakeholders approaches can be vital in creating channels for bottom-up political pressure, which may improve equity in the future.[16]

Yet incorporating market incentives in delivering public goods could result in significant and long-term adverse effects on equity. In societies where many face large poverty-related obstacles to responding to new incentives, the gap between the more privileged groups, who are able to take advantage of superior systems, and a poor majority left with either inferior services or no access at all, may increase social exclusion. It is difficult to imagine market reforms attaining a wide political legitimacy in such contexts.[17] Not only will this result in deep divisions within societies, but also among them, since countries where the majority is excluded from access to crucial services will not be able compete internationally. Although they would have difficulties competing in any event, it is plausible that the move toward market incentives could deepen already deep social cleavages and inequality and therefore impede growth.[18]

Finally, even failures to improve equity must be weighed in light of better institutional performance and political sustainability. Short-term equity trade-offs are often necessary to achieve improvements in quality, as can occur in education.[19] Where entire sectors are performing poorly, gradual or pilot improvements may increase quality for some people but not for others, as in the case of health care in Peru. Alternatively, new incentives that improve performance in some schools may not be taken up by the most disadvantaged ones, as happened with Chile's education reform. Yet if the overall system ultimately improves, it is likely that the poorest people or schools will eventually benefit as free riders, or can benefit from targeted policies in addition to the new incentives structures established by the reforms. And in other situations, efficiency and equity objectives can be met at the same time through removing distortions that benefit privileged groups at the expense of the poor. Examples include introducing competition into public utilities monopolies, which usually benefit wealthier urban groups; reallocating social expenditures from tertiary level services, such as universities and urban hospitals; and improving basic services such as primary school education and care provided by health posts.[20]

In addition, creating new stakeholders among a significant number of people (which may exclude the poorest) may still help the political sustainability of reforms. This was the case in virtually every country in this study. Sustaining market reforms long enough for them to yield growth is essential for reducing poverty. It is much easier to increase the poor's share of a growing pie than of a shrinking one.

Thus a bottom-line consideration may be that short-term trade-offs that improve institutional performance and the sustainability of reform may be a necessary cost for equity improvements in the future. But a societal and government commitment to making those improvements in the future must also be present. Such a promise was essential in Chile, which has traditionally been conscious of equity issues. It was also important in Bolivia, where an exceptional president made an explicit commitment to trade present equity gains for future ones, even at

a high political cost just before national elections. It is more difficult to imagine in Peru and Zambia, where such central government commitments to equity have traditionally been weak, and
the scale of equity challenges is much greater. In such contexts,
one can only hope that the new channels for pressure from the
bottom that have been created by stakeholders approaches can
increase equity in the future.

## Final Thoughts for Theory and Practice

Although there is broad public debate in many industrialized
countries about the appropriate role of private incentives in the
performance of public institutions, in many developing countries
such incentives are already in place. In some this is a result of explicit government strategies and reforms. In others it is a result of
bottom-up pressure and autonomous initiatives that have arisen
because public institutions have failed to provide essential services. The outcomes vary significantly across countries, particularly according to levels of poverty and inequality and to the existing capacity of public sector institutions, but some trends are
universal. For the most part, introducing new incentives and increasing voice and choice has at least some beneficial effects. The
challenge for policymakers is to use the approach to improve institutional performance, build attempts to improve equity into
the reforms from the beginning to minimize possible adverse effects, and present and explain reforms in a way that solicits broad
participation and ultimately political support for the market process.

There are certainly significant obstacles to meeting these
challenges. Sometimes a country's problems or situation overwhelms the best intentions in policy design. This is particularly
true of extremely poor countries with very weak administrative
capacity. Results will then vary within countries as well as
among them. In Zambia, for example, although a national health
care reform policy indeed existed, lack of administrative capacity
meant that policies were carried out haphazardly and often most
badly in the poorest and most remote areas. In such places it is
possible that extremely poor areas will be permanently marginal-

ized from participating in the change. Another possible result and a more optimistic one, based on the assumption that the marginal returns to improvements in institutional performance are very high when state capacity is extremely weak, is that the poor may ultimately benefit from these improvements as free riders, reversing the initial adverse effects on them. How extensive improvements are, and the extent of political and administrative obstacles to reaching the poorest people, will determine whether such an outcome is possible.

Although the experiences of the very poorest countries are important, they are not fully applicable to most countries implementing reforms. There are some common themes that emerge from experiences examined in this study that are applicable to most countries attempting to initiate stakeholder reforms. These themes are also relevant to the literature on the politics of reform and the political economy of growth more generally. First, private incentives that rely on introducing individual choice and voice into the performance of public institutions can succeed in improving performance and in creating new stakeholders. The existence of these new stakeholders has often made the reversal of reforms impossible, even in the midst of far-reaching political or economic change, as the experiences of Chile and the Czech Republic demonstrate. An important caveat is that attaining these goals has not always been free of inefficiencies. Vouchers or Bolivian-style capitalization may not be the most efficient way to privatize state-owned enterprises. But in both instances, the stakeholders approach generated the public support necessary to make them politically sustainable. And in all the cases in the study, reform reversals would have entailed far greater efficiency costs.

Second, equity outcomes vary according to the capacity of intended beneficiaries to respond to new incentives *and* according to policymakers' ability to educate the public about the reforms and to help the poor overcome poverty-related obstacles to participating. Even where there are short-term adverse effects on equity and inequalities increase, if stakeholders reforms improve institutional performance and the sustainability of market-led growth, they are contributing to future growth and poverty reduction. In more extreme instances, if the effects of the reforms severely worsen inequalities and undermine public support for market reforms, the policy framework may deteriorate, at high cost to future growth. Yet the experiences suggest that, on balance, new private markets for public goods are improving equity and therefore helping spur market-led growth. A more definitive theory about the equity implications of private markets for public goods, however, will not appear until much more research has been completed in a larger number of cases.

The dynamics of political economy often affect the design of reform programs and their outcomes, and not always equitably. If the poor have very weak political representation or the majority of the population does not have a tangible stake in the system being reformed, it will be difficult to generate political support for measures to compensate those harmed by reforms. In Chile the parties of the governing coalition had a strong stake in the political support of the poor and made addressing the problems of poor rural schools a priority. In Peru, in contrast, most workers are outside the formal social security system, and it would have been very difficult to generate public support for a fiscal commitment to poorer workers within the system. In education reform, however, because most Peruvians, who are also poor, depend on the public education system and there was a widespread public perception that education reform would be bad for the poor, a strong political constituency was able to block the implementation of a voucher-style system.

The absence of a definitive theory of the effects of private markets for public goods and the stakeholders approach provides a great deal of room for future experimentation, since there is no established recipe for success. Yet because clear guidelines are lacking and the results of reform depend on a complex interaction of market forces, actions of public institutions, and the nature of civil society, those carrying out reform programs (and those evaluating their efforts) must accept that outcomes will vary and may be unpredictable.

Despite the absence of established recipes or theories, there are some simple lessons that can enhance the chances of succeeding in improving institutional performance and building new stakeholders in market reform. The first is that private market approaches do not replace the state and indeed require an active government role in the administration, regulation, and monitoring of the public or private delivery of goods and services. Second, communication with the public and educating people about the reforms is essential to achieving broad participation. Third, paying attention from the beginning to the effects of the reforms on equity and introducing measures to correct for some of the typical poverty-related obstacles to the participation of the poorest people will not only result in greater equity but also in broader participation in and support for the reform process, particularly where poverty levels are high. Finally, no such approach to reform can succeed without a coherent set of macroeconomic policies in place, because the logic of the approach is inherently linked to market-led growth.

Finally, stakeholders reforms that entail the devolution of resources and responsibility from the center to local communities and institutions often take on a political dynamic of their own that makes them irreversible. For the center to let go of a certain amount of power is crucial to the success of the reforms, but letting go also implies losing some control over results. Government regulation and policies to help the disadvantaged participate in new systems can certainly moderate outcomes. Yet in the end the move to private markets for public goods requires central government willingness to forgo uniformity in outcomes in exchange for potential gains in the efficiency of public institutions and in the sustainability of market-led growth. Although there may be equity trade-offs in the short term, the experience of an increasing number of countries demonstrates that sustainable growth coupled with effective public institutions is the best recipe for permanently reducing poverty and inequality.

# Notes

## Chapter 1

1. The macroeconomic volatility of the 1980s was bad for both growth and income distribution. Without the reforms the trends toward greater inequality would have continued, and the distributional outcomes would have been far worse. See Juan Luis Londoño and Marcelo Szelesky, "Distributional Surprise after a Decade of Reforms: Latin America in the Nineties," paper prepared for IDB annual meeting, Barcelona, March 1997. Poverty outcomes, meanwhile, are directly related to growth trends in the region, with the exception of some "outlier" countries. See Samuel A. Morley, *Poverty and Inequality in Latin America* (Johns Hopkins University Press, 1994). See also William Easterly and Peter Monteil, "Has Latin America's Post-Reform Growth Been Disappointing?" World Bank, Washington 1995.

2. See "The Backlash in Latin America: Gestures against Reform," *Economist*, vol. 341 (November 30, 1996), pp. 19–21. For detail on how great inequality can lead to populist voting patterns, see Alberto Alesina and Roberto Perotti, "The Political Economy of Growth: A Critical Survey of the Recent Literature," *World Bank Economic Review*, vol. 8 (September 1994), pp. 351–72. Other empirical studies find that although there is no empirical relationship between democracy and income inequality, democracy is more likely to survive in regimes where income inequality is decreasing. See Adam Prezeworski and others, "What Makes Democracies Endure?" *Journal of Democracy*, vol. 7 (January 1996), pp. 39–55.

298

3. Reformist politicians have also fared better in these countries because the results of reform have created support for it. See Anders Aslund, Peter Boone, and Simon Johnson, "How to Stabilize: Lessons from the Post-Communist Countries," *Brookings Papers on Economic Activity*, no. 1 (1996), pp. 217–313. For a detailed survey of trends in poverty and inequality in the region, see Branko Milanovic, *Income, Inequality, and Poverty during the Transition* (Washington: World Bank, forthcoming).

4. See, for example, *Adjustment in Africa: Reform Results and the Road Ahead* (Washington and New York: World Bank and Oxford University Press, 1994); and David E. Sahn, ed., *Adjusting to Policy Failure in African Economies* (Cornell University Press, 1994).

5. Although the links between popular perceptions and voting are far from clear and are not consistent across countries, several studies suggest that people are more likely to vote for reform if they believe it will yield benefits rather than according to the costs of reform or how they are compensated. See Joan Nelson, "Poverty, Equity, and the Politics of Adjustment," in Stephan Haggard and Robert Kaufmann, *The Politics of Economic Adjustment: International Constraints, Distributive Conflicts, and the State* (Princeton University Press, 1992); and Carol Graham, *Safety Nets, Politics, and the Poor: Transitions to Market Economies* (Brookings, 1994). At a more general level, Margaret Levi and Richard Sherman demonstrate that when institutional systems structure incentives so that most people perceive that they can be winners—if not in the present, at least in the future—countries are more likely to have stable and efficient governments and economic systems. See "Rationalized Bureaucracy," paper prepared for the conference, "Economic and Political Institutions for Sustainable Development: Implications for Assistance," Washington, October 1994.

6. For the role of investments in human capital in growth, see Robert Barro, "Democracy and Growth," paper prepared for Harvard University and Universitat Pompeu Fabra Conference on Growth and Political Institutions, Barcelona, March–April 1995. See also Nancy Birdsall, David Ross, and Richard Sabot, "Inequality and Growth Reconsidered: Lessons from East Asia," *World Bank Economic Review*, vol. 9 (September 1995), pp. 477–508. See also Sebastian Edwards, "The Disturbing Underperformance of Latin American Economies," paper prepared for the Inter-American Dialogue Plenary Meeting, Washington, January 1997. For the role of institutions in encouraging sustained and broadly shared growth in East Asia, for example, see Jose Edgar Campos and Hilton L. Root, *The Key to the East Asian Miracle: Making Shared Growth Credible* (Brookings, 1996).

7. See Carol Graham and Moises Naim, "The Political Economy of Institutional Reform in Latin America," in Nancy Birdsall, Carol Gra-

ham, and Richard Sabot, eds., *Beyond Trade-offs: Market Reforms and Equitable Growth in Latin America* (Brookings and Inter-American Development Bank, forthcoming).

8. In addition, the erosion of public institutions has led to a tendency toward short-sighted behavior by most political actors in many developing countries. Barbara Geddes shows how people in less developed countries, for good reason and out of experience, tend to think that the outcomes of their interactions with the public sector will be unfair. Therefore cooperation in public sector reform is much less likely to evolve voluntarily, and politicians' incentives are skewed against reform. See *Politician's Dilemma: Building State Capacity in Latin America* (University of California Press, 1994).

9. For a description of the experience with safety nets during reforms in several regions, see Graham, *Safety Nets*.

10. Merilee Serrill Grindle, *Getting Good Government: Capacity Building in the Public Sectors of Developing Countries* (Harvard Institute for International Development, 1997), p. 7.

11. In the case of mass participation in privatization strategies, for example, "participation need not be a function of price, but charging a small fee enables governments to recoup some (or all) of the administrative costs, provides a strong psychological sense of value to the vouchers, and places responsibility for obtaining the vouchers on the recipients rather than the government." Stuart W. Bell, "Sharing the Wealth: Privatization through Broad-Based Ownership Strategies," World Bank Discussion Paper 285 (1995), p. 10.

12. The incentives facing politicians in the context of reform are discussed in detail in Barbara Geddes, "The Politics of Economic Liberalization," *Latin American Research Review*, vol. 30, no.2 (1995), pp. 195–214.

13. In a way this is analogous to Robert D. Putnam's concept of "social capital" (discussed later). See *Making Democracy Work: Civic Traditions in Modern Italy* (Princeton University Press, 1993).

14. One of the most common stakeholders approaches used worldwide is public participation in the privatization of state-owned enterprises. The success of such programs in making privatization politically feasible in countries ranging from Jamaica and Korea to the Czech Republic and Mongolia stands out in sharp contrast to the political obstacles that have plagued privatization in Russia and Hungary, for example, where ownership of shares has remained concentrated in the hands of the previous managers of state-owned enterprises. This conclusion is drawn from my participation in an Asia Foundation project comparing eastern European and east Asian transitions (1994–95) and discussions with the authors of the country papers: Russia—Boris Federov, former

finance minister and current member of parliament; Hungary and the Czech Republic—R. Friedman, A. Rapacynski, and J. Turkewitz, Central European Privatization Project; and Mongolia—Peter Boone, London School of Economics. The papers were published in Wing Thye Woo, Stephen Parker, and Jeffrey Sachs, eds., *Economies in Transition: Comparing Asia and Eastern Europe* (MIT Press, 1997). For a detailed study of privatization programs, see Bell, "Sharing the Wealth."

For the use of these programs in the OECD countries see, for example, David Owen, "Privatization Issue Comes to Haunt the Centre-Right," *Financial Times*, May 21, 1997, p. 4 (France); Andrew Hill, "Municipal Privatization: Councils Go to the Capital Markets," *Financial Times*, April 7, 1997 (Italy); "Blair Raises the Stake," *Economist*, January 13, 1996, pp. 25–26 (Britain); and Stephanie Flanders, "More Power to Local Authorities: Reformers Need to Guard against 'Devolution' Becoming a Byword for Anarchy," *Financial Times*, October 6, 1995, p. xiii (OECD in general). For an example in the United States, see Margaret Blair, *Wealth Creation and Wealth Sharing: A Colloquium on Corporate Governance and Investment in Human Capital* (Brookings, 1996). For a summary of Latin American experiences, see Mary M. Shirley, "Privatization in Latin America: Lessons for Transitional Europe," *World Development*, vol. 22 (September 1994), pp. 1313–23.

15. There is a certain analytical ambiguity in this definition. The stakeholders approach, as developed here, applies to the approach as both a feature of policies—that they are participatory and consumer driven—and as a mode of analysis—the use of the approach has effects on policy outcomes. The approach is part of a process of strengthening participation, and yet it is also contingent on certain outcomes: the creation of new stakeholders.

16. Recent research, for example, suggests that educational reforms that increase the relative strengths of parents rather than teachers in deciding the allocation of expenditures can lead to enormous gains in the cost effectiveness of schools because most education sectors allocate resources in a manner biased toward the welfare of teachers. "Crudely put, teachers lobby (and form unions, and strike, and write) and books and desks do not. Parents generally have been insufficiently strong on behalf of books. This implies that the main role of the estimation of educational production functions is not to inform an optimizing policymaker of the 'true' technical production function, but rather to provide the information necessary to encourage deeper educational reforms that change the structure of decisionmaking power." Lant Pritchett and Deon Filmar, "What Education Production Functions *Really* Show: A Positive Theory of Education Expenditures," Policy Research Department, World Bank, Washington, May 1997, p. 45.

17. A similar definition of stakeholders is found in Alejandra Gonzalez Ronzetti, "The Political Economy of Policy Change: Concepts for the Analysis of Health System Reform," London School of Tropical Medicine (1997). See also Edward Zajac, *The Political Economy of Fairness* (MIT Press, 1995).

18. The extent to which public awareness varies in regard to politics, regardless of the issues involved, is discussed in John R. Zaller, *The Nature and Origins of Mass Opinion* (Cambridge University Press, 1992).

19. I discuss the differences between the poor and the poorest in chapter 1 of Graham, *Safety Nets*. For a more detailed description, see Michael Lipton, "The Poor and the Poorest: Some Interim Findings," World Bank Discussion Paper 25 (1988).

20. In many of her writings, Joan Nelson has developed the hypothesis that for pro-poor reforms to be sustainable they must also be targeted to less poor but more politically powerful middle-income groups. See, for example, "Poverty, Equity, and the Politics of Adjustment," in Haggard and Kaufmann, *Politics of Economic Adjustment*. The author has developed a related hypothesis that it is possible to increase the political voice and relative importance of poorer groups (but rarely the poorest) through demand-based safety nets during fast-paced economic reform when the relative position of most interest groups is being challenged. The longer-term sustainability of this increase in political power, however, depends on more permanent institutional reforms. See Graham, *Safety Nets*.

21. See Ronzetti, "Political Economy of Policy Change."

22. One aspect of this approach, changing the behavior of providers and consumers, is called by Nancy Birdsall and Juan Luis Londoño a "horizontal" model for social service provision. The horizontal model does not focus on ownership of assets as its defining characteristic, but instead on rules-based incentives, which strengthens the interactions of consumers with providers. Critical traits of the model are equitable public financing (ensuring access for the poor); greater competition in the delivery of services within and between public and private sectors; and beneficiaries who are better informed, better represented, and more empowered. Like the stakeholders approach, the model increases the voice and choice of consumers and gives them access to a more competitive market of service providers (private or public). Equally important, it ensures that the poor have the ability to pay. This feature is also important to stakeholders strategies, although in practice it is not always put into place. For the horizontal model, see "No Trade-off: Efficient Growth via More Equal Human Capital Accumulation in Latin America," in Birdsall, Graham, and Sabot, *Beyond Trade-offs*.

23. It is beyond the scope of this study to evaluate exactly how much decentralization of authority is optimal, and there are many studies covering this subject. Although some decentralization is beneficial, too much can result in the capturing of policies and programs by local elites. See Paul Streeten, "The Political Economy of Fighting Poverty," Issues In Development, discussion paper 1, International Labour Office, Geneva, 1995; Gustav Ranis and Francis Stewart, "Government Decentralization and Participation," background paper prepared for the UNDP *Human Development Report*, 1994; and Rudolf Hommes, "The Conflicts and Dilemmas of Decentralization," paper prepared for the annual World Bank Conference on Development Economics, Washington, May 1995.

24. Albert Hirschman, *Exit, Voice, and Loyalty: Responses to Decline in Firms, Organizations, and States* (Harvard University Press, 1970), p. 101.

25. Hirschman, *Exit, Voice, and Loyalty*, p. 40.

26. The effectiveness of participation varies depending on the extent to which intermediaries are involved, for example. The involvement of local organizations can be very important in encouraging participation in projects that would otherwise be nonparticipatory. And the number of users also matters; it has an important interactive effect with participation. Increasing the number has a negative effect on project performance when projects are nonparticipatory. See Ritu Basu and Lant Pritchett, "The Determinants of the Magnitude and Effectiveness of Participation: Evidence from Rural Water Projects," Policy Research Department, World Bank, Washington, July 1994.

27. See Caroline Minter-Hoxby, "Does Competition among Public Schools Benefit Students and Taxpayers?" Department of Economics, Harvard University, October 1994. Minter-Hoxby uses exogenous variation in private school availability—by relying on religious schools rather than comparing socioeconomically differentiated areas with and without private school availability—to show that an increase in the number of private schools improves public school performance. Meanwhile studies by Eric Hanushek suggest that the trade-offs between improving quality and access are overstated because students are much more likely to attend and stay in school if quality is higher, even when controlling for students' abilities and earnings prospects. See Hanushek and Victor Lavy, "Dropping Out of School: Further Evidence on the Role of School Quality in Developing Countries," Rochester Center for Economic Research, Working Paper 345, March 1993.

28. Research has found that the primary benefit of introducing user fees is not fiscal but the increased accountability that users demand from the public sector. For certain services the increased use of voice had im-

portant beneficial effects on the quality and equity of public services. The nature of service delivery matters: nondifferentiated services such as water delivery face a greater free rider problem than do differentiated services such as education. For detail, see Samuel Paul, "Does Voice Matter? For Public Accountability, Yes," Policy Research Working Paper 1388, World Bank, Washington (December 1994). In contrast, in Zambia user fees discouraged the use of health care services. Although reform created a substantial number of new stakeholders, the fees excluded significant numbers of the poor. For detail, see Carol Graham, "Macroeconomic and Sectoral Reforms in Zambia: A Stakeholders Approach," Brookings and the World Bank, June 1995.

29. The effects of decentralized participation on equity, for example, are the subject of some debate because power structures in small communities are often conservative. There are two types of participation. Developmental participation is defined as active, broad-based local participation in making political demands as an end in itself. Instrumental participation is defined as a means to affect the appropriateness of decisions and increase the impact of public expenditures on efficiency, equity, and private initiative. Instrumental participation is more relevant to the allocation of social expenditures and may be beneficial even when elites dominate the process. For detail see Jeni Klugman, "Decentralization: A Survey of the Literature from a Human Development Perspective," HDRO occasional paper 13, UNDP (July 1994). Another important issue is that the opportunity costs of the poor's time are often undervalued because the costs are measured only by income. Yet those costs are often very high for certain of the poor, for example, single heads of households who often work more than one job and have little access to child care.

30. Graham, *Safety Nets*. See also Paul, "Does Voice Matter?"

31. In *Good Government in the Tropics* (Johns Hopkins University Press, 1997) Judith Tendler recounts the positive results of a government reform effort in one state in northeast Brazil where the participation of lower-level and local public sector workers in decisionmaking and implementation was encouraged. How such an approach can be carried out on a large scale in the central government is less clear. Arturo Israel, *Institutional Development: Incentives and Performance* (Johns Hopkins University Press/World Bank, 1987), explores how reform strategies, including exit, voice, and loyalty, differ between low-specificity, people-oriented sectors such as education and high-specificity, technically oriented sectors such as central banks. He finds that strategies to improve incentives for clients, beneficiaries, and lower-level staff are far more critical in people-oriented services.

32. Kathryn Stearns, "School Choice: Survival of the Fittest," *Washington Post*, November 24, 1995, p. A29.

33. Putnam, *Making Democracy Work*, p. 182.

34. This section on institutions draws directly from Graham and Naim, "Political Economy of Institutional Reform in Latin America," in Birdsall, Graham, and Sabot, *Beyond Trade-offs*. For different elements of this definition, see Sue E. S. Crawford and Elinor Ostrom, "A Grammar of Institutions," *American Political Science Review*, vol. 89 (September 1995), pp. 582–600; and Alberto Diaz-Cayeros, "Un Analisis Institucional del Papel del Estado," paper prepared for the Tinker Foundation Forum on the Role of the State in Latin America and the Caribbean, Cancun, Mexico, October 1996.

35. In a similar vein, Douglass North defines institutions as the formal and informal rules governing economic and social behavior, and sets of rules that reflect individual countries' histories and cultures. *Institutions, Institutional Change, and Economic Performance* (Cambridge University Press, 1990).

36. Alberto Alesina and Roberto Perotti use formal econometric methods to demonstrate that in societies where there are no institutional mechanisms to correct extreme inequality, the poor have greater incentives to engage in rent-seeking activities and to vote for populist politicians, both of which hinder investment and growth. See "The Political Economy of Growth: A Critical Survey of the Recent Literature," *World Bank Economic Review*, vol. 8 (September 1994), pp. 351–72.

37. See Silvio Borner, Aymo Brunetti, and Beatrice Weder, *Institutional Obstacles to Latin American Growth* (San Fransisco: International Center for Economic Growth, 1992); and Borner, Brunetti, and Weder, *Political Credibility and Economic Development* (St. Martin's Press, 1995).

38. Hirschman, *Exit, Voice, and Loyalty*, p. 101. Another, perhaps more classical, definition is found in James M. Buchanan, *The Demand and Supply of Public Goods* (Chicago: Rand McNally, 1968), p. 1: "People are observed to demand and to supply certain goods and services through market institutions. They are observed to demand and to supply other goods and services through political institutions. The first are called private goods; the second are called public goods."

39. See John Rawls, *A Theory of Justice* (Harvard University Press, 1971), p. 266.

40. Alternatively, the public nature of some goods depends on the scale of the community that is using them. The value of inoculations is indivisible across society because communicable diseases can spread very quickly. But other goods, such as spraying to eradicate mosquitoes, have an indivisible quality for the particular areas (most likely rural)

that have a mosquito problem; urban counterparts in a neighboring community receive little value from the exercise. See Buchanan, *Demand and Supply of Public Goods*. Another way of making this distinction is to consider the most indivisible goods such as defense *super* public goods and more divisible ones such as education and health care as *quasi* public goods. For detail on this distinction, see table 2 in Graham and Naim, "Political Economy of Institutional Reform in Latin America."

41. Yet another way of distinguishing the range of public goods is in terms of their carrying capacity. Defense, for example, is a *super* public good that covers all citizens in a national territory, regardless of their number. The public education system, in contrast, may be overwhelmed by an excessive number of students, and many of them may choose private education. This distinction is made by Jerome Rothenberg in the cases of congestion and pollution. All the users of public highways contribute to congestion and suffer its costs. In the case of pollution, however, some users, such as firms and smokers, pollute water and air, but all users suffer the costs because the goods are indivisible. See "The Economics of Congestion and Pollution: An Integrated View," *American Economics Review*, vol. 60 (May 1970), pp. 114–21.

42. Buchanan, *Demand and Supply of Public Goods*, p. 186.

43. Deepa Narayan and Lant Pritchett, "Cents and Sociability: Household Income and Social Capital in Rural Tanzania," paper prepared for the "Conference on Investment, Growth, and Risk in Africa," World Bank, Washington, April 1997, pp. 3–4.

44. For a good general analysis of voting trends during reform, see Susan C. Stokes, "Public Opinion and Market Reform: The Limits of Economic Voting," *Comparative Political Studies*, vol. 29 (October 1996), pp. 499–519. For detail on the Chilean experience, see Genaro Arriagada and Carol Graham, "Chile: Maintaining Adjustment during Democratic Transition," in Stephan Haggard and Steven Webb, eds., *Voting for Reform: Democracy, Political Liberalization, and Economic Adjustment* (Oxford University Press, 1994). For details on Peru, see Carol Graham and Cheikh Kane, "Opportunistic Government and Sustaining Reform: Electoral Trends and Public Expenditure Patterns in Peru, 1990–95," *Latin American Research Review*, vol. 33, no. 1 (1998), pp. 77–111.

45. This will obviously vary among societies because there are great differences in the degree of inequality that they are willing to tolerate. See, for example, Gosta Esping-Andersen, *The Three Worlds of Welfare Capitalism* (Princeton University Press, 1990).

46. The concept of marginalization, which has been used to describe the poor in the developing world, is related to *social exclusion*, which goes beyond the concept of income poverty and describes the

progressive rupturing of the relationship between individuals and society. This often occurs as a result of long-term unemployment and reflects the permanent rupture of broader social bonds. For a detailed description, see Gerry Rodgers, Charles Gore, and Jose B. Figueiredo, *Social Exclusion: Rhetoric, Reality, and Responses* (Geneva: International Labour Organization, 1995).

47. For a detailed discussion of the political trade-offs involved in compensating different income groups during economic reform, see Graham, *Safety Nets.*

48. Lant Pritchett and Jonah B. Gelbach, "More for the Poor is Less for the Poor: The Politics of Targeting," Policy Research Department, World Bank, Washington, June 1, 1997, pp. 24–25. For a broader discussion of the politics of targeted social welfare policies, see Theda Skocpol, "Universal Appeal: Politically Viable Policies to Combat Poverty," *Brookings Review,* vol. 9 (Summer 1991), pp. 28–33, and the response by Robert Greenstein in the same volume. This point is made more specifically about the targeting of social policy in Nancy Birdsall and Estelle James,"Efficiency and Equity in Social Spending: How and Why Governments Misbehave," World Bank Discussion Papers 274, Washington, May 1990.

49. See Graham and Naim, "Political Economy of Institutional Reform in Latin America."

50. See Michael Bruno and William Easterly, "Inflation's Children: Tales of Crises That Beget Reform," paper prepared for the 1996 annual meeting of the American Economics Association. This is particularly relevant with reforms such as autonomous central banks that lock in prudent macroeconomic management. On central bank independence, see Alex Cukierman, Steven Webb, and Bilin Neyapti, "Measuring the Independence of Central Banks and Its Effects on Policy Outcomes," *World Bank Economic Review,* vol. 6 (September 1992), pp. 353–93. For a discussion of the fate of rapid versus gradual reformers, see Anders Aslund, Peter Boone, and Simon Johnson, "How To Stabilize: Lessons from Post-Communist Countries," *Brookings Papers on Economic Activity,* no. 1 (1996), pp. 217–91.

51. See Graham, *Safety Nets.*

52. For a detailed discussion of these conclusions, as well as a review of the literature, see Barbara Geddes, "Politics of Liberalization."

53. See, for example, Stephan Haggard and Steven Webb, *Voting for Reform: Democracy, Political Liberalization, and Economic Adjustment* (Oxford University Press and the World Bank, 1994); and Karen L. Remmer, "The Political Economy of Elections in Latin America," *American Political Science Review,* vol. 87 (June 1993), pp. 393–407.

54. This latter point is made by Joan Nelson in "Poverty, Equity, and the Politics of Adjustment." Her study of sixteen "intense" adjusting governments found that they or their designated successors were reelected in about half the cases. Success was defined as attaining increases in real wage levels, which suggests the kind of growth response that the "crisis" study describes. For detail, also see Geddes, "Politics of Liberalization."

55. See Graham and Kane, "Opportunistic Government and Sustaining Reform."

56. Given economic conditions and the record of state performance, a school teacher in Peru or Venezuela, for example, is probably less likely to accept promises of real wage increases in the future than is a union member in Spain. For detail see Alan Angell and Carol Graham, "Can Social Sector Reform Make Adjustment Sustainable and Equitable?" *Journal of Latin American Studies*, vol. 27, pt. 1 (February 1995), pp. 189–219.

57. I discuss this in detail in Graham, *Safety Nets*. Haggard and Webb, *Voting for Reform*, also discuss the role of compensation, as does Joan Nelson, "Poverty, Equity, and the Politics of Adjustment." John Earle and Richard Rose, in a study of attempts to compensate workers in previously state-owned enterprises in Russia, come to similar conclusions about the difficulty of compensating the most directly affected losers. The authors find that antireform sentiments were strongest among this group, regardless of attempts to compensate them. In contrast, workers in new private firms tended to be the most in favor of reform. See "Ownership Transformation, Economic Behavior, and Political Attitudes in Russia," Center for International Security and Arms Control (CISAC) Discussion Paper, Stanford University, August 1996.

58. As early as Aristotle, philosophers have pondered the relative importance of equity issues. For a modern discussion on what the optimal fair distribution of income is, see Rawls, *Theory of Justice*. For an excellent analysis of how equity norms and practices develop in societies, see H. Peyton Young, *Equity: In Theory and Practice* (Princeton University Press, 1994). For different societies' tolerances for inequality, see Esping-Andersen, *Three Worlds of Welfare Capitalism*.

59. Rawls, *Theory of Justice*, p. 259.

60. See Young, *Equity*.

61. High levels of corruption during privatization in Russia, for example, not only delegitimated reform in the eyes of many but seem to have opened the door for further corruption and profiteering in both public and private sectors. But in the Czech Republic, where all citizens benefited equally—at least initially—from a voucher privatization that

was for the most part transparent, market reforms have maintained much broader public support and there have been fewer distributive conflicts. For Russia, see Anders Aslund, *Russia: The Making of an Economy* (Brookings, 1994). For the Czech Republic, see chapter 5 in this study.

62. See Birdsall, Ross, and Sabot, "Inequality and Growth Reconsidered"; Alesina and Perotti, "Political Economy of Growth"; Roland Benabou, "Unequal Societies," NBER Working Paper 5583, Cambridge, Mass., May 1996; Michael Bruno, Martin Ravaillion, and Lyn Squire, "Equity and Growth in Developing Countries: Old and New Perspectives on the Policy Issues," Policy Research Working Papers 1563, World Bank, Washington, January 1996; and Nancy Birdsall and Juan Luis Londoño, "Asset Inequality Does Matter: Lessons from Latin America," OCE Working Paper, Inter-American Development Bank, March 1997.

63. Much of this section is drawn from the introductory chapter of Birdsall, Graham, and Sabot, *Beyond Trade-offs*, and from Karla Hoff, "Market Failures and the Distribution of Wealth: A Perspective from the Economics of Information," *Politics and Society*, vol. 24 (December 1996), pp. 411–32.

64. Another example of market failure is in insurance and labor markets. In the absence of adequate social insurance mechanisms, workers seek to offset risk by legislating job security through the labor laws. Yet very rigid labor laws discourage job creation, which diminishes the incomes and opportunities of the poor.

65. See Nancy Birdsall and Estelle James, "Efficiency and Equity in Social Spending: How and Why Governments Misbehave," WPS 274, World Bank, Washington, May 1990.

66. For detail on how high inequality can lead to populist voting patters, see Alesina and Perotti, "Political Economy of Growth." For a view that questions median voter theory, in which the poor have equal political voice, see Benabou, "Unequal Societies."

67. See Rodgers, Gore, and Figueiredo, *Social Exclusion*.

68. Hilary Silver, "Reconceptualizing Social Disadvantage: Three Paradigms of Social Exclusion," in Rodgers, Gore, and Figueiredo, *Social Exclusion*, p. 7.

69. See Birdsall, Graham, and Sabot, *Beyond Trade-offs*; and Nancy Birdsall and Richard Sabot, *Virtuous Circles: Human Capital, Growth, and Equity in East Asia* (Brookings, forthcoming)

70. See Geddes, "Politics of Liberalization"; Remmer, "Political Economy of Elections in Latin America"; and Aslund, Boone, and Johnson, "How to Stabilize."

71. Jose Edgar Campos and Hilton L. Root, *The Key to the Asian Miracle: Making Shared Growth Credible* (Brookings, 1996), p. 1.

72. See, for example, Rudiger Dornbusch and Sebastian Edwards, "Macroeconomic Populism," *Journal of Development Economics*, vol. 32, no. 2 (1990), pp. 247–77; and Jeffrey Sachs, "Social Conflict and Populist Policies in Latin America," Occasional Paper 9, International Center for Economic Growth, ICS Press, San Francisco, 1990.

73. See Ricardo Hausmann and Liliana Rojas-Suarez, eds.,*Volatile Capital Flows: Taming Their Impact on Latin America* (Washington: Inter-American Development Bank, 1996).

74. For detail on inequality trends in the region, see Milanovic, *Income, Inequality, and Poverty during the Transition.*

75. See Birdsall and James, "Efficiency and Equity in Social Spending." The poor often pay much more for informal—and often inferior—services, purchasing water from trucks and using kerosene and candles instead of electricity, when they are denied access to public services. For evidence from Peru, see Blanca Adrianzen and George G. Graham, "The High Costs of Being Poor," *Archives of Environmental Health*, vol. 28 (June 1974).

76. Birdsall, Graham, and Sabot, *Beyond Trade-offs.*

77. Income inequality is measured by the Gini coefficient, which attempts to capture the extent to which a country's income distribution diverges from total equality. A Gini coefficient (or concentration ratio) of 0 is perfect equality, while a coefficient of 1 is perfect inequality. For developed countries, the Gini coefficient of earned pretax income tends to be around 0.4.

The coefficients for the countries in this study are Czech Republic, .270; Bolivia, .420; Peru, .449; Zambia, .462; and Chile, .565. See *World Development Report 1996: From Plan to Market* (World Bank and Oxford University Press, 1997), pp. 69, 196, 197.

The data for Peru and Chile are from 1994, for Zambia and Czech Republic from 1993, and for Bolivia, 1990. If public social expenditures and targeted income transfers were accounted for, Chile's Gini would probably be lower than those of Peru and Bolivia.

The urban Gini coefficients reported by ECLAC in the *Social Panorama of Latin America 1996* for Bolivia and Chile from 1994 are .434 and .479, respectively. The rural Gini coefficient is .414 for Chile. The lower Ginis from this source indicate discrepancies between the two sources of data.

78. While these assertions may be valid, they are difficult to validate, given the authoritarian nature of the regime at the time, which did not allow open political participation or dissent.

79. For a recent study done in the United Kingdom, see James Banks, Andrew Dilnot, and Hamish Low, "The Distribution of Wealth in the United Kingdom," Commentary 45, Institute for Fiscal Studies, London, 1994.

## Chapter 2

1. See, for example, Barry Bosworth, Rudiger Dornbusch, and Raul Laban, eds., *The Chilean Economy: Policy Lessons and Challenges* (Washington, DC: Brookings, 1994); Christian Larroulet, ed., *Private Solutions to Public Problems: The Chilean Experience* (San Fransisco: Center for International Private Enterprise, 1991); William Glade with Rossana Corona, eds., *Bigger Economies, Smaller Governments* (Boulder, Colo.: Westview Press, 1996); Dominique Hachette and Rolf Luders, *Privatization in Chile: An Economic Appraisal* (San Fransisco: International Center for Economic Growth, 1993); and Jose Joaquin Brunner and Cristian Cox, "Dinamicas de Transformacion en el Sistema Educacional de Chile," in Jeffrey M. Puryear and Jose Joaquin Brunner, eds., *Education, Equity, and Competitiveness in the Americas* (Washington: Organization of American States, 1995).

2. The Chicago Boys were called that because most received their training in economics at the University of Chicago. For a detailed discussion of how their role in the government changed after 1973, see Genero Arriagada Herrera and Carol Graham, "Chile: Sustaining Adjustment during Democratic Transition," in Stephan Haggard and Steven B. Webb, eds., *Voting for Reform: Democracy, Political Liberalization and Economic Adjustment* (Oxford University Press for the World Bank, 1994), pp. 242–89.

3. See Peter Diamond and Salvador Valdez-Prieto, "Social Security Reforms," in Bosworth, Dornbusch, and Laban, *Chilean Economy*, pp. 257–59, 273.

4. I discuss Chile's experience with targeted safety net programs in detail in *Safety Nets, Politics, and the Poor: Transitions to Market Economies* (Brookings, 1994), chap. 2.

5. See Graham, *Safety Nets*, pp. 26–27.

6. See Jose Piñera, *El Cascabel al Gato: La Batalla por La Reforma Previsional* (Santiago: Editorial Zig Zag, 1991).

7. There is disagreement about the extent of the reform's effects on the savings rate. See Giancarlo Corsetti and Klaus Schmidt-Hebbel, "Pension Reform and Growth," Policy Research Working Paper 1471, World Bank, Washington, June 1995.

8. The *subvenciones* differ slightly from vouchers in the strictest sense because parents never really received vouchers. Instead they were given the option to enroll in either public or state-subsidized private schools, and the schools received subsidies from the state for each pupil.

9. Budget Director Jose Pablo Arrellano, Ministry of Finance, presentation to Ministry of Finance/Inter-American Development Bank Workshop on Economic Growth and Social Equity, Santiago, July 1996.

10. Before the transition, criticism of economic policies was often carefully couched criticism of the authoritarian regime. See Arriagada and Graham, "Chile: Sustaining Adjustment during Democratic Transition."

11. Kevin Cowan and Jose de Gregorio, "Distribucion y Pobreza en Chile: Estamos mal? Ha Habido Progreso? Hemos Retrocedido?" Paper prepared for the Ministry of Finance/Inter-American Development Bank Workshop on Inequality and Growth, Santiago, July 1996, p. 3. Mario Marcel and Andres Solimano find that one of the principal variables explaining the decline in the income shares of the poorest quintiles during the 1980s was the increase in the unemployment rate. See "Distribution of Income and Economic Adjustment."

12. Christopher Scott, "The New Economic Model in Chile," London School of Economics, November 1994, p. 43.

13. See Graham, *Safety Nets*, chap. 2.

14. It is particularly notable that this tax reform was passed with the support of the conservative right as well as that of the Concertacion government in Congress.

15. Cowan and de Gregorio, "Distribucion y Pobreza en Chile," p. 4.

16. Marcel and Solimano, "Distribution of Income," p. 219.

17. Cowan and de Gregorio, "Distribucion y Pobreza en Chile."

18. This explains the difference between Chile's rankings by the World Bank, which uses individual income, and the Chilean government's continuous survey, the CASEN, which uses household income. See *World Development Report 1994* (Washington: World Bank, 1995); and Cowan and de Gregorio, "Distribucion y Pobreza en Chile."

19. Labor market variables are the most important explanatory variables for the income shares of the poorest and wealthiest quintiles, and minimum wage levels are closely associated with trends in the incomes of the poorest. See Scott, "New Economic Model," p. 43; and Marcel and Solimano, "Distribution of Income." See also Patricio Mujica and Osvaldo Larrañaga, "Politicas Sociales y de Distribucion del Ingreso en Chile," Documentos de Trabajo 106, Inter-American Development Bank, Washington, March 1992.

20. Social security is slightly less progressive: 12 percent of the resources go to the poorest 40 percent, and 60 percent of the resources for

state-sponsored assistance pensions go to the poorest 40 percent. Arrellano, presentation, July 1996.

21. An example of the effects of social expenditure is that while there was a deterioration in distribution from 1992 to 1994 caused by a necessary economic adjustment in 1994, it was less pronounced than the deterioration in pretransfer income distribution, suggesting that social expenditures had a mitigating effect. Cowan and de Gregorio, "Distribucion y Pobreza en Chile," p. 12.

22. Interview with Dagmar Razcynski, director of CIEPLAN, Santiago, December 12, 1996.

23. When asked if their country was progressing, stagnating, or decaying, respondents from Peru and Chile gave the most positive answers, 48 and 43 percent respectively, while those from Venezuela and Mexico gave the most negative answers (18 and 15 percent). For comparison, in Spain 36 percent believed the country was progressing. Chile was second highest after Brazil in ranking its economy's general situation, with 101 points compared to a regional average of 89 points (with an index of 100 for the average of the previous year). It was also among the five countries in which people ranked their personal economic prospects most optimistically: Colombia had 111 points, Brazil 107, Paraguay 106, Chile 105, and Bolivia 100. In general, the rankings for personal economic prospects were higher than those for the region. Opinion Publica Latinoamericana, "Informe de Prensa Encuesta Latinobarometro: 1996," Santiago, October 1996, pp. 7–8.

24. Meanwhile, two-thirds of respondents in the region believe that the current distribution of wealth is unfair. Latinobarometro, cited in Juan Luis Londoño and Marcelo Szekely, "Distributional Surprise after a Decade of Reforms: Latin America in the Nineties," paper prepared for the 1997 annual meeting of the Inter-American Development Bank, Barcelona.

25. The poor state of the health care system was one of the major issues in the 1993 presidential elections. See Alan Angell and Benny Pollack, " The Chilean Elections of 1993: From Polarization to Consensus," *Bulletin of Latin American Research*, vol.14 (May 1995), pp. 105–25. For fairly optimistic views of Chile's health care reforms, see Tarsicio Castañeda, *Para Combatir La Pobreza* (Santiago: Centro de Estudios Publicos, 1990); and Oswaldo Larrañaga, "Chile: A Hybrid Approach," in Elaine Zuckerman and Emmanuel de Kadt, *The Public-Private Mix in Social Services* (Washington: Inter-American Development Bank, 1997).

26. Before the reform in 1980 these rates were brought down to 33.5 and 41 percent, respectively. Hernan Buchi Buc, "Social Security Reform in Chile," in William Glade with Rossana Corona, eds., *Bigger Economies,*

*Smaller Governments: Privatization in Latin America* (Boulder, Colo.: Westview Press, 1996), pp. 59–88, esp. pp. 61, 64.

27. See Scott, "New Economic Model," p. 24; Buchi, "Social Security Reform," p. 69; and Carmelo Mesa-Lago, "Pension Reform in Latin America: Importance and Evaluation of Privatization Approaches," in Glade, *Bigger Economies*, pp. 89–137.

28. Scott, "New Economic Model," p. 28.

29. Interview with Sergio Baesa, president, AFP Santa Maria, Santiago, December 1996. See also Baesa, *Una Mirada al Sistema Privado de Pensiones: Quince Años Despues* (Santiago: Centro de Estudios Publicos, 1995).

30. See Baesa, *Mirada al Sistema Privado de Pensiones*. This is still very low. Other countries that have adopted variations on Chile's model allow for much more foreign investment. Bolivia, for example, allows for 10 to 50 percent of assets to be invested abroad. The appropriate level of foreign investment depends on the size of the domestic market and the benefits of risk diversification and return that can be gained. Seminar on the design of Bolivia's capitalization reforms, Harvard University, April 30, 1997.

31. Scott, "New Economic Model," pp. 23–29.

32. In June 1997, according to the Chilean Embassy in Washington, the minimum monthly wage level in Chile was $171.73, based on an exchange rate of 416 pesos to the dollar.

33. Scott, "New Economic Model," pp. 23–29; and Diamond and Valdez Prieto, "Social Security Reforms," p. 261.

34. Mesa-Lago, "Pension Reform in Latin America," p. 101.

35. Scott, "New Economic Model," pp. 26–27.

36. Interview with Jose Piñera, Santiago, December 1996. See also Jonathan Friedland, "Chile's Celebrated Pension-Fund System Has Growing Pains as Returns Decline," *Wall Street Journal*, August 12, 1997, p. A10.

37. Scott, "New Economic Model," pp. 24–28; Buchi, "Social Security Reform"; Piñera, *El Cascabel al Gato;* and Piñera, "Empowering Workers: The Privatization of Social Security in Chile," *Cato Letters*, no.10 (1996).

38. Corsetti and Schmidt-Hebbel, "Pension Reform and Growth." See also Diamond and Valdez-Prieto, "Social Security Reforms." The minimum pension, for example, may reduce savings as many low-income workers delay contributing so that they can be eligible for the minimum pension. Buchi, "Social Security Reform."

39. Interview with Jaime Ruiz-Tagle, director, Programa de Empleo y Trabajo (PET), Santiago, December 1996.

40. Mesa-Lago, "Pension Reform in Latin America," p. 133.

41. For a detailed description of the equity trade-offs in both systems, see Estelle James, "Pension Reform: Is There an Efficiency and Equity Trade-off?" in Nancy Birdsall, Carol Graham, and Richard Sabot, *Beyond Trade-offs: Market Reforms and Equitable Growth in Latin America* (Brookings and Inter-American Development Bank, forthcoming).

42. Ibid.

43. Friedland, "Chile's Celebrated Pension Fund System."

44. Vendors often receive a $50 to $100 commission for getting a worker to switch AFPs and often share the commission with their clients. A sum of $20, for example, is substantial for low-income workers in Chile. Interview with Sergio Baesa.

45. Diamond and Valdez-Prieto, "Social Security Reforms."

46. Ibid., p. 284. See also "Informe de Prensa: La Imagen Corporativa de las Administradores de Fondos de Pensiones," Market Opinion Research International Note, Santiago, August 1996.

47. Mesa-Lago, "Pension Reform in Latin America."

48. Interview with the principal architect of the reform, Jose Piñera, former minister of labor and social security, Washington, June 1996; and Piñera, *El Cascabel al Gato*.

49. Interview with Jose Piñera.

50. Piñera, *El Cascabel al Gato*.

51. Diamond and Valdez-Prieto, "Social Security Reform."

52. Interview with Alfonso Saran, counselor, Central Reserve Bank, and former member of the core reform team, Santiago, December 1996.

53. Diamond and Valdez-Prieto, "Social Security Reform," pp. 257–328.

54. Ibid., pp. 260–61, 265, 280.

55. Rolf J. Luders, "Massive Divestiture and Privatization: Lessons from Chile," *Contemporary Policy Issues*, vol. 9 (October 1991).

56. Piñera, *El Cascabel al Gato*, p. 125.

57. These surveys were taken in June 1996 in all cities with more than 40,000 inhabitants and covered 1,240 people in a nationally representative sample. See Market Opinion Research International (MORI), "Informe de Prensa: La Imagen Corporativa de las Administradores de Fondos de Pensiones" (August 1996), p. 2.

58. This proposition was confirmed by my interview with Alfonso Saran, Santiago, December 1996.

59. Interview with Martha Lagos, director, MORI, Santiago, December 1996.

60. Interview with Sergio Baesa.

61. See "Chile: Not so Wondrous Pensions," *Economist*, December 14, 1996, p. 46.

62. Varun Gauri, "The Politics of Education Reform in Chile," Ph.D. dissertation, Princeton University, 1996, p. 30. A revised version of the dissertation will be published by University of Pittsburgh Press in late 1998.

63. Tarsicio Castañeda, *Para Combatir La Pobreza* (Santiago: Instituto de Estudios Publicos, 1990); and Gauri, "Politics of Education Reform," pp. 33, 45.

64. For spending trends in the region, see Elaine Zuckerman and Emmanuel de Kadt, *The Public-Private Mix in Social Services* (Washington: Inter-American Development Bank, 1997).

65. Interview with Maria Theresa Infante, key figure in reforms by the Pinochet regime, Santiago, December 1996; and Taryn Rounds Parry, "Theory Meets Reality in the Great Voucher Debate," Department of Political Science, University of Georgia, 1996. This paper is in part based on empirical data I developed in conjunction with Donald Winkler of the World Bank and Alan Angell, "Improving the Quality and Equity of Education in Chile: The Programa 900 Esuelas and the MECE-Basica," in Antonia Silva, ed., *Implementing Policy Innovations in Latin America* (Washington, D.C.: Inter-American Development Bank, 1996), p. 2.

66. See the introduction by Elaine Zuckerman in Zuckerman and de Kadt, *Public-Private Mix.*

67. Rounds Parry, "Theory Meets Reality."

68. See Larrañaga, "Chile: A Hybrid Approach," p. 31.

69. Enrollment at the primary school level in Peru in the early 1990s was 88 percent, and at the secondary level 68 percent, although the enrollment of adults in secondary school inflates this figure. In Argentina, primary enrollment was 95.3 percent and secondary enrollment 53.5 percent. See the respective country chapters in Jeffrey M. Puryear and Jose Joaquin Brunner, *Educacion, Equidad, y Competitividad in las Americas* (Washington: Organization of American States, 1995).

70. Municipal primary schools had an average score of 58.3 percent correct answers in mathematics, while private subsidized schools had an average of 61.0 percent. In Spanish the respective averages were 60.7 and 64.5 percent. See Larrañaga, "Chile: A Hybrid Approach," p. 32.

71. Both Rounds Parry, "Theory Meets Reality," and Jorge Rodriguez, "School Achievement and Decentralization Policy: The Chilean Case," *Revista de Analisis Economica*, vol. 3 ( June 1988), pp. 75–88, find that differences in test scores remain significant even after controlling for socioeconomic differences. Gauri, "Politics of Education Reform," disputes the relevance of these results.

72. "Los Desafios de la Educacion Chilena Frente al Siglo 21," Comite Tecnico Asesor del Dialogo Nacional Sobre La Modernizacion

de le Educacion Chilena, Santiago, September 1994 (informally known as the Brunner Report), p. 9.

73. Although average SIMCE scores are higher in the subsidized private schools, the standard deviation is also higher, demonstrating more divergence in quality. Rounds Parry, "Theory Meets Reality."

74. Ibid.; and Caroline Minter Hoxby, "Does Competition among Public Schools Benefit Students and Taxpayers?" Department of Economics, Harvard University, October 1994. By focusing on religious schools instead of comparing areas with and without substantial private school availability, Minter Hoxby uses exogenous variation in private school availability to show that an increase in the number of private schools improves public school performance.

75. Brunner Report.

76. I am grateful to William Savedoff of the IDB and Estelle James of the World Bank for raising these issues on separate occasions.

77. Ernesto Schiefelbein, "Restructuring Education through Competition: The Case of Chile," *Journal of Educational Administration*, vol. 29, no. 4 (1991).

78. Gauri, "Politics of Education Reform."

79. Rounds Parry, "Theory Meets Reality."

80. Seventy-eighty percent of parents in the wealthy Santiago commune of Providencia send their children elsewhere to school. Although this level would undoubtedly be lower in poorer districts, there is a great deal of mobility in urban areas. Gauri, "Politics of Education Reform."

81. Interviews with Christian Cox, director, MECE program, Ministry of Education, December 1996; Maria Theresa Infante; and author's visit to and meetings with officials involved in El Salvador's EDUCO reform, including Cecilia Gallardo de Cano, minister of education, at the IDB Symposium on the Generation of Employment and Local Development, San Salvador, August 1996. For the effects of community participation in other countries, see Emmanuel de Kadt, "Thematic Lessons from the Case Studies," in Zuckerman and de Kadt, *Public-Private Mix*. Judith Tendler notes similar efficiency gains in public sector performance when lower-level public sector workers are given greater responsibility and nonfinancial rewards. See *Good Governments in the Tropics* (Johns Hopkins University Press, 1997).

82. Gauri, "Politics of Education Reform," pp. 13, 23. The sample was 726 households, in which there were 1,221 children in primary or secondary schools. Of these, 42.6 percent were attending private subsidized schools, 40.4 percent municipal schools, 14.8 percent private paid schools, and 2.5 percent corporation schools, a breakdown that compares well with the ministry's figures for the metropolitan area in 1992.

Gauri's econometric analysis found that the likelihood of children's attending high-quality schools increased by 8 percent if parents were informed and 9 percent if they believed they were entitled to send their children to better schools.

83. Interview with Maria Theresa Infante; and Larrañaga, "Chile: A Hybrid Approach."

84. See the introduction by Elaine Zuckerman in Zuckerman and de Kadt, *Public-Private Mix.*

85. Most economists assume that the opportunity costs of the poor's time are very low because they measure the costs by their earnings levels. Yet in relative terms these costs are very high and can preclude their participation in activities that require them to volunteer their time. The opportunity costs of time for a single head of household who works two jobs, for example, may not be large in terms of absolute income, but in relative terms the costs can make a tremendous difference to the household's welfare. In addition, these kinds of households are the least likely to have any child care support, increasing the time constraints on the head of the household.

86. Interview with Martha Lagos, director, Market Opinion Research International (MORI) , December 1996.

87. Gauri, "Politics of Education Reform."

88. For an excellent review of both programs, see Angell, "Improving the Quality and Equity of Education in Chile," in Silva, ed., *Implementing Policy Innovations in Latin America.*

89. Ibid., pp. 9, 15.

90. Ibid., pp. 11–12.

91. The reduction of 1 percentage point in the VAT is equivalent to 3 percent of the current account spending by the government. Presentation of Juan Pablo Arrellano at Ministry of Finance and IDB Conference, July 1996; and "Consolidation of Progress in Education: A New Proposal in Chile," Ministry of Finance and Ministry of Education, June 1996. Maintaining the VAT at this high level is not without opposition. Pamela Aravena, "El Pilar de la Reforma Educativa: Con La Tarea Incompleta," *El Mercurio,* March 9, 1997.

92. Presentation by Sergio Molina, Minister of Education, at Ministry of Finance and IDB Conference on Growth and Equity, Santiago, July 1996.

93. When the MECE program's World Bank funding runs out, for example, the government will continue to fund the rural MECE program. Interview with Christian Cox. Joan Nelson has written extensively about the difficulties of maintaining support for compensation programs favoring the poor when there are no spillover effects for non-poor groups. See "Poverty, Equity, and the Politics of Adjustment," in

Stephan Haggard and Robert Kaufmann, eds., *The Politics of Economic Adjustment: International Constraints, Distributive Conflicts, and the State* (Princeton University Press, 1992). A similar debate has occurred in the United States, where, with the exception of the highly successful Head Start program, targeted social welfare policies have seen their budgets dramatically curtailed. See Theda Skocpol, "Universal Appeal: Politically Viable Policies to Combat Poverty," *Brookings Review*, vol. 9 (Summer 1991), pp. 28–33; and Robert Greenstein, "Relieving Poverty: An Alternative View," pp. 34–35 in the same issue.

94. Interview with Ema Budinich, Centro de Estudios Publicos, Santiago, December 1996.

95. "De Municipios: Bajo Aporte a Elaboracion de Plan Educativo," *El Mercurio*, March 25, 1997, p. 5.

96. Viola Espinola, "The Decentralization of the Education System in Chile, 1980–1994," Inter-American Development Bank, Santiago, April 1995.

97. Interview with Patricio Cariola, director, Centro de Investigacion y de Desarrollo de la Educacion (CIDE), December 1996.

98. Larrañaga, "Chile: A Hybrid Approach," p. 28.

99. Interview with Christian Cox. See also Rene Cortazar, Nora Lustig, and Richard Sabot, "Economic Policy and Labor Market Dynamics in Latin America," in Birdsall, Graham, and Sabot, *Beyond Trade-offs*.

100. Interviews with Sergio Molina and Christian Cox.

101. Ibid.

102. "Desde Febrero Regira Alza de Rentas Docentes," *El Mercurio*, December 12, 1996, p. A1.

103. Interview with Sergio Molina. Some school directors do not want more responsibility because their pay is not increased when they are accorded it.

104. Interviews with Sergio Molina and Christian Cox.

105. Larrañaga, "Chile: A Hybrid Approach," p. 35.

106. Some of these issues may be addressed under the auspices of Juan Pablo Arrellano, who was brought in as education minister in late 1996 because of his reputation when he was deputy minister of finance as a good manager and as tough on the budget. Interview with Christian Cox.

107. An example of these are the Matte schools, special private schools that operate very effectively in poor areas but maintain selective admissions criteria. See Rounds Parry, "Theory into Practice."

108. More active community participation in private schools, for example, might help alleviate one concern about the shift to a primarily private system: that public schools are unique in their ability to produce common values.

109. See Eric Hanushek, ed., *Making Schools Work: Improving Performance and Controlling Costs* (Brookings, 1994).

110. Luders, "Massive Divestiture"; and Roberto Zahler, "Recent Southern Cone Liberalization Reforms and Stabilization Policies: The Chilean Case, 1974–1982," *Journal of Inter-American Studies and World Affairs*, vol. 25 (November 1983), pp. 524, 533.

111. Zahler, "Recent Southern Cone Liberalization," p. 538; and Patricio Meller, "Adjustment and Social Costs in Chile during the 1980s," *World Development*, vol. 19 (November 1991), p. 1559.

112. Luders, "Massive Divestiture," p. 1. See also Hachette and Luders, *Privatization in Chile*.

113. For detail see Vittorio Corbo and Andres Solimano, "Chile's Experience with Stabilization Revisited," in Michael Bruno, and others, eds., *Lessons of Economic Stabilization and its Aftermath* (MIT Press, 1991), pp. 57–91.

114. In 1982, as a result of a deep financial crisis, the Chilean government intervened in sixteen financial institutions, including those belonging to Chile's two largest financial groups, and gained control of about fifty of the nation's largest industries, insurance companies, mutual fund administrators, AFPs, and trading companies. These companies were then referred to as the "odd sector." Hachette and Luders, *Privatization in Chile*, p. 57.

115. See Luders, "Massive Divestiture," p. 5; and Hachette and Luders, *Privatization in Chile*, chap. 4.

116. In the United Kingdom under Margaret Thatcher the state-owned sector was reduced from 11.5 to 6.5 percent of GDP. Christian Larroulet, "Impact of Privatization on Welfare: The Chilean Case, 1985–1989," in Glade, *Bigger Economies*, p. 378.

117. Hachette and Luders, *Privatization in Chile*, p. 103. Jose Piñera, the architect of the social security reform, contends that the sequencing of the reforms was critical and that a virtuous circle was created because the privatized enterprises had a new channel for their stocks and the workers had the possibility of benefiting from productivity increases in the privatized companies through higher stock prices that increased the yield of their savings accounts in the AFPs. See "Empowering People," Testimony before the Senate Committee on Banking, Housing and Urban Affairs, Subcommittee on Securities, Washington, June 25, 1997.

118. Larroulet, "Impact of Privatization," p. 384.

119. Ibid., p. 387.

120. Ibid., pp. 376–77.

121. Ibid. See also Ben A. Pettrazini, "The Labor Sector: A Post-Privatization Assessment," in Glade, *Bigger Economies*, pp. 347–68.

122. For trends in social expenditure during this period, see Graham, *Safety Nets,* chap. 2.

123. Meller, "Adjustment and Social Costs," p. 1559.

124. This consensus became more feasible after the defeat of the Pinochet government in the 1988 plebiscite and when it became clear that the regime would abide by the results. Before then, criticism of economic policy was one of the few ways the opposition could issue public and carefully couched political criticisms of the regime. See Arriagada and Graham, "Chile: Sustaining Adjustment."

125. Alan Angell and Benny Pollack, "The Chilean Elections of 1989," *Bulletin of Latin American Research,* vol. 9, no. 1 (1990), pp. 1–24.

126. Although the opposition was cautious in its promises of increases in social expenditures and other alterations in the economic program, the government candidate, Hernan Buchi, promised, among other things, 1 million new jobs and the building of 100,000 new houses a year. Angell and Pollack, "Chilean Elections of 1989."

127. For detail, see Alejandra Gonzales Rosetti, "The Political Economy of Policy Change: Concepts for Health System Reform," London School of Hygiene and Tropical Medicine, May 1996.

128. There are a great many studies on the role of the state, and the list is too extensive to be covered here. For a discussion of the state's role in resolving issues of equity, see Gosta Eping-Andersen, *The Three Worlds of Welfare Capitalism* (Cambridge, Mass.: Polity Press, 1990). For the role of the state in developing economies and in countries in crisis, see Merilee Grindle, *Challenging the State: Crisis and Innovation in Latin America and Africa* (Cambridge University Press, 1996).

129. How matters of compensation and income distribution are dealt with during the initiation of market reforms may be critical in determining their future resolution, the course that reform takes, and the extent to which it is legitimized among most social groups. Perceptions of inequality are often as important as genuine trends in determining voter behavior, for example. For a discussion of the politics of compensation during reform, see Graham, *Safety Nets.* For a discussion of how unequal societies can be perpetuated even in democracies, see Roland Benabou, "Unequal Societies," NBER Working Paper 5583, Cambridge, Mass., May 1996.

## Chapter 3

1. I would like to thank Geoffrey Shepherd for logistical support and helpful comments on this chapter, Alan Angell and Cheikh T. Kane for useful insights, and Roberto Abusada, Patricia Arregui, and Richard Webb for helpful suggestions.

2. The so-called public choice approach to institutional reforms suggests that incorporating market incentives into the operation of public sector institutions will inevitably lead to better performance. The equity effects of that approach have been largely unexplored.

3. For detail on the Chilean experience, see Genaro Arriagada and Carol Graham, "Chile: Maintaining Adjustment during Democratic Transition," in Stephan Haggard and Steven Webb, eds., *Voting for Reform: Democracy, Political Liberalization, and Economic Adjustment* (Oxford University Press, 1994). For Peru see Carol Graham and Cheikh Kane, "Opportunistic Government or Sustaining Reform: Electoral Trends and Public Expenditure Patterns in Peru, 1990–95," *Latin American Research Review*, vol. 33, no.1 (1998), pp. 71–111.

4. This will obviously vary among societies because there are vast differences in the inequality that societies are willing to tolerate. See, for example, Gosta Esping-Andersen, *The Three Worlds of Welfare Capitalism* (Cambridge, Mass.: Polity Press, 1990).

5. For an illustration of the same dynamic in another country with a high poverty rate, see Carol Graham, "Macroeconomic and Sectoral Reforms in Zambia: A Stakeholders' Approach?" Poverty and Social Policy Department, World Bank, Washington, June 1995.

6. The savings rate was 12 percent in 1990 and 18 percent in 1996, while the investment rate (public and private) was 15 percent in 1990 and 24 percent in 1996. To be comparable to Chile's, savings rates should rise to about 25 percent. Figures are from Roberto Abusada, advisor to the finance minister, Lima, April 1997. The future growth payoffs that are likely from these trends as well as from the structural reforms are discussed in Felipe Ortiz de Zevallos, "The Promise and the Risks of Fujimorrow," *Hemisfile*, vol. 7 (January-February 1996), pp. 8–9.

7. This figure was also provided by Roberto Abusada, April 1997.

8. From 1979 to 1981 the number of workers in tax collection doubled while their salaries fell by 70 percent in real terms. For detail see Carlos Castro y Veronica Zavala, "Reforma de la Administracion Tributaria," in Agusto Alvarez and Gabriel Ortiz de Zevallos, eds., *Implementacion de Politicas Publicas en el Peru* (Lima: Editorial Apoyo, 1995).

9. An excellent and detailed description of these reforms is Philip Keefer, "Reforming the State: The Sustainability and Replicability of Peruvian Public Administration Reforms," World Bank, Washington, September 1995.

10. Alvarez and Ortiz de Zevallos, *Implementacion de Politicas Publicas*. For a good description of the conditions necessary for the reform of state-owned enterprises, see the chapter on politics in *Bureaucrats in Business: The Economics and Politics of Government Ownership* (New York:

University Press and the World Bank, 1995). The principal author of that chapter was Philip Keefer.

11. Kenneth M. Roberts, "Neoliberalism and the Transformation of Neopopulism in Latin America: The Peruvian Case," *World Politics*, vol. 48 (October 1995), p. 100. Roberts challenges the common assumption that populism and neoliberalism are incompatible and uses the example of the Fujimori government in Peru to support his argument.

12. The sector that grew the fastest in 1994 was construction, at 35 percent, then the fishing sector at 31.5 percent (second in the world after China in fishmeal production; it has now again reached the 1970s' high extraction levels). Mining was the slowest, up by only 4.6 percent, while manufacturing was up by 16.2 percent. For detail see Edgardo Favaro and Donna MacIsaac, "Who Benefited from Peru's Reform Program? Poverty Note," Latin America and Caribbean Region, World Bank, Washington, June 1995. Barings Securities rated Peru as the highest growth economy in Latin America. Cited in Stephen Fidler, "Survey of Peru: Post-Recovery Task Is to Heal Divisions," *Financial Times*, March 7, 1996, p. 1.

13. The poverty gap closed from 21 percent of the poverty line to 17.5 percent. From 1994 to 1996, while urban poverty increased from 38.1 percent to 41.9 percent, poverty fell in rural areas from 66.1 percent to 65.3 percent. This suggests that the upward trends for those years were indeed caused by the adjustment, which is more likely to have had immediate effects on urban areas. Figures are from the ENNIV (living standards) survey conducted periodically by the Instituto Cuanto, Lima, *Mil Quinientas Familias Dos Anos Despues: La Pobreza En El Peru*, 1994–1996, November, 1996, pp. 2, 6. These data became available in December 1996. See also Favaro and MacIsaac, "Who Benefited."

14. For detail on the decline in support for parties, see Carol Graham and Cheikh Kane, "Opportunistic Government or Sustaining Reform: Electoral Trends and Public Expenditure Patterns in Peru, 1990–1995," Brookings and World Bank, November 1995.

15. Francisco Sagasti and others, *Democracia y Buen Gobierno: Agenda Peru* (Lima: Editorial Apoyo, 1994), pp. 97, 43, 44, 67.

16. Even usually strong community organizations are affected by this trend. Some communal kitchens and other traditional urban organizations have noted a new reluctance to participate in communal efforts and a tendency to work in the *micro-empresas* or informal sector microenterprises, instead. This was noted by Cecilia Blondet of the Instituto de Estudios Peruanos at an Inter-American Dialogue conference on public sector reform in Lima, March 14–15, 1996.

17. Putnam compares differences in *civicness*, roughly defined as membership in social organizations such as local choral societies, and finds a significant relationship with differences in levels of economic development between the regions in the north and south of Italy. For detail see Robert Putnam, *Making Democracy Work: Civic Traditions in Modern Italy* (Princeton University Press, 1993).

18. Interview with Jaime Althaus, deputy editor, *Expreso*, Lima, October 11, 1995.

19. "Peru: The Dark Side of the Boom," *Economist*, August 5, 1995, pp. 22.

20. Sagasti and others, *Democracia y Buen Gobierno*, pp. 38, 39, 52.

21. Latinobarometro public opinion survey cited in Stephen Fidler, "Survey of Peru."

22. Instituto Cuanto, 1994.

23. Sagasti and others, *Democracia y Buen Gobierno*, p. 42.

24. Underemployment is roughly defined as earning less than $240 a month. For detail, see Sagasti and others, *Democracia y Buen Gobierno;* and "World Bank Poverty Assessment," World Bank, Washington, 1993.

25. The relationship between politics and public expenditure allocations under the Fujimori regime is discussed in detail in Graham and Kane, "Opportunistic Government" (1998).

26. Rafael Hidalgo, "La Torta Social," *Caretas* (September 28, 1995), pp. 24–25.

27. "Ministerio de la Presidencia Concentra 22.6% del Presupuesto," *El Comercio*, October 7, 1995, p. A6.

28. Interview with Javier Abugattas, special advisor for social policy, Ministry of Economics and Finance, Lima, October 6, 1995.

29. Interview with Guillermo Lopez de Romaña, director, Nutrition Research Institute, Lima, October 10, 1995.

30. In national opinion polls people ranked the provision of school infrastructure as the most important achievement of the Fujimori government after the defeat of Shining Path, with stabilizing inflation much lower in importance. For detail on this and expenditure trends and voting, see Graham and Kane, "Opportunistic Government" (1998), pp. 75, 99.

31. See Graham and Kane, "Opportunistic Government" (1998), pp. 91–94.

32. For the early history of Foncodes, see Carol Graham, *Safety Nets, Politics, and the Poor: Transitions to Market Economies* (Brookings, 1994).

33. Julianna Weissman, presentation on Foncodes, World Bank, Washington, March 27, 1996.

34. Foncodes, *Nota Mensual*, November 1994; and interview with Manuel Vara, minister of the presidency, Lima, October 11, 1995.

35. The program was recently cited as a model of success at the 1995 annual Bank-Fund meetings. "Banco Mundial Destaca Programas de Ayuda Social en el Peru," *El Comercio*, October 8, 1995.

36. The food is a specially designed, locally produced breakfast product. See Santiago Cueto, Enrique Jacoby, and Ernesto Pollitt, "Breakfast Prevents Delays of Attention and Memory Functions among Growth Retarded Children," Department of Pediatrics, University of California at Davis and Instituto de Investigacion Nutricional, Lima, January 4, 1996; and Enrique Jacoby, Santiago Cueto, and Ernesto Pollitt, "Benefits of a School Breakfast Program among Andean Children in Huaraz, Peru," *Food and Nutrition Bulletin*, forthcoming. There are plans to expand the program to preprimary school children.

37. Interview with Manuel Vara. Interviews with Patricia Teullet, administrator for the program at the Instituto de Investigacion Nutricional, Lima, September 1994; and Jaime Althaus, "Un Proyecto Alimentario Modelo: Desayunos Escolares," *Expreso*, July 10, 1994.

38. The program has a $10 million budget for the next two years, half from the government and half from external donors. Observers have cited it as a novel and successful program. For a detailed description see Rosario Valdeavellano, "Recompensacion Social Mas que Compensacion Social," *Paginas*, vol. 20 (April 1995), pp. 24–35. See also Keefer "Reforming the State." I also discussed the program with Manuel Vara in an interview.

39. This was certainly a complaint of the administrators of the school breakfast program. Interviews with Patricia Teullet. For detail on the program's troubled relations with NGOs, see Graham, *Safety Nets*.

40. Interview with Manuel Vara.

41. Administrative costs are 1 percent of the ministry's total budget. The Education Ministry spends more than 90 percent of its budget on recurrent costs. For details on the Ministry of the President's budget, see "Ministerio de la Presidencia Concentra 22.6% del Presupuesto."

42. Donald R. Winkler, "Decentralization in Education: An Economic Perspective," discussion paper, Population and Human Resources Department, World Bank, Washington, November 1991. For detail on how resources reallocated to local groups can strengthen their voice vis-à-vis the center and create new bases of support for reform, see Graham, *Safety Nets*.

43. A recent study of decentralized development funding in Mexico, for example, found that the funds only had a beneficial development impact where local governments were already both internally decentralized and accountable to their citizens. See Jonathon Fox and Josefina Aranda, "Decentralization and Rural Poverty in Mexico: Muni-

cipal Solidarity Funds and Community Participation in Oaxaca," paper prepared for the annual meeting of the Latin American Studies Association, Washington, September 28–30, 1995.

44. For a good review of discrimination against indigenous groups, see Alison Brysk and Carol Wise, "Liberalization and Ethnic Conflict in Latin America," *Studies in Comparative International Development*, vol. 32, no. 2 (1997), pp. 76–104.

45. Stephanie Flanders, "Decentralizing Governments: Rolling the Frontiers of the State Downwards," *Financial Times*, October 6, 1995, p. 13.

46. Winkler, "Decentralization in Education."

47. Imagine, for example, the opportunity costs of time for the working head of a poor, single head of household with several children in attending extended community meetings.

48. Winkler, "Decentralization in Education."

49. Ibid.

50. Sagasti and others, *Democracia y Buen Gobierno*, pp. 83, 89, 90.

51. A good example of this is the complaint, written to the Ministry of the Economy, of one mayor in a remote rural district regretting his lack of ability to respond to the initiatives of the Social Expenditure Targeting Program because there was no post office in his district and most correspondence for the program is by mail. Letter from Alcalde Mariano del Pilar Ogarte, Paccaretambo District, Cusco, October 3, 1995; and interview with Javier Abugattas, principal advisor for social policy, Ministry of Economics and Finance, Lima, October 6, 1995.

52. Interview with Hugo Diaz, advisor to the Education Ministry, Lima, October 5, 1995.

53. See Graham and Kane, "Opportunistic Government" (1998), p. 96.

54. Interview with Ivan Rivera, advisor to the Minister of Economics and Finance, Lima, October 12, 1995.

55. "Peru: Dark Side of the Boom," *Economist*, August 5, 1995, p. 23.

56. Even the Ministry of Economics and Finance ran into difficulties with Foncodes when it attempted to involve the institution in a matching grants program with the local governments. Interview with Roberto Abusada, advisor to the economics minister, Lima, October 5, 1995.

57. This discussion of education reform draws heavily on three comprehensive studies: Patricia McLaughlan de Arregui, "Dinamica de la Transformacion del Sistema Educativo en el Peru," *Notas Para El Debate*, no. 12 (Lima: GRADE, 1994), pp. 53–94; Teresa Tovar, Hugo Diaz, and Manuel Iguiñiz, *Educacion Peruana: El Futuro Posible* (Lima: Tarea, 1995); and *Politicas Educativas: Propuestas Para el Debate* (Lima: Tarea, 1994).

58. Sagasti and others, *Democracia y Buen Gobierno, pp. 42, 56.*

59. Arregui, "Dinamica de la Transformacion," p. 54.

60. See Nancy Birdsall, David Ross, and Richard Sabot, "Inequality and Growth Reconsidered," paper presented to the American Economics Association, March 1994.

61. Erik Hanushek, ed., *Making Schools Work: Improving Performance and Cutting Costs* (Brookings, 1994).

62. The level of technical, science, and engineering degrees is 31 percent, a level that is higher only in Chile and Argentina among countries in the region. In Europe the level is 35 percent. See Arregui, "Dinamica de la Transformacion."

63. Pedro Francke Ballvé, "La Educacion Publica Basica y Los Pobres," *Revista Tarea,* no. 35 (June 1995), pp. 3–8.

64. The total increases to 19.5 percent if one adds what is transferred to the regions via the Ministry of the Presidency. See Rafael Hidalgo, "La Torta Social," *Caretas,* September, 28 1995, pp. 24–25.

65. Arregui, "Dinamica de la Transformacion," p. 57; and interview with Hugo Diaz, senior advisor to the Education Ministry, Lima, October 5, 1995.

66. "Educacion: Cero Conducta," *Caretas,* November 4, 1993, pp. 38–41.

67. For a detailed explanation of the coup, see Carol Graham, "Economic Austerity and the Peruvian Crisis: The Social Costs of Autocracy," *SAIS Review,* vol. 13 (Winter-Spring 1993), pp. 45–60. See also Philip Mauceri, "State Reform, Coalitions, and the Neoliberal Autogolpe in Peru," *Latin American Research Review,* vol. 30, no. 1 (1995), pp. 7–37.

68. Interview with Hugo Diaz.

69. Interviews with Manuel Iguiñiz, president, TAREA, Lima, October 9, 1995; and Gloria Helfer, former minister of education, Lima, October 11, 1995.

70. "Discurso de Sergio Molina Silva, Ministro de Educacion en Inauguracion Ano Escolar 1995," Santiago, March 6, 1995.

71. Interview with Luis Carlos Gorritti.

72. Interview with Hugo Diaz.

73. Arregui, "Dinamica de la Transformacion," p. 78.

74. "Padres de Familia Mantiene Lucha por no Privatizacion de un Colegio," *El Pueblo,* Arequipa, October 1, 1994; and Gloria Helfer, "Se Puede Silenciar Al Huaracan Educativo? Los Dolores de Nuestra Senora," *La Republica,* October 21, 1994.

75. For detail see Graham and Kane, "Opportunistic Government" (1998), p. 103.

76. Interview with Manuel Iguiñiz.

77. For detail on this, see Graham and Kane, "Opportunistic Government" (1995).

78. Interview with Luis Carlos Gorritti, coordinator, Foro Educativo, Lima, October 4, 1995. This point was also made by Hugo Diaz, Lima, October 5, 1995.

79. Chapter by Hugo Diaz in Tovar, Diaz, and Iguiniz, *Educacion Peruana*; and interview with Jose Quelopana, secretary general, Ministry of Education, Lima, October 9, 1995.

80. Of particular concern are the 17,000 single-teacher schools in rural areas. See the chapter by Hugo Diaz in Tovar, Diaz, and Iguiniz, *Educacion Peruana*.

81. A pilot program proposed by the World Bank would test different management models in urban and rural schools in poor areas. Although the government has expressed interest in the program since early 1994, it has yet to be implemented. Meanwhile the prime minister noted in his inaugural speech that schools would have responsibility for their own budgets. See "Exposicion del Senor Presidente del Consejo de Ministros y Ministro de Educacion, Dr. Dante Cordova Blanco ante el Congreso de la Republica," August 22, 1995.

82. Interview with Jose Quelopana.

83. Ernesto Cuadra, "Presentation on Education Reforms in Peru," World Bank, Washington, March 27, 1996.

84. INIDEN, *Nota Mensual*, Enero 1995.

85. For an excellent analysis of the role of SUTEP during the military government, see Alan Angell, "Classroom Maoists: The Politics of Schoolteachers under Military Government," *Bulletin of Latin American Research*, vol. 1, no. 2 (1982).

86. Interview with Patricia Arregui, executive director, Grupo de Analisis de Desarrollo Economico (GRADE), October 11, 1995.

87. Interview with Hugo Diaz.

88. Interview with Luis Carlos Gorritti.

89. Some literature suggests that involving unions in education policy has positive results on performance. See, for example, Sam Morley and Antonia Silva, "Problems and Performance in Primary Education Systems: Why Do Systems Differ?" paper prepared for the 1995 annual meeting of the Latin American Studies Association, Washington. A recent study in the United States, however, suggests that the presence of teachers' unions explains how public schools can simultaneously have more generous inputs and worse performance, and that the trend is stronger when public schools dominate the market. Caroline Minter-Hoxby, "Teachers' Unions and the Effectiveness of Policies Designed to Improve School Quality," Harvard University, July 1995.

90. Interview with Luis Carlos Gorritti.

91. However, there are administrative problems involved, such as the relationship with the community and the lack of banking centers in many provinces.

92. There has been a great deal of progress in developing pre-primary education, and the system is now a "vanguard on the continent," with 48 percent of children aged 3–5 enrolled. Interview with Luis Carlos Gorritti; and Arregui, "Dinamica de la Transformacion."

93. In the 1980s the public health budget fell by 50 percent in real terms, and the number of operating health centers in Peru fell from 5,000 to 4,000. Because workers needed to supplement falling real wages with alternative sources of income, the hours of attention at health posts fell to an average of six a day. Interview with Juan Jose Vara and Alberto Sobrevilla, Ministry of Health, Lima, March 12, 1996.

94. In Peru, in contrast with many other countries, fees have traditionally been charged for services and drugs, and are not a result of market-oriented reforms. Previously, these fees were channeled to and administered by the regional authorities (UTES), and the health facilities ultimately received 40–70 percent of the revenues that they generated. See Patricia Paredes-Solari, "Shared Administration in Primary Health Care Facilities: The Case of Peru," Johns Hopkins University, School of Hygiene and Public Health, 1995.

95. The latter three tend to be community members with some familiarity with health issues, such as retired doctors or representatives of NGOs.

96. Paredes-Solari, "Shared Administration."

97. See "Decreto Supremo No. 001-94-SA: Salud," El Peruano, May 2, 1994.

98. Carl E. Taylor, "Report to the Honorable Minister of Public Health of Peru: An Evaluation of CLAS—A New Component in Health Care Reform in Peru," Johns Hopkins University, January 2–15, 1996.

99. People found out about the CLAS through the newspapers, contact with public health personnel, and contact with other communities at regional meetings. Interview with Patricia Paredes-Solari, Johns Hopkins University, Baltimore, March 19, 1996.

100. Interview with Juan Jose Vara and Alberto Sobrevilla; and Taylor, "Report to the Honorable Minister." This evaluation by Taylor, one of the world's experts on local-level public health care, was based on qualitative evaluations of the operations of sixteen CLAS in four subregions in January 1996.

101. Results of La Encuesta Nacíonal sobre Medicíon de Niveles de Vida (ENNIV) 1996 survey, Instituto Cuanto, Lima, December 1996. These figures disproportionately reflect the attendance of lower-income

groups, meanwhile, because the survey excluded the IPSS and military facilities, which primarily attend to urban workers or the military.

102. Interviews with Juan Jose Vara and Dr. Alberto Sobrevilla; Patricia Paredes-Solari; Carl Taylor, Johns Hopins University, Baltimore, April 9, 1996; and Taylor, "Report to the Honorable Minister."

103. Interviews with Juan Jose Vara and Alberto Sobrevilla; Patricia Paredes-Solari.

104. Paredes-Solari, "Shared Administration."

105. Taylor, "Report to the Honorable Minister."

106. Taylor, "Report to the Honorable Minister."

107. This is stressed in Taylor, "Report to the Honorable Minister."

108. Taylor, "Report to the Honorable Minister."

109. Rosemary Thorp and others, "Challenges for Peace: Towards Sustainable Social Development in Peru," report prepared for the Inter-American Development Bank, Washington, 1994; and interview with Jaime Freunt, minister of health, Lima, September 1994.

110. In contrast to the flood of information about the private system, not all of which was accurate, no information about the public system was made available. Interview with Carlos Diaz Aliaga.

111. For detail on state personnel increases under the APRA government, see Carol Graham, *Peru's APRA: Parties, Politics, and the Elusive Quest for Democracy* (Boulder: Lynne Rienner, 1992).

112. Jose Danos and others, *Sistema Privado de Pensiones: Desafios y Respuestas* (Lima: CEDAL Ediciones, 1994), p. 13 (my translation).

113. Julio Castro, "Defender La SNP Para Modificarlo"; and Kurt Bermeo, "Una Caracterizacion del Sistema Privada de Pensiones," in Danos and others, *Sistema Privado de Pensiones*.

114. Superintendencia de Administradoras Privadas de Fondos de Pensiones, *Memoria 1994*, Lima, 1995; and interview with Maximo Vega Centeno, director, Department of Economics, Universidad La Catolica, and Maria Antonia Remenyi, La Catolica, Lima, October 10, 1995.

115. The Peruvian experience stands in sharp contrast to the experiences of other countries, where reform of social security systems has been far more controversial. This stems from the small percentage of the labor force that was covered by the scheme, the widespread agreement that the previous system was bankrupt, and the political consensus on the macroeconomic reform program.

116. Interview with Carlos Boloña, former finance minister, Lima, October 12, 1995 (my translation).

117. Interviews with Carlos Boloña and Enrique Diaz Ortega.

118. Interview with Maximo Vega Centeno and Maria Antonia Remenyi.

119. Superintendencia de Administradoras Privadas de Fondos de Pensiones, *Boletin Informativo Mensual*, No. 08-95, Lima, August 31, 1995. See also Richard Lapper, "New Deal Fuels Price Rises," *Financial Times*, March 7, 1996, p. 2.

120. These fears were reasonable given that the Ministry of Economics was already responsible for the debts of the IPSS to the remaining workers, as well as the payment of recognition bonds. With the creation of the private scheme, the management of IPSS pensions was transferred to the ministry, in the Oficina de Normalizacion Previsional (ONP), modeled on a similar system in Chile. This debt is growing as those workers with the higher contribution rates switched to the private system. The highest-income 20 percent that left accounted for 60 percent of contributions. See Danos and others, *Sistema Privado de Pensiones*. Eventually these fiscal costs may be eased by plans that allow for different funding mechanisms, such as the Citizen Participation Scheme, which proposes to allow workers to cash in their recognition bonds for shares in enterprises that are auctioned off through the plan. Interview with Enrique Diaz Ortega.

121. This was worsened by the 1994 collapse of the CLAE market, a large informal savings plan.

122. Even supporters of the Fujimori regime could have doubts about the likelihood of future governments recognizing these bonds at their full value.

123. To be eligible for a recognition bond, workers had to have been contributing to the IPSS in the previous six months and to have contributed for a total of forty-eight months in the past ten years. The maximum bond was 60,000 soles. See Danos and others, *Sistema Privado de Pensiones*. See also "ONP Tramitara los Bonos de Reconocimiento," *El Comercio*, October 8, 1995. Of the total that joined the private system, 582,588 have the right to a recognition bond, but only 4,547 of those are in the 61 to 67 age range, implying a relatively small fiscal burden in the short term. And of the 600,000 who said that they had rights to bonos in the future, only 23,000 had formally registered their right, presumably because they lacked data to prove their contribution record.

124. Because most workers in the new system joined without a minimum, it would be relatively simple to introduce a minimum plan with strong conditions, such as at least fifteen years of contributions, which would limit the fiscal implications yet counter the popular dislike created by the absence of a minimum. The minimum must be backed by the government resources, however, since taxing individual accounts to finance it would run counter to the objective of encouraging individual savings. The government has yet to address the issue in a serious manner. Interview with Enrique Diaz Ortega.

125. Because there are some 30,000 new entrants into the formal private sector each year, these figures indicate substantial switching from the public system. There is no difference, however, in the basic traits of the workers that joined the new program: they tend to be relatively young (less than 45 years), and their average income is above $450 a month. Interview with Enrique Diaz Ortega; and "El Sistema Privado de Pensiones en 1995," *Aporte*, February, 1996, pp. 10–11.

126. "Sistema de Pensiones no Desaparecera" and "Debe Establecerse Edad Minima Para Pensionistas del D.L. 20530," *Expreso*, March 10, 1996, p. 4A.

127. Superintendencia de Administradoras Privadas de Fondos de Pensiones, *Boletin Informativo Semanal*, no. 37-95, Lima, October 2–8, 1995, and no. 10-96, March 4–10, 1996.

128. Superintendencia de Administradoras Privadas de Fondos de Pensiones, *Boletin Mensual Informatico*, no. 08-95, Lima, August 31, 1995. The fund administrators placed several conditions on switching, however, to prevent another expensive advertising campaign and to avoid the high transaction costs of large numbers of people switching randomly from fund to fund. In Chile, one in every four workers switches, which adds very high administrative costs to the system. Fund administrators are actually planning to propose a law that would provide financial incentives for remaining in one AFP for a fixed period of time. Interview with Enrique Diaz Ortega.

129. Interviews with Maximo Vega Centeno and Maria Antonia Remenyi; and with Cesar Aliaga, legal advisor, Centro de Asesoria Laboral del Peru (CEDAL), Lima, October 9, 1995.

130. Of the initial 9 percent in the IPSS, 3 percent went to pensions, 3 percent to FONAVI, and 3 percent to the IPSS. Employers contributed 18 percent. Now it is 11 percent to pensions, while the employer contributes 9 percent to FONAVI and 9 percent to the IPSS. The AFP was 10 percent to pensions, 2 percent to commission, 1 percent to the solidarity bond to the IPSS, and 1.6 percent for life insurance. The AFP rates are now 8 percent to pensions, 2 percent to commission, 0 to IPSS, and 1.4 percent to life insurance. For detail see "Mas Cargos Sobre Los Trabajadores," *Actualidad Economica*, no. 165 (July 1995).

131. The government seems to have backed off the decision to prohibit new entrants into the public system, at least temporarily.

132. "El Sistema Privado de Pensiones en 1995," *Aporte*, February, 1996, pp. 10–11.

133. "Perfiles Atitudinales: Evaluacion Cualitativa," *AFP Horizonte*, Lima, August-September 1995.

134. Interview with Jaime Shimabukuru, technical coordinator, Citizen Participation Scheme, Lima, October 10, 1995.

135. Cheikh Kane, "Policy Note: Reform of Peru's Pension System," Poverty and Social Policy Department, World Bank, Washington, June 1995.

136. The study comprised 100 workers from income levels B and C (group C earns less than $500 per month, while B earns less than $1,000). "Perfiles Atitudinales: Evaluacion Cualitativa," *AFP Horizonte*, Lima, August-September 1995.

137. A survey of informal sector workers taken in the late 1980s found that they did not want to join the public system because of the low value of the pensions, the time lost waiting in line to get services, and time lost in traveling to the town center to get services. Carmelo Mesa-Lago, *La Seguridad Social y el Sector Informal* (Santiago: Prealc, 1990).

138. Another example of this is Zambia, where a comprehensive health reform and decentralization program had caused the poor to refrain from using health care posts. Because of some of the traditional obstacles facing the poor, such a lack of adequate access to information, as well as weak administrative capacity on the part of the government, critical elements of the reform, such as an exemptions clause for those that could not pay user fees and for children under five, were not clear. Thus a theoretically progressive reform ended up falling short because the nonmarket reasons for the poor's not being able to participate or benefit were not adequately addressed. See chapter 6.

139. The strategy of the current fund administrators is to increase the capital base of the AFPs first, then develop strategies to attract lower-income, informal sector workers. Interview with Carlos Diaz Aliaga.

140. Interview with Enrique Diaz Ortega.

141. More recently the agency that administers the program, CO-PRI, had its institutional positioning switched. It was previously responsible to the minister of mines, but since March 1996 it responds to the more powerful prime minister. Interview with Jaime Shimabukuru, techincal coordinator for the Participation Program, Lima, March 14, 1996.

142. Sally Bowen, "Small Investors Pushed Aside in Peru Telecom Privatisation," *Financial Times*, July 4, 1996, p. 12; and Bowen, "Peruvians Rush to Buy Luz del Sur Shares," *Financial Times*, November 25, 1996, p. 22.

143. "Peru: The Dark Side of the Boom," *Economist*, August 5, 1995, p. 21.

144. "Culmino venta de Acciones al Publico en Cementera," *Gestion*, June 6, 1995, p. 13.

145. Interview with Agusto Alvarez, senior investigator, APOYO, and principal advisor to Citizen Participation Program, Lima, October 5, 1995.

146. Interview with Javier Tovar, executive director, Citizen Participation Program, Lima, October 12, 1995.

147. Interview with Roberto Abusada.

148. Although recognition bonds would have been an attractive way to reduce the government's large debt to the public pension system, the Economics Ministry's (understandable) reluctance to issue them too quickly has slowed the development of this option. If the option is allowed, it will give preference to older and lower-income workers who have already joined AFPs. Interview with Jaime Shimabukuru, Citizen Participation Program, Lima, October 6 and October 10, 1995, and March 14, 1996.

149. Interview with Javier Tovar.

150. Interview with Jaime Shimabukuru.

151. Unpublished document, Citizen Participation Campaign, Lima, October 1995.

152. Interview with Nilda Zavaleta, street saleswoman, in "Como Comprar Acciones Sin Tener Mucho Dinero," *Nuestra Casa*, August 1994 (my translation).

153. Interviews with Marilu Alegria de Gutierrez and Walter Zavaleta Alvarado in "Trujillanos Forman Cola Para Comprar Acciones de Cementos Norte Pacasamayo," *La Industria*, November 24, 1994 (my translation).

154. Unpublished participant survey, Citizen Participation Program, Lima, October 1995.

155. Headlines in *Ojo* and *La Republica*, November 23, 1994, and December 11, 1994 (my translation).

156. Interview with Jaime Shimabukuru.

157. Citizen Participation Program, Participant Survey, 1994.

158. Interview with Carlos Montoya; and "Nuevo Cronograma de Privatizacion No Afectara Programa de Participacion Ciudadana," *Gestion*, January 24, 1996, pp. 1–2.

159. "Venderan Entre un 10 percent y 15 percent de Acciones Estatales de Edelnor y Luz del Sur," *El Comercio*, April 6, 1995, p. E1.

160. Interview with Jaime Althaus, deputy editor, *Expreso*, October 11, 1995.

161. Interview with Javier Tovar.

162. Interviews with Jaime Shimabukuru; and Augusto Alvarez, APOYO, and advisor to the Citizen Participation Program, March 12, 1996. See also "Banco de Credito Barrio Con Wiese, Interbanc, y Continental," *Expreso*, January 30, 1996.

163. Bowen, "Small Investors"; Sally Bowen, "Lima Hangs up on Hopeful Share Buyers," *Financial Times*, July 4, 1997; and "Participacion Ciudadana Oficializo el Recorte," *Expreso*, July 5, 1997.

164. Bowen, " Peruvians Rush to Buy Luz del Sur Shares."

165. Information provided by Apoyo, S.A., the consulting firm that advised the program on public relations and other logistics for the Telefonica sale, Lima, June 1996.

166. Estimated values from the Citizen Participation Program, March 1996.

167. Carlos Montoya, for example, the former head of COPRI, noted a substantial slowing in the pace of COPRI's activities after his end-1995 departure. Interview, March 15, 1996.

168. Of those interviewed in a survey conducted by a private firm, EIPIM, 66 percent were against privatizing PetroPeru for national sovereignty reasons, 23.1 percent were in favor, and 10.4 percent had no opinion. "Tercera Encuesta Confirma Que Mayoria de Peruanos Defiende Empresa Estatal," *La Republica*, February 25, 1996, p. 1.

169. The questionnaire being developed seems designed to reach the lower-income strata, if not the lowest. Unpublished questionnaire, APOYO, Lima, October 1995.

170. Interview with Augusto Alvarez.

171. Interviews with Jaime Shimabukuru; and Cesar Mosquera Leyva, "AFP y Venta de Empresas Estales," *Actualidad Economica*, no. 165, June 1995, p. 62.

172. Interviews with Carlos Montoya and Jaime Shimabukuru.

173. "Trabajadores de Empresas Privatizadas Compraron Acciones por US$36.38 million," *El Peruano*, May 22, 1995, p. B1.

174. In the 1989–90 fiscal year, state-owned enterprises lost $4.2 billion, enough revenue to pave 42,000 km of roads or build 14,000 schools. And since 1991 the government has earned more than $5 billion through privatizations. See Stephen Fidler, "Privatisations," *Financial Times*, March 7, 1996, p. 3.

# Chapter 4

1. I wish to thank Kris McDevitt and Gualberto Rodriguez for research assistance and Jeffrey Sachs of Harvard University for his early willingness to support this research. Jose Valdez, Evette Lopez, and William Blacutt of the Bolivian Ministry of Capitalization provided logistical support and information about the capitalization program, and Ricardo Godoy of Harvard University and Ramiro Salinas from the National Secretariat of Pensions gave helpful comments.

2. For detail, see Carol Graham, *Safety Nets, Politics, and the Poor: Transitions to Market Economies* (Brookings, 1994), chap. 3.

3. The 1992 creation of Unidad de Analisis de Politicas Sociales (UDAPSO), a support organization within the Ministry of Planning, marked the intent of the government to incorporate the operations and approach of the FIS more permanently into the public sector. See Manuel Contreras, "Capacity Building in the Social Policy Analysis Unit in Bolivia: Reflections of a Practitioner," in Merilee Grindle, ed., *Getting Good Government: Capacity Building in the Public Sectors of Developing Countries* (Harvard University Press, 1998).

4. When the NEP was introduced and the tin mining industry dismantled, 30,000 to 70,000 workers lost their jobs and the COB lost much of its power. As many miners went into coca-growing activities, the COB was increasingly dominated by campesinos and teachers. See "Bolivia: El Dificil Proceso de Transformacion," dossier 57, Institute for European-Latin American Relations, Madrid, September 1996.

5. High inflation tends to hurt the poor the most because they have the fewest ways to protect themselves from it. Wealthier groups are able to transfer assets abroad and use other devices to protect themselves and sometimes even benefit from policy swings. Thus establishing macroeconomic stability increases equity. For details, see Nancy Birdsall, Carol Graham, and Richard Sabot, eds., *Beyond Trade-offs: Market Reforms and Equitable Growth in Latin America* (Brookings and Inter-American Development Bank, forthcoming), particularly the chapter by Michael Gavin and Ricardo Hausmann.

6. Juan Antonio Morales, "Bolivia and the Slowdown of the Growth Process," in Leila Frishtak and Izak Atiyas, *Governance, Leadership, and Communication: Building Constituencies for Economic Reform* (Washington: World Bank, 1996), pp. 15–16.

7. ESF wages were at the average for unskilled construction workers. It makes little sense from the standpoint of either poverty relief or politics to concentrate all safety net benefits on relatively privileged losers, as the tin miners were, because they are unlikely to be as well off immediately after reform as they were before, particularly given the levels of compensation available under the fiscal constraints of stabilization. See Graham, *Safety Nets*, chap. 3.

8. The 1991 privatization law allowed for the privatization of more than one hundred state-owned enterprises. Not more than twenty-five were privatized, and they were small, by 1994. See A. Morales, "Bolivia and the Slowdown." The performance contracts between the Bolivian government and large "strategic" state-owned enterprises were introduced in 1990 to help restructure the firms to be more efficient and competitive. See Richard D. Mallon, "State-Owned Enterprise Reform through Performance Contracts: The Bolivian Experiment," *World Development*, vol. 22 (June 1994), pp. 925–34.

9. Although total investment was equivalent to about 20 percent of GDP (a threshold value) in Peru, Colombia, and Ecuador according to IFC (International Finance Corporation) statistics, in Bolivia it was 6 percent. The weighted average for all developing countries is 23.4 percent. The IFC report is discussed in "Venezuela and Bolivia Rates below Average," Knight-Ridder Information, Latin America News, March 7, 1996. Investments in human capital—education in particular—are increasingly recognized as crucial to sustainable economic growth. See, for example, Nancy Birdsall, David Ross, and Richard Sabot, "Inequality and Growth Reconsidered: Lessons from East Asia," *World Bank Economic Review*, vol. 9 (September 1995), pp. 477–508; and Roland Benabou, "Unequal Societies," NBER working paper 5583, Cambridge, Mass., May 1996. Bolivia's rural illiteracy rate of 36 percent is closer to standards for Sub-Saharan Africa than for Latin America. See Sally Bowen, "Andean Struggle for Reform," *Financial Times*, May 1, 1996, p. 12..

10. I discuss this and the role of foreign aid in supporting or undermining domestic political consensus in "Making Foreign Aid Work," co-authored with Michael O'Hanlon, *Foreign Affairs* (July-August 1997), pp. 96–104.

11. For detail on this point, see Rene Antonio Morales, "Bolivia's Silent Revolution," *Journal of Democracy*, vol. 8 (January 1997), pp. 142–56.

12. The growth projections are from a CGE (computable general equilibrium) model constructed by UDAPE (Unidad de Analisis de Politicas Economicas), La Paz, 1997.

13. For comparison, in Peru tax receipts were 4 percent of GDP when Alberto Fujimori took over in 1990 and, as a part of the macroeconomic reform program, increased to 14.3 percent by 1996 (Ministry of Economics and Finance figures, April 1997).

14. R. A. Morales, "Bolivia's Silent Revolution"; and *Informe Nacional al Congreso*, Republica de Bolivia, 1995–96.

15. J. A. Morales, "Bolivia and the Slowdown."

16. R. A. Morales, "Bolivia's Silent Revolution," p. 151.

17. R. A. Morales, "Bolivia's Silent Revolution."

18. Nathaniel C. Nash, "Bolivian Assured of Presidency as Foe Concedes," *New York Times*, June 10, 1993, p. A13.

19. Initial support for both parties may have increased slightly at the time of their leaders' deaths out of sympathy or solidarity, as was demonstrated by the surge in support for UCS in the 1993 elections and the massive turnout for Palenque's funeral in La Paz in March 1997. The personalist nature of both these parties' leadership suggests that this support is unlikely to last.

20. In addition, the populist movement has not been particularly effective at mobilizing latent concerns about ethnocultural cleavages. Be-

cause of the reforms undertaken by the 1952 revolution, the trend in Bolivia has been toward incorporating Indian peoples, respecting diversity and traditional cultures, rather than moving toward Indian separatism. Sanchez de Lozada's vice president, Victor Hugo Cardenas, is an Aymara Indian. See R. A. Morales, "Bolivia's Silent Revolution."

21. The term of the president was also increased from four years to five. See IRELA,"Bolivia: El Dificil Proceso."

22. Peter McFaren, "Ex-Dictator May Win Bolivian Election," AP Wire Service, June 2, 1997; and "Bolivia Names Ex-Dictator President," *New York Times*, August 6, 1997, p. A8.

23. "Bolivia Arrests Strikers," *New York Times*, April 20, 1995, p. A11.

24. "Public Workers Riot in Bolivian Capital," *New York Times*, April 3, 1996, p. A9; and "Workers Bitter at Pay and Privatization Tie Up Bolivian Capital," *New York Times*, March 28, 1996, p. A7.

25. The 60 percent figure is a UNDP estimate, cited in IRELA, "Bolivia: El Dificil Proceso," p. 28. The 70 percent figure is slightly high because it is based on basic needs indicators rather than income. See "Bolivia Poverty, Equity, and Income: Selected Policies for Earning Opportunities for the Poor," report 15272-BO, World Bank, Washington, 1996. See also Wilson Jimenez and Ernesto Yanez, "Ingresos Familiares Urbanos en un Contexto de Crecimiento," UDAPSO, La Paz, April 1997.

26. *World Development Report, 1995* (Washington: World Bank, 1995).

27. IRELA, "Bolivia: El Dificil Proceso," p. 30; and *World Development Report 1996* (Washington: Oxford University Press and World Bank, 1996).

28. Contreras, "Capacity Building."

29. Gary Fields and others, "A Decomposition of Labor Income Inequality in Bolivia," Harvard Institute for International Development, Boston, April 1997, p. 9. Another factor, for which there are not yet data, is discrimination against indigenous people. For a general review of this issue in the Andean countries, see Alison Brysk and Carol Wise, "Liberalization and Ethnic Conflict in Latin America," *Studies in Comparative International Development*, vol. 32, no. 2 (1997), pp. 76–104.

30. Manuel Contreras, "Genesis, Formulacion, Implementacion, y Avance de la Reforma Educativa en Bolivia," Harvard Institute for International Development and Universidad Catolica Boliviana, La Paz, 1997, p. 8.

31. These figures are based on opinion polls conducted and elaborated by the Universidad Catolica in the major cities in the country. See Contreras, "Genesis," p. 15.

32. Interview with Manuel Contreras, Universidad Catolica and Harvard Institute for International Development and former head of the Unidad de Analisis de Politicas Sociales (UDAPSO), La Paz, March 11, 1997.

33. The difficulties of carrying out institutional reform are discussed in Carol Graham and Moises Naim, "The Political Economy of Institutional Reform," in Birdsall, Graham, and Sabot, *Beyond Trade-offs.*

34. This point was raised by Manuel Contreras at an informal discussion with the president and his advisors sponsored by Harvard University, Cambridge, April 30, 1997.

35. See, for example, "ADN: Lineamientos-Programa de Gobierno," *La Razon*, March 12, 1997, p. B2.

36. For the relationship between growth and poverty reduction in the region, see Michael Bruno, Martin Ravaillion, and Lyn Squire, "Equity and Growth in Developing Countries: Old and New Perspectives on the Policy Issues," Policy Research Working Papers 1563, World Bank, Washington, January 1996. For the role of investments in human capital, see Birdsall and Sabot, "Inequality and Growth"; and Benabou, "Unequal Societies."

37. I discuss these issues in detail in Graham, *Safety Nets,* chap. 3.

38. Interview with Eduardo Antelo, UDAPSO, La Paz, March 10, 1997.

39. Apparently Sanchez de Lozada was also influenced by the U.S. experience in establishing social security in the aftermath of the Great Depression. Informal discussions with international advisers to the president, Cambridge, Mass., April 30, 1997.

40. Interview with Alfonso Robello, minister of capitalization, La Paz, March 11, 1997.

41. Carl Honore, "Modern World Closing in on Rural Bolivia: Many Lack Electricity, But They May Get Pensions," *Miami Herald*, September 25, 1995, p. A10.

42. Presentation by Ministry of Capitalization team at the World Bank, Washington, June 23, 1997; and presentation by Luis Paz of MIT at a Harvard meeting with President Gonzalo Sanchez de Lozada on the Plan de Todos reforms in which I participated, April 30, 1997.

43. Presentation by Edgar Saviria, one of the architects of the reform, at the World Bank, Washington, June 23, 1997.

44. *Informe Nacional al Congreso, 1995–96*; and Ministry of Capitalization statistics.

45. Ministry of Capitalization figures, 1997.

46. Interview with Hugo Vits, Bolivia representative of Consorcio Enron/Shell, La Paz, March 12, 1997.

47. Presentation by Edgar Saviria, June 23, 1997.

48. *Informe Nacional al Congreso, 1995–96.*

49. Presentation by Edgar Saviria, and several conversations with Jose Valdez, subsecretary for promotion, Ministry of Capitalization, La Paz, March 1997, and Washington, June 1997.

50. Figures from the National Secretariat of Pensions, La Paz, 1997; and interview with Theresa Vargas, director of standards, National Secretariat of Pensions, La Paz, March 12, 1997. The estimated debt of the complementary funds was $9 million. See Luis Carlos Jemio, "The New Pension System in Bolivia," paper prepared for the Harvard University seminar "The Reform Process in Bolivia," April 30, 1997.

51. Jemio, "New Pension System," p. 8; and interviews with the pension reform team in La Paz in March 1997 and Washington in May 1997. Although the reform thus results in a net "savings," there are obviously short-term versus long-term expenditure trade-offs involved.

52. Under the previous system the state paid 1.5 percent and the employer paid 4.5 percent of the 14.82 percent rate. Figures from the National Secretariat of Pensions.

53. Interview with Jose Valdez, subsecretary for promotion, Ministry of Capitalization, La Paz, March 10, 1997.

54. Those in the banking sector could retire earlier, at 50 and 45 years, respectively, but were required to make a greater number of contributions during their employment period. National Secretariat of Pensions data, La Paz, March 1997.

55. National Secretariat of Pensions, 1997.

56. Interview with Theresa Vargas.

57. Interview with Theresa Vargas.

58. Sally Bowen, "Pension Law Starts Bolivian Strike," *Financial Times*, November 12, 1996, p. 9.

59. Interview with Theresa Vargas; and interview with Elvira Lopez, director for consolidation of complementary funds, National Secretariat of Pensions, La Paz, March 11, 1997.

60. Interview with Elvira Lopez.

61. This issue was raised by Laurence Kotlikoff at the April 30 Harvard meeting with President Sanchez de Lozada. Although many countries would also want to keep a higher percentage of the funds at home due to reasons of national interest or national pride, the size of the Bolivian market would make it difficult for the AFPs to meet a guaranteed rate of return. Another view, raised by Daniel Lessard, is that Bolivia is too small to worry about having capital markets; it should have an adequate banking system and then "free-ride" on world capital markets. President Sanchez de Lozada believed that political pressure would aim toward Chile-style requirements for investments in local companies. The exact amount that could be invested abroad is agreed upon annu-

ally by the AFPs and the Central Bank, albeit within the 10 percent to 50 percent margin.

62. National Secretariat of Pensions, 1997.

63. Lally Weymouth, "Dictator Turned Democrat," *Washington Post*, October 22, 1997, p. A21.

64. Interview with Jose de la Fuente, general manager for AFP Banco Bilbao Viscaya, La Paz, March 12, 1997.

65. "Entel Bajo Su Oferta de Inversiones Para el '97," *La Razon*, March 13, 1997, p. B4.

66. Recent research suggests that the poor are more likely to make additional sacrifices in consumption to save for their children's education if there are employment opportunities available that make the investments worthwhile. See Nancy Birdsall and Richard Sabot, "Inequality, Savings, and Growth," Williams College and Inter-American Development Bank, November 1995.

67. This point was made by Daniel Lessard at a Woodrow Wilson Center conference on Bolivia's capitalization reforms held in Washington, May 19, 1997.

68. Laurence Whitehead, "Bolivia's Capitalization Programme: Taking Neoliberal Precepts One Step Further," paper prepared for Ministry of Capitalization Conference, Miami, April 12, 1997, pp. 15, 17.

69. Ibid., p. 7.

70. *Informe Nacional al Congreso, 1995–96.*

71. Interview with Jorge Blanes, director, Centro Boliviano de Estudios Multi-Disciplinarios (CEBEM), La Paz, March 11, 1997.

72. J. A. Morales, "Bolivia and the Slowdown."

73. Gabriel Escobar, "Change in Bolivia: No One Said It Would Be Popular," *Washington Post*, April 17, 1996, p. A28.

74. Interview with Hugo Vits, local representative for Enron/Shell, La Paz, March 12, 1997.

75. J. A. Morales, "Bolivia and the Slowdown."

76. Interviews with Elvira Lopez; and Jorge Harriague, executive director, Procurement Division, Bolivian Ministry of Capitalization, Washington, May 6, 1996. Even President Sanchez de Lozada cites inadequate communication, in part due to not having enough time, as being one of the major flaws of the program. He noted this in a presentation at the Brookings Institution, Washington, May 2, 1997.

77. Interview with Claude Bessi, superintendent for the electricity sector, La Paz, March 10, 1997.

78. Interviews with Elvira Lopez; and Jorge Harriague.

79. Interview with Hugo Vits.

80. Interview with John Vega, administrative and financial manager, Empresa Electrica Guaracachi, Santa Cruz, March 13, 1997.

81. "Si Usted Tiene Mas de 65 Anos, Aliste Su Carnet de Identidad, el Bonosol Llegara el 2 de Mayo," *La Razon*, March 13, 1997, p. 20.

82. Presentation at the World Bank by Edgar Saviria, one of the principal architects of the capitalization reform, Washington, June 23, 1997. Interviews with bonosol recipients appeared in "Durante el Cobro del Bonosol los Ancianos Recibieron Atencion Medica," *Hoy*, May 6, 1997, p. 6; "Risas y Lagrimas en un Dia Diferente Para 4885 Beneficiarios," *Hoy*, May 6, 1997, p. A4; Jose Medrano C., "El Pago del Bonosol," *Los Tiempos*, May 7, 1997, p. B2; "Incredulidad y Alegria en Sucre," *Hoy*, May 6, 1997; and "Dos Mil Quinientos Beneficiados en Trinidad," *Hoy*, May 6, 1997, p. A4.

83. Interviews with Hugo Vits, John Vega, and Jose Maria de la Fuente.

84. The rationale for this is to encourage new investment, which will be matched by locally generated revenue to cover operating costs. By 2001, municipalities will have to allocate 85 percent of their own revenues to investment, a requirement that may be too high for effective operations and impinges on their new autonomy by restricting their independence over locally generated resources. For a detailed discussion of this see John Stith, "Strategies for National Influence toward Municipal Investment Decisions in Bolivia," paper prepared for the John F. Kennedy School of Government, Harvard University, and to UDAPSO, La Paz, April 1997, pp. 4, 7.

85. For details see "Popular Participation and Rural Decentralization in Bolivia," report prepared for the Swedish International Development Agency (SIDA), La Paz, November 1996; and Fernando Ruiz Mier and Bruno Giussani, "La Decentralizacion y el Financiamiento de la Provision de Servicios de Educacion y Salud en Bolivia," UDAPSO, La Paz, 1997.

86. Interview with one of the few observers of this process, La Paz, March 1997.

87. SIDA, "Popular Participation."

88. See Kathleen O'Neill and others, "The First Two Years of 'Popular Participation' in Bolivia: A Case Study in Policy Reform," UDAPSO and Harvard Institute for International Development, November 1996. Although ideally municipal governments would rely less on transfers and more on local resources, in the short term this would be difficult to achieve for most rural municipalities, where the majority of their population lives below the poverty line.

89. For detail see George Gray Molina, "Social Investments under Popular Participation in Bolivia: Explaining Municipal Investment Choices," UDAPSO/HIID, La Paz, November 1996; and SIDA, "Popular Participation."

90. Ibid.

91. Ibid., p. 4. These figures come from a study conducted by the author and a research team affiliated with HIID and UDAPSO. They compiled a database of fiscal, political, social, and demographic traits of the 311 municipalities in the country from 1994–1996. They also conducted more qualitative field studies in 40 rural municipalities in 5 departments throughout the country. As always in cases where it is difficult to collect accurate and comprehensive data, a word of caution about the accuracy of the data is in order.

92. Nearly all municipalities met the first requirement in 1996, but only 47 percent met the economic development requirement and only 37 percent met both. Enforcement of this regulation was very lax, however, and no municipality was officially cited as violating the requirement in 1996. See Stith, "Strategies for National Influence," pp. 9–10.

93. Gray Molina, "Social Investments," p. 5.

94. Ibid., p. 11.

95. Ibid., pp. 11–12; and interview with Gray Molina, La Paz, March 11, 1997.

96. See O'Neill and others, "First Two Years." There are several other funds in addition to the FIS, but in general they are relatively inefficient and ineffective. The Fondo de Desarrollo de Campesinsos, for example, spent more on operating costs in its first three years ($3 million) than in disbursements ($2 million), a record that seems to support the frequent criticism that the fund is politicized and riddled with corruption. Interview with Nico Van Niekerk, special adviser for NGO issues to the Economics Ministry, La Paz, March 13, 1997.

97. Interview with Hugo Frias, director, Secretariat for Popular Participation for Santa Cruz, Santa Cruz, March 13, 1997.

98. Communities with more grassroots organizations tend to invest more in civil works and infrastructure projects, while those with fewer organizations invest more in education. In part this reflects differences in education levels: less educated people seem to want more education. It also reflects the greater organizational capacity required for implementing larger civil works and infrastructure projects. Jean Paul Faguet, "Participatory Planning and Decentralization: Assessing Local Government Performance," Ph.D. dissertation, London School of Economics, 1996.

99. SIDA, "Popular Participation." In addition to its overall study, the report relies on in-depth field studies conducted in four "representative" municipalities. Also, interview with Nico Van Niekerk, special adviser for NGO Issues, Ministerio de Hacienda, La Paz, March 13, 1997.

100. The Andean tradition of *rotacion de cargos* or rotation of posts, for example, does not lend itself to accumulating experience and can be an obstacle to leadership development. Some indigenous communities

also have much more rigid internal structures and are much more hesitant to cooperate in joint leadership structures than are others. See SIDA, "Popular Participation"; and Jose Blanes, Rolando Sanchez, and Jose Rodolfo Arias, "Impactos Socio-Politicos de la Implementacion de la Ley de Participacion Popular En Las Comunidades Rurales de La Paz," CEBEM, March 1996.

101. See O'Neill and others, "First Two Years."

102. This was the case in Cotoca in Santa Cruz, for example, where, according to the president of the committee, the mayor sent a group of thugs to intimidate the vigilance committee, which was challenging his use of public resources for personnel ventures. The committee's attempts to solicit a response from the center, meanwhile, received no reply. Apparently a similar situation occurred in neighboring Puñate. Interview with Señora Tania Cronenbold Suarez, vigilance committee president, Cotoca, Santa Cruz, March 13, 1997. This account was confirmed by reports of similar instances elsewhere. See, for example, "Guarayos Muestra Su Rostro Indigena," La Razon, March 13, 1997, p. A12. See also Blanes, Sanchez, and Arias, "Impactos Socio-Politicos."

103. Interview with Jorge Blanes, CEBEM, March 12, 1997. Blanes cites instances where in polls of up to fifty campesinos in a rural La Paz municipality, not one knew a member of the vigilance committee. A more general survey found that 42 percent of those surveyed did know someone on the committee. See George Gray Molina and Carlos Hugo Molina, "Popular Participation and Decentralization in Bolivia: Building Accountability from the Grass Roots," paper prepared for the Harvard Seminar to Evaluate the Reforms in Bolivia, Cambridge, Mass., April 30, 1997.

104. IRELA, "Bolivia: El Dificil Proceso," p. 31.

105. See Gray Molina, "Popular Participation."

106. In Santa Cruz, for example, some NGOs told people that they had a right to claim their per capita expenditure allocations individually and that they could demand them from the program secretariat, which created all sorts of problems for the program administration. Interview with Hugo Frias, Santa Cruz, March 13, 1997.

107. Interview with Torres Goita, MNR senator, La Paz, March 11, 1997.

108. One such example was in the municipality of Independencia in Cochabamba, where the rural unions were at the forefront of the opposition and disinformation campaign until March 1995, when, under the umbrella of the United Left and the Asamblea Para la Soberania de los Pueblos, they defeated the MIR-ADN incumbents and took over the municipality. SIDA, "Popular Participation."

109. For details on this dynamic in Peru, for example, see Carol Graham and Cheikh Kane, "Opportunistic Government or Sustaining Reform: Electoral Trends and Public Expenditure Patterns in Peru, 1990–95," *Latin American Research Review*, vol. 33, no.1 (1998), pp. 71–111. Even in Chile, where parties are traditionally strong, local elections are influenced less and less by national party competition. I would like to thank Alan Angell for raising this point.

110. For detail, see SIDA, "Popular Participation."

111. Ibid., p. 45.

112. Interview with George Gray Molina, UDAPSO/HIID, La Paz, March 11, 1997.

113. Interview with Hugo Frias, secretary general for Popular Participation for Santa Cruz, Santa Cruz, March 13, 1997.

114. SIDA, "Popular Participation."

115. This problem is less marked in education because teachers apparently do attend their assigned posts. Interview with Hugo Frias. This problem was also noted by the president himself in an informal meeting in Cambridge, Mass., April 30, 1997. He noted the political difficulties entailed in devolving the responsibility for hiring and firing to the local level, difficulties that could have jeopardized the reform.

116. See Ruiz and Giussani, "La Decentralizacion y el Financiamiento." See also Manuel Contreras, "Genesis, Formulacion, Implementacion, y Avance de la Reforma Educativa en Bolivia," Harvard Institute for International Development and Universidad Catolica Boliviana, La Paz, 1997.

117. Interview with George Gray Molina, UDAPSO, March 11, 1997.

118. A recent study found that variables such as illiteracy, lack of health care, and shortages of water and sanitation services had no significant effects on the investment decisions of municipalities. See Stith, "Strategies for National Influence."

119. Ruiz and Giussani, "La Decentralizacion y el Financiamiento," p. 12.

120. For example, no municipality's 1996 budget was deemed in violation of the decree by the Finance Ministry. See Stith, "Strategies for National Influence," p. 9.

121. Ibid., p. 14. One criticism of the program is that excess rigidity in financing has led to a reduced quality of health care in certain instances.

122. Interview with Jean Paul Faguet, London School of Economics and the World Bank, La Paz, March 11, 1997.

123. SIDA, "Popular Participation."

124. Interview with Nico Van Niekerk, La Paz, March 13, 1997.

125. See Graham and Naim, "Political Economy of Institutional Reform."

126. Interview with Manuel Contreras, former director, UDAPSO, La Paz, March 11, 1997.

127. A July 1996 poll found that 48 percent of the population approve of the education reform, while 45 percent approved of Popular Participation. Nationwide poll conducted by the National Secretariat of Participation, cited in Contreras, "Capacity Building."

128. See Graham and Kane, "Opportunistic Government."

## Chapter 5

1. I thank Mitchell Orenstein and Jiri Vecernik for helpful comments on this chapter, and Branko Milanovic, Nancy Sherwood Truitt, and Jiri Vecernik for providing me with valuable contacts in the Czech Republic.

2. The so-called public choice approach to institutional reforms suggests that introducing market incentives into the operations of public sector institutions will invariably lead to better performance.

3. This will obviously vary among societies because they differ in their tolerance for inequality. See Gosta Esping-Andersen, *The Three Worlds of Welfare Capitalism* (Princeton University Press, 1990).

4. *Public goods,* as used here, is broader than the purely economic definition. For a discussion of the public goods delivered by public sector institutions, goods that range from "super" public to "quasi" public, see Carol Graham and Moises Naim, "The Political Economy of Institutional Reform in Latin America," in Nancy Birdsall, Carol Graham, and Richard Sabot, eds., *Beyond Trade-offs: Market Reforms and Equitable Growth with Latin America* (Inter-American Development Bank/Brookings, forthcoming).

5. In January 1993 in the so-called velvet divorce, the former Czechoslovakia split into two independent republics: Slovakia and the Czech Republic.

6. Mitchell Orenstein, "Out of the Red: Building Capitalism and Democracy in Post-Communist Europe," Ph.D. dissertation, Yale University, May 1996, p. 82.

7. The poverty rate is according to the government's legal minimum. See Jiri Vecernik, *Markets and People: The Czech Reform Experience in Comparative Perspective* (Aldershot: Avebury Press, 1996). There are lower estimates, of less than 1 percent, according to a regionally comparable poverty line of $4 a day, as well as higher ones, according to the European Community's minimum line. See also Branko Milanovic, *Income, Inequal-*

*ity, and Poverty during the Transition* (Washington: World Bank, forthcoming). The investment rating was from Standard and Poor's. See "Survey on the Czech Republic," *Financial Times*, June 26, 1996.

8. As of September 1995 the Czech Republic had the largest number of registered enterprises relative to population of any of the former communist economies: 68.4 per 1,000 people. Hungary had 51 per 1,000 and Poland 27.6. The EU average is 43. "Emerging Market Indicators," *Economist*, November 9, 1996, p. 124. The Republic also had one of the highest savings rates (as a percentage of GDP), 21.2 percent versus 18.8 in Poland and 17.1 in Hungary. "Tigers or Tortoises?" *Economist*, October 26, 1996, p. 140. See also "Emerging Market Indicators," *Economist*, January 4, 1997.

9. Ivka Kalus-Bystricky and Pedro Pick, "The Reform Process in the Czech Republic: A Progress Report and a Tale of One Company," in H. Shaughnessy, eds., *Privatization and Economic Development in Eastern Europe and the CIS: Investment, Aquisition, and Managerial Issues* (Boston: John Wiley, 1994), p. 47.

10. Ibid. Indeed, Klaus was notorius for his disregard for foreign advisors. And as if to confim his position, a survey of the performance of privatized enterprises shows that bilateral and multilateral aid has in general been poorly received in the Czech Republic, while consultants hired and paid for by the firms themselves have been used much more productively.

11. For a discussion of the trade-off between kinds of expenditures, see Carol Graham, *Safety Nets, Politics, and the Poor: Transitions to Market Economies* (Brookings, 1994). For details on pension expenditures in the region see Mark Kramer, "Social Protection Policies and Safety Nets in East-Central Europe: Dilemmas of the Post-Communist Transformation," paper prepared for the National Academy of Sciences Task Forces on Social Sector Reforms in Economies in Transition, Washington, September 19–20, 1996.

12. Interview with Pedro Pick, former director, Arthur D. Little, Prague, and consultant, Patria Finance, Prague, October 15, 1996. For a good description of unemployment trends in the Czech Republic see Jan Svejnar, Katherine Terrell, and Daniel Munich, "Unemployment in the Czech and Slovak Republics," in Jan Svejnar, ed., *The Czech Republic and Economic Transition in Eastern Europe* (San Diego: Academic Press, 1995), pp. 285–316.

13. "Czech Republic," *Financial Times Survey*, December 6, 1996.

14. Interviews with Jan Mladek, former deputy minister of the economy, Prague, October 17, 1996; and Martin Kupka, director of research, Patria Finance, Prague, October 16, 1996. See also "Czech Republic," *Financial Times Survey*, June 16, 1996; Vincent Boland, "Czech PM

Exploits Budget Win," *Financial Times*, October 11, 1996, p. 3; and "Emerging Market Indicators," *Economist*, January 4, 1997.

15. This is made worse because most funds are close-ended so that companies cannot profit by issuing new shares, which would also be an incentive to improve performance. See John Coffee, "Institutional Investors in Transitional Economies: Lessons from the Czech Experience," discussion paper, Transition Economies Division, Policy Research Department, World Bank, Washington, 1994, p. 94.

16. Interview with Vladimir Benacek, Institute of Social Sciences, Prague, October 17, 1996. See also Vladimir Benacek, "Capital Hoarding, Postponed Bankruptcies, and the Financial Capital for the Restructuring of Czech Manufacturing," paper prepared for Seminar on European Integration, Vienna, July 6, 1995. See also Anthony Robinson, "Czech Republic: Sell-Offs Now Give Cause for Concern," *Financial Times*, December 6, 1996, p. 3..

17. Vincent Boland, "Czech PM's Cliffhanger Victory Fails to Dispel Survival Fears," *Financial Times*, June 12, 1997, p. 3; Christine Spolar, "Czech Premier Acts to Restore Confidence," *Washington Post*, April 17, 1997, p. A25; and Vincent Boland, "Survey—Czech Industry and Finance: Capital Markets: Reforms Promised," *Financial Times*, May 14, 1997, p. 6.

18. Interview with Dusan Triska, deputy to Minster Klaus for several years and the architect of the voucher privatization, Prague, October 15, 1996.

19. For an excellent and detailed discussion of these political trends, see Orenstein, "Out of the Red."

20. Ibid.

21. All citizens older than age 18 in October 1991 were eligible. Participation was 5.98 million people in the Czech Republic and 2.59 in Slovakia. For more detail, see Roman Frydman, Andrzej Rapaczynski, and John S. Earle, eds., *The Privatization Process in Central Europe* (London: Central European University Press, 1993).

22. Interview with Jiri Pehe, director of research, Open Media Resources Institute, Prague, October 17, 1996.

23. More than 50 percent of people surveyed at the time thought that all state-owned enterprises should be privatized, and more than 50 percent also thought that vouchers were the appropriate method of privatization. See Vecernik, *Markets and People*.

24. Interview with Jiri Pehe.

25. See Vecernik, *Markets and People*, p. 205; and Orenstein, "Out of the Red," p. 200.

26. For details on Poland, see Graham, *Safety Nets*, chap. 7.

27. Orenstein, "Out of the Red," p. 97.

28. See Jiri Vecernik, "Old and New Economic Inequalities: The Czech Case," *International Review for Comparative Public Policy*, vol. 7 (1996), pp. 147–75. Vecernik describes a latent tension between the service class in the public sector and government restrictions that disproportionately affect workers such as teachers and doctors.

29. A former advisor to Klaus and a principal architect of the voucher program noted that after six years people were tired of the government, and people in the government were also tired. Interview with Dusan Triska.

30. Interviews with Zdenek Bakala, chairman, Patria Finance, Prague, October 16, 1996; and Jiri Pehe.

31. Interview with Jiri Pehe.

32. The 1993 Constitution called for the creation of a Senate, to replace the previous Upper House, which was nationally based and included both Czech and Slovak representatives. The new Czech assembly has 81 members, elected in a first-past-the post system. Voter turnout was very low in the Senate elections: 35 percent versus 76.4 percent in the June elections for the lower house. One reason was the general lack of enthusiasm for the new assembly, which many observers thought was superfluous. In addition, the vote took place in a complicated two-round system that was poorly understood by the average voter. See "Czechs Snub Senate Polls amid Confusion and Sleaze," *Central Europe Online*, November 18, 1996; "Czech Social Democrats Squabble over Poll Setback," *Central Europe Online*, November 19, 1996; and Supplement on the Czech Republic, *Financial Times*, December 6, 1996.

33. See Vecernik, *Markets and People*. Also, interview with Ladislav Venys, director, Center for Democracy and Free Enterprise, Prague, October 16, 1996.

34. Interviews with Jan Mladek, former deputy minister of the economy and current advisor to the CDDS; and Martin Kupka, director of research, Patria Finance, October 16, 1996.

35. The percentage of people agreeing that privatization should continue at any price fell from 28 percent to 18 percent from mid-1992 to the end of 1993. At the end of 1994, some 54 percent of people felt that the property was in the wrong hands. See Vecernik, *Markets and People*, p. 156.

36. Interview with Dusan Triska.

37. For detail, see Orenstein, "Out of the Red"; and Kevin Done and Vincent Boland, "Financial Times Survey: The Czech Republic," *Financial Times*, November 22, 1995.

38. This point was raised in a discussion in Washington with Joel Hellmann, Harvard University, October 29, 1996.

39. For a detailed discussion, see Petr Mateju and Blanka Rehakova, "Turning Left or Class Realignment? Analsyis of the Changing Relationship between Class and Party in the Czech Republic, 1992–1996," Social Trends Working Papers, Institute of Sociology, Prague, January 1996.

40. Vecernik, *Markets and People.*

41. Poverty figures are from Milanovic, *Income, Inequality, and Poverty during the Transition*, p. 78. The poverty line he uses is $4 a day or $120 a month, adjusted for purchasing power parity. Although this is higher than the World Bank's absolute poverty line of $1 a day, it is lower than the social minimum income—and therefore the official poverty line—of most transition economies. If one were to use the Czech "living minimum" line, the poverty rate would be 2.9 percent of households or 3.5 percent of persons. See Vecernik, *Markets and People*, p. 99. For unemployment, see Kramer, "Social Protection Policies." The figures are for 1995.

42. If adjusted household income is used to calculate the Czech Gini, then it is much lower (.24). Adjusted income does not change the Ginis as much in either Poland or the OECD countries. See Vecernik, *Markets and People*, p. 85.

43. Eighty percent of those surveyed in 1995 were against any increase in taxes, even for better social benefits. Ibid., p. 77.

44. One of the most comprehensive of these is Milanovic, *Poverty and Income Inequality during the Transition.*

45. Most of the figures on poverty and inequality presented here are based on survey research conducted by Jiri Vecernik, director, Institute of Sociology of the Academy of Sciences, Prague. Vecernik's institute has conducted a biannual survey, "Economic Expectations and Attitudes," since May 1990. The sample is 1,200 adults, with a two-step quota sampling procedure whereby the region and size of the locality were defined in the first step, and gender, age, and education in the second. Vecernik has also used other surveys, including "The Dismantling of the Safety Net and Its Political Cosequences," October 1991, conducted by the Institute of East-West Security Studies, New York. The sample is the Czech Republic (1,187), Slovakia (817), Hungary (1,500), and Poland (1,491). In addition, he has used the Luxembourg Income Study database; D. Treiman and I. Szeleyni, UCLA, "Social Stratification in Eastern Europe after 1989" (national samples of the Czech Republic, Hungary, Slovakia, Poland, Russia, and Bulgaria, with about 5,000 respondents in each country); and SOCO, the Social Consequences of Transition survey, conducted in early 1995 on about 1,000 household

random samples in the Czech Republic, Hungary, Poland, Slovakia, and the former East Germany, initiated and coordinated by the Institute for Human Sciences, Vienna.

46. Vecernik, "Old and New Economic Inequalities," p. 12.

47. There are 50,000 guest workers in Prague alone, which is equivalent to 2 percent of the labor force. Interview with Pedro Pick; and Vecernik, "Old and New Economic Inequalities."

48. Marie Vavrejnova and Ivana Moravcikova, "The Czech Household Sector in Transition," in Jan Svejnar, ed., *The Czech Republic and Economic Transition in Eastern Europe* (San Diego: Academic Press, 1995), p. 318.

49. Ibid.

50. Vecernik, "Old and New Economic Inequalities."

51. This line is higher than the World Bank's absolute minimum of $1 a day, but lower than the social minimum or legal poverty line in most transition economies. See Milanovic, *Income, Inequality, and Poverty.*

52. Vecernik, *Markets and People;* and Vecernik, "Old and New Economic Inequalities."

53. Jiri Vecernik, "Incomes in Central Europe: Distributions, Patterns, and Perceptions," *Journal of European Social Policy,* vol. 6, no. 2 (1996), p. 116.

54. Vecernik, "Old and New Economic Inequalities."

55. Vecernik, *Markets and People,* p. 127.

56. Ibid.

57. See Petr Mateju and Nelson Lim, "Who Has Gotten Ahead after the Fall of Communism: The Case of the Czech Republic," *Czech Sociological Review,* vol. 3 (Fall 1995); and Thesia I. Garner, "Changing Welfare in a Changing World? Income and Expenditure Inequalities in the Czech and Slovak Republics," in S. Jenkins, A. Kapetyn, and B. van Praag, eds., *The Distribution of Welfare and Household Production: International Perspectives* (forthcoming). For a definition of the Gini coefficient, see note 77, chap. 1.

58. The group in between is the north central European countries, Germany, and the Netherlands, with Ginis of .25–.32. Vecernik, *Markets and People,* p. 85.

59. Gardner, "Changing Welfare in a Changing World?"

60. Vecernik, "Old and New Economic Inequalities."

61. Vecernik, "Incomes in Central Europe," pp. 115–16.

62. Ibid., p. 116.

63. Ibid., pp. 117–18.

64. Mateju and Lim, "Who Has Gotten Ahead," p. 124.

65. Vecernik, "Incomes in Central Europe."

66. Erik Hanley and others, "The Making of Post-Communist Elites in Eastern Europe," Institute of Sociology working papers, Prague, March 1996, p. 35.

67. Blanka Rehakova and Klara Vlachova, "Subjective Mobility after 1989: Do People Feel a Social and Economic Improvement or Relative Deprivation?" *Czech Sociological Review*, vol. 3 (Fall 1995), pp. 157–77.

68. Jiri Vecernik, "Economic and Political Man: Hardships and Attitudes in the Czech Republic and Central Europe," *Czech Sociological Review*, vol. 3, no. 2 (1995).

69. Many of these points were raised by Jan Hartl, director of the public opinion polling firm, STEM, in an interview, Prague, October 15, 1996.

70. For an excellent discussion of these isses, see Jan Hartl, "Social Policy: An Issue for Today and Tomorrow," *Czech Sociological Review*, vol. 3 (Fall 1995), pp. 209–19.

71. Mitchell Orenstein, "Transitional Social Policy in the Czech Republic and Poland," *Czech Sociological Review*, vol. 3 (Fall 1995), p. 184.

72. Vecernik, *Markets and People*.

73. The Czech government still spends $7 billion a year on heating subsidies. Interview with Josef Kotrba, senior researcher, Center for Economic Research and Graduate Education, Charles University (CERGE), Prague, October 16, 1996. Housing subsidies, meanwhile, are actually regressive because under communism the nomenklatura had preferential access to subsidized housing, and their continued presence skews the development of an efficient housing market.

74. Christopher Heady, Najma Rajah, and Stephen Smith, "Tax Reform and Economic Transition in the Czech Republic," *Fiscal Studies*, vol. 15 (1994), p. 70.

75. Vavrejnova and Moravcikova, "Czech Household Sector in Transition," p. 321.

76. Vecernik, *Markets and People*. For a description of the slighly haphazard manner that social assistance benefits are distributed in Poland, see Graham, *Safety Nets*, chap. 7. For a description of the effectiveness of targeted benefits, see chapter 2 in the same volume.

77. Mark Kramer, "Social Protection," p. 38.

78. See Orenstein, "Out of the Red."

79. Despite the departure of some women from the labor force, the rates of participation in the labor force and of unemployment are still the same for women as for men. See Kramer, "Social Protection," p. 39.

80. See Jan Svejnar, Kathering Terrell, and Daniel Munich, "Unemployment in the Czech and Slovak Republics," in Svejnar, ed., *The Czech Republic and Economic Transition in Eastern Europe*.

81. For a detailed description, see Orenstein, "Out of the Red."

82. The lifting of restrictions has caused some inflation and a decrease in the competitiveness of Czech exports, contributing to the current account deficit. Interview with Jan Mladek.

83. In Poland the number of pensioners increased by 45 percent from 1989 to 1994, and the number of contributors dropped by 15 percent. In the Czech Republic these rates were a more modest 10 percent and 12 percent, respectively. See Kramer, "Social Protection," pp. 30–35.

84. Ibid, pp. 31, 32. One-quarter of the Czech rate is paid by employers; in the United States, half is paid by employers. Poland's rate is 45 percent and is paid totally by employers.

85. Interview with Jiri Pehe.

86. "Old and Unaffordable," *Economist*, April 30, 1996, p. 41.

87. Heady, Rajah, and Smith, "Tax Reform and Economic Transition," pp. 64–80.

88. Orenstein, "Transitional Social Policy," p. 186.

89. Interviews with Michal Mejstrik, director, Institute for Social Studies, Charles University, Prague, October 16, 1996; and Jan Hartl.

90. Orenstein, "Transitional Social Policy," p. 186.

91. Interviews with Jiri Vecernik, research director, Institute of Sociology, Academy of Sciences, Prague, October 14, 1996; and Martin Kupka. Another reason that the government might have been reluctant to press for a fully funded system is that private pension funds in the Czech Republic were expropriated by the Nazis during World War II and a second time by the communists, an experience that may create concern about private funds among some of the population. Interview with Jan Mladek.

92. See Orenstein, "Transitional Social Policy"; and Vecernik, *Markets and People*.

93. Vecernik, "Incomes in Central Europe"; and Orenstein, "Out of the Red."

94. Interview with Dusan Triska.

95. Interview with Timothy Garton-Ash, Oxford, October 18, 1996.

96. Interview with Jiri Pehe.

97. It is telling that the Social Democrats now support the new supplementary private pension funds because they want to use some of the proceeds to support the National Pension Fund. They recognize that the private funds are likely to generate a better return than the public system. Interview with Jan Mladek.

98. Vecernik, "Old and New Economic Inequalities." Vecernik's findings are supported by those of Rehakova and Vlachova, "Subjective Mobility."

99. Kramer, "Social Protection," p. 23.

100. The population that participated in all of the then Czechoslovakia was 8.5 million. The second wave began in 1994 in the Czech Republic alone. For a good description, see Kalus-Bystricky and Pick, "Reform Process in the Czech Republic"; and Josef Kotrba, "The Privatization Process in the Czech Republic: Players and Winners," in Svejnar, ed., *The Czech Republic and Economic Transition in Eastern Europe*, pp. 159–98.

101. See Kalus-Bystricky and Pick, "Reform Process in the Czech Republic"; and Kotrba, "Privatization Process in the Czech Republic."

102. Kotrba, "Privatization Process in the Czech Republic," pp. 175–76.

103. See Kalus-Bystricky and Pick, "Reform Process in the Czech Republic."

104. Interview with Dusan Triska.

105. Kalus-Bystricky and Pick, "Reform Process in the Czech Republic"; and interview with Dusan Triska.

106. Kotrba, "Privatization Process in the Czech Republic"; and Kalus-Bystricky and Pick, "Reform Process in the Czech Republic," p. 60.

107. See Coffee, "Institutional Investors in Transitional Economies," p. 31.

108. Interview with Michal Mejstrik.

109. See Radek Lastovicka, Anton Marcinin, and Michael Mejstrik, "Corporate Governance and Share Prices in Voucher Privatized Companies," in Svejnar, ed., *The Czech Republic and Economic Transition in Eastern Europe*, p. 203.

110. See Karla Brom and Mitchell Orenstein, "The Privatized Sector in the Czech Republic: Government and Bank Control in a Transitional Economy," *Europe-Asia Studies*, vol. 46, no. 6 (1994), pp. 893–928.

111. See ibid for a detailed account of ownership concentration, by fund and by financial institution.

112. Lastovicka, Marcinin, and Mejstrik, "Corporate Governance," pp. 199–209.

113. Coffee, "Institutional Investors," p. 28.

114. Ibid., pp. 30–31.

115. Interview with Dusan Triska.

116. Interview with Josef Kotrba.

117. See Coffee, "Institutional Investors," pp. 7, 8; and Peter Rutland, "Economic, Legal, and Political Dilemmas of Privatization in Russia," *Transnational Law and Contemporary Problems*, vol. 5 (Spring 1995).

118. See Rutland, "Economic, Legal, and Political Dilemmas." For another example of insider domination, see Nevenka Cuckovic, "Privatization Process and its Consequences for Distribution of Welfare: The

Case of Croatia," paper prepared for the EACES Conference on Privatization and Distribution, Trento, March 3–4, 1995.

119. Kotrba, "Privatization Process in the Czech Republic."

120. Approximately 55 to 60 percent of those surveyed thought all firms should be privatized in 1991–93 and that the pace of privatization should be rapid. Vecernik, *Markets and People*, pp. 155–59.

121. For detail, see Vincent Boland, "Czech Finance and Investment: Consolidation Process under Way," *Financial Times*, April 26, 1996, p. 4.

122. Vecernik, *Markets and People*, p. 159.

123. The survey was conducted by Patria Finance. Interview with Martin Kupka. See also Coffee, "Institutional Investors"; and Brom and Orenstein, "Privatized Sector in the Czech Republic."

124. Interview with Pedro Pick.

125. Ibid. For detail on labor and capital hoarding, see interview with Benacek.

126. Interview with Jan Mladek. For detail on how different social groups behaved in terms of keeping or selling their shares or going through a fund, see Vecernik, *Markets and People*, chap. 7.

127. Interview with Jan Mladek.

128. Interview with Pedro Pick.

129. Anton Marcincin and Dmitri Shemetilo, "Investment Funds' Strategies and Performance of Shares," Institute for Economic Studies, Charles University, Prague, *Privatization News Letter of the Czech Republic and Slovakia*, nos. 33-34 (April-May 1995); and Brom and Orenstein, "Privatized Sector in the Czech Republic."

130. Coffee, "Institutional Investors," p. 6.

131. Matthew Bishop and John Kay, *Does Privatization Work? Lessons from the UK* (London: London Business School, 1988).

132. Barbara G. Katz and Joel Owen, "Optimal Voucher Privatization Fund Bids When Bidding Affects Firm Performance," *Journal of Comparative Economics*, vol. 24 (February 1997), pp. 25–43.

133. Jeffrey R. Gates, "Revolutionizing Share Ownership: The Stakeowner Economy," *Demos Arguments*, no. 8 (1996), p. 28.

134. See "Privatisation in Europe: Is the Price Right?" *Economist*, November 23, 1996, pp. 87–88.

135. Interview with Dusan Triska.

136. Ibid.

137. Zeman refused to participate, calling the program "a repetition of the old comminist myth of ownership of the people and by the people." Vincent Boland, "Penchant for Witty Illusions," *Financial Times*, November 22, 1995.

138. See the surveys in Vecernik, *Markets and People*, chap. 7.

139. John S. Earle and others, "Mass Privatization, Distributive Politics, and Popular Support for Reform in the Czech Republic," Central European University Privatization Project, February 1997. These results were based on a survey of 1,459 Czech adults taken in January 1996.

140. Also important in electoral terms were the tens of thousands of small businesses that were returned to their original owners through the restitution. These companies have performed better than the privatized enterprises, which has created a strong base of support for the government among the new owners. Sample surveys find that those who received property in the restitution program, for example, were more likely to support reform, markets, democracy, and reformist politicians. Earle and others, "Mass Privatization." See also interviews with Zdenek Bakala, chairman, Patria Finance, Prague, October 16, 1996; Jan Mladek; and Jiri Pehe.

141. Earle and others, "Mass Privatization"; and Vecernik, *Markets and People*, chap. 7.

142. Interview with Jan Hartl.

143. See Coffee, "Institutional Investors"; and interview with Vladimir Benacek, "Capital Hoarding."

144. Vecernik, *Markets and People*, p. 153.

145. Ibid., pp. 154, 157.

146. See Graham, *Safety Nets*. See also Anders Aslund, Peter Boone, and Simon Johnson, "How to Stabilize: Lessons from the Post-Communist Countries," *Brookings Papers on Economic Activity*, no. 1 (1996).

147. Interview with Jan Mladek.

148. *Hospodarske Noviny*, various editions.

149. Vecernik, *Markets and People*, chap. 7.

150. Ibid.

151. Interview with Jan Hartl.

152. Interview with Josef Kotrba.

153. "Economic Expectations and Attitudes Survey," in Vecernik, *Markets and People*.

154. *Hospodarske Noviny*, several editions.

155. Coffee, "Institutional Investors."

156. Interview with Josef Kotrba.

157. Coffee, "Institutional Investors," p. 35.

158. Vecernik, *Markets and People*, chap. 7.

159. Ibid.

160. Branko Milanovic, "Privatization in Post-Communist Societies," *Communist Economies and Economic Transformation*, vol. 3, no. 1 (1991); and Bishop and Kay, *Does Privatization Work?*

161. Orenstein, "Out of the Red," p. 123.
162. Interview with Michal Mejstrick.
163. Interview with Dusan Triska.
164. Interview with Zdenek Bakala.

## Chapter 6

1. I would like to thank Theo Lippeveld of HIID and Ravi Rannan-Eliya of the Harvard School of Public Health for helpful comments on an earlier draft, Virginia Bond of the University of Hull for sharing her valuable survey data with me, Alan Dock of the World Bank for facilitating the field research for this chapter, and Gerard Kambou of HIID/Zambia for providing me with updated fiscal data.

2. These points are raised and elaborated by Nicholas van de Walle, "Economic Reform and Democracy: Crisis and Opportunity in Africa," *Journal of Democracy*, vol. 6 (April 1995), pp. 128–41.

3. Ibid., p. 129. Van de Walle suggests that institutional development may ultimately be more important than specific economic policies.

4. A related issue is the extent to which the introduction of fees at a level that has little relevance to cost recovery gives users a genuine stake in the process. I thank Roger Hay of the Food Studies Group at Oxford University for raising this point.

5. The most extensive evaluation on nongovernment health care provision in Zambia concludes that incomes are too limited and population too sparse to support full-time private practice in rural areas, and that even in urban areas demand is restricted to high-income groups. The study also concluded that the failure of private providers to supply cost-effective services of public health care may not be that important, if failure allows the Ministry of Health to divert resources from meeting social demand for higher-quality services in urban areas and devote the resources to poor rural areas. This indicates the limits to using cost recovery and exit options to build stakeholders among the poor majority in Zambia. For detail see Peter Berman and others, "Zambia: Non-Governmental Health Care Provision," paper prepared for Data for Decisionmaking Project, Harvard University, and Africa Bureau, USAID, Boston, January 1995.

6. "Zambia Poverty Assessment," Southern Africa Department, World Bank, Washington, 1994.

7. For detail on the subsidies, see Carol Graham, *Safety Nets, Politics, and the Poor: Transitions to Market Economies*, pp. 161–62.

8. The relatively independent Bank of Zambia, which was set up during attempts at reform during the 1980s, has also been important in

controlling inflation. The Zambian Revenue Authority was set up in 1994 with a great deal of fanfare in an attempt to improve revenue collection, although its record has been disappointing. For detail see Nicholas van de Walle and Dennis Chiwele, "Democratization and Economic Reform in Zambia," Michigan State University Working Papers 9, November 15, 1994, p. 31.

9. Bruce R. Bolnick, "Establishing Fiscal Discipline: The Cash Budget in Zambia," in Merilee S. Grindle, ed., *Getting Good Government: Capacity Building in the Public Sectors of Developing Countries* (Harvard University Press, forthcoming).

10. The bailout of Meridien Bank, for example, was opposed by some donors, but the government believed it had little alternative to avert a general and much more damaging crisis in the financial sector. Pressure from public sector workers for salary increases has been increasing as their real wages continue to decline.

11. Information on the fiscal situation was kindly provided by Gerard Kambou of the Harvard Institute for International Development (HIID) and the Ministry of Finance in Zambia.

12. Oliver Sassa, "Structural Adjustment and Governance Capacity in Zambia, 1983–1994," paper presented to IMF Conference on Governance, Washington, November 9–11, 1994; and Clive Gray and Bruce R. Bolnick, "Equity and Growth through Economic Research in Africa: Public Strategies for Growth Component," Research Prospectus 1, Project Eager/PSG, USAID and Harvard Institute for International Development, December 15, 1995.

13. When the government withdrew from maize marketing in 1992 the private sector was facing a serious credit crunch and in the absence of government support did not take over the government's role in purchasing wholesale maize. Thus a substantial amount of harvested maize was not purchased that year. For detail see ibid.

14. High real interest rates and high returns on government-issued treasury bonds have attracted bank investment, reducing the availability of credit for private sector firms. For detail see ibid.

15. For detail see ibid.; and van de Walle and Chiwele, "Democratization and Economic Reform in Zambia." Other very poor and land-locked countries, such as Ghana and Bolivia, have also experienced a lower than expected investment response after the initiation of significant macroeconomic reforms. This may be a result of natural disadvantages, such as lack of a port, or lack of investor confidence because of high levels of economic or political instability under previous governments.

16. Interview with Chris Adam, Centre for the Study of African Economies, Oxford University, Oxford, April 21, 1995.

17. ZCCM generates 90 percent of Zambia's foreign exchange, but remains a very inefficient producer, with a producing cost of

82 cents per pound of copper, which is almost double that of Chile (the world's largest producer). Leslie Crawford, "Fulcrum of the Economy," *Financial Times*, Survey of Zambia, October 24, 1994, p. 13. There are some indications that the government is addressing this matter, such as the recent appointment of a privatization team for ZCCM. But the government showed obvious displeasure when Deputy Minister of Mines Panda took a stance on the method by which ZCCM should be privatized, which indicated that there was as yet no clear agreement on the issue. Interviews with Gedion Nkogo, resident representative, World Bank, Lusaka, April 24, 1995; and Oliver Sassa, director, Institute for African Studies, University of Zambia, Lusaka, April 24, 1995.

18. Chris Adam, interview, April 21, 1995.

19. The PSRP promised to cut the civil service by 25 percent in three years and improve conditions for the remaining workers. In 1992, 15,000 poorly paid manual workers without job security were laid off, but since then there has been little progress. Indeed, some observers note that the civil service has grown because the government is replacing retirees rather than letting their positions fade out. Interview with James Polhemus, Democracy Project advisor, USAID, Lusaka, April 24, 1995.

20. Zambia Poverty Assessment (1994). This conclusion was confirmed by the author's interviews with government officials, nongovernmental organizations, and academic researchers in Lusaka, April 1995. See also "Hear the Cry of the Poor: A Pastoral Letter on the Current Suffering of the People of Zambia," Catholic Secretariat, Lusaka, July 1993.

21. The increasing prevalence of AIDS, for example, has effects far beyond the individual deaths. The epidemic is prevalent in young adults, who are the primary income earners for most households. Thus an AIDS death often leaves large numbers of orphaned children or dependent elderly without a source of income. Other households in the community, usually the wealthiest, often take on the responsibility for supporting the orphans, a responsibility which then substantially reduces the living standards of those households. Interview with Virginia Bond of the Project on Community Capacity to Prevent AIDS, Lusaka, April 26, 1995. This project recently undertook a survey of 613 of the 676 households in the Chiawa area (2,389 sq km) of Kufue district and found household coping capacity and community organizational capacity very weak in comparison with other countries. See Virginia Bond, "Death, Dysentery, and Drought: Coping Capacities of Households in Chiawa," Working Paper 7, Project on Community Capacity to Prevent, Manage, and Survive HIV/AIDS, Karolinksa Institutet, University of Hull, and University of Zambia, August 1993; and Virginia Bond and S. Wallman, "Report on the 1991

Survey of Households in Chiawa," Working Paper 5 in the same series, August 1993.

22. Bond, "Death, Dysentery, and Drought"; and Bond and Wallman, "Report on the 1991 Survey."

23. Those that left were Emmanuel Kasonde, Guy Scott, Humphrey Mulemba, and Arthur Wina. Kasonde and Wina then formed the National Party in August 1993. The main supporters of reform that remained in the Chiluba government were Patel in Trade, Zuka in Agriculture, Penza in Finance, and Tembo in the Central Bank. There have also been subsequent political clashes between some of them. For detail see van de Walle and Chiwele, "Democratization and Economic Reform in Zambia." These trends were also noted in an interview with Oliver Sassa, director, Institute for African Studies, University of Zambia, Lusaka, April 24, 1995.

24. Clive Gray and Bruce R. Bolnick, "Equity and Growth through Economic Research in Africa: Public Strategies for Growth Component," Research Prospectus, USAID and Harvard Institute for International Development, December 15, 1995, p. 98.

25. Van de Walle and Chiwele, "Democratization and Economic Reform in Zambia."

26. Policymaking under UNIP was often a struggle between the civil service bureaucracy and the party. In the late 1980s, when the government attempted a move toward more market-oriented policies, the balance of power shifted from the party to the ministries; then it shifted back when a command economy was again imposed in 1987. Robert Bates and Paul Collier, "The Politics and Economics of Policy Reform in Zambia," in Robert Bates and Anne O. Krueger, eds., *Political and Economic Interactions in Economic Policy Reform: Evidence from Eight Countries* (Oxford: Basil Blackwell, 1993), pp. 387–443.

27. This is most notable but not limited to the behavior of one of Chiluba's most important loyalists and now current health minister, Michael Sata. As minister of local government he was notorious for his attacks on UNIP property and the like; as minister of health he withheld funds from an important immunization project because it was run by a woman with links to UNIP. Various interviews, Lusaka, November 1991 and April 1995. Chiluba's imposition of a state of emergency in late 1992 in response to rumors that UNIP was embroiled with the military in plotting a coup has also been criticized by many observers as unnecessary and heavy-handed. Graham, *Safety Nets*, chap. 6. As the 1996 elections approached, the government made a series of attempts to derail the candidacy of Kaunda, including passing a constitutional amendment that made his candidacy illegal.

28. This conclusion is drawn from the author's interviews with various members of the government, including Emanuel Kasonde, minister of finance, Lusaka, November 15, 1991; and Jacob Mwanza, acting governor, Central Bank of Zambia, Washington, June 1, 1995.

29. "Zambia Poverty Assessment," World Bank.

30. Bates and Collier, "The Politics and Economics of Policy Reform in Zambia."

31. Interview with Philip Alderfer, doctoral candidate, University of Michigan, Lusaka, April 25, 1995. These conclusions are based on Alderfer's research on the role of the National Assembly and on his close following of the political campaigns of several MPs in the assembly.

32. "Zambian Government May Deport Ex-President as Illegal Alien," *New York Times*, October 19, 1995, p. A7.

33. Mark Ashurst and Tony Hawkins, "Donors Perturbed by Zambian Polls: Multi-Party but Flawed," *Financial Times*, November 18, 1996, p. 7.

34. In Chingole 55 percent of registered voters voted in 1991 but only 15 percent in 1995. In Mwande 42 percent voted in 1991 and 21 percent in 1995. Interview with James Polhemus, democracy/governance advisor, USAID, Lusaka, April 24, 1995. These rates are particularly striking because there has been no update of the electoral register since before the 1991 elections, and as many as 35 to 40 percent of Zambians are apparently not registered. Interview with Peter Henriot, St. Ignatius Church, Lusaka, April 27, 1995. However, voter turnouts tend to fall between general elections, particularly when the opposition is weak, in most Westminster-style electoral systems. I thank Ravi Rannan-Eliya for raising this point.

35. In Chingole, where wealthy businessman and MP Enoch Kavindale was running for the MMD and apparently spent a large amount of money on his campaign, the MMD won with 5,000 votes versus 300 for the NP. Interview with James Polhemus, April 24, 1995.

36. "Zambia: So That's Democracy?" *Economist*, November 23, 1996, p. 82; and Donald G. McNeil Jr., "President Is Re-Elected in Zambia, but Vote Is Called Tainted," *New York Times*, November 21, 1996, p. A15.

37. The extent of Chiluba's electoral margin is telling: he took 76 percent of the popular vote, as well as 125 of 150 parliamentary seats. Graham, *Safety Nets*, p. 150.

38. For detail on policy learning, see Bates and Collier, "The Politics and Economics of Policy Reform in Zambia."

39. The government, meanwhile, which has until now relied on the support of a unified ZCTU, may prefer a single union federation but is

reluctant to step in. Ketson Kandafula, "Break-Away Unions Worry ZCTU," *Zambia Daily Mail*, April 27, 1995.

40. Van de Walle and Chiwele, "Democratization and Economic Reform in Zambia."

41. These observations are drawn from interviews with people that have been working with grassroots projects for a long time. These include Clare Barkworth, technical advisor, Social Recovery Project, April 24, 1995; John Milimo, University of Zambia, April 25, 1995; and Peter Henriot, St. Ignatius Church, April 27, 1995. This gradual change in expectations is also reflected in the beneficiary assessments conducted by John Milimo and his colleagues for the Social Recovery Project. A recent evaluation of the Food for Work Program, meanwhile, demonstrates how quickly this change can be reversed and dependency on government handouts reestablished. Richard Saba, and others, "Food for Work in Zambia," evaluation prepared for The Study Fund, Social Recovery Project, Lusaka, April 1995.

42. This was evidenced, for example, by Chiluba's criticisms of donors and international financial institutions on an April 1995 international tour.

43. The importance of the 1980s "policy learning" in making macroeconomic reform successful in the 1990s is raised by van de Walle and Chiwele, "Democratization and Economic Reform in Zambia."

44. Ibid., pp. 9, 41; and Sassa, "Structural Adjustment and Governance Capacity in Zambia."

45. Michela Wrong, "Zambia: Crown Jewels Earmarked for Foreign Buyers," *Financial Times Survey*, March 4, 1997, p. 1; and Mark Ashurst, "Profile: Valentine Chitalu: Chief Executive of the Zambia Privatization Agency—Critical Role in the Economy's Rescue," *Financial Times Survey*, March 4, 1997, p. 4.

46. Theo Lippeveld, "Review of Population and Health Policies in Burkina Faso," report prepared for Harvard Institute for International Development Report to the Government of Burkina Faso, Cambridge, Mass., March 1996, p. 7.

47. The study of household coping capacity in the Chiawa area of Zambia by Bond, "Death Dysentery, and Drought," and Bond and Wallman, "Report on the 1991 Survey of Households in Chiawa," found that it was very weak. Officials from the Food for Work program, for example, were cited as noting that locals often overestimated how long their food reserves and income would last. The Chiawa study found that public understanding of AIDS was extremely limited, with a majority attributing AIDS deaths to witchcraft; that no solidarity was demonstrated by the community in the face of a dysentery epidemic; and that there was poor response to external efforts to encourage people to dig

pit latrines to dispose of disease-spreading waste. Only when material incentives (in the form of food for work) were provided was there a response. See also V. Bond and P. Ndubani, "Indicators of Health in Chiawa," Working Paper 3 in the above series (1993). This contrasts sharply with other countries such as Peru, where houseold coping capacity and community solidarity remains very strong despite high levels of poverty. For example, in Peru in the aftermath of a 1990 shock adjustment program, voluntary community organizations were credited with providing a massive feeding and relief effort that was critical to protecting the welfare of the poorest groups. And public education efforts in the face of a 1991 cholera epidemic succeeded in maintaining the death rate at 1.5 percent, while in Zambia the death rate from cholera is over 10 percent. Graham, *Safety Nets*, chap. 4.

48. "Zambia Poverty Assessment," World Bank.

49. Swedish technical support for the health reform unit provided the team a way to get visibility and some autonomy. The importance of such an opportunity in a large and underfunded public administration should not be underestimated. The deputy minister, Katele Kalumbe, meanwhile, is cited by many observers as being critical in providing the necessary leadership and commitment to the process. Interviews with Ian Hopwood, former UNICEF resident represenative in Lusaka, Washington, April 10, 1995; Mark Stirling, current UNICEF representative, Lusaka, April 26, 1995; and several members of the World Bank country team, April 1995.

50. Ian Hopwood, "Policy Formulation and Health Sector Reform: Lessons from Zambia and Guinea," UNICEF, Washington, March 1995.

51. The *Implementation Guidelines* are described in detail in David Booth and John Milimo, "Coping with Cost Recovery in Basic Services (Health and Education) in Poor Communities in Zambia," report prepared for SIDA/Development Studies unit, Stockholm University, Lusaka, April 1995.

52. Interview with Michael Soko, deputy to the permanent secretary, National Commission for Development Planning, Lusaka, April 26, 1995.

53. A similar dynamic also occurred in early 1995 when the health care reform bill was due to be presented to Congress. The reform team and the relevant donors clearly wanted the bill to go to Congress. But Minister Sata delayed the presentation of the bill until the summer session, a move that risked losing substantial donor support. There were probably several reasons for Sata's move. He sought to maintain more centralized control over the process and altered the bill to retain subtantial regulatory power in the hands of the ministry. He may also have been trying to reassert control of the relationship with the donors, who

clearly preferred to deal with the deputy minister. These conclusions are drawn from interviews with representatives of the donors in both Lusaka and Washington in April 1995, as well as with Zambian academics who follow the reform process.

54. The point about the utility of user fees in generating quick and visible results was raised by Ian Hopwood in an interview, Washington, April 8, 1995.

55. Most of the evidence comes from a study recently sponsored by the Swedish International Development Agency (SIDA) on the effects of user fees: David Booth and John Milimo, "Coping with Cost Recovery." The report was based on a pilot survey and then more in-depth fieldwork in two poor urban compounds and two poor rural communities. I also discussed the results of the study with John Melimo, one of the principal investigators for the study, University of Zambia, Lusaka, April 25, 1995, and Virginia Bond, another primary investigator, Lusaka, April 26, 1995. An earlier study by Sally Lake of UNICEF found drops of up to 98 percent in one of the poorest urban income areas, Chainda, with little recovery. Hospital visits fell from 22,663 a month to no more than 359 a month between July and August 1993. See Sally Lake, "User Charges in the Health Sector: Some Observations on the Zambian Experience," UNICEF, Lusaka, August 1994.

56. This flexibility was the practice in Chongwe, where I attended a district development committee meeting and also interviewed Mr. Msole, district officer for health, April 26, 1995. This was noted on a wider scale by Booth and Milimo, "Coping with Cost Recovery." Rural mission hospitals tended to be the most flexible of the rural health-service providers, perhaps due to their longer-term experience with fee requirements.

57. "Participatory Poverty Monitoring: Draft Summary Report," prepared for the SIDA Workshop on Coping with Cost Recovery by the Participatory Assessment Group, World Bank Social Recovery Project, Lusaka, May 1995; and Booth and Milimo, "Coping with Cost Recovery."

58. Interview with Roger Hay, Food Studies Group, University of Oxford, Oxford, April 21, 1995.

59. Mark Stirling, UNICEF resident representative, presentation to the minister of health, April 24, 1995. A national prepayment plan was announced for hospitals on April 1, 1994, but its implementation has been ad hoc and haphazard. See also "U.S. AID Child Health Project," draft project paper, USAID, Lusaka, 1995.

60. The most comprehensive study on health care financing in Africa is R. Paul Shaw and Charles C. Griffin, *Financing Health Care in Sub-Saharan Africa through User Fees and Insurance* (Washington: World Bank, 1995).

61. I would like to thank Roger Hay for raising this point. The most comprehensive study done on the effects on user fees in Zambia, sponsored by SIDA, confirms the various reports that use of services among the poorest groups has fallen dramatically. See Booth and Milimo, "Coping with Cost Recovery."

62. Lippeveld, "Review of Population and Health Policies." See also R. Sauerborn, A. Nougtara, and E. Latimer, "The Elasticity of Demand for Health Care in Burkina Faso: Differences among Ages and Income Groups," *Health Policy and Planning*, vol. 9, no. 2, (1994), pp. 185–92.

63. In April 1995, US$1 = 800 kwacha. Outpatient visits vary from 200 to 1,000 kwacha. In Chiwana, for example, the traditional healer charges 100 kwacha, while a visit to the health post costs 500 kwacha. At this time, the daily minimum wage in Zambia was 570 kwacha. Interview with Virginia Bond, member of research team and coauthor, "SIDA Report on Cost Recovery," Lusaka, April 26, 1995; and Booth and Milimo, "Coping with Cost Recovery."

64. Booth and Milimo, "Coping with Cost Recovery," p. 57.

65. The evidence was provided by Ravi Rannan-Eliya of the Harvard School of Public Health. In China, fees on admissions were set at less than 10 percent of unit costs.

66. Booth and Milimo, "Coping with Cost Recovery," p. 16. This point was also noted in USAID, "Child Health Project." President Chiluba himself has often stated that the fees are intended to change the attitudes of Zambians toward government and service delivery. He made such a statement in an address to CSIS, Georgetown University, Washington, April 10, 1995.

67. Booth and Milimo, "Coping with Cost Recovery," p. 42.

68. "Participatory Poverty Monitoring: Draft Summary Report."

69. Hopwood, "Policy Formulation and Health Sector Reform." In addition, I interviewed the district officer in charge of such a board, Mr. Mole, Chongwe district, April 26, 1995.

70. John Milimo, "Beneficiary Assessment for Zambia Poverty Assessment," Southern Africa Department, World Bank, Washington, 1994; "Participatory Poverty Monitoring: Draft Summary" (1995); and interview with John Milimo, University of Zambia, Lusaka, April 25, 1995. Also interview with Virginia Bond, Lusaka, April 26, 1995. Bond has conducted extensive research in Chiawa as well as more cursory studies in several poor Lusaka compounds.

71. This is one of the conclusions of the SIDA study, Booth and Milimo, "Coping with Cost Recovery." The willingness to pay for drugs rather than consultations is not unique to Zambia in Africa, and is also noted in Shaw and Griffin, *Financing Health Care in Sub-Saharan Africa.*

Differences among priorities in Zambians' willingness to pay for services were also discussed in interviews with Sue Durston, health and education representative for the Overseas Development Agency, Lusaka, April 26, 1995; and John Milimo.

72. Interview with John Milimo.

73. "Zambia Poverty Assessment," World Bank. The Bamako Initiative was a cost-sharing plan launched by ministers of health in Africa in 1987 that aims to involve communities in managing and financing health care. See Shaw and Griffin, *Financing Health Care in Sub-Saharan Africa*. For detail on broader public expenditures, see Booth and Milimo, "Coping with Cost Recovery."

74. I attended the first such meeting of a district development committee on April 26, 1995, in Chongwe. Although the committee members took their responsibilities seriously and met in an orderly fashion, it was clear that their activities were in the nascent stages, that they were still waiting for directives from the center, and that there was as yet no real coordination with the health care management boards.

75. John Kelly, "Below the Poverty Line in Education: A Situation Analysis of Girl Child Education in Zambia," UNICEF, Lusaka, December 1994, pp. viii, 22.

76. "Zambia Poverty Assessment," World Bank.

77. Booth and Milimo,"Coping with Cost Recovery"; also "World Poverty Assessment," World Bank.

78. For detail, see Alan Angell and Carol Graham, "Can Social Sector Reform Make Adjustment Sustainable and Equitable?" *Journal of Latin American Studies*, vol. 27, pt. 1 (1995), pp. 189–219.

79. These examples were noted by Ravi Rannan-Eliya, and the figures are from data he provided from the Central Bank of Sri Lanka; and from *The East Asian Miracle* (Washington: World Bank, 1994).

80. Geoffrey Lungwangwa, "Prospects of Private Entrepreneur Investment in Primary Education in Zambia," paper prepared for the Study Fund of the Social Recovery Project, Lusaka, August 1993.

81. Booth and Milimo, "Coping with Cost Recovery."

82. Lungwangwa, "Prospects of Private Enterpreneur Investment"; and Kelly, "Below the Poverty Line in Education."

83. Education is allocated 2.5 percent of GNP in terms of total expenditure. Although primary education received 40 to 45 percent of these expenditures in the early 1980s, by the 1990s this share had fallen to 28 to 32 percent. See Kelly, "Below the Poverty Line in Education."

84. Lungwangwa, "Prospects of Private Entrepreneur Investment." This was also confirmed by my interview with a rural primary school teacher, Mr. Mwaketembala, in Chongwe, April 26, 1995.

85. One theory is that the overemphasis on providing desks is linked to corruption in procurement.

86. The at times elitist nature of the PTA is noted in Kelly, "Below the Poverty Line"; and Booth and Milimo, "Coping with Cost Recovery."

87. For the communication efforts in the early months of the government, see Graham, *Safety Nets*, chap. 6.

88. Van de Walle and Chiwele, "Democratization and Economic Reform in Zambia."

89. This seems to be the case with the social marketing program for oral rehydration salts (ORS), where a strong relationship exists between the level of awareness of private providers that supply ORS and the level of use of private providers by pharmacies. Berman and others, "Zambia: Non-Governmental Health Care Provision."

90. "Zambia Poverty Assessment," World Bank.

91. Polls in urban areas have found that roughly equivalent proportions could read either Bemba or English, suggesting the need for dissemination in languages other than English. Only 35 percent of rural women listened to radio and 23 percent read a newspaper, again suggesting the need for other forms of information dissemination. USAID, "Zambia Child Health Project," Lusaka, 1995. A study in Chiawa, for example, found that only 22 percent of households had a radio or cassette player, with an unknown number of those in working condition. Bond and Wallman "Report on the 1991 Survey of Households in Chiawa."

92. Van de Walle and Chiwele, "Democratization and Economic Reform in Zambia," pp. 30–46.

93. See, for example, Carol Graham, "Strategies for Enhancing the Political Sustainability of Reform in Ukraine," ESP Discussion Papers 50, World Bank, Washington, January 1995.

94. Bond and Wallman, "Report on the 1991 Survey of Households in Chiawa"; and interviews with the directors of safety net programs as well as with NGOs and academic researchers in Lusaka and environs, November 1991 and April 1995.

95. Interview with Clare Barkworth, technical advisor to the Social Recovery Project, Lusaka, April 24, 1995; and presentation by the SRP Management Team, World Bank, Washington, May 12, 1995. Ninety-four percent of the SRP's activities and funding is devoted to community initiatives; 3 percent to monitoring poverty; and 3 percent to poverty analysis.

96. See Mavis Sikota, Nelson Nyangu, and Charlotte Harland, "Review of Selected NGOs, Government, and Donor Activities in the Social Sector," paper prepared for the Study Fund of the Social Recovery Project, Lusaka, January 1994; and Booth and Milimo, "Coping with Cost Recovery."

97. For detailed descriptions of these effects see Graham, *Safety Nets*.

98. See, for example, "Preventing Famine: Zambia in the 1991/92 Drought," Network Paper 2, ODI-Euron, London, 1994.

99. Richard Saba and others, "Food for Work Programme in Zambia," paper prepared for the Study Fund of the Social Recovery Project, Lusaka, April 1995.

100. Ibid.

101. These effects were noted by the managers of the Social Recovery Project in interviews in April 1995 in Lusaka, as well as by Saba and others, "Food for Work."

102. Sikota, Nyangu, and Harland, "Review of Selected NGOs." The limited nature of autonomous NGO capacity was also noted in an interview with James Polhemus, USAID, Lusaka, April 24, 1995.

103. Milimo, "Beneficiary Assessment." The assessment also cited the problems participation would pose for some community members if they were overworked, such as very poor mothers who had to contribute their labor to rural health posts in order to get their children medical care.

104. The potential of for-profit health care services to develop in Zambia, for example, is very limited because of the focus on curative care and poverty and low population densities. For-profit programs would likely serve only upper-income urban groups. See Berman and others, "Zambia: Non-Governmental Health Care Provision."

## Chapter 7

1. For example, the central role of institutions in addition to market-oriented policies in fostering sustained, equitable growth in East Asia is increasingly recognized. See Jose Edgardo Campos and Hilton L. Root, *The Key to the East Asian Miracle: Making Shared Growth Credible* (Brookings, 1996). See also Silvio Borner, Aymo Brunetti, and Beatrice Weder, *Institutional Obstacles to Latin American Growth* (San Francisco: International Center for Economic Growth, 1992).

2. Various studies have found weak economic growth in countries with great inequality of income and assets. In such contexts the poor face strong obstacles and disincentives to contributing to growth, especially in making critical investments in education that would allow their children to participate in future growth. See, for example, Nancy Birdsall, David Ross, and Richard Sabot, "Inequality and Growth Reconsidered: Lessons from East Asia," *World Bank Economic Review*, vol. 9 (Sep-

tember 1995), pp. 477–508; Alberto Alesina and Roberto Perotti, "The Political Economy of Growth: A Critical Review of the Recent Literature," *World Bank Economic Review*, vol. 8 (September 1994), pp. 351–72; and Robert Barro and Xavier Sala-I-Martin, *Economic Growth* (McGraw-Hill, 1995). For a detailed discussion of the difficulties that great inequality poses for the poor's participation in growth, see the introductory chapter in Nancy Birdsall, Carol Graham, and Richard Sabot, *Beyond Trade-offs: Market Reforms and Equitable Growth in Latin America* (Brookings Institution/Inter-American Development Bank, forthcoming). For a dissenting view, see Lant Pritchett, "Where Has All the Education Gone?" Policy Research Department, World Bank, Washington, 1996.

3. State-centered approaches have been successful in some contexts; Costa Rica is a notable example. Yet they require at least minimum administrative capacity, which is precisely what the poorest countries lack.

4. See Merilee Grindle, *Challenging the State: Crisis and Innovation in Latin America and Africa* (Cambridge University Press, 1996). Unfortunately, as Grindle notes, the state is unable to fill this role in many developing countries. The political and economic crisis of the 1980s severely eroded state capacity in many developing countries.

5. The literature on the role of the state is too extensive to be covered here. For a discussion of the state's role in resolving issues of equity, see Gosta Eping-Andersen, *Three Worlds of Welfare Capitalism* (Cambridge, Mass.: Polity Press, 1990).

6. How compensation and distribution problems are dealt with during the implementation of market reforms may be critical in determining their future resolution, the course that reform takes, and the extent to which it is legitimized among most if not all social groups. Perceptions of inequality are often as important as genuine inequalities at such times. For a discussion of the politics of compensation during reform, see Carol Graham, *Safety Nets, Politics, and the Poor: Transitions to Market Economies* (Brookings, 1994). For a discussion of how unequal societies can be perpetuated, even in democracies, see Roland Benabou, "Unequal Societies," NBER Working Paper 5583, Cambridge, Mass., May 1996. For a discussion of how equity norms and principles increase economic efficiency by avoiding continual distributive conflicts, see H. Peyton Young, *Equity: In Theory and Practice* (Princeton University Press, 1994).

7. James Q. Wilson, "Can the Bureaucracy Be Regulated?" in John J. DiIulio Jr., ed., *Deregulating the Public Service: Can Government Be Improved?* (Brookings, 1994), p. 59.

8. For a review of the different approaches to institutional reforms taken by different disciplines, see Carol Graham and Moises Naim, "The

Political Economy of Institutional Reforms," in Birdsall, Graham, and Sabot, *Beyond Trade-offs*.

9. See Samuel Paul, "Does Voice Matter? For Public Accountability, Yes," PRWP 1388, World Bank, Washington, December 1994.

10. I would like to thank Carl Taylor of Johns Hopkins for pointing out this side of financing stakeholders strategies. Interview with Carl Taylor, Johns Hopkins University School of Public and International Health, Baltimore, April 9, 1996.

11. An important caveat in the case of Chile is that the teachers union was alienated from the reform by the authoritarian Pinochet regime and thus remained opposed to it after the transition to democracy. At that point, while they were not able to reverse the voucher system, they were able to push for significant modifications. See chapter 2.

12. For detail on Chile's experience with targeted policies, see Graham, *Safety Nets*, chap. 2.

13. For the dramatic example of Venezuela, see Moises Naim, *Paper Tigers and Minotaurs: The Politics of Venezuela's Economic Reforms* (Washington: Carnegie Endowment for International Peace, 1993).

14. Conversation with Juan Luis Londoño, former Minister of Health, Colombia, and adviser to the CLAS program, Washington, July 1997.

15. Estelle James, "Equity and Efficiency Trade-offs in Social Security Reforms," in Birdsall, Graham, and Sabot, *Beyond Trade-offs*.

16. I discuss the potential of such new channels in detail in Graham, *Safety Nets*.

17. Because the concept of social exclusion is fairly new, at least in the political economy literature, there is no established link between it and political instability. For details on the concept, see Gerry Rodgers, Charles Gore, and Jose B. Figueiredo, *Social Exclusion: Rhetoric, Reality, and Responses* (Geneva: International Labour Organization, 1995).

18. For the effects of ethnic and social fragmentation on growth, see William Easterly and Ross Levine, "Africa's Growth Tragedy: Policies and Ethnic Division," Policy Research Department, World Bank, Washington, April 1996.

19. See Eric Hanushek, *Making Schools Work: Improving Performance and Controlling Costs* (Brookings, 1994).

20. For a discussion of these potential equity and efficiency gains, see Birdsall, Graham, and Sabot, *Beyond Trade-offs*. For a much less optimistic view see Albert Berry, "The Income Distribution Threat in Latin America," *Latin American Research Review*, vol. 32, no. 2 (1997), pp. 3–40.

# Index

371